Dōgen

Dōgen

Textual and Historical Studies

Edited by

STEVEN HEINE

OXFORD
UNIVERSITY PRESS

OXFORD
UNIVERSITY PRESS

Oxford University Press, Inc., publishes works that further
Oxford University's objective of excellence
in research, scholarship, and education.

Oxford   New York
Auckland   Cape Town   Dar es Salaam   Hong Kong   Karachi
Kuala Lumpur   Madrid   Melbourne   Mexico City   Nairobi
New Delhi   Shanghai   Taipei   Toronto

With offices in
Argentina   Austria   Brazil   Chile   Czech Republic   France   Greece
Guatemala   Hungary   Italy   Japan   Poland   Portugal   Singapore
South Korea   Switzerland   Thailand   Turkey   Ukraine   Vietnam

Published by Oxford University Press, Inc.
198 Madison Avenue, New York, New York 10016

www.oup.com

Oxford is a registered trademark of Oxford University Press

Library of Congress Cataloging-in-Publication Data
Dogen : textual and historical studies / edited by Steven Heine.
p.   cm.
Includes bibliographical references and index.
ISBN 978-0-19-975446-5 (hardcover : alk. paper)—ISBN 978-0-19-975447-2 (pbk. : alk. paper)
1. Dogen, 1200–1253. I. Heine, Steven, 1950–
BQ 9449.D657D66   2012
294.3'927092—dc23   2011023577

1 3 5 7 9 8 6 4 2

Printed in the United States of America
on acid-free paper

Contents

Dōgen

Dōgen Studies on Both Sides of the Pacific

Steven Heine

This volume brings together a series of ten state-of-the-art essays by leading scholars from both sides of the Pacific, who carry out textual and historical studies of Zen Master Dōgen (1200–1253), the founder of the Japanese Sōtō sect. Dōgen's life and thought is seen in relation to the Chinese Chan influences he absorbed, as well as the impact he exerted on Buddhist thought and culture in Japan. The book contributes to the advancement of specialized scholarship on Dōgen and the Chan/Zen school more generally as seen in the context of East Asian religions and their connections to developments of Buddhism in Song dynasty China and Kamakura-era Japan, as well as current academic, intellectual, and cultural trends.

The aim of *Dōgen* is to inform the reader regarding the nature of Dōgen's writings as a whole, including various versions of his texts, especially the *Shōbōgenzō* and several of its fascicles, in particular, as well as the sermons and discourses in the *Eihei kōroku* that express his views on core practices and rituals, such as reading the sutras (*kankin*), diligent training in zazen meditation (*shikan taza*), the kōan realized in everyday life (*genjōkōan*), or using supranormal powers (*jinzū*). Essays in this book also analyze the historical significance of this seminal figure; for example, how he appropriated Chan sources and the ways in which he is comparable to or in conflict with the teachings of Dahui, Hongzhi, and Yanshou, all of whom were important Chinese monks, in addition to Japanese Zen predecessor Eisai, considered the founder of the Rinzai sect, who preceded Dōgen in traveling to study Buddhism on the mainland. The book also looks at the ways in which Dōgen influenced subsequent developments in the Sōtō sect, as well as its understanding of its founder, including scholarship on and celebrations of the significance of their first patriarch's life and thought.

The collection features contributions by two eminent Japanese scholars from the Buddhist Studies Department at Komazawa University, the premier research institution in Japan: Ishii Shūdō, one of the most eminent scholars of Song Chinese Chan sources in Japan; and Ishii Seijun, a Dōgen specialist who is currently president of the university. These are accompanied by eight chapters by Western scholars who have trained extensively at Komazawa University, in large part through the mentorship of Ishii Shūdō and Ishii Seijun, as well as other prominent professors including Kagamishima Genryū, Kawamura Kōdō, and Yoshizu Yoshihide, or collaborated with its faculty and graduates in the field of Zen studies. These include William M. Bodiford, author of *Sōtō Zen in Medieval Japan*, who contributes two chapters in addition to two articles I have written, along with one chapter each by Carl Bielefeldt, who has published *Dōgen Manuals of Zen Meditation*; T. Griffith Foulk, one of the co-editors of the Sōtō Translation Project; Taigen Dan Leighton, who has translated major works by Dōgen; and Albert Welter, a specialist on Chinese Buddhist studies who also has expertise in medieval Japan.

Background of Dōgen Studies

Studies of Dōgen in the West began four decades ago with early translations of some of his main writings by Reihō Masunaga, Jiyu Kennett, Yūhō Yokoi, Masao Abe/Norman Waddell, and Kosen Nishiyama/John Stevens, among others. During the 1970s, numerous fascicles of the *Shōbōgenzō* appeared in English for the first time, along with other works, including *Shōbōgenzō zuimonki* and *Hōkyōki*, and important shorter pieces such as *Bendōwa* and "Tenzokyōkun." In addition, several important historical and philosophical studies were produced, including Hee-Jin Kim's *Dōgen Kigen—Mystical Realist*, Takashi James Kodera's *Dōgen's Formative Years in China*, and Tom Kasulis's *Zen Action/Zen Person*, which discussed Dōgen extensively. "The Zen Philosopher," an influential review article by Kasulis published in *Philosophy East and West* in 1978, gave a good assessment of the state of the field at the time. Kasulis stressed the need to develop a solid corps of Western scholars, armed with linguistic skills and historical tools, who would be able to benefit from recent advances by a host Japanese researchers working on Dōgen.

During the ensuing decades, considerable progress would be made in various aspects of Chan/Zen studies, particularly on heretofore obscure topics ranging from the Northern school to Tang and Song dynasty Chan movements in China, as well as to developments of Zen in the Edo and Meiji eras in Japan, in addition to the role of Zen in Korea and Vietnam. How has the study of Dōgen fared during this fruitful phase in the advancement of scholarship on East Asian Buddhism?

Since the formative stage of Dōgen studies in the West, a stream of translations has continued to come forth, and now multiple complete versions of the *Shōbōgenzō* are in print, with several more in the pipeline, although the definitive edition is yet to be published since it is very difficult to balance the need for notations and other scholarly apparatus that explicate the text with readability and a refinement of rhetoric that captures the flavor of the original. Other major writings, including the *kanbun* materials of *Eihei kōroku* and the monastic instructions of *Eihei shingi*, as well as Dōgen's poetry collection, have appeared in reliable versions, and several anthologies present sets of writings in translation centering around his views of Buddhist theory or practice in regard to meditation, nature, or monastic rules. Many of the shorter works in Dōgen's collected writings (*Dōgen zenji zenshū*, the generic title used for several Japanese editions, as will be explained in some of the articles) are now available. There have also been several outstanding historical studies, including those by contributors to this book, which situate the significance of Dōgen's works in appropriate socioreligious contexts.

However, there remains a tendency in some approaches to Dōgen Studies to be lacking in historical specificity and verifiability, and in general, the rapid development of the field has often meant that a few key topics are discussed and debated extensively, while there has not been an opportunity in other instances to create detailed scholarly works on significant specialized topics. What still needs to be developed—or, to put it in another way, some of the lacunae that are to be filled by this volume—revolves around issues of interpretive depth and breadth. Expanding the field in both of these directions through scholarship that is accessible to Western readers requires an intimate yet critical and nuanced familiarity with the latest developments of research projects in Japan. All of the contributors to this volume represent and epitomize the trend of drawing on up-to-date resources dealing with Chan/Zen generated by the Japanese academy.

Several articles carefully examine Dōgen's texts in novel ways, such as one demonstrating the diversity and authenticity (or lack thereof) of the various editions of the *Shōbōgenzō* that have been collected over the centuries, beginning with the time of the initial composition and creation of the text. Four other contributions take up a particular fascicle, or even single passage of one of his discourses, and explore the multiple levels of meaning in terms of how this illumines Dōgen's oeuvre and approach to Buddhist ritual practice as a whole. Moreover, the five historically-based articles in *Dōgen* significantly broaden our understanding of his relation to classical Chan/Zen schools in China and the introduction of Zen into medieval Japan, particularly at the time of the formation of Sōtō Zen, as well as the ways Dōgen's persona and major works have been appreciated and appropriated in the early modern and contemporary periods.

Chapter Summary

The first chapter in Part I on the topic of Textual Studies is "Textual Genealogies of Dōgen" by William M. Bodiford. This piece makes a unique and important contribution to the field as a reference essay that critically introduces, surveys, and evaluates the main texts by Dōgen, including the major editions of the *Shōbōgenzō*, in order to correct many current misimpressions. Bodiford's chapter, derived from a careful examination of Japanese scholarship, will quickly become essential material for anyone laboring in the field of Chan/Zen studies. It examines in fine detail the multiple writings attributed to Dōgen and the various extant versions. A special focus is placed on the several editions and redactions of the *Shōbōgenzō* that contain different numbers of fascicles, a topic that has received relatively little discussion in Western studies. Bodiford shows how the 12-fascicle, 28-fascicle, 60-fascicle, 75-fascicle, and 95-fascicle *Shōbōgenzō* texts, among others, were formed, and which of the editions are reliable. He also demonstrates the relation between the *Kana Shōbōgenzō* and *Mana Shōbōgenzō* texts. He assesses the authenticity or corruption, as well as the scholarly relevance of each version for conducting research on Dōgen's writings. In addition, this chapter surveys the versions of the *Shōbōgenzō zuimonki*, *Eihei kōroku*, *Eihei shingi*, along with other key texts by Dōgen.

The next chapter is "What Is on the Other Side? Delusion and Reality in Dōgen's 'Genjōkōan.'" Here, I deal with one of the most frequently cited but still controversial and contested passages in Dōgen's corpus, in which he argues, "When perceiving one side, the other side is concealed" (alternative rendering: "When one side is illumined, the other side is dark") in the context of discussing the role of sense perceptions in the experience of enlightenment. The "Genjōkōan" fascicle, which was one of the earliest *Shōbōgenzō* compositions that appears as the opening section of the mainstream 75-fascicle edition is anomalous because it is a rare example of a document by Dōgen that was addressed as an epistle to a lay disciple, rather than to his monastic community. Its teaching focuses on three themes expressed in the enigmatic initial paragraph on the polarities of sentient beings and buddhas, life and death, and delusion and realization. The key passage in question deals with the third antimony and has traditionally been interpreted as indicating that realization represents the thorough penetration of a single object (*ippō gūjin*) beyond delusion. I seek to reveal a more nuanced view by drawing on recent approaches and philosophical debates conducted by Japanese scholars Kurebayashi Kōdō, Yoshizu Yoshihide, Matsumoto Shirō, and Ishii Seijun, who demonstrate in various ways that the passage indicates a complex interweaving of the states of enlightenment and nonenlightenment. I conclude by presenting a position that articulates a constructive compromise overturning one-sided expositions of the passage.

The third piece in the collection is the chapter, ""Just Sitting"? Dōgen's Take on Zazen, Sutra Reading, and Other Conventional Buddhist Practices," by T. Griffith Foulk. This chapter is based on a close reading of passages in the *Shōbōgenzō* and elsewhere on sutra reading, which is one of the practices that Dōgen says is unnecessary in the oft-quoted passage attributed to his mentor Rujing, cited in *Bendōwa* (also found in *Hōkyōki* and "Gyōji"): "You can only succeed by just sitting, without a need to make use of burning incense, prostration, recitation of buddha names, repentance ceremonies, reading scriptures, or ritual incantations." Foulk shows from the ritual practices he followed that Dōgen did not mean to reject literally any of those standard Buddhist training methods. Why, then, does he disparage them? The answer is actually simple and clear, Foulk argues, and is well illustrated in "Kankin": one should engage in all practices, ideally without attachment to them, but even with attachment if one has not figured out yet what nonattachment really is. Nonattachment for Dōgen is insight into the emptiness of dharmas, which in plain English means the ultimately false (albeit useful) nature of all conceptual categories, starting with the category of "thing." From that point of view, all practices (including zazen or sitting meditation) are rejected because, after all, there is no such thing as "practice"—it is just a conventional category—and yet all practices are also accepted and endorsed.

The fourth chapter in Part I is my "A Day in the Life: Dōgen's View of Chan/Zen Lineage in *Shōbōgenzō* 'Gyōji,'" which points out that "Gyōji" is one of several *Shōbōgenzō* fascicles that is unique in varying ways. The majority of fascicles focus on Mahayana Buddhist doctrines explicated in terms of kōan literature, which Dōgen often radically reinterprets. The "Gyōji" fascicle contains some of this element, especially in the opening passage, which is a philosophical discourse on the meaning of zazen practice related to time, metaphysics, and ethics. For the most part, however, the fascicle provides a hagiographical discussion of 35 patriarchs in the Zen lineage, from Indian Buddhist figures Sakyamuni, Mahakasyapa, and Parsva to first Chinese patriarch Bodhidharma and numerous Chan leaders, culminating in Caodong (Jp. Sōtō) master Furong Daokai and, of course, Dōgen's mentor Rujing, who receives special attention. The main portion of the fascicle is much closer to transmission of the lamp style texts than any other work in Dōgen's corpus, much like the *Denkōroku* by Keizan, and reflects his particular interest in highlighting the importance of zazen. However, "Gyōji" is not a text that advocates "just sitting" (*shikan taza*) in a way akin to the *Fukanzazengi* or *Shōbōgenzō* "Zazengi," which both offer specific admonitions and instructions on how to meditate. Instead, "Gyōji" expresses a broad vision of how strict adherence to discipline underlies and is the necessary condition for meditation. The forms of discipline include the austerities of the 12 *dhuta* practices (Jp. *zuda* or *zudagyō*) or a commitment to spiritual independence and integrity while living in thatched

huts on remote peaks to abandon worldly temptations, as frequently evidenced
through the supranormal power to overcome indigenous spirits. For example,
Dōgen praises Mahakasyapa not for receiving Sakyamuni's flower, as in the prototypical Zen narrative, but for being an extraordinary representative of *dhuta*-
based asceticism, as portrayed in early Buddhist literature. He also sums up the
merit of several masters, such as Jingqing Daofu, Sanping Yichong, and Changqing Daan, based on their supranormal skill in being able to dispense with the
need to be served food or of being able to be seen by local gods.

The last chapter in Part I is Taigen Dan Leighton's "Dōgen's Approach to
Training in *Eihei kōroku.*" Leighton's chapter makes several important contributions to this book. First, as the co-translator of a monumental translation of the
Eihei kōroku, which is arguably Dōgen's most important body of work from the
period of his career when he was ensconced in Eiheiji temple (since the *Shōbōgenzō*
was for the most part composed before then), Leighton highlights the role of
Chinese writing (*kanbun*) and of sermons delivered in the Dharma Hall (*jōdō*) in
Dōgen's overall style of teaching. These techniques were appropriated by Dōgen
from his travels to China and studies of Chan sources, and were delivered to an
audience of trainees who were likely unfamiliar with Chinese Buddhism. Also,
Leighton explains the significance of several particular discourses included in the
text that emphasize the way in which Dōgen instructed his disciples in the art of
practicing meditation, as well as the relation between the contemplative life and
other aspects of monastic institutional rituals. Another important implication of
Leighton's article is his exegetical method; that is, the creative way in which he
teases out of various *Eihei kōroku* passages their implications for religious practice, which was, after all, the primary goal behind Dōgen's pedagogy and literary
style.

Part II, on Historical Studies, opens with "Dōgen Zen and Song Dynasty
China," by Ishii Shūdō. This chapter explores the relationship between Dōgen's
thought and that of leading Song Chan thinkers of the Caodong (Sōtō) and Linji
(Rinzai) lineages, particularly the intense rivalry between the approaches of
Silent Illumination (Ch. *mozhao chan*, Jp. *mokushō zen*) and Kōan-Introspection
(Ch. *kanhua chan*, Jp. *kanna zen*). Silent Illumination Chan refers to the Chan
style of Hongzhi, a fellow disciple with Zhenxie of Danxia and a member of the
same Caodong order as Dōgen's teacher, Rujing. Although not necessarily align-
ing himself with this view, it is clear that the style Dōgen disagreed with most
strongly was introspecting the kōan Zen, represented by the illustrious Linji master Dahui (1089–1163), whom Dōgen both praised and excoriated in various
writings. Ishii's article addresses the following questions that are critical to Dōgen
studies: What kind of attributes characterized the paths of Silent Illumination
and Kōan-Introspection during the Song Dynasty? What connection does
Dōgen Zen, which resulted from his importation of Song Chan to Kamakura

Japan, have with the various Song schools and approaches? In short, Ishii considers the characteristics of Dōgen Zen against the currents of Chinese Chan history and ideology in order to understand and explicate the influences Dōgen received, as well as the unique features of religious practice he formulated and promulgated.

The seventh chapter in the volume, "Zen Syncretism: An Examination of Dōgen's Zen Thought in Light of Yongming Yanshou's Chan Teaching in the *Zongjing lu*" is by Albert Welter. This chapter examines the syncretic Zen teachings of Yanshou, a highly influential Chinese monk who is sometimes overlooked in these discussions, and Dōgen, who founded the Sōtō sect based on his studies in China. Welter contends that the rubric of "pure Zen" (*junsui zen*), by which early Zen in Japan is often judged, was not inherent to the period but was framed largely in reaction to political demands that the Zen sects faced during the Tokugawa era, when the Zen school was downgraded to outsider status as Confucian and Shinto traditions were being promoted. The category of purity, therefore, had little to do with the teachings propagated by Zen's two founders. Furthermore, the article contends that underlying the apparently different paths of Yanshou and Dōgen are many points of commonality. In contrast to "pure Zen," Yanshou and Dōgen subscribed to a style of Zen that may be called syncretic by fostering connections with the larger Buddhist, and in the case of Yanshou, even non-Buddhist traditions. The article serves not only to rehabilitate the maligned category of "syncretic Zen," and thus restore an often neglected tradition, but it also provides an analysis of syncretism as an analytical tool in the study of religion by applying this methodology to the cases of Yanshou's and Dōgen's thought.

The next chapter is "Disarming the Superpowers: The *Abhijna* in Eisai and Dōgen" by Carl Bielefeldt, which examines the two early Kamakura era Zen giants, in the context of more general Mahayana Buddhist teachings. This article, which has a resonance with Albert Welter's focus on Yanshou in addition to the attention given to supranormal powers by my chapter and to ritualism by T. Griffith Foulk, highlights the role of Dōgen and Eisai in transmitting Chan to Japan, with its distinctive spiritual environment. According to Bielefeldt, the real powers of the Chan masters in Song Chinese literary records, or what made them alien and dangerous to the established Buddhist community, were precisely their dismissal of the traditional use of the supranormal powers or *abhijna* (*jinzū*) as detailed in early Buddhist lore, and thus their refusal to play by the rules of standard buddhology. Eisai tried to downplay this danger by appealing to the circumstances and threat of the Final Age (*mappō*) and by invoking the authority of monastic law as the only legitimate avenue by which to achieve enlightenment. Dōgen, on the other hand, handled the problem by reaffirming the Chan masters' fidelity to orthodox esoteric buddhology and their consequent subjection to the higher metaphysical laws of the cosmic body. That is, Eisai attempted to turn the seminal Chan tricksters into sober Vinaya specialists who were off meditating in their monasteries, whereas, through very different means but with rather similar effect, Dōgen sought to transform them into a new kind of ritual master who was skilled in enacting the way of the Buddha. Thus transformed, the Chan master could now become a familiar figure in the Japanese theological scene—somewhat eccentric, perhaps, in his style of ritual practice, but hardly a threat to the established order.

This chapter is followed by William M. Bodiford's second contribution to this volume, "Remembering Dōgen: Eiheiji and Dōgen Hagiography." Here, Bodiford explains that Dōgen occupies a prominent place in the history of Japanese religions and is primarily remembered as the founder of the Sōtō school of Zen Buddhism. As such, he is afforded high status as one of the most significant Buddhists in Japanese history. His image adorns countless altars in temples and households affiliated with the Sōtō school, and he is the subject of numerous biographies and studies. His works are available in multiple editions and translations, and his ideas are taught in university classrooms, in and outside Japan, as being representative of authentic Japanese spirituality. In these respects, appropriations of Dōgen exemplify many aspects of founder worship, a widespread practice among diverse sectarian religious organizations in Japan. This chapter examines the process and function developed during the years for the remembrance of Dōgen, or the ways in which his memory has been used and developed over time, including the religious rituals and historical vicissitudes that helped elevate Dōgen to his present position of prominence. It uses the example of Dōgen to illustrate how new historical identities are constructed in response to social imperatives and institutional struggles. Furthermore, Bodiford argues that we cannot fully understand Japanese religions in general and Sōtō Zen, in particular, unless we become more sensitive to the ways in which these historical, social, and institutional factors shape our received images of the past.

The final chapter is "New Trends in Dōgen Studies in Japan," by Ishii Seijun, a leading historian and interpreter of Dōgen's life and works in the Japanese academy, has lectured extensively in the West. Ishii shows that there are two major currents in the study of the teachings and institutional legacy of Dōgen in modern Japan, called Sōtō Shūgaku in Japanese and referred to here as Sōtō Theology. One current is internal or derived from forces, as well as from the work of scholar-monks within the tradition; it strives to secure orthodoxy. The other is external, or stems from philosophers and lay followers outside the institution who wish to be innovative and comparative in their approaches. The first current is the traditionalistic approach undertaken within the Sōtō school, which began in the Edo period and was designed to construct the identity of Sōtō sectarians as legitimate successors to Dōgen's ideas and monastic system. This current has focused on the revival of monastic regulations, and it produced the *Eihei shingi* as a single collection of Dōgen's writings on rules. The second major current in the study of Dōgen began after the Meiji restoration of 1868, when the Japanese Zen schools looked to intellectuals for assistance in the face of the government's policy of National Shintoism (Kokka Shintō). Tanabe Hajime and Akiyama Hanji, both of the Kyoto school of Japanese philosophy, did not treat the *Shōbōgenzō* as a sacred canon of the Sōtō school, but rather as an ideological or philosophical work. That is, Dōgen's thought as indicated in *Shōbōgenzō* was separated from Sōtō Theology, and it became an independent academic subject. In addition, in the Meiji period when Lay Buddhism prospered, Ōuchi Seiran and Daidō Chōan were representative of lay-oriented Sōtō school leaders of the time. In 1891, Ōuchi compiled a new canon for lay believers by selecting eloquent and appropriate passages from the *Shōbōgenzō*. This new canon, called *Shushōgi*, has been used in most Sōtō sect rituals since then.

Note on Contributions and Formatting

Several of the chapters in *Dōgen: Textual and Historical Studies* have appeared in earlier versions. One chapter was published in English in a collection produced in Japan: Carl Bielefeldt's "Disarming the Superpowers: The *Abhijna* in Eisai and Dōgen" originally appeared in *Dōgen zenji kenkyū ronshū,* edited by Daihonzan Eiheiji Daionki Kyoku (Fukui-ken: Eiheiji, 2002), pp. 1018–1046. Two chapters are revised versions of publications that appeared previously in journals: Steven Heine's "A Day in the Life: Dōgen's View of Chan/Zen Lineage in *Shōbōgenzō* 'Gyōji'" is a significantly expanded version of a review essay appearing in the *Japanese Journal of Religious Studies* 35/2 (2008): 363–372; William M. Bodiford's "Remembering Dōgen: Eiheiji and Dōgen Hagiography" is a revision of an article published in the *Journal of Japanese Studies* 32/1 (2006): 1–21. In addition, Ishii Shūdō's "Dōgen Zen and Song Dynasty China" is a translation by Albert Welter with revisions of a chapter taken from his *Dōgen Zen no seiritsu shiteki kenkyū* (Tokyo: Daizō shuppansha, 1991), pp. 293–335.

Also, the transliteration of some Japanese and Chinese names and terms, particularly in titles of fascicles of the *Shōbōgenzō*, can be quite varied in terms of whether they are sorted as one or more words, and by other distinguishing factors including pronunciation and capitalization. An editorial decision was made to seek some consistency but also to allow discrepancy and variation among articles to stand when it was considered appropriate to a contributor's research on source materials. Furthermore, many of the chapters cite different editions of Dōgen's collected works, which are all called *Dōgen zenji zenshū* in the original Japanese; readers are advised to check the relevant endnotes to see which editor or version is being followed in the respective articles. Finally, in the glossary there is a general list of Sino-Japanese terms used in several or more articles that is followed by the terms contained in each chapter. Items in the general list for the most part have been deleted from the list for the chapters.

CONTRIBUTORS

CARL BIELEFELDT is Evans-Wentz professor of Religious Studies at Stanford University, and co-editor of the Sōtō Zen Text Project

WILLIAM M. BODIFORD is professor of Asian Languages and Cultures at the University of California in Los Angeles, and author of *Sōtō Zen in Medieval Japan*

T. GRIFFITH FOULK is professor of Religion at Sarah Lawrence College, and co-editor of the Sōtō Zen Text Project

STEVEN HEINE is professor and director of Asian Studies at Florida International University, and author of *Did Dōgen Go To China?*

ISHII SEIJUN is professor of Buddhist Studies and president of Komazawa University in Tokyo, and author of *Zen mondō nyūmon*

ISHII SHŪDŌ is professor of Buddhist Studies at Komazawa University in Tokyo, and author of *Dōgen Zen no seiritsu shiteki kenkyū*

TAIGEN DAN LEIGHTON teaches Buddhism online at the Graduate Theological Union, and is co-translator of *Dōgen's Extensive Record*

ALBERT WELTER is professor of Religion and Culture at the University of Winnipeg, and author of *Monks, Rulers, and Literati*

ACKNOWLEDGMENTS

The editor thanks Cynthia Read and the staff at Oxford University Press for their support, the anonymous readers who made helpful suggestions, a variety of colleagues in the field too numerous to name for inspiration, as well Jennylee Diaz, Maria Sol Echarren, and Gabriela Romeu for their editorial assistance.

PART ONE

Textual Studies

I

Textual Genealogies of Dōgen

William M. Bodiford

Since 1975, when Hee-Jin Kim published his groundbreaking study of Dōgen, English-language scholarship on Dōgen has appeared in an ever-greater quantity, quality, and variety of methodological approaches. Regardless of approach, scholars invariably interpret Dōgen through published compilations of his writings. Beginning with the *Honzan* edition of the *Shōbōgenzō* (completed ca. 1815; revised edition 1906), new editions of Dōgen's works have appeared regularly: in volume 1 of the *Sōtōshū Zensho* (Complete Works of the Sōtō School, 1929) and its revised edition (1970; abbreviated as "SZ 1929" and "SZ 1970" respectively); the Ōkubo Dōshū compilation of 1930, reprinted in 1944 as *Teihon: Dōgen Zenji Zenshū* (Dōgen's Collected Works: Definitive Edition, 2 vols.); in his completely new compilation, also titled *Dōgen Zenji Zenshū* (3 vols., 1969–1970; reprinted 1989; abbreviated as "DZZ 1969"); another completely new compilation, also titled *Dōgen Zenji Zenshū* (7 vols., 1988–1993; abbreviated as "DZZ 1988"), compiled by Kagamishima Genryū and others; and a revised compilation with translations into modern Japanese, titled *Dōgen Zenji Zenshū: Genbun taishō Gendaigoyaku* (17 vols. projected, Kagamishima 1999–present; abbreviated as "DZZ 1999"), also compiled by Kagamishima Genryū and others. This long list could be many times longer if it were to include editions that contain only one or a few of the many individual works attributed to Dōgen.

The above editions of Dōgen's writings were not created equal. Each has its own characteristics and limitations, based on their selection of manuscript sources and the choices made by their editors. They were compiled in accordance with methods of textual criticism that assume the existence of an original text (archetype), whether extant or not, actually authored by Dōgen. In other words, the manuscript versions upon which the published text is based—and in regard to which editors might provide notes on textual variations—simply constitute witnesses to the stages of development (or alteration) that the archetype presumably has suffered at the hands of subsequent copyists and editors. In recent decades, the publication of new editions of historical sources based on this kind of textual criticism has revolutionized our understanding of Dōgen's biography (e.g., see the discussion of *Kenzeiki* in Chapter 9 on "Remembering Dōgen"). At the same time, though, the actual techniques used for editing Dōgen's writings raise a host of issues that heretofore have not been fully considered. The text-critical apparatus, with its notes on textual variations, tends to confer on modern published editions an aura of authenticity and finality that they do not deserve. The textual genealogies of Dōgen are not as simple as the modern editions might lead us to assume. People who study Dōgen and translate or analyze his writings, therefore, should approach published editions with an informed awareness of their limitations.

Editors of Dōgen's writings must confront three main tasks. First, they routinely adapt the format of the original text to make it more accessible to modern readers. At the very least, these adaptations include converting rare or abbreviated Chinese glyphs into standardized modern forms, converting the Japanese *katakana* syllabary into its corresponding *hiragana* form, and adding voiced marks (*dakuon pu*) to selected *kana* glyphs, or reducing the size of others as an aid to reading. Frequently, it also includes adding punctuation to break the text into clauses and sentences, adding phonetic glosses in small type (ruby) to indicate pronunciations, and adding interlinear "markup" (*kunten*; i.e., marks that signal semantic arrangement) to Chinese passages to indicate how they should be parsed into Japanese word order. Sometimes (but less often nowadays), the adaptations also include correcting perceived mistakes in the original text to bring it into conformity with standard editions of Chinese texts, commentaries, or the editor's notions of correct grammar.

These seemingly innocuous adaptations have the power not just to transform the format of a text from medieval norms to modern ones but also to strongly influence how it will be interpreted. Even small changes in punctuation, pronunciation, or markup can generate major differences. Linguistic evidence disappears and meanings slip. The way that these adaptations and emendations have been implemented after the language reforms of the 1950s differ from the way that they were implemented in editions published between 1865 and 1949, and they also differ from the editorial changes exhibited by editions published during the Tokugawa period. Nonetheless, the Tokugawa influence remains strong. Some editors (e.g., Ōkubo Dōshū) strive to adhere to the format of the earliest textual witnesses, but most editors rely on Tokugawa period (or later) commentaries to determine how the text should be adapted.

Second, editors must decide on what titles to attach to individual texts and whether or not those individual texts should stand alone or be included as part of some larger work. A couple of examples will serve to illustrate this task. The first example is that Dōgen never wrote a work titled *Eihei Shingi* (Eihei [Dōgen]'s Rules of Purity). The work that we now know by that title first came into existence in 1667, when Kōshō Chidō (d. 1670) published a collection of five short texts (two of which previously had been published as individual works) under the title *Dōgen Zenji Shingi*. When this edition was reprinted in 1794, one of the texts was split apart to create a new compilation with a total of six parts. In 1969, when Ōkubo Dōshū compiled his edition of *Dōgen's Collected Works* (DDZ 1969), under the category of "Shingi" (Rules of Purity) he included the texts previously published by Kōshō Chidō, plus six more texts for a total of 12. Of the works included in these three editions (1667, 1794, or 1969), only two actually have the word "*shingi*" in their titles. None of these compilations include the many books from Dōgen's *Shōbōgenzō* (e.g., *Ango, Senmen*, etc.) that also concern monastic rules of purity. By its very existence, the *Eihei Shingi* thus misleads unwary readers in at least two ways. It implies that Dōgen intended to author his own monastic rules (*shingi*) and that this work (the *Eihei Shingi*) contains his most important instructions on this topic. Neither implication is true.

The second example is that Dōgen never wrote a work titled *Dōshin* (The Heart of the Way), but the *Honzan* edition of the *Shōbōgenzō* includes a book with that title. It first appeared in the version of the *Shōbōgenzō* compiled by Kōzen (1627–1693). Kōzen found two very different versions of the *Shōbōgenzō* book *Butsudō* (The Way of the Buddha). Unable to decide between the two versions, he included both books in his version of the *Shōbōgenzō* but changed the name of one book to *Dōshin*. He thereby disguised the relationship between the two texts and misled readers into assuming that Dōgen addresses the same themes in two separate books (rather than in a revised version of an earlier work).

Kōzen's decision to keep both versions brings us to the third task that editors of Dōgen's writings confront: They must decide which versions of his writings to include or exclude. Many of the writings attributed to Dōgen exist in more than one version. Sometimes the relationship between alternative versions is unclear. In a few key cases, however, diplomatics indicates a chronological sequence in which one version preserves an earlier draft while its alternative version represents a subsequent revision. The fact that Dōgen revised and rewrote his compositions demonstrates that he played a direct role in their compilation and editing. Furthermore, it undermines much of the evidence for traditional chronologies of Dōgen's writings. A work with an early date of composition might survive only in a revised form that postdates another work that carries a later date of composition. For this reason, the traditional chronological arrangements of Dōgen's writings (as found, for example, in the *Honzan* edition of the *Shōbōgenzō*) cannot be trusted.

The existence of alternative versions raises tricky questions. What criteria should be used to select one or the other version as *the* textual archetype? When should a compilation include both versions? If multiple versions are to be included, then how should they be labeled? Editors should explain the rationale for their choices, but seldom do so. They rarely alert readers to the existence of alternative texts and never in a helpful manner.

Consider, for example, *Raihai Tokuzui* (Getting the Marrow by Doing Obeisance). Published editions of the *Shōbōgenzō* all include two versions of this text, with an excerpt from the alternative version appended to the end of the standard version. The appended excerpt attracts much attention today for its favorable endorsement of women. Few readers realize, however, that the insertion of this excerpt disrupts the intended structure of *Shōbōgenzō* or that there exists only a single manuscript witness for the excerpt, which is part of a problematic collection of miscellaneous texts. The alternative version of *Raihai Tokuzui* first should be evaluated in terms of those other miscellaneous works. Then, on the basis of that examination, readers can decide how to interpret its novel statements in relation to other versions of the *Shōbōgenzō*. Placing the excerpt within another version of the *Shōbōgenzō* renders the alternative version of *Raihai Tokuzui* more accessible to readers, but prevents them from being able to analyze its original context. To date, only one of Dōgen's works, his *Fukan Zazengi* (Principles of Sitting Zen), has been carefully analyzed and translated in light of its alternative versions and related texts (see Bielefeldt 1988).

Scholars working in Japan generally possess greater awareness of these three editorial tasks and the issues they present. Graduate seminars on historical texts at Japanese universities frequently require students to compare published editions against manuscript witnesses. In some cases, advanced graduate students and their instructors conduct on-site investigations of archives and temple libraries where they photograph manuscripts. Noteworthy texts will be analyzed in seminars and edited for publication as a typeset edition. This experience teaches new scholars not only the requisite skills for reading and editing manuscripts for publication, but also to develop a healthy skepticism regarding the editorial policies of other scholars.

Today, scholars working on Dōgen's writings can conduct this kind of archival investigation without going to Japan. Beginning with the publication of *Eihei Shōbōgenzō Shūsho Taisei* (Compendium of *Shōbōgenzō* Manuscripts; 27 vols., 1974–1984; abbreviated as "E-SBGZ-ST"), almost all the important manuscript witnesses for Dōgen's writings have been published as photographic facsimiles with textual notes and, in many cases, transcriptions that faithfully reproduce the original text in its unaltered, raw format. It is now possible for scholars anywhere in the world to fully consider the textual genealogies of Dōgen's writings and to consult the manuscript witnesses before trusting and citing a modern edition.

The survey below provides a brief overview of the textual genealogies for the variant versions of the main works attributed to Dōgen. Initially, I compiled these notes only for my own reference. I never intended to provide a complete or detailed survey of every manuscript witness. I do not discuss the *Fukan Zazengi* (for which, see Bielefeldt 1988), minor texts, or ones that lack alternative witnesses. Although still incomplete, I hope that this survey will nonetheless prove useful to others. It consists of the following six sections:

A. *Shōbōgenzō* (as a collection of kōans)
B. Hōkyōki
C. Recorded Sayings
D. Zuimonki
E. Bendōwa
F. *Shōbōgenzō* (as a collection of thematic books)

A. Shōbōgenzō *(As a Collection of Kōans)*

This work consists of a three-fascicle collection of 301 kōan copied from Chinese sources and titled *Shōbōgenzō*, with a preface by Dōgen dated 1235. Ishii Shūdō (1985) has demonstrated that the primary source for 129 of the kōan in this collection derive from the first edition of the *Zongmen Tongyao* (1179), a Chinese kōan collection that was lost in China and all but unknown in Japan. Although commonly referred to as "Dōgen's Chinese-language (*Shinji* or *Mana*) *Shōbōgenzō*," one should assume neither that Dōgen authored the text (he only compiled it) nor that it was read as Chinese—since its manuscript witnesses all include interlinear "markup" (*kunten*) to indicate how its Chinese word order should be interpreted as Japanese. It is available in three main versions:

A-1. *Nenpyō Sanbyakusoku Funōgo*, facsimile (E-SBGZ-ST vol. 14) of the woodblock edition published in 1767: This version consists of the so-called "three-hundred cases" (*sanbyaku soku*) with commentary by Shigetsu Ein (1689–1764). Because this publication includes many emendations to the wording of the kōans, critics who compared this text with Dōgen's other writings initially rejected its attribution to Dōgen. Scholars who accepted the underlying kōan collection as Dōgen's compilation noted that its existence is mentioned by Menzan Zuihō (1683–1769) in his 1742 essay on the authenticity of Dōgen's writings, the *Shōbōgenzō Byakujaketsu* (leaf 3a, E-SBGZ-ST vol. 20), and in the funeral record of Tsūgen Jakurei (1322–1391; *Zoku Sōtō Zensho* Shingi 29). This debate ended with the discovery of the Kanazawa Bunko manuscript below (A-2).

A-2. *Shōbōgenzō*, facsimiles of the Kanazawa Bunko manuscript dated 1287 (fasc. 2 only; E-SBGZ-ST vol. 1) and the Jōkōji manuscript dated 1481 and recopied in 1715 (E-SBGZ-ST vol. 1): When the Kanazawa Bunko manuscript first appeared in print (in *Kanazawa Ibun*, edited by Ōya Tokujō, 1934), it provided conclusive evidence for the early existence of a kōan collection titled *Shōbōgenzō* compiled by Dōgen because it was the only textual source then known to be in agreement with the versions of certain kōan quoted by Dōgen. Once it was linked to the *Zongmen Tongyao*, it helped establish the conclusion that Dōgen quotes Chinese texts faithfully more often than not (Ishii 1985).

A-3. *Shōbōgenzō*, critical edition compiled by Kawamura Kōdō (1987, pp. 119–199) based on A-1 and A-2 as well as on three additional manuscript witnesses: the Shinbōji manuscript. (ca. 1500s), Eishōji manuscript (ca. early 1600s), and Jōrokuji manuscript (fasc. 1 only; ca. 1760s). A simplified version of this edition appears in DZZ 1988 vol. 5.

B. Hōkyōki

This work consists of Dōgen's record of his private interviews with Rujing (1163–1267). If the *Zuimonki* is to be regarded as a work by Dōgen, then the *Hōkyōki* should be regarded as a work by Rujing. Dōgen kept it private so that its existence remained unknown until Ejō (1198–1280) discovered it after Dōgen's death. Two versions are significant:

B-1. *Hōkyōki*, woodblock edition published in Meiwa 8 (1771) by Menzan Zuihō: This version is known as the "widely circulated" (*rufu*) edition since it has been reprinted in popular editions (e.g., *Sōtō Zensho* 1970 Shūgen 2; in the Iwanami Bunko series in 1938). Menzan states that his version is based on the 1326 manuscript by Daichi (1290–1366), but it deviates repeatedly from that source, which is now available as a facsimile (E-SBGZ-STZS vol. 4). Menzan's edition should not be used as a source for studying Dōgen. Nonetheless, many of its emendations and additions appear in the English translation by Takashi James Kodera (1980).

B-2. Facsimile (E-SBGZ-ST vol. 26 Shiryōshū; E-SBGZ-STZS vol. 4) of the Zenkyūin manuscript in the handwriting of Dōgen's disciple Ejō, with a postscript dated 1299 by Giun (1253–1333): This manuscript is the archetype from which all other witnesses descend. It should be the starting point for any study of the *Hōkyōki*. It is the source text used for most recent printed editions (e.g., DZZ 1969 vol. 2; DZZ 1988 vol. 7; DZZ 1999 vol. 16).

C. Recorded Sayings

Prior to the 20th century, the general public knew of Dōgen's teachings primarily on the basis of his recorded sayings (*goroku*). In Japanese Zen, the genre of *goroku* refers only to records of monastic pronouncements, sermons, poetry, and dedications composed in literary Chinese. Japanese remarks (like those preserved in the *Zuimonki*) are excluded. The reputations of Zen teachers rested in no small part on their skill in composing erudite Chinese prose and poesy. For this reason, Dōgen's spiritual descendents expended great effort to publish his recorded sayings in a properly edited and corrected form. Today, they exist in three main versions:

C-1. *Eihei Gen Zenji Goroku*, woodblock edition published in 1358 by Donki and reprinted 1648: Dōgen's disciple Giin (1217–1300) carried Dōgen's recorded sayings to China in 1264, where he asked Rujing's disciple Wuwai Yiyuan (d. 1266) to edit them. Because Wuwai abridged the edited text to about one-tenth the size of Dōgen's "extensive record" (*kōroku*), it is known as his "abridged record" (*ryakuroku*). Giin also collected literary endorsements from the well-known Buddhist teachers Xutang Zhiyu (1185–1269) and Tuigeng Dening. The abridged text, along with the endorsements, was published at Eiheiji 90 years later by Donki. It contains sermons from Kōshōji and Eiheiji temples, as well as Dōgen's *Fukan Zazengi, Zazenshin*, and poetry. This abridged record is the text that revealed Dōgen's teachings to a general audience from the 14th to the 17th centuries. In recent years, it has gained notoriety because it uses the phrase "dropping mind and dust" instead of the expected "sloughing body and mind" (both pronounced in Japanese as "*shinjin datsuraku*"). It is reprinted in many modern editions (e.g., SZ 1970 Shūgen 2; DZZ 1988 vol. 5; Ōtani 1991; and DZZ 1999 vol. 13). Finally, note that the word "*Gen*" in the title represents a polite form of address in which the first glyph of a proper name (i.e., in this case, the "*dō*" of "Dōgen") is omitted.

C-2. *Eihei Dōgen Oshō Kōroku*, facsimile (Ōtani 1991) of the woodblock edition published in 1673 by Manzan Dōhaku (1636–1714): Consisting of ten fascicles, this extensive record is the text that revealed Dōgen's teachings to a general audience from the late 17th to the early 20th centuries. It contains sermons from Kōshōji, Daibutsuji, and Eiheiji temples, as well as Dōgen's *Fukan Zazengi* and poetry. No manuscript witnesses exist for this version of Dōgen's recorded sayings, a fact suggesting that Manzan Dōhaku himself is responsible for its many emendations. Some of these emendations seem to have been based on Dōgen's abbreviated record, but there is no evidence to support the suggestion that Manzan reproduced a version of Dōgen's extensive record that had been edited by Wuwai Yiyuan. Manzan's version is the subject of many traditional commentaries (see Itō 1964) and is the source text for the printed version in SZ 1970 vol. 1 Shūgen 2.

C-3. *Dōgen Oshō Kōroku*, facsimile (Ōtani 1989) of the ten-fascicle Eiheiji manuscript copied in 1598 by Monkaku (d. 1615): This version most faithfully preserves the original format of Dōgen's extensive record, including its textual errors. The sermons from Kōshōji temple compiled by Dōgen's disciple Senne, for example, do not necessarily follow a chronological sequence (unlike the sermons for Daibutsuji and Eiheiji, which do), and mistakes in quotations and Chinese diction abound. Quotations from Dōgen's recorded sayings that appear in early Sōtō sources agree precisely with the wording found in Monkaku's copy, not with either the abbreviated record or Manzan's edition. Moreover, unlike the 1673 Manzan edition, Monkaku's copy shows no signs of having been altered in response to the doctrinal controversies of the Tokugawa period. It is the textual basis for a number of other manuscript copies and is the source text for the printed versions in DZZ 1968 vol. 2, DZZ 1988 vols. 3–4, and DZZ 1999 vols. 10–13.

D. Zuimonki

This work was not authored by Dōgen, but by his disciple Ejō (1198–1280). It consists of Ejō's record of his private interviews with Dōgen at Fukakusa near Kyoto. The title "*Shōbōgenzō Zuimonki*" is somewhat of a misnomer. It derives from an unsigned postscript by one of Ejō's disciples, which says that Ejō "recorded as he listened" (*zuimon kiroku*) and that he kept these records among his copies of Dōgen's *Shōbōgenzō* written in *kana* (or *keji*). Since the *Zuimonki* was not written by Dōgen and was never meant to be a part of the works to which Dōgen attached the title "*Shōbōgenzō*," I avoid using that label. Today, the *Zuimonki* often is regarded as an accessible introduction to Dōgen's teachings. It is important to remember, however that although the words were spoken by Dōgen, the editing and selection of topics reflects Ejō's own interests as a recently converted follower of the Darumashū. The numerous passages in the *Zuimonki* concerning precepts, for example, reflect the existence of deep conflicts between Darumashū and Dōgen regarding the significance of ordinations and morality. Three versions of the *Zuimonki* are significant:

D-1. *Shōbōgenzō Zuimonki*, facsimile (E-SBGZ-ST vol. 4) of the woodblock edition published in Keian 4 (1651) and reprinted 1669: Although it occasionally appears in modern editions (e.g., SZ 1970 Shūgen 2), this early published version has been relatively ignored by scholars. It played an important role in introducing Dōgen to a popular audience during the early Tokugawa period. Today, its main value lies in the fact that it bears witness to a line of transmission different from either of the two versions listed below. For this reason, scholars imagine that manuscripts of the *Zuimonki* must have circulated in three separate lines of transmission. It is important to note, however, that no early manuscript witnesses exist for this version.

D-2. *Shōbōgenzō Zuimonki*, woodblock edition published in Meiwa 7 (1770) by Menzan Zuihō: No early manuscript witnesses exist for this version of the *Zuimonki*. It is known as the "widely circulated" (*rufu*) edition since it has been reprinted in editions for a popular audience (e.g., as part of the Iwanami Bunko series in 1929). It is the source text used for almost all the English translations of the *Zuimonki*. In spite of its near-canonical status, it should be avoided for most scholarly purposes because its order of fascicles and record of Dōgen's autobio-graphical details differ substantially from the more reliable Chōenji manuscript.

D-3. Facsimile (E-SBGZ-ST vol. 4) of the Chōenji manuscript dated 1380 and recopied in 1644: This version most faithfully preserves the format of the original text down to reproducing medieval-period spellings of names and terms. Most significant for the study of Dōgen's life and teachings, the order of fascicles and autobiographical details found in the Chōenji manuscript differ from either of the two woodblock editions. For these reasons, scholars now cite the Chōenji version exclusively. The Chōenji manuscript is the source text for the printed versions of the *Zuimonki* included in DZZ 1968 vol. 2, DZZ 1988 vol. 7, DZZ 1999 vol. 16, and the *Nihon Bungaku Taikei* volume (no. 81) on the *Shōbōgenzō* published by Iwanami Shoten (Nishio 1965). Several other manuscript witnesses of the *Zuimonki* survive (see Azuma 1980; E-SBGZ-STZS vols. 1 and 2), but they contribute little additional information.

E. Bendōwa

Bendōwa presents Dōgen's introduction to Zen Buddhism in a relatively easy to understand didactic dialog, written in the Japanese vernacular and addressed to a general audience. Since the late 19th century, Sōtō teachers have afforded it special attention, grouping it together with the *Shōbōgenzō* books *Genjōkōan* and *Busshō*, as one of the three essential texts (known by the collective designation "*Ben-Gen-Butsu*") for understanding Dōgen's Zen. It is included as book 1 of the *Honzan* edition of the *Shōbōgenzō* (ca. 1815; revised edition 1906), but neither Dōgen nor his disciples regarded it as such. It does not appear in any of the four basic *Shōbōgenzō* compilations (i.e., in 60, 75, 12, or 28 books). Therefore, it should be regarded as an independent work. *Bendōwa* exists in two versions:

E-1. *Bendōwa*, facsimile (E-SBGZ-ST vol. 4) of the woodblock edition published in Tenmei 8 (1788) by Gentō Sokuchū (1729–1807): This version of the *Bendōwa* consists of 18 questions and answers. It is based on a manuscript (now lost) that once existed at Daijōji monastery. Several earlier copies of that copy exist: *Bendōwa* is included as part of the supplement (*shūi*; fascicle 20) to the 1689 manuscript of the *Shōbōgenzō* in 89 (84 + 5) books compiled by Manzan Dōhaku at Daijōji (E-SBGZ-ST vol. 7), and two manuscript copies survive from the hand of Manzan's disciple Sotō (or Bankō) Dōki (d. 1757), one dated 1750, at Myōgonji, and one dated 1755, at Kyokuden'in (E-SBGZ-STZS vol. 2). The Tenmei 8 woodblock edition is the source text for the printed versions of the *Bendōwa* included in the *Nihon Bungaku Taikei* volume (no. 81) on the *Shōbōgenzō* (Nishio 1965) and the *Nihon Shisō Taikei* volume (no. 12) on Dōgen (Minzuno 1972) published by Iwanami Shoten, as well as in DZZ 1969 vol. 1, DZZ 1988 vol. 2, and

DZZ 1999 vol. 1. According to a commentary on *Bendōwa*, the *Bendōwa Monge* (leaves 1–2; in E-SBGZ-STZS vol. 17, p. 397) by Menzan Zuihō, the first person in the Sōtō Zen community to learn of the existence of the *Bendōwa* was Gesshū Sōko (1630–1698), the abbot of Daijōji and the teacher of Manzan Dōhaku.[1] Gesshū supposedly heard of the *Bendōwa* from a nobleman who possessed a holograph by Dōgen, which the nobleman then permitted Gesshū to copy. Gesshū's copy became a secret treasure at Daijōji, and the supposed holography by Dōgen has never been seen again.

E-2. *Bendōwa*, facsimile (E-SBGZ-ST vol. 4) of the Shōbōji manuscript dated 1332 and recopied in 1515: This version of the *Bendōwa* consists of 19 questions and answers. It was unknown by the general public until 1959, when Etō Sokuō (1888–1958) first published a transcript. Since the Tenmei 8 (1788) version enjoys near canonical status in the Sōtō tradition, the Shōbōji manuscript is usually dismissed as an initial draft. This judgment seems to rest more on the prestige of the *Monge* commentary than on the literary qualities of the texts themselves. The Sōbōji manuscript is the source text for the printed edition in DZZ 1969 vol. 1 (labeled as an "alternative text," *beppon*) and DZZ 1988 vol. 2 (labeled as a "draft version," *sōan hon*). Recently, the entire bound volume of the Shōbōji manuscript has become available as a full-color facsimile (SBGZ-Zatsubun 2010). In addition to the *Bendōwa,* it also contains a dharma talk (*hōgo*) by Keizan Jōkin (1264–1325) and copies of other documents related to his community.

F. Shōbōgenzō *(As Thematic Books)*

Since the early 20th century, the *Shōbōgenzō* (hereafter abbreviated as "SBGZ") has become the preeminent source for Dōgen's teachings. The SBGZ, however, is not just a single text, or even just different versions of one text. It consists of many different books (*maki* or *kan*), which are bound together as ordered fascicles (*sasshi*) of the whole.[2] Dōgen composed the books of the SBGZ not as independent works, but as related parts of a larger whole that consists of a beginning, middle, and end. Dōgen repeatedly revised the individual books, and he rearranged their order at least two or three times. Subsequent generations compiled new versions of Dōgen's SBGZ, adding or rejecting individual books and rearranging them thematically or chronologically. To make sense of the complex textual genealogies of the SBGZ, I rely on the exhaustive research by Kawamura Kōdō (1980 and 1987), as well as on the facsimiles in E-SBGZ-ST (27 vols., 1974–1982) and E-SBGZ-STZS (10 vols., 1989–2000), the compilations of which he supervised. Kawamura's conclusions, although convincing to me, are by no means the only possible interpretations of the evidence regarding origins, dates, and filiation of the manuscripts. I alone am responsible for any errors.

Extant versions of the SBGZ can be grouped into: The Four Basic Compilations, Other Premodern Manuscript Compilations, and Printed Editions of the SBGZ. I also provide two appendixes: tables of contents for each of the four basic compilations, and an index of the titles for the individual books of the SBGZ.

The Four Basic Compilations

Four basic compilations constitute the starting point for any study of the SBGZ. For convenience, they are known, in chronological order, as the *Shōbōgenzō* in 60, 75, 12, or 28 books. Prior to Kawamura's research, scholars assumed that Dōgen's disciples or their disciples had edited and compiled these versions. When editors compiled a modern printed edition, they mixed and matched books from any one of the four compilations, selecting those that they assumed to be earliest or the best. They gave preference to holographs by either Dōgen or Ejō, without regard to whether the manuscripts in question represented an initial draft, a revised draft, or a rewritten work. In short, they produced hybrid compilations that failed to accurately represent any previously existing SBGZ.

Kawamura has demonstrated that Dōgen himself compiled the SBGZ both in 60 books and in 75 books. The 60-book version represents Dōgen's earlier arrangement, the books of which Dōgen subsequently revised and rearranged to produce the 75-book version. Manuscript copies of the SBGZ books *Gyōji* in Dōgen's handwriting and *Busshō* in Ejō's handwriting (for facsimiles of both, see E-SBGZ-ST vol. 26 Bekkan), for example, agree in wording with other manuscript witnesses for the 60-book version. But they also contain many interlinear annotations that reveal how these books were to be revised and rewritten. These revisions agree with the wording found in the manuscript witnesses of the 75-book version.

The 60- and 75-book versions each exist in the form of multiple manuscript witnesses. The 12- and 28-book versions exist as only a single manuscript witness apiece. Modern critical editions should respect these different lines of development. SBGZ editions should be edited by comparing manuscripts that represent the same edition (i.e., SBGZ in 60 books with other 60-book manuscripts, and SBGZ in 75 books with other 75-book manuscripts). Then it would be possible to study (or translate) both versions on their own terms and make meaningful comparisons and contrasts between them. In brief, the four basic compilations are as follows:

F-1. SBGZ in 60 books: Although commonly referred to as having 60 books, it actually consists of 59 books with each half of the book *Gyōji* counted individually. Its manuscripts usually are written in the *hiragana* version of the Japanese syllabary. Many of its books contain postscripts by Ejō. Prior to Kawamura's research, Sōtō scholars had assumed that this version was compiled by Giun

(1253–1333) because Giun composed a verse commentary (*Honmokuju*; in E-SBGZ-ST vol. 20) for each of the 60 books. This version seems to have been handed down mainly within the Jakuen lineage based at Eiheiji monastery (where it was copied by the Jakuen-line monks Sōgo in 1381, Zenkō in 1400, and Kōshū in 1479). Later copies also were handed down among other lineages: extant copies are dated 1468 (Tafukuan ms., E-SBGZ-STZS vol. 3), 1491, 1510 (Tōunji ms., E-SBGZ-ST vol. 6), 1686 (Seiryūji ms., E-SBGZ-STZS vol. 3), and 1751 (Myōshōji ms., E-SBGZ-ST vol. 7). It formed the basis of the SBGZ in 78 books compiled by Tenkei Denson (see F-8).

F-2. SBGZ in 75 books: In this version, the two halves of *Gyōji* are counted together as a single book. Its manuscripts usually are written in the *katakana* version of the Japanese syllabary and lack any postscripts by Ejō. The order and structure of the 75-book version remains close to that of the 60-book one. Fifty SBGZ books are common to both versions, of which 32 books have the same numerical position. It also contains 25 new books not found in the 60-book version. Of the nine books deleted from the 60-book edition, seven reappear in the 12-book edition (see F-3) and two books (*Hokke ten Hokke* and *Bodaisatta Shishōhō*) seem to have been discarded altogether. This version was handed down at Yōkōan (a.k.a., Yōkōji) monastery near Kyoto, where it was the subject of the *Goshō* commentaries by Senne and Kyōgō (ca. 1263 and ca. 1308, in E-SBGZ-ST vols. 11–14), as well at Sōjiji and other temples associated with the Gasan lineage. Extant copies are dated 1488 (Kenkon'in ms., E-SBGZ-ST vol. 1), 1512 (Shōbōji ms., E-SBGZ-ST vol. 1), 1547 (Ryūmonji ms., E-SBGZ-ST vol. 2), 1626, 1677 (Kōunji ms., E-SBGZ-ST vol. 3), 1690 (Hōkyōji ms., E-SBGZ-ST vol. 2), 1714 (Eiheiji ms., E-SBGZ-ST vol. 20), 1738, and 1774. This version formed the basis of the 84-book (75 + 9) version by Bonsei (see F-5).

F-3. SBGZ in 12 books, Yōkōji manuscripts. (E-SBGZ-ST vol. 1) dated 1420 and recopied in 1446: Also known as the "new draft" (*shinsō*), this is the compilation that Dōgen reportedly was writing shortly before he died. It consists of five new books, plus seven books from the 60-book compilation (which had not been included in the 75-book version). Significantly, the order of the books seems to reflect a new arrangement. Whereas both the 60- and 75-book compilations end with books on monastic life, this compilation begins with books that stress the importance of monasticism. Although all but one of these 12 books had been included in subsequent compilations, this 12-book edition as a whole remained unknown until a single manuscript of it was discovered at Yōkōji monastery in 1936. It contains the only manuscript of the SBGZ book *Ippyakuhachi Hōmyō Mon*. It also contains the only version of the book *Hachi Dainin Gaku* that includes the now famous postscript by Ejō (although Kenzei, 1415–1474?, of the Jakuen lineage also quotes from it), in which Ejō explains that *Hachi Dainin Gaku* is the 12th and final book in Dōgen's new draft; Dōgen had been revising

SBGZ books for the new draft until illness forced him to stop; and the new draft was to have consisted of 100 books. Every one of these statements raises questions: In contrast to the "new draft," what is the "old draft" (the 60-book or 75-book or both editions)? Why had previous books been revised, and what possible revisions had been planned but not implemented? Which previous books would have been kept, and which ones excluded from the new 100-book edition?

F-4. SBGZ in 28 books, Eiheiji manuscript (E-SBGZ-ST vol. 1), possibly dating from the middle of the 14th century: Also known as the "secret" (*himitsu*) SBGZ, this version contains 26 separate books, of which one book (*Shin Fukatoku*) is repeated twice and one book (*Butsudō*) appears in two variant versions (one of which was later titled *Busshin* in the *Honzan* edition). Some of its books (e.g., *Butsudō, Raihai Tokuzui, Shin Fukatoku*, etc.) differ substantially from other manuscript witnesses. It seems to have been compiled as a supplement to the 60-book version since many of its books were taken from the 75- and 12-book editions. Twenty-two of its books (23 if the repeated one is counted twice) still retain book numbers marking their original locations. Of these, 17 are from the 75-book edition, four are from the 12-book edition, and one (*Yuibutsu Yobutsu*) has a book number (38) corresponding to no known compilation. Note that five of the 28-book edition's books lack any number, and two of them (Bukkōjōji and Shisho) lack the title "SBGZ." Note also that the SBGZ in 28 books should not be confused with the kōan collection with the same title (*Himitsu Shōbōgenzō*), falsely attributed to Keizan Jōkin.

Other Premodern Manuscript Compilations

Sōtō monks of subsequent generations combined books from the four basic compilations to produce new versions of the SBGZ of various sizes (e.g., 78, 84, 89, 90, 95, or 96 books), each of which also exist as multiple manuscript witnesses. The evolution of these versions reflects changing attitudes toward Dōgen and his teachings. Some compilations include other independent works which, although attributed to Dōgen, do not appear in the four basic compilations and which were never previously labeled as being part of "Dōgen's *Shōbōgenzō*." These include, for example, *Bendōwa, Jikuin Mon, Jūundō Shiki*, and *Shōji*. Some compilations include a SBGZ book titled *Baika Shisho* (E-SBGZ-ST vol. 4) or *Chinzo* (ZSZ vol. 1 Shūgen Hoi) that modern scholars regard as apocryphal. Among the premodern compilations, the following have been especially influential:

F-5. SBGZ in 84 (75 + 9) books compiled by Bonsei (d. 1419): This compilation consists of the SBGZ in 75 books plus a separate group (*besshū*) of five fascicles containing nine books added from the 60-book version: *Sanjigō, Hokke ten Hokke, Bodaisatta Shishōhō, Shiba, Hotsu Bodai Shin, Kesa Kudoku, Shukke Kudoku, Kuyō Shobutsu*, and *Kie Buppōsō Bō*. Extant manuscripts are dated 1644

(Chōenji ms., E-SBGZ-ST vol. 4), 1658 (Daineiji ms., E-SBGZ-STZS vol. 3), 1680 (En'ōji ms., E-SBGZ-ST vol. 5), and 1718.

F-6. SBGZ in 89 (84 + 5) books, Daijōji manuscript (E-SBGZ-ST vol. 7) compiled by Manzan Dōhaku (1636–1714) in 1689: Manzan's version represents the first attempt during the Tokugawa period to compile a comprehensive and chronological edition of the SBGZ. Thereafter, until the publication of the *Honzan* edition, Manzan's version was the most widely copied version of the SBGZ. In this respect, Manzan began the process of creating the SBGZ as we know it today. His edition includes a supplemental (*shūi*) fascicle with five additional books: *Bendōwa, Jūundō Shiki, Jikuinmon, Jukai*, and *Hachi Dainin Gaku*. It lacks three other books: *Shizen Biku, Shōji*, and *Ippyakuhachi Hōmyō Mon*. Although Manzan based his compilation on Bonsei's SBGZ in 84 books, Manzan arranged the books in chronological order. The fact that he rejected the traditional order of the 75 books indicates that he believed that it was not based on Dōgen's intentions.

F-7. SBGZ in 96 books, Komazawa University Library manuscript (E-SBGZ-ST vol. 8) compiled by Kōzen: While serving as abbot of Eiheiji, Kōzen attempted to create a new version of the SBGZ even more comprehensive and more complete than the one compiled by Manzan Dōhaku. He integrated Manzan's supplemental books into the overall chronological order and added seven additional books: *Go Shin Fukatoku* (variant version of *Shin Fukatoku*), *Shōji, Dōshin* (variant version of *Butsudō*), *Shizen Biku, Yuibutsu Yobutsu*, and the spurious book *Chinzo*. His version lacks one book (*Ippyakuhachi Hōmyō Mon*). Kōzen repeatedly revised the chronological order of the books so that a final version was never produced. Nonetheless, his efforts became the basis for the *Honzan* edition (see F-9).

F-8. SBGZ in 78 (59 + 18) books compiled by Tenkei Denson (1648–1735): Tenkei believed that the SBGZ in 60 books had been compiled by Giun as the original and most authoritative version. The first 59 books in Tenkei's version are the same as in the 60-book version except for three alterations: *Mitsugo* replaces *Daigo, Shukke* replaces *Shukke Kudoku*, and *Zazengi* and *Zazenshin* form a single book. In a separate group (*besshū*), Tenkei included 18 books from the 75- and 12-book versions: *Menju, Shisho, Daigo, Tashin Tsū, Sesshin Sesshō, Raihai Tokuzui, Bukkyō* (Buddhist Teachings), *Sansuikyō, Shohō Jissō, Ō Saku Sendaba, Bukkyō* (Buddhist Scriptures), *Butsudō, Jishō Zanmai, Shunjū, Ten Hōrin, Zanmai Ō Zanmai, Dai Shugyō*, and *Sanjūshichibon Bodai Bunpō*. Tenkei explicitly rejected ten books: *Senjō, Den E, Busso, Shin Fukatoku, Baika, Hachi Dainin Gaku, Shizen Biku, Jinshin Inga, Jukai*, and *Shukke Kudoku*. His text lacked one book (*Ippyakuhachi Hōmyō Mon*). Tenkei compiled his version of the SBGZ while writing his *Benchū* commentary during the years 1726 to 1729. A few years earlier, in 1722, the government had banned publication of the SBGZ, which prevented Tenkei from ever preparing his commentary for print. When the *Benchū* was finally published in 1875, many sections of Tenkei's commentary were altered to avoid angering his opponents. The version subsequently reprinted in the *Shōbōgenzō Chūkai Zensho* (Jinbo 1957; see F-11) is even more unreliable since it accompanies the official *Honzan* edition, whereas Tenkei's comments were intended to accompany his revised and rewritten version of the SBGZ books. The only reliable version of the *Benchū* now available is the facsimile copy by his disciple Ryūsui Nyotoku (E-SBGZ-ST vol. 15).

Printed Editions of the SBGZ

F-9. The *Honzan* edition in 90 books (ca. 1815) and revised *Honzan* edition in 95 books (1906): This is the version that first introduced the SBGZ to a general audience. The *Honzan* edition is based on the SBGZ in 96 books compiled by Kōzen, but only 90 books were released. One book (*Chinzo*) was eliminated because of doubts as to its authenticity, and five other books (*Den E, Busso, Shisho, Jishō Zanmai,* and *Jukai*) were considered too secret to be released to the general public. These five books were added to the revised 1906 edition. It lacks one book (*Ippyakuhachi Hōmyō Mon*), which had not yet been discovered.

F-10. SZ 1929 and revised SZ 1970 editions: The original edition of the *Sōtōshū Zensho* (Complete Works of the Soto School, 1929) contains a SBGZ in 96 books consisting of the revised *Honzan* edition plus the spurious book *Chinzo*. The revised edition (1970) deleted *Chinzo*. Both editions lack *Ippyakuhachi Hōmyō Mon*. A supplemental series, *Zoku Sōtōshū Zensho* (1974), includes *Ippyakuhachi Hōmyō Mon* and *Chinzo* (ZSZ vol. 1). Although the 1970 edition corrected many of the earlier version's typos, for Dōgen's writings, even the 1970 edition has been superseded by more recent publications, such as DZZ 1969, DZZ 1988, E-SBGZ-ST, E-SBGZ-STZS, and Ōtani 1981 and 1991.

F-11. *Shōbōgenzō Chūkai Zensho* (Collected Commentaries on the SBGZ, 1956), edited by Jinbo Nyoten (1880–1944) and Andō Bun'ei (1883–1958): This 11-volume series edits together individual paragraphs from SBGZ books with corresponding passages from as many as 31 different types of commentarial sources. Despite its convenience, the many textual discrepancies and typographical errors in this work render it all but useless for serious scholarly work. Today, it has been completely surpassed by the commentarial sources reprinted as facsimiles in the E-SBGZ-ST series.

F-12. DZZ 1969 edited by Ōkubo Dōshū (1896–1994): The SBGZ books are arranged as an "old draft" (*kyūsō*) consisting of 75 (plus four alternative) books, a "new draft" (*shinsō*) consisting of 12 (plus one alternative) books, and a supplement (*shūi*) consisting of five (plus one alternative) books: *Bendōwa,*

Shōji, Yuibutsu Yobutsu, Hokke ten Hokke, and *Bodaisatta Shishōho.* The new draft uses the SBGZ in 12 books (Yōkōji ms. copied in 1446, E-SBGZ-ST vol. 1) as its source text, but the so-called "old draft" constitutes a hybrid compilation in which Ōkubo edits together manuscript witnesses representing the SBGZ in 60 and 75 books. A noteworthy feature of this compilation is the care with which Ōkubo strove to retain the original textual characteristics of the manuscript witnesses. It spite of its hybrid nature, therefore, this edition remains one of the few printed sources that attempts to reproduce the texts in their original form.

F-13. *Nihon Shisō Taikei* edition (vols. 12–13) published by Iwanami Shoten (Minzuno 1972), edited by Mizuno Yaoko: This edition consists of *Bendōwa* plus the SBGZ in 75 and 12 books. The 12-book version uses the Yōkōji manuscript copied in 1446 (E-SBGZ-ST vol. 1) as its source text, and the 75-book version uses the Tōunji manuscript copied in 1510 (E-SBGZ-ST vol. 6). Since the Tōunji manuscript consists of the SBGZ in 60 books, Mizuno supplements it with books from other manuscript witnesses to create a hybrid compilation. In this version, many editorial changes were made (e.g., in the glosses, etc.) to benefit modern readers. It contains explanatory notes by a literary critic (Terada Tōru), rather than by Buddhist scholars.

F-14. DZZ 1988 (vols. 1–2), edited by Kawamura Kōdō: This edition consists of four groups of texts: an old draft (*kyūsō*) of 75 books, a new draft (*shinsō*) of 12 books, a separate group (*besshū*) of nine uncollected (*mishūsei*) books, and a supplement (*shūi*) of seven initial drafts (*sōan hon*). The separate group consists of *Bendōwa, Jūundō Shiki, Hokke ten Hokke, Shin Fukatoku* (a.k.a., *Go Shin Fukatoku*), *Bodaisatta Shishōhō, Jikuin Mon, Yuibutsu Yobutsu, Shōji,* and *Butsudō* (a.k.a., *Dōshin*). The initial drafts consist of *Bendōwa, Shisō, Bukkōjōji, Senmen, Henzan, Daigo,* and *Sanjigō.* The old draft uses the Ryūmonji manuscript copied in 1547 (E-SBGZ-ST vol. 2) as its source text, whereas the new draft uses the Yōkōji manuscript copied in 1446 (E-SBGZ-ST vol. 1). This version contains the only printed edition of the SGBZ in 75 books for which every one of its books is based on the same manuscript witness (the 1547 Ryūmonji ms.), which also consists of the SBGZ in 75 books. This edition attempts to satisfy two audiences. On the one hand, it provides a historically accurate arrangement of the texts for scholars and, on the other hand, it edits them with modern glyphs and glosses, revised punctuation, and translations of Chinese passages to aid general readers. Although scholars will want to begin with this edition, many still will find it useful to consult Ōkubo Dōshū's edition (DZZ 1969 vol. 1) and the facsimiles in E-SBGZ-ST (vols. 1–2).

F-15. DZZ 1999 (vols. 1–9, of which only 1–7 have appeared), edited and translated into modern Japanese by Mizuno Yaoko: This edition uses the text previously prepared by Mizuno for the *Nihon Shisō Taikei* edition discussed above (F-13) with minor corrections and revisions.

Appendix 1: Tables of Contents for Each of the Four Basic Compilations
SBGZ in 60 Books

Table of Contents	Location in Other Compilations		
	75 Book	12 Book	Honzan
SBGZ no. 1. Genjō Kōan	1		3
SBGZ no. 2. Maka Hannya Haramitsu	2		2
SBGZ no. 3. Busshō	3		22
SBGZ no. 4. Shinjin Gakudō	4		37
SBGZ no. 5. Sokushin Zebutsu	5		6
SBGZ no. 6. Gyōbutsu Iigi	6		23
SBGZ no. 7. Ikka Myōju	7		4
SBGZ no. 8. Sanji Gō		8	84
SBGZ no. 9. Kobutsushin	9		44
SBGZ no. 10. Daigo	10		26
SBGZ no. 11. Zazen Gi	11		58
SBGZ no. 12. Hokke ten Hokke			17
SBGZ no. 13. Kaiin Zanmai	13		31
SBGZ no. 14. Kūge	14		43
SBGZ no. 15. Kōmyō	15		36
SBGZ no. 16. Gyōji (Part 1)	16		30
SBGZ no. 17. Gyōji (Part 2)	16		30
SBGZ no. 18. Kannon	18		33
SBGZ no. 19. Kokyō	19		20
SBGZ no. 20. Uji	20		11
SBGZ no. 21. Juki	21		32
SBGZ no. 22. Tsuki	23		42
SBGZ no. 23. Zenki	22		41
SBGZ no. 24. Gabyō	24		40
SBGZ no. 25. Keisei Sanshoku	25		9
SBGZ no. 26. Bukkōjōji	26		28
SBGZ no. 27. Muchū Setsumu	27		38

(continued)

Appendix 1: *(continued)*

Table of Contents	Location in Other Compilations		
	75 Book	12 Book	Honzan
SBGZ no. 28. Bodaisatta Shishōhō			45
SBGZ no. 29. Inmo	17		29
SBGZ no. 30. Kankin	30		21
SBGZ no. 31. Shoaku Makusa	31		10
SBGZ no. 32. Sangai Yuishin	41		47
SBGZ no. 33. Dōtoku	33		39
SBGZ no. 34. Hotsu Bodai Shin		4	70
SBGZ no. 35. Jinzū	35		25
SBGZ no. 36. Arakan	36		34
SBGZ no. 37. Henzan	57		62
SBGZ no. 38. Kattō	38		46
SBGZ no. 39. Shiba		9	85
SBGZ no. 40. Hakujushi	40		35
SBGZ no. 41. Kesa Kudoku		3	12
SBGZ no. 42. Hou	71		78
SBGZ no. 43. Kajō	59		64
SBGZ no. 44. Ganzei	58		63
SBGZ no. 45. Jippō	55		60
SBGZ no. 46. Mujō Seppō	46		53
SBGZ no. 47. Kenbutsu	56		61
SBGZ no. 48. Hosshō	48		54
SBGZ no. 49. Darani	49		55
SBGZ no. 50. Senmen	50		56
SBGZ no. 51. Ryūgin	61		65
SBGZ no. 52. Soshi Seirai I	62		67
SBGZ no. 53. Hotsu Mujō Shin	63		69
SBGZ no. 54. Udonge	64		68
SBGZ no. 55. Nyorai Zenshin	65		71
SBGZ no. 56. Kokū	70		77
SBGZ no. 57. Ango	72		79
SBGZ no. 58. Shukke Kudoku		1	86
SBGZ no. 59. Kuyō Shobutsu		5	87
SBGZ no. 60. Kie Buppōsō Bō		6	88

(continued)

SBGZ in 75 Books

Table of Contents	Location in Other Compilations		
	60 Book	28 Book	Honzan
SBGZ no. 1. Genjō Kōan	1		3
SBGZ no. 2. Maka Hannya Haramitsu	2		2
SBGZ no. 3. Busshō	3		22
SBGZ no. 4. Shinjin Gakudō	4		37
SBGZ no. 5. Sokushin Zebutsu	5		6
SBGZ no. 6. Gyōbutsu Iigi	6		23
SBGZ no. 7. Ikka Myōju	7		4
SBGZ no. 8. Shin Fukatoku		3	18
		4	19
SBGZ no. 9. Kobutsushin	9		44
SBGZ no. 10. Daigo	10		26
SBGZ no. 11. Zazen Gi	11		58
SBGZ no. 12. Zazen Shin			27
SBGZ no. 13. Kaiin Zanmai	13		31
SBGZ no. 14. Kūge	14		43
SBGZ no. 15. Kōmyō	15		36
SBGZ no. 16. Gyōji (Part 1)	16		30
Gyōji (Part 2)	17		
SBGZ no. 17. Inmo	29		29
SBGZ no. 18. Kannon	18		33
SBGZ no. 19. Kokyō	19		20
SBGZ no. 20. Uji	20		11
SBGZ no. 21. Juki	21		32
SBGZ no. 22. Zenki	23		41
SBGZ no. 23. Tsuki	22		42
SBGZ no. 24. Gabyō	24		40
SBGZ no. 25. Keisei Sanshoku	25		9
SBGZ no. 26. Bukkōjōji	26	1	28
SBGZ no. 27. Muchū Setsumu	27		38
SBGZ no. 28. Raihai Tokuzui		8	8
SBGZ no. 29. Sansuikyō		14	14
SBGZ no. 30. Kankin	30		21

(continued)

Appendix 1: *(continued)*

Table of Contents	Location in Other Compilations		
	60 Book	28 Book	Honzan
SBGZ no. 31. Shoaku Makusa	31		10
SBGZ no. 32. Den E		12	13
SBGZ no. 33. Dōtoku	33		39
SBGZ no. 34. Bukkyō (Teachings)		13	24
SBGZ no. 35. Jinzū	35		25
SBGZ no. 36. Arakan	36		34
SBGZ no. 37. Shunjū			66
SBGZ no. 38. Kattō	38		46
SBGZ no. 39. Shisho		19	16
SBGZ no. 40. Hakujushi	40		35
SBGZ no. 41. Sangai Yuishin	32		47
SBGZ no. 42. Sesshin Sesshō		27	18
SBGZ no. 43. Shohō Jissō		6	50
SBGZ no. 44. Butsudō		7	93
		9	49
SBGZ no. 45. Mitsugo		15	51
SBGZ no. 46. Mujō Seppō	46		53
SBGZ no. 47. Bukkyō (Scriptures)		25	24
SBGZ no. 48. Hosshō	48		54
SBGZ no. 49. Darani	49		55
SBGZ no. 50. Senmen	50		56
SBGZ no. 51. Menju		26	57
SBGZ no. 52. Busso		22	15
SBGZ no. 53. Baika			59
SBGZ no. 54. Senjō			7
SBGZ no. 55. Jippō	45		60
SBGZ no. 56. Kenbutsu	47		61
SBGZ no. 57. Henzan	37		62
SBGZ no. 58. Ganzei	44		63
SBGZ no. 59. Kajō	43		64
SBGZ no. 60. Sanjūshichibon Bodai Bunpō		11	73
SBGZ no. 61. Ryūgin	51		65

(continued)

Table of Contents	Location in Other Compilations		
	60 Book	28 Book	Honzan
SBGZ no. 62. Soshi Seirai I	52		67
SBGZ no. 63. Hotsu Mujō Shin	53		69
SBGZ no. 64. Udonge	54		68
SBGZ no. 65. Nyorai Zenshin	55		71
SBGZ no. 66. Zanmai Ō Zanmai		10	72
SBGZ no. 67. Ten Hōrin		16	74
SBGZ no. 68. Dai Shugyō		18	76
SBGZ no. 69. Jishō Zanmai		17	75
SBGZ no. 70. Kokū	56		77
SBGZ no. 71. Hou	42		78
SBGZ no. 72. Ango	57		79
SBGZ no. 73. Tashin Tsū			80
SBGZ no. 74. Ō Saku Sendaba			81
SBGZ no. 75. Shukke		24	83

SBGZ in 12 Books

Table of Contents	Location in Other Compilations		
	60 Book	28 Book	Honzan
SBGZ no. 1. Shukke Kudoku	58		86
SBGZ no. 2. Jukai		21	94
SBGZ no. 3. Kesa Kudoku	41		12
SBGZ no. 4. Hotsu Bodai Shin	34		70
SBGZ no. 5. Kuyō Shobutsu	59		87
SBGZ no. 6. Kie Buppōsō Bō	60		88
SBGZ no. 7. Jinshin Inga		5	89
SBGZ no. 8. Sanji Gō	8		84
SBGZ no. 9. Shiba	39		85
SBGZ no. 10. Shizen Biku		23	90
SBGZ no. 11. Ippyakuhachi Hōmyō Mon			
SBGZ no. 12. Hachi Dainin Gaku			95

(continued)

Appendix 1: *(continued)*
SBGZ in 28 Books

Table of Contents*			75 Book	12 Book	Honzan
1		Bukkōjōji	26		28
2	SBGZ	Shōji			92
3	SBGZ no. 8.	Shin Fukatoku	8		18
4	SBGZ no. 8.	Shin Fukatoku			19
5	SBGZ no. 87.	Jinshin Inga		7	89
6	SBGZ no. 42.	Shohō Jissō	43		50
7	SBGZ	Butsudō			93
8	SBGZ	Raihai Tokuzui	28		8
9	SBGZ no. 44.	Butsudō	44		49
10	SBGZ no. 66.	Zanmai Ō Zanmai	66		72
11	SBGZ no. 60.	Sanjūshichibon Bodai Bunpō	60		73
12	SBGZ no. 32.	Den E	32		13
13	SBGZ no. 34.	Bukkyō (Teachings)	34		24
14	SBGZ no. 29.	Sansuikyō	29		14
15	SBGZ no. 45.	Mitsugo	45		51
16	SBGZ no. 67.	Ten Hōrin	67		74
17	SBGZ no. 69.	Jishō Zanmai	69		75
18	SBGZ no. 66.	Dai Shugyō	68		76
19		Shisho	39		16
20	SBGZ no. 12.	Hachi Dainin Gaku		12	95
21	SBGZ no. 2.	Jukai		2	94
22	SBGZ no. 52.	Busso	52		15
23	SBGZ no. 10.	Shizen Biku		10	90
24	SBGZ no. 75.	Shukke	75		83
25	SBGZ no. 47.	Bukkyō (Scriptures)	47		52
26	SBGZ no. 51.	Menju	51		57
27	SBGZ no. 42.	Sesshin Sesshō	42		18
28	SBGZ no. 38.	Yuibutsu Yobutsu			91

Location in Other Compilations spans the 75 Book / 12 Book / Honzan columns.

* The Table of Contents reflects the actual textual designation that appear in the manuscript.

Appendix 2: Title Index for Individual Books of the Shōbōgenzō

Book Title	60 Book	75 Book	12 Book	28 Book	Honzan
Ango	57	72			79
Arakan	36	36			34
Baika		53			59
Bendōwa					1
Bodaisatta Shishōhō	28				45
Bukkōjōji	26	26			28
Bukkyō (scriptures)		47		25	52
Bukkyō (teachings)		34		13	24
Busshō	3	3			22
Busso		52		22	15
Butsudō		44		9	49
Butsudō (variant)				7	93
Daigo	10	10			26
Dai Shugyō		68		18	76
Darani	49	49			55
Den E		32		12	13
Dōshin (originally "Butsudō")				7	93
Dōtoku	33	33			39
Gabyō	24	24			40
Ganzei	44	58			63
Genjō Kōan	1	1			3
Go Shin Fukatoku				4	19
Gyō Butsu Iigi	6	6			23
Gyōji (part 1)	16	16			30
Gyōji (part 2)	17	16			30
Hachi Dainin Gaku			12	20	95
Hakujushi	40	40			35
Henzan	37	57			62
Hokke ten Hokke	12				17

(continued)

Appendix 2: *(continued)*

Book Title	60 Book	75 Book	12 Book	28 Book	Honzan
Hosshō	48	48			54
Hotsu Bodai Shin	34		4		70
Hotsu Mujō Shin	53	63			69
Hou	42	71			78
Ikka Myōju	7	7			4
Inmo	29	17			29
Ippyakuhachi Hōmyō Mon			11		
Ji Kuin Mon					2
Jinshin Inga			7	5	89
Jintsū	35	35			25
Jippō	45	55			60
Jishō Zanmai		69		17	75
Jukai			2	21	94
Juki	21	21			32
Jūundō Shiki					5
Kaiin Zanmai	13	13			31
Kajō	43	59			64
Kankin	30	30			21
Kannon	18	18			33
Kattō	38	38			46
Keisei Sanshoku	25	25			9
Kenbutsu	47	56			61
Kesa Kudoku	41		3		12
Kie Buppōsō Bō	60		6		88
Kobutsu Shin	9	9			44
Kokū	56	70			77
Kokyō	19	19			20
Kōmyō	15	15			36
Kūge	14	14			43
Kuyō Shobutsu	59		5		87
Maka Hannya Haramitsu	2	2			2
Menju		51		26	57

(continued)

Book Title	60 Book	75 Book	12 Book	28 Book	Honzan
Mitsugo		45		15	51
Muchū Setsumu	27	27			38
Mujō Seppō	46	46			53
Nyorai Zenshin	55	65			71
Ō Saku Sendaba		74			81
Raihai Tokuzui		28			8 .
Raihai Tokuzui (variant)				8	
Ryūgin	51	61			65
Sangai Yuishin	32	41			47
Sanjigō	8				84
Sanjigō (rewritten)			8		
Sanjūshichibon Bodai Bunpō		60		11	73
Sansuikyō		29		14	14
Senjō		54			7
Senmen	50				56
Senmen (rewritten)		50			
Sesshin Sesshō		42		27	18
Shiba	39		9		85
Shin Fukatoku		8		3	18
Shin Fukatoku (variant)				4	19
Shinjin Gakudō	4	4			37
Shisho		39		19	16
Shizen Biku			10	23	90
Shoaku Makusa	31	31			10
Shohō Jissō		43		6	50
Shōji				2	92
Shukke		75		24	83
Shukke Kudoku	58		1		86
Shunjū		37			66
Sokushin Zebutsu	5	5			6
Soshi Seirai I	52	62			67
Tashin Tsū		73			80
Ten Hōrin		67		16	74
Tsuki	22	23			42

(continued)

Appendix 2: *(continued)*

Book Title	60 Book	75 Book	12 Book	28 Book	Honzan
Udonge	54	64			68
Uji	20	20			11
Yuibutsu Yobutsu				28	91
Zanmai Ō Zanmai		66		10	72
Zazen Gi	11	11			58
Zazen Shin		12			27
Zenki	23	22			41

BIBLIOGRAPHY

Azuma Ryūshin, ed., *Go shahon eiin: Shōbōgenzō zuimonki* (*Shōbōgenzō zuimonki*: Facsimiles of Five Manuscripts). Tokyo: Keibunsha, 1980.

Bielefeldt, Carl, *Dōgen's Manuals of Zen Meditation*. Berkeley: University of California Press, 1988.

Dōgen zenji zenshū (Dōgen's Collected Works), 2 vols. Ōkubo Dōshū, ed. Tokyo: Chikuma shobō, 1969–1970. Rpt., Tokyo: Rinsen Shoten, 1989.

Dōgen zenji zenshū (Dōgen's Collected Works), 7 vols. Comp. Sakai Tokugen, Kagamishima Genryū, and Sakurai Shūyū, comp. Tokyo: Shunjūsha, 1988–1993.

Dōgen zenji zenshū: Genbun taishō gendaigoyaku (Dōgen's Collected Works: Original Texts with Modern Translations), 15 vols. to date. Comp. Kagamishima Genryū et al., comp. Tokyo: Shunjūsha, 1999–present.

Eihei Shōbōgenzō shūsho taisei (Dōgen's *Shōbōgenzō*: Complete Manuscript Series), 27 vols. Kawamura Kōdō, ed. Tokyo: Taishūkan Shoten, 1974–1982.

Eihei Shōbōgenzō shūsho taisei, Zokushū (Dōgen's *Shōbōgenzō*: Complete Manuscripts, Continued Series), 10 vols. Kawamura Kōdō, ed. Tokyo: Taishūkan Shoten, 1992–2000.

Ishii Shūdō, "*Shūmon tōyōshū to Shinji Shōbōgenzō*" (Dōgen's *Shōbōgenzō* in Chinese and the *Zongmen tongyaojí*), *Shūgaku kenkyū*, vol. 27 (1985): pp. 58–65.

Itō Shunkō, ed, *Eihei kōroku chūkai zensho* (Collected Commentaries on Dōgen's Extensive. Record), 4 vols. Tokyo: Kōmeisha, 1964.

Kawamura Kōdō, "*Shōbōgenzō*," i." In *Dōgen no chosaku* (Textual Works by Dōgen) 1980–1987, pp. 2–73.

Kim, Hee-Jin, *Dōgen Kigen: Mystical Realist*. Tucson: Published for the Association for Asian Studies by the University of Arizona Press, 1975. Rpt. Eihei Dōgen: Mystical Realist. With a foreword by Taigen Dan Leighton. Boston, M.A.: Wisdom Publications, 2004.

Kodera, Takashi James, *Dogen's Formative Years in China: An Historical Study and Annotated Translation of the Hōkyō-ki*. London: Routledge and Kegan Paul, 1980.

Kōza Dōgen (Lectures Aabout Dōgen), vol. 3. Kagamishima Genryū and Tamaki Kōshirō, eds. Tokyo: Shunjūsha, 1980.

Mizuno Yaoko, ed., *Dōgen*. In Mizuno Yaoko, ed., Nihon shisō taikei (Outlines of Japanese Thought), vols. 12–13. Tokyo: Iwanami Shoten, 1972.

Nishio Minoru, et al., eds., *Shōbōgenzō, Shōbōgenzō zuimonki*. Nihon bungaku taikei (Outlines of Classical Japanese Literature), vol. 81. Tokyo: Iwanami Shoten, 1965.

Ōtani Teppu, ed., *Manzan-bon Eihei kōroku, Sozan-bon taikō* (Dōgen's Extensive Record: The Manzan Edition, with comparisons to the Eiheiji Manuscript). Tokyo: Ichihosha, 1991.

Ōtani Teppu, ed., *Sozan-bon Eihei kōroku* (Dōgen's Extensive Record: The Eiheiji Manuscript). Tokyo: Ichihosha, 1989.

Ōya Tokujō, ed., *Kanazawa ibun* (Documents from the Kanazawa Library), 3 vols. Kyoto: Benridō, 1934.

Shōbōgenzō chūkai zensho (Collected Commentaries on the *Shōbōgenzō*), 11 vols. Jinbo Nyoten and Ando Bun'ei, eds. Tokyo: Shōbōgenzō chūkai zensho kankōkai, 1956–1957.

Shōbōgenzō no seiritsu shiteki kenkyū (Studies on the Historical Development of Dōgen's *Shōbōgenzō*), Tokyo: Shunjūsha, 1987.

Shōbōgenzō zatsubun hensan iinkai, ed., *Shōbōgenzō zatsubun: Shōbōji-bon* (Miscellaneous *Shōbōgenzō Texts*: The Shōbōji Temple Manuscripts). Tokyo: Shunjūsha, 2010.

Sōtōshū zensho kankōkai, ed. *Sōtōshū Zensho* (Complete Works of the Soto School), 19 vols. Tokyo: Kōmeisha, 1929–1935.

Sōtōshū zensho kankōkai, ed., *Sōtōshū Zensho* (Complete Works of the Soto School). Revised and corrected edition, 25 vols. Tokyo: Sōtōshū shūmuchō, 1970–1973.

Zoku sōtōshū zensho kankōkai, ed., *Zoku Sōtōshū Zensho* (Complete Works of the Soto School, Continued), 10 vols. Tokyo: Sōtōshū shūmuchō, 1974–1977.

2

What Is on the Other Side?

DELUSION AND REALIZATION IN DŌGEN'S
"GENJŌKŌAN"

Steven Heine

The Question of Consistency

Even by the standards of Dōgen, whose works abound in paradoxes, ambiguities, and apparent inconsistencies, "Genjōkōan" (Spontaneous Realization of Zen Enlightenment), often included as the first fascicle in his main collection, the *Shōbōgenzō*, stands out for the way it is entangled in at least a couple of levels of contradiction.[1] One main area of incongruity has to do with its place in Dōgen's oeuvre and the magnified sense of importance often ascribed to the fascicle despite its very much anomalous origins and style of composition that may seem to call into question—or, conversely, perhaps, reinforce—its exalted status. Is "Genjōkōan" as central as is often stated by commentators, who claim that it epitomizes all of Dōgen's teachings in one relatively short piece of writing? Perhaps this is the case, but the matter needs to be explored and explained from a neutral standpoint that examines Dōgen's works holistically, rather than argued primarily from the perspective of transmitting sectarian rhetoric, as is often the case, whereby long-established views derived from medieval Japanese Buddhist panentheistic theology are uncritically repeated.

Another level of contradiction, which is the primary theme of this chapter, involves some basic internal inconsistencies or apparent discrepancies of meaning within the text itself, especially concerning a key passage:

> When perceiving one side, the other side is concealed
> 一方を證するときは一方はくらし.

"Genjōkōan" has traditionally been understood as advocating an outlook of all-encompassing, seamless realization experienced without obstruction or partiality. What, then, is the significance of Dōgen's contrasting of revealment and concealment, or light (*shō*) and dark (*kurashi*), and by extension wisdom and ignorance, in relation to apparent proclamations of universal enlightenment? Does this passage support or somehow oppose the main standpoint of the fascicle?

The sentence about two seemingly opposite sides that are generated by the process of human perception of external phenomena may appear controversial and possibly out of place within the context of the paragraph or subsection in which it is contained, and it can also be contrasted with other key passages in the fascicle. This sentence concludes a short paragraph that begins:

> In seeing forms by engaging body–mind and hearing sounds by engaging body–mind, although things are perceived intimately, this is not like an image reflected in a mirror and it is not like the moon in water 身心を擧して色を見取し、 身心を擧して聲を聽取するに、 したしく會取すれども、 かがみに影をやどすがごとくにあらず、 水と月とのごとくにあら.

Because all punctuation considered standard in modern editions was imposed on the text retrospectively by later editors, one cannot be sure how to break up the sentence and, therefore, what is implied by the simple yet important word, "this," which has no direct grammatical equivalent in the original. Although it obviously references human perception, it is not clear whether the process represents the standpoint of enlightenment or unenlightenment, although traditionally it has been seen as the former because of the passage's emphasis on "intimate" knowing.

However, dividing the translation into two sentences with the second beginning, "Even so, this is not like . . ." might lend the passage a somewhat different flavor that could be interpreted to highlight a disjunction with or departure from the realm of enlightenment. The paragraph's rejection of the simile of the moon also seems to conflict with the assertion made a couple of paragraphs later that, "A person experiencing enlightenment is like the moon reflected in water," 人のさとりをうる、 水に月のやどるがごとし.[2] Furthermore, the reference in this passage to engaging body–mind may not be consistent with the image echoed in the fascicle's very next paragraph, which states that Buddhist practice is a matter of "studying the self by forgetting the self," 自己をならふといふは、 自己をわするるなり, which is enabled by "casting off body–mind (*shinjin datsuraku*) of self (*jiko*) as well as body–mind of others," 自己の身心および他己の身心をして脱落せしむるなり.

Do the various semantic components of the paragraph contradict or complement one another, and conflict with or reinforce other passages in "Genjōkōan"?

In exploring and evaluating this issue of translation and interpretation, I will first examine the traditional view expressed in *Goshō*, the earliest *Shōbōgenzō* commentary, composed in 1308 by Dōgen's disciple Senne and his follower Kyōgō, which has constituted the orthodox position for centuries and is endorsed by several modern exponents. This standpoint, which has greatly infused many of the current translations of the fascicle and discussions of the topic in Western literature, argues without hesitation that the sentence is question is consistent in expressing an absolutist view of enlightenment. *Goshō* finds an inner consistency in the sense that the darkness of the apparent other side of perception indicates the profundity and obscurity of transcendental wisdom, or the merging of all phenomena into oneness. In this sense, the image of concealment forms an ironic expression that supplements the remainder of the text's emphasis on universal, unlimited enlightenment.

However, newer interpretations challenging orthodoxy have been offered by several prominent Sōtō Zen commentators from Komazawa University, the sect's leading institution of higher learning, which houses the largest department of Buddhist Studies (Komazawa Daigaku Bukkyōgakubu) in Japan. In the early 1990s, a book published posthumously containing the writings of Kurebayashi Kōdō, a towering figure in postwar sectarian studies who had learned from giants like Nishiari Bokusan, and who tried to interpret *Goshō* for the modern world, helped to start a movement to revisit and reinterpret "Genjōkōan." Kurebayashi pursued a compromise that seeks to reconcile orthodoxy with contemporary scholarly trends regarding Zen theory and practice along with comparative philosophy and religious thought.[3] Although Kurebayashi's conclusions, heavily influenced by Nishiari's *Shōbōgenzō keiteki*,[4] which he edited, are in the end not so distant from those of *Goshō*, within a few years after the publication of his book three "Young Turks" emerged at the University, including Yoshizu Yoshihide, Matsumoto Shirō, and Ishii Seijun, to further the debate.[5] Each of these scholars has sought in varying ways to carve out an innovative relativist position regarding the passage on the two sides of perception that stands in contrast to interpretations based on the absolutism of sectarian orthodoxy. These interpreters argue that, even in the realm of enlightenment, opposites continue to intermingle from the standpoint of multiperspectivism that characterizes the content of the fascicle more generally.

A critical review and assessment of traditional and modern scholarship sets the stage for presenting my own interpretation of the meaning of the key passage for understanding "Genjōkōan." This view, which combines the most constructive aspects of absolutism and relativism, is based on the notion of "horizonality," or the idea that the range of human perception even for the enlightened is characterized by finitude yet allows for enhancing and transforming this limitation as the basis of attaining transcendence.

Status of the Fascicle

Let us first consider the initial level of contradiction concerning the status of the fascicle in Dōgen's oeuvre. On the one hand, "Genjōkōan" does appear to hold a prestigious position as acknowledged and propagated by Dōgen himself. It serves as the opening section of the mainstream 75-fascicle version of the *Shōbōgenzō* that was endorsed by *Goshō*, whose main author, Senne, was privy to private conversations in which Dōgen purportedly discussed his philosophy, and it is also the first fascicle of the important 60-fascicle version edited by Eiheiji's fifth patriarch, Giun, in the middle of the 14th century. According to the colophon in the modern edition of Dōgen's collected writings, the *Dōgen zenji zenshū*, "Genjōkōan" was written in mid-autumn of 1233 (the eighth month of the first year of Tempuku), making it one his earliest compositions.[6]

Even more interesting is the way the colophon suggests that Dōgen was still editing the fascicle 20 years after it was composed in 1252, which turned out to be a year before his death and over half a decade since he had authored any other writings included in the 75-fascicle edition.[7] If this were the case, it would make the endeavor of revising "Genjōkōan" one of Dōgen's final—perhaps even the very last—acts of involvement in the composition and organizing of the main version of the *Shōbōgenzō*. Furthermore, according to their notation about the colophon, it is conjectured by the *Dōgen zenji zenshū* editors that, at this late period, Dōgen (who, we can imagine, may have already felt sick and had a sense that his days were numbered in advance of his demise) was not only editing "Genjōkōan" but also arranging the order and sequence of the entire text. Thus, he was the one—rather than a subsequent handler, such as Dōgen's main disciple and scribe/attendant, Ejō—who placed the fascicle in a favored position.

In addition, the status of "Genjōkōan" is highlighted by the fact that it is often referred to as one of the "big three" fascicles; that is, it forms a part of the crucial "Ben-Gen-Butsu" trio, along with "Bendōwa" and "Bu[t]s[u]shō," in conveying the heart of Dōgen's teachings.[8] This point is complicated in that "Bendōwa," written in 1231, is not included in the 75-fascicle edition of the *Shōbōgenzō*, although it is the first section of the all-inclusive 95-fascicle edition that was created in the Edo period in order to gather into a single unit all of the Japanese vernacular writings in Dōgen's collection. Even among these three important fascicles, however, "Genjōkōan" is seen to play a special role. Kyōgō has argued that "Genjōkōan" sets up a thematic unity that is carried out all the way through "Shukke," the last section of the 75-fascicle *Shōbōgenzō*.[9] As Norman Waddell and Masao Abe point out in citing Nishiari's frequently cited commentary, *Shōbōgenzō keiteki*, "Many have written about the difficulties, beauty, and unobtainable depths of *Genjōkōan*. Nishiari Bokusan, an eminent Sōtō teacher of the Meiji era, calling it one of the most difficult of all the fascicles, said, 'This is Dōgen's skin, flesh, bone, and marrow. His entire teaching begins and ends with this fascicle, the other 95 fascicles are all offshoots of this one.'"[10]

As a testament to the importance of "Genjōkōan," not only are there a couple of dozen translations available in print or on the internet, which is the case with numerous sections of the *Shōbōgenzō* by now, but there are at least three books in English dedicated to interpreting this fascicle, although all of these involve a Japanese author or co-author who is primarily a cleric/teacher of practitioners, yet has also contributed to modern scholarship.[11] John Daido Loori, the founding leader of the Zen Mountain Monastery, who co-authored and provided illustrative photographs for the first book published in English in the 1970s with his mentor and longtime head of the Los Angeles Zen Center, Taizen Maezumi, once commented, "'Genjōkōan'" (The Kōan of Everyday Life) is the first and defining chapter of Master Dōgen's *Shōbōgenzō*. It is said that this section sums up all of the later fascicles. The writing is pithy and lyrical, each paragraph filled with a lifetime worth of teachings. [The fascicle's teachings] examine our everyday life as a way of boundless clarity, pointing out that the very barriers hindering us are the gates leading us to freedom."[12] To sum up and highlight the fascicle's prominent role, newcomers to the study or practice of Sōtō Zen in the West are often instructed that if they are going to start by reading one and only one piece by Dōgen, it should be "Genjōkōan."

Although all of this evidence seems to point overwhelmingly in the direction of the fascicle's significance, the contradictory nature of the role of "Genjōkōan" among Dōgen's collected works is indicated by several factors. The single main point concerns the anomalous quality of the text, which is distinct from all of Dōgen's writings in the *Shōbōgenzō* and elsewhere in his complete collection. These texts were almost always sermons or other forms of expression such as essays, poems, kōan commentaries, or monastic instructions delivered to monks in training either at Kōshōji temple in Kyoto, from 1233 to 1243, or at Eiheiji temple in the Echizen mountains, from 1243 to 1253. Instead, according to the colophon, this was an epistle written to an otherwise unknown lay disciple named Yōkōshū of Chinzei (Kyushu).[13] It has been conjectured that he was an official attached to Dazaifu, the government outpost located in northern Kyushu that dealt with foreign affairs and national defense. The circumstances surrounding the composition of "Genjōkōan" are obscure, but it is presumed that Dōgen must have met Yōkōshū during his return from China in 1227, when he landed and probably spent some time in Kyushu and may have also established a temple in the area. Dōgen either continued communicating with the layman for a few years by post, or Yōkōshū may have visited the master in the capital in the early 1230s, as he was beginning to form a new Zen movement.

Like all of the fascicles in the *Shōbōgenzō*, "Genjōkōan" is written in Japanese vernacular, but unlike almost all the other sections, for the most part, it does not rely on citing and making interlinear comments on Chan texts. However, there is a citation and discussion of an anecdote culled from a transmission of the lamp record in the final two paragraphs about a monk waving a fan in the breeze to show the importance of ongoing religious practice.[14] Nevertheless, the inspiration for the epistle probably came more from Chinese rather than Japanese sources. When Dōgen was in China, he must have recognized that a major approach of the Chan abbots was to be in touch with lay followers, particularly scholar-officials and literati who often visited the temple's main hall for a ceremonial vegetarian banquet or to listen to sermons and engage in informal discussions of doctrine that was often expressed through elegant Song-style poetry.

Chan abbots also offered spiritual advice to a variety of laypersons, especially through eulogies delivered orally or through the composition of letters and verse at the time of a family member's death; these included words of consolation and comfort through evoking the meaning of the Dharma.[15] Such an outreach effort was particularly endorsed by Dahui in the 12th century, who was a leader of the Five Mountains system of temples, including for a time Mount Tiantong, which Dōgen later visited, and it is evident from the Chinese-style verses (*kanshi*) he composed during his travels that Dōgen participated in this kind of ministry.[16] It is likely that Dōgen expected to continue such efforts in Japan but fairly quickly realized that the fledgling Zen movement in his native country, which had to compete for the attention and approval of authorities with established Buddhist sects, needed first to establish a strong monastic presence before embarking on proselytizing for a lay audience. Thus, he abandoned the use of epistle writing after the first such endeavor, but must have continued to value the original product composed in this style.

Furthermore, when considering the role of "Genjōkōan" in terms of the sequence of the *Shōbōgenzō* fascicles, given the extent to which the text was in the hands of editors from the time of Ejō through the Edo period—when defining sectarian identity as required by the shogunate was a crucial factor that often led to various kinds of theoretical and practical institutional revisionism—it can well be argued that Dōgen's intentions are not at all clear from the relatively meager scraps of evidence currently available. Thus, it would be misleading to read too much into a few scattered, cryptic comments, as in a colophon that was likely added by an editor who may have sought with hindsight to justify the placement of the fascicle or had some other kind of priority or agenda in including the remark.

Whether or not "Genjōkōan" was placed as the opening for the 75-fascicle *Shōbōgenzō*, whose order somewhat follows the chronology of the composition of the fascicles, simply because it was the first piece that was written or for complex ideological reasons in that it is summative of the entirety, its literary style is markedly different from the rest of the text. But what about the function of

"Genjōkōan" in terms of its aims in communicating doctrinal content compared to other components of the *Shōbōgenzō*? Does this fascicle, after all, serve as an ideal introductory statement that provides a concise, cogent, and compelling overview and synopsis of the whole work, or is it too inconsistent and variable for this purpose? My argument is that the fascicle does indeed epitomize Dōgen's approach in many important ways, but this is based in large part on how it integrates a view of the paradoxical, relativist intertwining of ignorance and wisdom, or of the partiality of enlightenment that has been overlooked by the traditionalist quest to emphasize exclusively the consistency of the entire fascicle and all of its seeming incongruities as an endorsement of absolutism.

Literary and Doctrinal Structure

As Yoshizu Yoshihide points out, as an epistle to a layperson, one might expect that "Genjōkōan" would be fairly straightforward and thus fairly easy to understand, but he and nearly all other commentators, both traditional and modern, agree that this is hardly the case.[17] Even though the fascicle was written for a nonspecialist, its meaning is considered elusive and mysterious. Most interpreters agree that its main purpose is to teach the importance of religious practice (*shūgyō*), especially zazen meditation, which is highlighted by the discussion of the kōan case about waving a fan; however, its doctrinal details have been appropriated in many different ways. Perhaps the enigmatic and ambivalent nature of the text is precisely the element that contributes to the way the fascicle captures the essence of Dōgen's multifaceted collection of writings.

Multifaceted Opening Paragraph

Much has been written regarding the way "Genjōkōan" starts off in contradictory fashion with a deliberately puzzling and difficult to grasp introductory paragraph consisting of four sentences, particularly in the seemingly quixotic relation of the final statement to the previous three:

> When all dharmas are Buddha Dharma, that means there is delusion and enlightenment, there is practice, there is life, there is death, there are all buddhas, and there are sentient beings. When the myriad dharmas are without self, there is no delusion or enlightenment, no buddhas, no sentient beings, no birth or extinction. Because the Buddha Way springs out of abundance and lack, there is birth and extinction, there is delusion and enlightenment, there are beings and buddhas. Nevertheless, even though this has been said, flowers fall to our sadness and weeds spring up only to

our chagrin. 諸法の佛法なる時節、 すなはち迷悟あり、 修行あ
り、 生あり、 死あり、 諸佛あり、 衆生あり。 萬法ともにわ
れにあらざる時節、 まどひなくさとりなく、 諸佛なく 衆生
なく、 生なく滅なし。 佛道もとより豐儉より跳出せるゆゑ
に、 生滅あり、 迷悟あり、 生佛あり。 しかもかくのごとく
なりといへども、 花は愛惜にちり、 草は棄嫌におふるのみ
なり.

The first three sentences represent a series of inconsistencies in affirming, then denying, and finally affirming again the existence of three sets of polarities: delusion versus realization, life versus death (or birth versus extinction), and buddhas versus sentient beings.[18] Although each of the sentences has a different structure, with the first two referring to the notion of "when" (*jisetsu*) there is unity with the truth in slightly varying fashion and the third evoking transcendence by using another kind of metaphor, it seems clear that the aim of this sequence is to invoke the Zen logic (or nonlogic), as initially expressed by Tang master Qingyuan, of "mountains are mountains, mountains are not mountains, and mountains are mountains." That is, the dichotomies exist but in a misleadingly superficial way for those who are just beginning to engage in Buddhist practice. In the next stage of spiritual development, for those who are in the midst of training, polarities seem to dissolve and disappear altogether; but, from the standpoint of attaining enlightenment and undergoing post-realization cultivation, the polarities reemerge and must be reckoned with as part of the authentic process of ongoing spiritual attainment.

Therefore, the overall message of the first three sentences is that the polarities, for better or worse, are alive and well, and do exist before, during, and after the experience of enlightenment, but these are not to be understood in the ordinary sense of constituting mutually opposed and everlastingly separable distinctions. Furthermore, it must be acknowledged that even one who has gained genuine spiritual insight cannot escape from and is compelled to continually grapple with the realm of duality. This sphere encompasses one basic natural polarity (life versus death) that characterizes reality, along with two anthropocentric polarities (delusion versus realization and buddhas versus beings) that mark the human quest to overcome ignorance by attaining wisdom. Or, another view is that the passage sets up an objective polarity, in that reality is based on the cycles of living/birth and dying/extinction, contrasted with one basic subjective polarity, which is based on whether or not the objective polarity is fully comprehended; that is, it shows the divergence and possible convergence between impermanence (*mujō*) and nonself (*muga*).[19]

What is the significance of the overarching dichotomy of nonduality, in the sense that all distinctions are surmounted from the standpoint of wisdom, and duality, in that even the wise must grapple with sliding back into ignorance while still struggling to overcome it? That is where the seemingly innocuous final sentence can be seen as crucial for interpreting the significance of the first paragraph as a whole and as a key to unlocking the inscrutability of "Genjōkōan." According to traditional interpretations of the sentence that follow the lead of the commentary of *Goshō*, the relation between nonduality and duality—as symbolized by the term *genjōkōan*, which is taken to signify "ultimate reality in which all things exist in their distinctive individuality [*an*] and are at the same time identical [*kō*] in their 'presencing' [*genjō*] or manifesting of suchness"[20]—is a matter of the sameness of differences and the differences of sameness, or of the unity of the equality of inequality and the inequality of equality.

Since the way the final sentence of the first paragraph, with its natural symbolism, is interpreted seems to be a strong indicator of how the passage on the revealed and concealed sides of perception is viewed, it is important to indicate the significance of an alternative interpretation. The orthodox view argues that that each and every aspect of human and natural existence, including falling flowers and flourishing weeds, as well as the ways people respond to these phenomena, pertains to the interior experience of enlightenment. The limitation of this approach is that it tends to collapse the distinction by identifying subjective awareness with objective reality, rather than highlighting a continuing creative dialectical tension between these realms. Thus, orthodoxy tends to project a degree of triumphalism that claims to embrace—yet in a subtle way dismisses—differences and inequality in favor of the priority of sameness or equality.

In contrast to the traditional emphasis, my approach builds in part on the view held by Kurebayashi Kōdō, who stresses that, for historical reasons since the time of *Goshō*, the Sōtō sect has played down the role of "kōan" in the title of the fascicle, largely because this school became associated with *shikan taza* or just-sitting (zazen-only) practice, whereas the Rinzai sect was identified as the kōan-based school of Zen.[21] Although by no means rejecting the *Goshō* interpretation, Kurebayashi argues that, from a contemporary vantage point, this level of meaning of "Genjōkōan" needs to be recovered and highlighted. Following that lead, I maintain that the final sentence regarding human reactions to the coming and going of natural phenomena, both desired and undesired, serves a kōan-like function of steering the discussion of the polarity of subjectivity and objectivity away from a logical response and toward an allusive metaphor, drawing from the East Asian religio-aesthetic tradition that at once seeks to affirm and to undermine the realm of the emotions of joy and despair in reacting to the vagaries of living and dying.[22] This view puts more emphasis on differences or gives a preference to contrast, conflict, and contradiction instead of the one-sided focus on identity that is found in the conventional interpretation.

In other words, the objective reality of life-and-death neither trumps nor is subsumed by subjective awareness regarding whether or not one awakens to an appropriate understanding of reality. Just as, according to other passages in "Genjōkōan," self-learning is paradoxically fulfilled through self-forgetfulness and the abiding dharma-position (*jū-hōi*) encompasses and yet is cut off from before and after (*zengo saidan*), Zen enlightenment includes and is free from longing and regret; it contains both an aversion and a profound resignation to suffering, as well as a desire for release without expectation or clinging. Intense emotional attachment that is spontaneously disturbed by sorrow and simultaneously detached from the tribulations of evanescence, or is independent of egoistic clinging and interdependently linked to the suffering experienced by all beings, is seen as the basis of the initial and sustained resolve that seeks to cultivate and renew realization beyond the (statically conceived of) attainment of enlightenment.

The final sentence of the first paragraph of "Genjōkōan" does not state a truth that is reducible to formula, but naturalistically conveys the perplexing yet inspiring encounters of the contradiction of pursuing release yet finding it directly through ephemeral beauty and lyric melancholy rather than philosophical reflection. From this standpoint, the loneliness of emotional response is seen as the fulfilled locus of spiritual renewal. When one opposes the flux by wishfully seeking a state of immutability or stagnation, Dōgen points out that the result tends to be just the reverse—heightened frustration—in that flowers still fall and weeds flourish, causing even more pain than before. To accord genuinely with reality is to accept uncompromisingly and resign oneself to the flux and to struggle urgently against the grief it causes by seeking a realization of nonself. However, even the effort to overcome self must be abandoned through uncompromising renunciation, but self cannot be cast off without continual aesthetic-emotional attunement to the sorrow from which it seeks release.

Therefore, the sentence about longing and despair reflects the issue of Dōgen's "primal question" (as framed in another text from the early 1230s, *Fukanzazengi*: What is the need for renewed practice if Buddha-nature is innate?), but from the perspective of having resolved—while still remaining deeply disturbed by—that ongoing concern. It articulates the initial and naïve yet profound longing for release which he and all Buddhist seekers share by suggesting a distinct value judgment about what should be promoted or prevented (flowers are preferable to weeds), as well as the sense of futility when this effort falls short in the face of impermanence (flowers still fall, and weeds keep growing). The sentence could be rewritten as the following: "Even so, to learn the Dharma is to be sorrowful about transiency. To be sorrowful is to transcend sorrow (as a source of attachment) and to realize impermanence as the nonsubstantiality of all phenomena." But, the complexity and depth of the sentence lies in its utter simplicity. It is a kind of kōan because it presents a disturbing and puzzling ambiguity whereby question and answer, problematic and resolution, speech and silence are intermingled. The sentence also expresses what Dōgen seems to mean by the term *genjōkōan* as the manifestation of each occasion in which one encounters, is moved by, and seeks to subdue but cannot fully overcome the effects of transiency.

Struggle Between Delusion and Enlightenment

The opening paragraph sets the stage for interpreting the remainder of "Genj-ōkōan" in that the way one views its final sentence as evoking either enlighten-ment (*satori*) or a mixture of delusion (*mayoi*, also pronounced *madoi*, or *mei*) with realization very likely forecasts the reading of the last sentence of the para-graph about the duality of human perception, in addition to other passages. To put this matter in perspective by making a key hermeneutic point that has not been noted by previous commentaries as far as I am aware, the structure of the entire fascicle can best be understood in terms of the way it carries out an analysis of the three polarities expressed in the very first sentence. Although "Genjōkōan" is not constructed systematically in the sense that there are more or less clear, consecutive divisions that move forward in a relatively straightforward "a-b-c" fashion, since the themes and imagery for each polarity are very much overlap-ping and interwoven throughout the text, it is nevertheless possible and useful to demarcate the main sections and various points of transition between portions of the fascicle.

Most translations differ, sometimes significantly, in the ways they configure the paragraphs. Following the opening four sentences of the first paragraph, in the rest of the text Dōgen exploits in novel ways typical Zen metaphors of moon representing calmness or aloofness and form or color symbolizing attachments, as well as fire standing for passions and ash for detachment. The next several para-graphs, including the passage about the two sides of perception, deal with the first polarity of delusion and realization.[23] Then, there are a couple of paragraphs that focus on life-and-death in relation to temporality by evoking the metaphor of a boat moving in relation to the seemingly shifting but static shoreline and offering an extended discussion of the connections, as well as disconnections, between firewood and ash. After this section, the rest of the fascicle treats the polarity of buddhas and beings by coming back to the metaphor of the boat and shore, this time with an emphasis on the multiplicity of perspectives regarding the sea, and adding a lengthy passage on the analogy of birds flying in the air and fish swim-ming in the water. As indicated, the two subjective polarities are so interwoven that, instead of highlighting three thematic areas, it might be preferable to refer to the early and concluding sections of the fascicle emphasizing the duality of subjective awareness as being either enlightened or unenlightened, in contrast to the duality of the objective reality of living and dying featured around the middle of "Genjōkōan."

Thus, the key juncture in "Genjōkōan" is the doctrine of the dharma-position, which is introduced in the context of the firewood and ash metaphor, because it is precisely how one receives and accepts the objective polarity of life-and-death unfolding each and every moment in relation to before-and-after that determines subjective awareness, or whether one remains a deluded sentient being or becomes an enlightened buddha. The various passages of the fascicle move back and forth between explicating delusion and demonstrating realization. The relation between these polarized realms is, in turn, based on the underlying connection—whether characterized by harmony or discord—between the self and the myriad dharmas (alternatively: "ten thousand things").

According to "Genjōkōan," fully realized buddhas are those who let things come forward and are enlightened about delusion, or who attain enlightenment beyond enlightenment without realizing they are buddhas. But they continually reconfirm their status by forgetting the self through casting off body–mind and inwardly receiving the transmitted Dharma, which they feel is somehow still lacking in their pursuit of ongoing realization. Hopelessly deluded beings, on the other hand, carry themselves forward to things and are deluded about enlightenment or compound delusion within delusion by trying to stay consciously aware of their status. In seeking the Dharma outside of themselves, they fail to renew their practice, yet feel complacently that what they have accomplished is sufficient. However, Dōgen's intention in drawing out these distinctions is not to set up a hard-and-fast dichotomy; buddhas and beings are very much interwoven, in that the former must emerge from the ranks of the latter and continue to struggle with those challenges, whereas beings need to cultivate their practice in order to seek to attain transcendence while actualizing the innate capacity to transform into the buddhas.

The Traditional View of Perception Based on Ippō Gūjin

It is in the context of highlighting the need to come to terms with the subjective polarity regarding delusion and realization that the passage about human perception appears in the fascicle. Before considering various interpretations traditional and modern, let us take a look at a couple of basic translation issues. First, the sentence is often rendered by two passive clauses as in, "When one side is perceived, the other side is concealed," but the first clause uses the infinitive (*shōsuru*), which justifies the active tense. Second, because the word used in the second clause refers to darkness, the first clause is often rendered with an image of light or illumination as in, "When illuminating one side, the other side is dark," but such a translation tends to imply a standpoint of attaining enlightenment that may seem to violate the apparently deliberate ambiguity of the sentence.

I basically agree with Thomas Cleary's rendering, "when you witness one side, one side is obscure,"[24] since this version both includes the active verb and avoids the allusion to brightness; however, the use of "you witness," while by no means inaccurate, favors seeing over hearing and also personalizes the activity in a way that may go against the grain of the original grammar. Also useful is William Bodiford's, "Illuminating one side obscures the other side."[25] In order to capture the intention of the title and contents of the fascicle, which highlight the interplay of wisdom and ignorance, as well as of fullness and partiality, my translation seeks to evoke Heideggerian imagery of the dynamic interplay of revealing, which always harbors a layer of concealment that in turn is ever seeking to break through the barriers to disclose itself, at least partially.

Another key element in the passage that is difficult to capture in English is that three verbs—"seeing" (*mito*), "hearing" (*chōshu*), and "understanding" (*eto*)—each consist of a compound that includes the main word accompanied by the suffix 取. This term is used in Chinese Buddhist texts as the equivalent of the Sanskrit term *upadana*, which means clinging or attachment and implies being seduced or betrayed by illusion. Although it cannot be ascertained that he intended it this way, the accumulated effect of using this term seems to indicate that the type of perception of which Dōgen speaks is a limited and deficient kind, or that an element of uncertainty must be taken into account in interpreting the passage.

Given that the sentence highlights the complementary or conflicting sides of revealment and concealment, and in the text appears after the negation of the simile of moon-in-the-water that is associated with enlightenment in a subsequent passage, it would appear to be easy to argue that the paragraph on perception based on engaging body–mind refers to the state of unenlightenment or ignorance. This would stand in contrast to the casting off of body–mind (*shinjin datsuraku*) mentioned in the very next paragraph on self-forgetting that leads to the attainment of enlightenment. However, such an interpretation has traditionally been neglected or dismissed in favor of a viewpoint that tends to diminish or suppress contradiction and difference by seeing all passages in "Genjōkōan" as affirming the sameness or equality of enlightenment.

Goshō's Approach

Since the early 14th century, the orthodox sectarian interpretation recorded in the earliest *Shōbōgenzō* commentary written by Senne and Kyōgō has generally been accepted as the most accurate and influential understanding of the sentence in question. As its title suggests, the original commentary by Senne, known as *Shōbōgenzō kikigakishō*, claims authority in that it was based on notes taken during the disciple's personal conversations (*kikigaki*) with Dōgen.[26] According to

Goshō, Kyōgō's remarks, which further comment on the records of his teacher's sessions, the originals of which have been lost, the sentence about perception refers exclusively to the realm of enlightenment because it means that if a person completely comprehends one particular thing and its Buddha Dharma—taking into account the dual use of the term *hō* 法 in its specific epistemological (phenomena or things) and general metaphysical (law or truth) senses—they will be able to comprehend completely all things or dharmas in harmonious conjunction with the whole of Buddha Dharma. This view follows the notion of *ippō-gūjin*, or the thorough investigation or total exertion of a single dharma, which is alluded to near the end of the fascicle. Although the notion of *ippō-gūjin* is not explicitly stated in "Genjōkōan" but is extrapolated by Senne/Kyōgō through evoking phrases from two different though consecutive sentences, the main passage that is claimed to articulate this doctrine reads,[27] "As someone practices the Buddha Way, expressing one dharma penetrates that one dharma and encountering one practice carries out that one practice," 人もし佛道を修證するに、 得一法 、 通一法なり、 遇一行、 修一行なり.[28] Some translators including Cleary, Yasutani, and Okumura insert the word "completely" or "fully" to modify the penetration of the dharma, although this seems to represent an overreach that is not explicitly indicated by the text. Also, Sōtō Zen's promotional materials often stress that "Genjōkōan" advocates thoroughly attaining and penetrating one single dharma or one single practice.

Therefore, according to *Goshō*, the word *ippō* 一方 translated as "one side" is understood as having the identical meaning as *ippō* 一法 or "one dharma," which has the same pronunciation. This conflation seems to represent the kind of philosophical pun Dōgen frequently uses and implies that the earlier passage on perception also evokes *ippō-gūjin*. From the standpoint of this interpretation, there is neither limit nor partiality in human perception, such that Dōgen expresses the concept of the oneness of the person and the object, thereby denying a separate existence of either. Moreover, the sentence, "When perceiving one side, the other side is concealed," expresses that all things have become aligned with one whole Dharma. *Goshō* asserts that the sentence indicates the notion of *ippō-gūjin* because when a person intimately perceives things by engaging the whole body and mind—again, the term "whole" is introduced into some translations and also intimate knowing is identified with intuition as a higher form or spiritual insight—he will realize the truth of the Dharma of the object. Since nothing exists outside of the Dharma, "one side" (*ippō*) is perceived as complete. Moreover, there will be no "other side"; thus, it is dark, but this darkness, like the "mystery" (Ch. *xuan*, Jp. *gen*) of profundity and depth mentioned at the conclusion of the first chapter of the *Daodejing*, indicates absolute truth beyond divisions. Similarly, in the "Kōmyō" fascicle, Dōgen cites a passage from Yunmen suggesting that the brightest radiance is the same as the deepest darkness of ignorance, although here Dōgen's comments ironically in a way that may cast doubt on the notion of absolutism implied in the source passage.[29]

In sum, *Goshō* argues that Dōgen expresses the state of enlightenment through the sentence, "When perceiving one side, the other side is concealed," which is compatible with the notion of a universal oneness or all-pervading Buddha-nature that declares all things of the world are co-existing interdependently and harmoniously. This approach seems to reflect the fact that Senne and Kyōgō—whose stream within the Sōtō sect may have stayed behind or quickly returned to Kyoto when Dōgen and his other disciples moved to the Echizen mountains in the summer of 1243—were very much influenced by the prevailing theology in the world of early medieval Japanese Buddhism—original enlightenment thought (*hongaku shisō*). This doctrine was associated with the Tendai sect established on Mount Hiei, where Dōgen was ordained and first studied before experimenting with Zen and traveling to China to gain enlightenment under Rujing.[30] Traditional accounts of Dōgen's great doubt about original enlightenment suggest that he distanced himself from the school in which he was trained. However, in accord with the panentheistic, one-is-all and all-is-one orientation of Tendai thought, *Goshō* asserts that if a person realizes the whole truth of one particular dharma or thing, then this specific moment of perception leads to a realization of the entire Dharma of all things.

The *Goshō* approach to the perceptual unity of subjectivity and objectivity that partakes of universal oneness is supported by several modern Sōtō commentators, including Hakuun Yasutani, who maintains that water and moon are "not two separate things that have become one" for the "actual experience of enlightenment is a completely different matter" of how to "manifest absolute reality (*genjōkōan*).[31] According to Yasutani, who translates the sentence about seeing sights and hearing sounds with the phrase "whole body and mind," Dōgen's sentence about perception implies *ippō-gūjin*: "It's the whole thing, being complete with one, exhausting everything with one."[32] Moreover, Shohaku Okumura similarly argues that the passage "means that we are living as a part of the entirety of all things."[33] For Okumura, although we refer to "self," it is not an island or an isolated unit but rather an entity that encompasses all beings or vice-versa as part of "wondrous reality of interdependent origination."[34]

Kurebayashi and the Relativization of "Genjōkōan"

Although perhaps only intending in small part to turn from the traditional absolutist view that is transmitted by Yasutani and Okumura, Kurebayashi has helped to question sectarian orthodoxy about "Genjōkōan" and to open the door to a complex and in some ways more compelling hermeneutic path based on a relativist view of the fascicle, including the sentence about the two sides of perception, which is treated for nearly a quarter of the length of Kurebyashi's book. The book is based on a series of lectures given in his home after retiring from teaching, which were edited by his wife, who was herself a well-known figure at Komazawa University. *Genjōkōan wo kataru* was published in 1992, four years after his death, with a preface explaining the origins of the work by the then eminent senior Dōgen scholar, Kagamishima Genryū, who has since passed away.[35]

This study was followed in short order by those of Young Turk scholars, including Yoshizu Yoshihide, who spoke of being motivated in part by Kurebayashi;[36] Ishii Seijun, who commented on Yoshizu's analysis of the passage; and Matsumoto Shirō, whose book on Dōgen responded to the arguments put forth by both of these scholars. All of the commentators who published interpretive materials of the fascicle in the 1990s deny that the passage about perception is intended strictly as an expression of the doctrine of *ippō-gūjin*, which constitutes an affirmation of the absolute, and argue instead that it highlights the inevitable partiality in perceiving things, as well as the intersection of delusion and realization.

One of the innovations that Kurebayashi initiates in interpreting "Genjōkōan" is to evoke the term *kōan* in two ways that were not previously being utilized in Sōtō sect discourse: one more general and abstract, and the other more concrete and specific. Despite the fact that Dōgen and other medieval masters in the Sōtō tradition made extensive use of kōan commentaries in their preaching, since the Edo period, the sect had come to define itself as the *shikan taza* tradition, in contradistinction to the Rinzai sect's emphasis on kōan-based pedagogy. Breaking this mold, Kurebayashi stresses that the contents of the fascicle, which are elusive and perplexing, function as a "manifesting kōan" or "kōan which reveals itself" (*genjō shite iru kōan*), thereby suggesting that the text harbors unrevealed and mysterious elements of meaning like the puzzling, riddle-like paradigmatic cases found in the main Song dynasty kōan collections (see Figure 2.1).

The second way that Kurebayashi emphasizes the term kōan is to compare some of the passages with the records of paradigmatic kōan cases. In particular, Kurebayashi draws an association regarding the sentence on perception with case 26 in the *Wumenguan* (Jp. *Mumonkan*) known as "Two Monks Roll Up the Screen," 二僧卷簾. According to the brief case record, "When the monks assembled before the midday meal to listen to his lecture, the great master Fayan of Qingliang pointed at the bamboo blinds. Two monks simultaneously went and rolled them up. Fayan said, 'One gain, one loss.'" 清涼大法眼、因僧齋前上參。眼以手指簾, 時有二僧、同去卷簾。眼曰、一得一失。[37]

Although Kurebayashi does not mention this, the kōan is similar to *Wumenguan* case 11, in which Zhaozhou interviews two hermits in their caves, and when both respond to his inquiry in identical fashion by raising a fist, the master applauds one and vilifies the other.[38] These two kōans suggest a pattern in which an identical response to a query is given opposite evaluations, whereas another

一　一
失　得

FIGURE 2.1 *Wumenguan* Case 26. From Kurebayashi, *Genjōkōan wo kataru*, p. 75.

pattern is that opposite responses are given the same evaluation, as when Zhaozhou says "go have a cup of tea" in several different dialogues no matter what his disciples are doing.

According to Kurebayashi, Fayan's retort in case 26, which indicates that "One has wisdom and the other does not," highlights the idea that the "Genjōkōan" passage about perception can be seen to encompass the relativism of a wrong side contrasted with a correct side, depending on timing and circumstance. Thus, there is always a misperception or element of delusion embedded in all acts of perception. However, another way of understanding the standpoint Kurebayashi puts forward has a nearly opposite implication in that it must be recognized that at any and every moment of perception there is also always a correct side. When seen in this context, Kurebayashi's argument may seem to reinforce the message of *Goshō* and also stands in accord across sectarian lines with the *Wumenguan* prose commentary's suggestion that there is an ultimate sense of oneness or non-discrimination beyond polarity: "Now, tell me, which of the two monks gained and which lost? If anyone has one eye, he will see through National Teacher Qingliang's failure. However, I warn against discussing gain and loss."[39]

Furthermore, Kurebayashi's interpretation is close to that of *Goshō* in that he features the notion of the "one side" (*hitotsu no koto*) of perception as a kind of oneness of subjectivity and objectivity in which singularity equals totality in a way that seems to deny the possibility for misperception or error. A simple but ingenuous illustration included in an earlier part of the book, which is used to highlight the doctrine of nonsubstantiality by showing how seemingly everlasting mountains are just as impermanent and "without self" (*ware ni arazaru*) as the flowing waters, can also be taken to represent Kurebayashi's more or less traditional approach that equalizes form and emptiness, as well as part and whole (Figure 2.2).

Moreover, the meaning of the term "dark" in the passage about perception is not directly addressed in Kurebayashi's discussion, so that it seems from the context of his writing that darkness is considered to be nothing other than "illumination." Finally, Kurebayashi notes that the image of the water and moon is used variably by Dōgen in different parts of the fascicle and other writings, but he feels that this is not necessarily a philosophical inconsistency. If anything is limited or partial, according to Kurebayashi, consistent with the notion of Zen as a special transmission that is not reliant on words or letters, it is the metaphors of the mirror and moonlight that serve as somewhat misleading rhetorical devices, in this case for separation rather than indivisibility, and not the process of human perception, which invariably remains untainted—yet partial—for the enlightened.

FIGURE 2.2 "All things are impermanent." From Kurebayashi, *Genjōkōan wo kataru,* p. 33.

Young Turks' Emphasis on the Unavoidability of Delusion

The three Young Turks, beginning with Yoshizu, who was stimulated by Kureba-yashi's manner of introducing the notion of relativism into discussions of "Genjōkōan" that were previously dominated by the absolutist view, all claim that the image of darkness in the sentence about perception refers to a lack of aware-ness. By way of refuting *Goshō*'s *ippō-gūjin*-oriented reading, the three scholars maintain that the passage expresses the state of "delusion" or the innate partiality of perception even for the enlightened. For these interpreters, there is invariably a factor of unknowability in that the human capacity to perceive and understand is limited and potentially deficient.

This view is reflected in a well-known saying used extensively in Chan litera-ture—for example, in a capping phrase comment on case 4 of the *Biyanlu* (Jp. *Hekiganroku*)—which suggests in somewhat tongue-in-cheek fashion that a Zen master can be compared to "someone carrying a board across the shoulder," or a person with tunnel vision.[40] The image of the board indicates that one's ability to view things in all directions is blocked, although there is also a Chan saying, per-haps just as tongue-in-cheek, about "growing an eye on the top of one's head" as a symbol of an all-seeing capability. A focus on innate perceptual limitations is reinforced by another passage in "Genjōkōan," particularly noted in Ishii's discus-sion, which speaks of traveling out to sea so that the shoreline can no longer be seen and becomes unrecognizable and unknowable to the disabled beholder.

Yet, each of the Young Turks in the end interprets the sentence, "When per-ceiving one side, the other side is concealed," somewhat differently. How far each of these scholars goes in emphasizing the dark side, so to speak, determines their overall interpretation of the fascicle. Yoshizu claims that one side referred to in the source passage indicates "external" phenomena and the other side represents "self," whereas Matsumoto states that one side refers to "vision" and the other side to "hearing," and Ishii argues that one side is "self" and the other side indicates what is "beyond the horizon." After examining these interpretations in light of the approaches of *Goshō* and Kurebayashi, I will present my own view that tries to synthesize traditional and contemporary, and absolutist and relativist readings of the passage in terms of the notion of horizonality.

Yoshizu's View

Yoshizu, a specialist in studies of Huayan Chan (Jp. Kegon Zen) who is also well versed but has not published extensively on Dōgen, was the first interpreter to argue in a straightforward manner that the sentence on perception expresses the standpoint of delusion rather than *ippo-gūjin*. He stresses that the passage points out the narrow-mindedness and one-sidedness of the discernment of things by all humans, including the enlightened. According to Yoshizu's reading, the one side that is perceived or revealed consists of external things (*gaikyo*) and the other side that is concealed or represents the realm that stands in the darkness is our inner self (*jiko*). In putting forward this interpretation, he offers an insightful explanation of why there is an apparent inconsistency regarding the moon-in-the-water simile used in the sentence on perception and a later passage:

> We think that we have perceived objects by seeing their forms and by hearing their sounds with our body–mind. However, the relationship between our understanding and our selves (body–mind) is not the same as the relationship between the moon and its reflection on the water. When we see a reflection in a mirror, we are aware of the reflection of ourselves and the mirror itself together, and recognize both our reflection and the mirror itself simultaneously. Also, the water that is illuminated by the moon and the moon itself that is reflected on the water occur at the same time. But these types of relationships do not exist when we perceive external things like sounds or forms. When we recognize only the external, our attention is focused solely on one side, which is to verify, comprehend, and perceive external things. At this juncture, however, attention is not being paid to the other side—our individual selves. Therefore, the attention toward our own body–mind remains in the darkness, so that our self is left unexamined.[41]

Yoshizu further relates the simile of the moon-in-the-water to an earlier sentence in the fascicle, "The myriad dharmas advancing and confirming the self is realization," 万法すすみて自己を修証するはさとりな. That is, the moon (or Dharma) illuminates (or provides the wisdom of enlightenment to) any given drop of water (or particular person or phenomenon) on which it shines and is reflected. Yoshizu goes on to state that, "When perceiving one side, the other side is concealed," is another way of expressing the point indicated in the second part of the above sentence, "Carrying the self forward to confirm the myriad dharmas is delusion," 自己をはこびて万法を修証するを迷とす. This illustrates the limitation and partiality of human perception when it seeks to impose itself on the external world, as well as the unfortunate yet inevitable tendency toward a lack of self-examination. Therefore, according to Yoshizu, the sentence that follows right after the paragraph about perception, "To study the Buddha way is to study oneself," 仏道をならうといふは、自己をならふ也, indicates that the other side that remains in the darkness is one's self, which needs to be studied. In the process of doing so, the self must be transcended, as suggested in the very next sentence, "To study the self is to forget the self . . . and be confirmed by all

dharmas," 自己をならふといふは、 自己をわするるなり ... 萬法に證
せらるるなり.[42]

Matsumoto's View

Following the lead set by Yoshizu in claiming that the passage about perception is
an expression of delusion, yet disagreeing with him about some of the implications of this argument, Matsumoto suggests that the notion of one side refers to
"forms," that is, visible things or sights (*iro*), whereas the other side refers to
"sounds," or audible things (*koe*).[43] Matsumoto's views on Dōgen are rather complicated and constitute a relatively small but important part of his overall project
of promoting Critical Buddhism (*Hihan Bukkyō*), which seeks to criticize any
and all notions found in various streams of East Asian Buddhism, including Sōtō
Zen, which seem to stray from a strict adherence to the basic Buddhist view of
karmic causality as the key moral principle guiding human behavior.[44] According
to Matsumoto and his colleague Hakamaya Noriaki, the early writings of Dōgen
tend to be linked to Tendai original enlightenment thought and the related doctrine of the universal Buddha-nature (*busshō*), which could be taken to imply that
humans can forego moral responsibility since they will partake of the ultimate
reality regardless of the consequences of their actions. But Dōgen gradually
moved away from this approach and, by the later period in the 1240s, when he
composed the text known as the 12-fascicle *Shōbōgenzō*, Dōgen embraced what
Critical Buddhism considers to be the authentic Buddhist view by going against
the tide of mainstream East Asian Buddhist ideology to emphasize the principle
of moral causation.

Matsumoto's approach to understanding "Genjōkōan" in the context of his
overall critique of the Chan/Zen school is based on distinguishing two views
of Buddha-nature theory: immanental Buddha-nature (*busshō naizai ron*),
which sees all sentient beings possessing ultimate reality (a view explicitly
rejected by Dōgen in the "Busshō" fascicle), and phenomenal Buddha-nature
(*busshō kenzai ron*), which sees ultimate reality manifested in all sentient
beings. According to Matsumoto, while still in the opening stages of his career
in the early 1230s, after returning from studies in China but before establishing
his first main Zen temple in Kyoto, in "Genjōkōan" and other examples Dōgen
started to make a dramatic breakthrough from the misguided view of immanental Buddha-nature that was prevalent in both the Chinese Chan and Japanese Tendai schools to an improved, although still in the final analysis, deficient
view of phenomenal Buddha-nature. Matsumoto provides a detailed examination of this transition, expressed in "Genjōkōan," which endorses the standpoint of practical Buddha-nature (*busshō shūken ron*) (in the sense of practicing
meditation through zazen-only).[45] The sentence, "When perceiving one side,

the other side is concealed," is applauded as a central part of this development.[46] Ironically, Matsumoto's appreciation of the passage about delusion is just as great, but is generated for reasons nearly opposite to that of *Goshō* and its modern exponents.

To explain and support his interpretation, Matsumoto suggests removing the clause that negates the similes of moon and mirror, which he feels is a distraction from the primary ideas of the passage, in order to view consecutively the two main thoughts on the matter of perception being expressed by Dōgen. The result of this abbreviation reads:

> In seeing forms by engaging body–mind and hearing sounds by engaging body–mind, although things are perceived intimately, when perceiving one side, the other side is concealed, 心身を挙して色を見取し、 心身を挙して声を聴取するに、 したしく会取すれども、 一方を証するときは一方はくらし.

Matsumoto points out that, in the grammatical structure in the first part of the sentence above, we find three nouns, including body–mind, forms, and sounds. Therefore, it is a natural thought process to insert the latter two terms into the meaning of the following clause, "when perceiving one side, the other side is concealed." The effect of this substitution is to replace the two nouns, "one side" and "the other side," which seem to have opposite meanings that can be contrasted. Thus, Matsumoto offers a unique reading of the final sentence of the original paragraph as, "When perceiving forms, sounds are concealed,"[47] and this could just as well be reversed.

Matsumoto agrees with Yoshizu's understanding that "perceiving dharmas intimately," したしく会取見取する, and "carrying the self forward to confirm the myriad dharmas," 万法を自己をはこぶ, are the same kind of actions that are described as delusory in "Genjōkōan." He further states that "the human actions of seeing, listening, and perceiving are defined as potentially unenlightened activities which lead to delusion."[48] Matsumoto understands that the misguided direction of "humans moving toward all dharmas," 人から諸法へ, is described by Dōgen as a delusory state and constitutes the opposite of "all dharmas moving toward humans," 諸法から人へ, which is indicated as representing the experience of enlightenment throughout the text of "Genjōkōan."[49] He asserts that if one takes actions that lead to the wrong direction, the Dharma will not reside in humans. In this way, "whole Dharma" remains unknown, such that only "one part of the Dharma" will be known as "one side." Therefore, the overall meaning of the sentence, "When perceiving one side, the other side is concealed," equals "only one part of the Dharma is known, and the rest remains unknown."[50]

Ishii's View

Although Ishii's publications on "Genjōkōan" preceded and influenced Matsumoto, I treat him last because his approach, which focuses on the role of the
horizon as a delimiting factor in the process of perception, becomes a spring-
board for the interpretation I wish to develop. According to the reading of the
key sentence by Ishii, a Dōgen specialist who has consistently tried to emphasize
the interwoven quality of the master's diverse body of writing at various stages in
his career, one side represents "self" and the other side indicates what is "beyond
the horizon."

To put forth his argument, Ishii stresses the need to pay attention to the sentence that is contradicted by the rejection of the moon-in-the-water simile, "A
person getting enlightened is like the moon reflecting in the water," 人のさとり
をうる、 水に月のやどるがごとし. This is one of the main expressions of
Dōgen's definition of the enlightenment experience, indicating that a sentient
being can attain authentic awareness in order to become a buddha. However,
Ishii points out that enlightenment is not the real moon itself, which serves
merely as a rhetorical device. He further argues that Dōgen maintains it is impossible for anyone to recognize all phenomena, so that the awareness of even an
enlightened person is limited. An understanding of human limitation is described
by Dōgen as, "When you have still not fully realized the Dharma in body–mind
you think it sufficient. When the Dharma fills body and mind, you feel some
lack," 心身に法いまだ参飽せざるには、 法すでにたれりとおぼゆ。
法もし心身に充足すれば、 ひとかたはたらずとおぼゆるなり.

Another crucial passage, according to Ishii, contains a different simile used to
describe the boundaries and partiality of human perception, which literally reads,
"sailing in the midst of the sea without mountains" (*yamanaki kaichū*). The implication of this passage—variously translated as "where no land is in sight," the
"ocean beyond sight of land," and "into a broad and shoreless sea"[51]—suggests
that when a person is in a boat floating in the middle of the waters, so that the
shoreline recedes from view and even the tallest mountains way off in the distance can no longer be seen, he tends to misrepresent the context of the situation
and believe that he is the only one in existence at that time and is located at the
center of the world, occupying the sole viable vantage point available. This adven-
turer recognizes only himself and the objects in the immediate, visible surround-
ings. Although mountains are indeed present beyond the horizon that delimits
his perception, their existence is unrecognizable in a classic case of "out of sight,
out of mind."

Thus, the traveler perceives the waters "as a circle only, without any other
characteristics. But," according to Dōgen, "the great sea is not a circle or any
other particular shape because its qualities are inexhaustible," ただまろにのみ

みゆ、さらにことなる相みゆることなし。しかあれど、この大海、
まろなるにあらず、 方なるにあらず、 のこれる海徳つくすべか
らざるなり. In another passage near the end of the fascicle that similarly deals
with the limitations of perception, Dōgen maintains that, "Since this is the very
place where the unfolding of the Way occurs, the limits of knowability cannot be
determined because the emerging and practice of knowing is simultaneous with
the thorough investigation of the Buddha Dharma," これにところあり、み
ち通達せるによりて、 しらるるきはのしるからざるは、 このしる
こ との、 佛法の究盡と同生し、 同参するゆゑにしかあるなり.
Therefore, Ishii maintains that the word "dark" is used by Dōgen not to indicate
enlightenment, as in *Goshō*'s view, but to describe the insufficiency of human
awareness or delusion, and he further argues that whatever exists in darkness are
invisible and unknowable objects, such as the rest of the ocean and the mountains
beyond the horizon (*nokori no kaitoku santoku*).[52]

According to Ishii, to determine whether the simile of the moon-in-the-
water can be used to express either enlightenment or delusion, the meaning
of "engaging body–mind" (*shinshin wo kosu*) needs to be examined. The
point of the conflict among various interpretations of the passage centers on
whether this seemingly positive activity is necessarily turned into the negative result of delusion. For Ishii, this is the case because of the aim of the act
of "perceiving the myriad dharmas intimately," 万 法をしたしく会取見取
すること. It can be said that this action is the same as "carrying the self," 自
己をはこ ぶ, to confirm the Dharma, which is defined as a delusion by
Dōgen.[53] Furthermore, the activity of "engaging body–mind" is the opposite
behavior to that of, "When buddhas are truly buddhas, there is no need for
them to perceive they are buddhas," 諸仏のまさしく諸仏なるときは、
自己は諸仏なりと覚知する ことをもちぬ. Engaging body–mind will
not lead the person toward the experience of enlightenment but will have the
negative effect of creating a cloud of delusion that represents a potential set-
back for enlightened awareness and must be overcome by renewed effort.

Conclusion
Whither Light Amid the Dark?

The following table provides an overview of the main ingredients of the various
traditional and modern interpretations, including the compromise standpoint I
am about to unfold.

Whereas *Goshō* emphasizes the notion that any and all perception is potentially pure and complete for the enlightened, in that perceiving any particular
object or one dharma reveals the entirety or the whole Dharma, the approach of

Interpreter	Standpoint
GOSHŌ	ABSOLUTE (No MAYOI)
ippō gūjin or one side equals one dharma	
KUREBAYASHI	RELATIVIZES ABS. & MAYOI
one side has it, the other side does not	
YOSHIZU	MAYOI re Self-Awareness
one side is external; the other side is self	
MATSUMOTO	MAYOI re Perception
one side is vision; the other is hearing	
ISHII	MAYOI re the Unknown
one side is self; the other is beyond the horizon	
HEINE	MAYOI inseparable w/ ABSOLUTE
the finite transcendence of horizonality	

the Young Turks can be summed up in the following straightforward way that tries to make explicit some of the ambiguity of the original passage in the fascicle: "When seeing forms or hearing sounds, the act of perceiving is intimate because all perception engages body–mind. However, perception is not necessarily enlightened awareness, which is like the moon reflected in the water or an image seen in a mirror, since when perceiving one side, as if going forth to confirm things and failing to be aware of the lack of truth, the other side is concealed."

My approach seeks a constructive middle ground that finds some degree of truth in both absolutist and relativist standpoints by stressing that there is, in one sense, no possibility of complete understanding even after self-forgetfulness takes place, in that even a buddha "carries a board across the shoulder." But there are also momentary instances of perception that involve full absorption in the realm of forms and sounds, whereby a focus on a specific sensation, such as seeing or hearing a drop of water, is fulfilled, so that crossing the horizon for that perceptual instant helps one realize a state of transcendence that is itself transient, ever shifting, and thus challenging to uphold.[54] Therefore, I both agree and disagree with the *ippō-gūjin*-oriented interpretation of *Goshō* and with the *mayoi*-oriented interpretations of the Young Turks, but I am especially influenced by Ishii's emphasis on the role of the horizon in defining at once the capabilities and limitations of the act of perception for the enlightened and unenlightened.

Perception and Nonperception

Although, as mentioned in the discussion of Kurebayashi's interpretation, *Wumen-guan* case 26 emphasizes the relativity of making judgments, another Chan dialogue first introduced into the analysis of the passage on perception by Nishiari and extensively examined by Kurebayashi highlights the matter of whether perceiving can, at least in some extraordinary cases, or cannot, because it is necessarily bound by the realm of attachment (as suggested by early Buddhist thought), become a vehicle for the experience of enlightenment. This anecdote cited by Kurebayashi involves master Xiangyan, who is sweeping the grounds of the temple as he performs daily chores when a pebble suddenly strikes a bamboo, making a clunk sound, and he abruptly drops the broom in an epiphanous moment of astonishment.[55] This is actually one of several prominent examples, as Nishiari shows, in the Chan literary tradition when a master reports that he has a satori experience from a special moment of perception.[56] The satori comes either through hearing sounds, such as Jingqing's spontaneous reaction to the pitter-patter of raindrops, which also recalls Bashō's haiku about the sound of the water (*mizu no oto*) when a frog leaps into an ancient pond, or seeing sights, such as Lingyun during an arduous mountain journey observing a spring peach blossom coming into bloom while discarding all his doubts, or Huineng counseling two monks who are debating the meaning of a flag moving in the wind that the movement takes place in their minds (see Figure 2.3).

FIGURE 2.3 Xiangyan and the pebble sound. From Kurebayashi, *Genjōkōan wo kataru*, p. 105.

Although Kurebayashi does not mention this, it is important to recognize that Dōgen comments extensively on the anecdotes regarding Xiangyan, Lingyun, and Jingqing, as well as Huineng, in a variety of sources, including the *Mana Shōbōgenzō* (cases 17, 155, and 286, respectively); several *Shōbōgenzō* fascicles, especially "Udonge" on Lingyun and Xiangyan; a number of sermons and kōan verse commentaries recorded in the *Eihei kōroku*; evening discourses included in the *Shōbōgenzō zuimonki*; and his Japanese waka poetry collection.[57] Supplementing this, in "Keisei sanshoku," which is one of several *Shōbōgenzō* fascicles that deals with the theme of how external forms and sounds, particularly in the pristine natural environment, can stimulate a Zen awakening and also mentions Lingyun, Dōgen opens by citing a naturalist verse from famed Song poet Su Shi. One of the prominent literati who interacted with Zen Buddhism extensively, Su Shi received approval for the following verse from his Chan meditation master on Mount Lu in the Huanglong school, Changzong (Jp. Jōsō), who was considered the second coming of Mazu (Jp. Baso), and its content is also evoked in one of Dōgen's waka on the *Lotus Sutra*:[58]

> The valley stream's rushing sound is the eloquent tongue of Buddha:
> The mountain's vibrant colors are nothing other than the form of Buddha.
> With the coming of night, I heard the eighty-four thousand songs,
> But with the rising of the sun, how am I ever to offer them to you?

In general, Dōgen's comments about the examples of Xiangyan, Jingqing, and Lingyun, as well as Su Shi's lyric, are overwhelmingly positive and supportive—and not at all skeptical or dismissive—regarding the efficacy of satori-like moments of perception in attaining a spiritual breakthrough.[59] In fact, he frequently compares these instances to Sakyamuni's experience at the dawn of his awakening when he gazed at the morning star with single-minded concentration free from hindrance or distraction. Nishiari Bokusan points out that when Lingyun perceived the peach blossoms, there was nothing else that intruded upon that all-encompassing experience in which "the entire ground and sky became peach blossoms," but if he had perceived something similar with cherry blossom then this would have represented the moment of *ippō-gūjin*.

In *Eihei kōroku* 1.36, Dōgen comments on the anecdote about Lingyun with the verse, "The high skies of spring now darken,/The green colors of the fields are clear,/Amid the ten million peach blossoms,/Where can we find the 'spirit clouds' (the literal meaning of Lingyun, 靈雲)?"[60] In addition to a couple of *kanshi* poems regarding Lingyun and other examples, Dōgen also writes eloquently of Chan perceptivity in his waka poetry; for example, a Japanese verse with the headnote, "Becoming enlightened upon seeing the peach blossoms" ("Kentōkagodō"):

Haru kaze ni	Petals of the peach blossom
Hokorobi ni keri	Unfolding in the spring breeze,
Momo no hana	Sweeping aside all doubts
Edaha ni wataru	Amid the distractions of
Utagai mo nashi	Leaves and branches.[61]

According to another waka, which recalls imagery of the moon to suggest that enlightenment is manifested in particular, natural, temporal and locative settings:

Yo no naka wa	To what shall
Nani ni tatoen	I liken the world?
Mizudori no	Moonlight reflected
Hashi furu tsuyu ni	In dewdrops,
Yadoru tsukikage.	Shaken from a crane's bill.[62]

Furthermore, inspired by Rujing, Dōgen expounds extensively in prose and poetic commentary on seeing and smelling the beauty of plum blossoms, which flourish and exude an intoxicating fragrance in late winter when there is still snow on the ground, as a symbol of eternal hope and renewal.[63]

This trend of affirming extraordinary acts of momentary perception that pervades Dōgen's various writings indicates that the *ippō-gūjin* approach of *Goshō* probably cannot be considered off base and discardable, as the Young Turks seem to suggest, but must be accepted as valid and integrated into an overall interpretation of "Genjōkōan." However, it is also very interesting and important to note that the kōan commentary literature that greatly influenced Dōgen does suggest at least a note of irony concerning the issue of whether perception is conducive to awakening, and this material tends to support the Young Turks' skeptical standpoint.

For example, the full dialogue of "Jingqing and the Raindrops" included in *Biyanlu* case 46, which is frequently cited by Dōgen, indicates the inevitable role of delusion that is part and parcel of his experience: "Jingqing asked a monk, 'What is that sound outside?' The monk said, 'That is the sound of raindrops.' Jingqing said, 'People live in an upside-down world. They lose themselves in delusion and only pursue [outside] objects.' The monk asked, 'What about you, Master?' Jingqing said, 'I was on the brink but did not lose myself in such delusions.' The monk said, 'What does it mean about being on the brink of losing yourself in such delusions?' Jingqing said, 'Stepping out looks easy, but attaining liberation is difficult.'"[64]

Another example of a kōan highlighting the undeniable role of delusion during the process of perception is *Wumenguan* case 16, "The Seven-Piece Robe as the Bell Sounds," in which Wumen's prose comment recommends that one should mistrust and stay detached from moments of perceiving things that may seem out of the ordinary. The main case is deceptively simple: "Yunmen said, 'The world is vast and wide. Why do you put on your seven-piece robe at the sound of the bell?'" According to Wumen's commentary:

> In studying Zen, you should not be swayed by sounds and forms. Even though some say they have attained insight when hearing a sound or seeing a form, this is simply the ordinary way of perceiving things. Don't you know that the authentic Zen practitioner commands sounds and controls forms at each and every moment? If you claim to be liberated, just tell me: Does the sound come to the ear or does the ear go to the sound? If both sound and silence fade off and are forgotten, at such a juncture how can perception be explained? Listening with your ear is not perception. To perceive intimately, you should hear with your eye.

In the first two sentences, Wumen questions, if not altogether negates, the kinds of momentary perceptual experiences that Lingyun, Xiangyan, and Jingqing claim have led to their respective attainments of enlightenment. However, in the rest of the passage, he does not deny that perception can be a key to genuine understanding, so long as it is based on the self-control of Zen meditation, which is capable of experiencing synesthesia by seeing sounds (or hearing colors), an image also evoked in some of Dōgen's reflections on Chan dialogues.[65] Furthermore, in characteristically ambivalent fashion, Wumen's verse comment maintains that the efficacy of perception is paradoxically at once affirmed and denied, along with equality and inequality, as well as awakening and nonawakening:

會則事同一家	If you are awakened, all things are one and the same,
不會萬別千差	If you are not awakened, all things are varied and distinguished.
不會事同一家	If you are not awakened, all things are one and the same;
會則萬別千差	If you are awakened, all things are varied and distinguished.

The Finite Transcendence of Horizonality

Does the mixed understanding of the role of perception represented in various kōan commentaries seem to echo and reinforce, or to undermine and negate Dōgen's complex view of the other side of concealment as expressed in "Genjōkōan"? How does the juxtaposition of these various kinds of Zen literature affect an interpretation of the fascicle? In *Shōbōgenzō* "Daigo," Dōgen comments extensively on a dialogue dealing in similar fashion with the thorny problem of the relation between delusion and realization. According to this case record, a monk asks, "What is it like when a greatly enlightened person is nevertheless deluded?," and the master responds, "A shattered mirror never reflects again; a fallen flower never returns to the tree."

According to Hee-Jin Kim's analysis, Dōgen's reading of this case is parallel to the message expressed in the "Genjōkōan" sentence, "When perceiving one side, the other side is concealed." Dōgen emphasizes not the irreversibility implied by the master's response—in "Udonge," for example, Dōgen cleverly notes Rujing's comment that "Lingyun gained enlightenment upon seeing the blossoms in bloom, but I gained enlightenment upon seeing them fall." In Kim's reading, from the standpoint of their common existential predicament, all humans, including the enlightened and the deluded, continually confront "the *interface* of delusion and enlightenment in their dynamic, non-dual unity [which] is extremely complex, elusive, and ambiguous."[66] Furthermore, Kim suggests, "The relationship between delusion and enlightenment is such that one is not the simple negation or absence of the other, nor does one precede or succeed the other," so that, "A greatly enlightened person is further greatly enlightened, and a greatly deluded person is still greatly enlightened as well."[67] Whereas the enlightened one is in but not of the world of delusion and the deluded one is in but not of the world of enlightenment, both parties are constantly shifting, transitioning, and transforming themselves for better or worse in terms of their apparent opposite, which not only conflicts with but remains integral to their own realm.

The complex and potentially productive yet innately limited role that perception plays in the process of awakening the authentic mind is expressed by Dōgen in the following waka poem. The poem plays off the image of the full moon used as a symbol in the Buddhist tradition, including in "Genjōkōan," for the universality of Buddha-nature, and in Court poetry, for the often uncontrollable emotions of longing and regret while seeking consolation through natural scenery and for the inevitability of change in term of daily and seasonal cycles that can lead to revitalization and rejuvenation:

Ōzora ni	Contemplating a clear moon
Kokoro no tsuki o	Reflecting a mind as empty as the open sky—
Nagamuru mo	Drawn by its beauty,
Yami ni mayoite	I lose myself
Iro ni medekeri	In the shadows it casts.

The poem highlights the underlying connection between a personal attraction to form and color and the development of a spiritual realization of formlessness by focusing on the word *medekeri* (lit. "love" or "attraction") in the final line, *iro ni medekeri* (lit. "attracted to form"). This phrase reinforces Dōgen's emphasis on the role of an emotional attunement to natural beauty. The word *medekeri* (also pronounced *ai*), which also appears in the final sentence of the first paragraph of "Genjōkōan" as part of the compound word *aijaku* (sadness) concerning the falling of flowers, indicates either desirous or compassionate love, depending on the context; both meanings seem implicit here.

This waka contains other terms that are highly suggestive from a Buddhist standpoint: *ōzora* (the "open sky," symbolizing emptiness or nonsubstantiality); *iro* ("form," the first of the five aggregates that constitute human existence, and the objects of desire); and *mayoi* (to "lose myself" in the ensnarements of self-imposed ignorance or delusion, a concept that is paradoxically identified with enlightenment in Mahayana Buddhist thought). The latter two terms are featured in "Genjōkōan." Through this imagery, the poem asserts the productive interplay between moon and mind, light and dark, and delusion and awakening. To be drawn by the moon for the beauty of its form and color (*iro*) is misleading (*mayoi*) but can become a self-surpassing experience if it leads to an understanding that the moonlight, as the source of illumination, mirrors the enlightened mind free of distractions (*ōzora*).

The aim of the Zen Buddhist religious experience is to purify and liberate the individual mind in order to reach an attunement with the holistic truth of concrete reality beyond the distinction of form and formless. In his interpretation of such doctrines as *sangai-yuishin* (triple world is mind only), *sokushin-zebutsu* (this very mind is itself the Buddha), and *shinjingakudō* (learning the Way through the mind), Dōgen argues that the universal mind, as the ground of phenomenal reality, is neither an independent possession nor an entity that views the world as a spectator from a distance. Rather, it is indistinguishable from "walls, fences, tiles, and stones," "mountains, rivers, and earth," or "sun, moon, and sky." Therefore, the perspective of perception is determined by the interior condition or the level of authentic subjectivity attained through a realization of the universal mind by observing transient forms and sounds. The observer must cast off his or her status as mere observer and become fully immersed in perceiving the unfolding of the impermanence of living and dying. Since the incessancy of change is inalterable, it is incumbent on the mind of the beholder to transform any negative impression of cynicism or pessimism on the part of the individual mind into, first, a positive outlook of creative resignation, and, ultimately, a transcendental awareness such that negativity is converted into a lyrical, holistic standpoint.

In a similar vein, renowned waka poet, critic, and editor Fujiwara Teika, who was Dōgen's contemporary in the Kyoto religio-literary world, argues that the value of poetic composition is a reflection of the ability of the mind to be actively involved with time and nature, so that "mind and words function harmoniously like the right and left wings of a bird." In the following waka, Teika examines the role of the perception of sounds and forms, "Why blame the moon?/For whether gazing on its beauty/Summons tears,/Or whether it brings consolation,/Depends upon the mind alone." He suggests that the apparent difference between delusion and realization is a matter of attitude, and that the perception of beauty can lead in either—or in some cases, both—direction(s).

In responding to the light of the moon, according to Dōgen's verse, even a mind originally or potentially clear (*ōzora*) invariably becomes lost (*mayoi*) in the shadows of forms (*iro*). This imagery resonates with the relativist view of "Genjōkōan" expressed by the Young Turks. Therefore, the verse shows that an intense focus on one particular thing, by engaging body–mind, can lead to being absorbed in a level of intimacy, which may seem lost in the misty approximation that characterizes perceptivity. This experience eclipses all other things that one needs and wants to see and hear at the very same time as the moonlight is taken in. Just as the shadow is a partial reflection of the true source, interaction with concealed brightness is also edifying yet limited. Thus, emotions represent both turmoil and the inspiration to awaken from the bondage they cause. The self must continually lose itself in the shadowy world of impermanence to ultimately realize itself liberated from yet still involved in the unceasing process of continual change.

Teika and Dōgen concur that the mind can be either mired in deception or rectified and liberated from distraction and vacillation based on the realization of the mind's capacity to overcome its self-imposed attachments. They see the authentic mind arising from a discipline or cultivation of contemplative awareness, which requires the proper physical posture (just-sitting) and scrupulous concentration, but culminates in a spontaneous or effortless experience. As indicated in the poems of both Dōgen and Teika, the genuine subjectivity of the mind can be understood only in terms of a holistic view of nature symbolized by the moon. It is the experience and description of nature by the authentic subject that seizes on and determines the relativity of the illusion and the truth of impermanent phenomena.

For Dōgen, in "Genjōkōan" and other writings, perception is necessarily delimited by a boundary of the horizon. But this border is ever shifting as one travels from land to sea and back—first locating with the eyes, then losing sight of, and then seeing once again the mountains—and the horizon therefore allows for breakthrough moments of seemingly ordinary yet remarkable perceptual experiences, such as Lingyun viewing the peach blossom or Xiangyan hearing a stone strike a bamboo, anecdotes celebrated throughout Dōgen's writings.[68] These momentary perceptions, which cross the gaps between partiality and wholeness, as well as possibility and impossibility, transcend specificity and enable a level of spiritual awareness that penetrates and even leaps beyond, yet without claiming to deny, the inevitable presence of the horizon. A text such as *Eihei kōroku* 1.52 reflects Dōgen ambiguity regarding the role of perception by concluding with the rhetorical questions addressed to the assembly of monks in attendance at the sermon: "What is it that you call sounds and forms? Where can sounds and forms now be found?"[69] Therefore, the views of *Goshō* and its contemporary followers, as well as of the Young Turks, instigated by Kurebaya-hi's ruminations are, at least temporarily and tentatively, reconciled by the paradoxical notion of horizonality as encompassing both limited expanse and borderless boundary.

3

"Just Sitting"?

DŌGEN'S TAKE ON ZAZEN, SUTRA READING, AND OTHER CONVENTIONAL BUDDHIST PRACTICES

T. Griffith Foulk

Dōgen has often been cast by modern scholars as the leading proponent of a "pure" form of Zen practice—one in which various conventional Buddhist ceremonies and rituals are eschewed, no "syncretistic" borrowing of elements from the Pure Land or Esoteric Buddhist traditions is tolerated, and no concessions are made to the demands of the laity for funerals, memorials, and offering services for the spirits of their ancestors. The erroneous nature of that depiction, and the not-so-hidden agenda of the Japanese scholars who formulated it in the century following the Meiji Restoration, are matters that I have addressed in some detail in previous publications.[1] There is no need in the present chapter to rehash my arguments concerning those matters, but I do wish to revisit what is without question the single most compelling (and, I believe, the *only*) piece of concrete historical evidence we have that lends any credence at all to the aforementioned image of the "purist" Dōgen.

The evidence I refer to is the famous, often-quoted passage from Dōgen's *Bendōwa*, written in Japanese, in which he says: "From the start (*hajime yori*) of your consultation (*sanken*) with a wise teacher (*chishiki*), have no recourse (*mochiizu*) whatsoever (*sarani*) to burning incense (*shōkō*), prostrations (*raihai*), buddha-mindfulness (*nenbutsu*), repentances (*shusan*), or sutra reading (*kankin*). Just (*tadashi*) sit (*taza*) and attain the sloughing off of mind and body (*shinjin datsuraku suru koto wo eyo*)."[2] This passage occurs just after an assertion by Dōgen that all the buddhas and ancestral teachers of the Zen lineage who uphold the buddha-dharma regard sitting upright (*tanza*) in self-enjoyed *samādhi* (*jijuyū zanmai*) as the true path that led to their own awakening (*kaigo*), and that sitting upright is the "marvelous means" (*myōjutsu*) employed by all the masters and disciples in India and China who attained realization (*satori*). Given that context, the passage in question appears to state quite clearly that sitting upright in self-enjoyed samādhi—the practice of zazen—is crucial to attaining the "sloughing off of mind and body," which in Dōgen's usage is a synonym for satori or awakening, and that the various other practices named are either unnecessary or perhaps even obstacles to achieving that goal. The passage would thus seem to provide solid evidence in support of those modern spin doctors who have claimed that Dōgen dispensed with all the superstitious beliefs, arcane doctrinal formulations, and religious rituals that other Zen Buddhist monks of his day embraced—including practices such as upholding moral precepts, studying sutras and commentaries, devotional worship, prayer, merit-making, and so on—and that he took instead a "single practice" approach in which he stressed "just sitting" (*shikan taza*) in meditation.

The problem with this interpretation is that it privileges the aforementioned passage from *Bendōwa* as the essence of Dōgen's teachings and ignores the extensive body of writings in which he not only endorses a wide range of conventional Buddhist practices, but explains in detail exactly how they are to be performed in the daily life of a monastery. In point of fact, all of the particular practices that Dōgen dismisses in that passage—incense burning, prostrations, buddha-mindfulness, repentances, and sutra reading—are explicitly and enthusiastically promoted by him in a number of his other works.

In the first half of this chapter, I document that fact in some detail. I then address the question that naturally arises when we consider the passage from *Bendōwa* within this broader frame of reference: What did Dōgen mean by issuing such apparently contradictory recommendations for Buddhist practice? How can we, as students and interpreters of his teachings, resolve that contradiction? Given the preponderance of historical evidence that points to Dōgen's embrace of all the conventional Buddhist practices he encountered in the large public monasteries of Song dynasty China, is the passage from *Bendōwa* something that we should dismiss as an anomaly, an offhand remark that he did not really mean? Could that passage even be an interpolation by later editors of something that Dōgen himself never actually said?

Neither of those explanations are viable, for Dōgen repeated the passage, using nearly identical words, in seven of his other writings: once in the *Hōkyōki* (Record of the Hōkyō Era), a diary of his personal exchanges with his teacher Rujing at the Tiantong Monastery during the Baoqing (Jp. *Hōkyō*) era of the Song dynasty; three times in his *Shōbōgenzō* (Treasury of the True Dharma Eye); and three times in the *Eihei kōroku* (Extensive Record of Eihei), a collection of Dōgen's remarks made from the abbot's high seat during convocations in a dharma hall (*jōdō*), his exchanges with disciples, verse comments on kōans, and so on. What is noteworthy about these additional occurrences is that, in six of the seven instances, Dōgen explicitly attributed the admonition to "just sit" (*shikan taza*) and "make no use of incense burning . . . etc." to his teacher Tiantong Rujing, whom he quoted using classical Chinese. It is virtually certain, therefore, that the passage from *Bendōwa* is actually Dōgen's translation into Japanese of a saying that originated with Rujing. This complicates the central question I raise in this chapter—what did Dōgen mean by issuing such apparently contradictory recommendations for Buddhist practice?—because we cannot assume that when Dōgen quoted his teacher he was also speaking for himself.

It could be argued that by translating Rujing's dictum and presenting it without attribution as instruction to his students in *Bendōwa*, Dōgen was not only endorsing it but in effect making it his own. In most of the other instances in which Dōgen cited Rujing's saying, however, he was "raising" (*kyo*) it as a topic to be commented on, not merely offering it as practical advice from an authoritative source. That is to say, he treated Rujing's dictum as an "old case" (*kosoku*) or "precedent" (*kōan*): a nugget of wisdom attributed to an old master that is hard to understand on the face of it and therefore demands interpretation. What this means is that Dōgen himself implicitly recognized the tension that existed between his teacher Rujing's admonition to "make no use of incense burning . . . etc." and the actual Buddhist practices that were standard procedure in the great public monasteries of Song China, including the Tiantong Monastery where Dōgen trained and Rujing was abbot.

In the second half of this chapter, I cite each of the eight occurrences of Rujing's dictum in its immediate textual context and analyze Dōgen's interpretation of it. In aggregate, the passages in question show that Dōgen himself struggled at first to make sense of the dictum, that he changed his view of it over time, and that what Rujing meant by "just sitting" may have been different from the understanding that Dōgen eventually arrived at.

Conventional Buddhist Practices Embraced by Dōgen

Most of Dōgen's writings on monastic discipline are actually commentaries on the *Rules of Purity for Chan Monasteries* (Ch. *Chanyuan qinggui*, Jp. *Zennen shingi*).[3] Some modern Japanese scholars have argued that the *Rules of Purity for Chan Monasteries* represented a form of Chan monastic practice that had already degenerated since the "golden age" of the Tang dynasty, and that Dōgen was a purist who rejected the "syncretic" and "worldly" aspects of Song Chan found in that text,[4] but there is no evidence of that in any of his writings. In virtually every case, Dōgen cites the *Rules of Purity for Chan Monasteries* as an authoritative work that his disciples should understand and follow to the letter. He disparages unnamed monks in Japan who are ignorant of or refuse to follow that model, and he criticizes individual Chinese monks for various shortcomings, but he never voices any disapproval of the forms of Buddhist monastic practice that he encountered in Song China. The particular practices that Dōgen apparently dismissed in *Bendōwa* are all found throughout the *Rules of Purity for Chan Monasteries*, and he clearly embraced all of them. Let us consider each of those practices in turn.

Burning Incense

The burning of incense (*shōkō*) in a brazier set on an offering table before an altar on which buddhas, bodhisattvas, devas, ancestors, or other deities are enshrined is a ubiquitous feature of East Asian Buddhist ritual and was already well established as such when Dōgen visited Song China. The burning of fragrant wood may have originated as a substitute for burnt offerings of meat from sacrificial animals, which was practiced both in the brahmanic worship of devas in ancient India and in rites for nourishing ancestral spirits in pre-Buddhist China. In any case, whatever is offered by fire disappears from the human realm, and the smoke apparently conveys it to the heavens, where the devas and spirits reside. In Buddhism, the burning of incense was adopted as a means of worshipping buddhas and other sacred beings that does not involve taking life. Being expensive, however, the burning of incense does involve "sacrifice."[5] In Buddhist terms, the offering of incense to a buddha, bodhisattva, ancestor, or other spirit enshrined on an altar is conceived as a good deed (*gō*) that produces merit (*kudoku*). Because it counteracts bad odors, incense smoke also came to be understood as a purifying agent. In Buddhist rituals that involve "censing" (*kō ni kunjiru*) offerings and official documents in incense smoke, the trope of purification is clearly at play. The burning of incense is also interpreted metaphorically in some Buddhist texts as an analogue for karmic retribution: just as the smell of incense spreads and lingers long after the act of burning it is finished, the performance of good deeds has far-reaching beneficial consequences that "perfume" the world.

In Dōgen's writings on monastic discipline, references to burning incense appear so often that to catalogue all the occurrences here is out of the question. In "Ango," to cite but one of those writings, the "ceremony of burning incense" (*shōkō gyōji*) as an offering is discussed in at least four different ritual contexts,[6] and it is clear that Dōgen fully endorses the Chinese custom of appointing an incense-burning acolyte (*shōkō jisha*) to serve as one of the five main assistants to the abbot.[7] The recipients of incense offerings mentioned in Dōgen's writings include figures enshrined on altars in a monastery, such as the earth spirit (*dojijin*) and the Sacred Monk (*shōsō*);[8] the ancestral teachers (*soshi*) of the Zen lineage; Dōgen's own deceased teacher Rujing; a monk's living teacher, when making a formal request of him; the current abbot and other senior officers of a monastery, in the context of thanking them for a kindness shown; the three treasures (*sanbō*) of buddha, dharma, and sangha; and sutras (*kyō*), monastic robes (*kesa*), and inheritance certificates (*shisho*), which are material objects that represent the Buddha's teachings, the Buddhist sangha, and the Zen lineage, respectively. The practice of burning incense, especially when it takes place before an altar, is often connected with other types of offerings (*kuyō*), mainly those of food, drink, and merit (*kudoku*) that is generated by chanting sutras, dharanis, and buddha names; the merit is dedicated (*ekō*) to the figure enshrined in conjunction with prayers for various benefits. The practice of burning incense, moreover, is so often conjoined with that of making prostrations that Dōgen seems at times to treat "burning incense and making prostrations" (*shōkō raihai*) as a single unit of ritual behavior. I cite examples of his use of that expression below.

Prostrations

The term that I translate here as "prostrations" (*raihai*) can be rendered more literally as a "bow" or "prostration" (*hai*) that is rendered as a sign of "respect" or "courtesy" (*rai*). Standing alone, the word *hai* has the basic meaning of "to bow," but its connotations in Chinese and Japanese include "saluting," "showing deference," "calling on a superior," "supplication," and "worship." In the East Asian Buddhist tradition, the physical act of making prostrations involves getting down on one's knees and elbows, lowering one's forehead to the floor, and turning one's hands palm up to symbolically take the feet of the Buddha. Quite apart from its Buddhist context, the social meaning of that posture as a sign of submission and humility (if not humiliation) is a human universal, and the making of prostrations has a psychological effect even if the practitioner regards it as a mere formality or "empty ritual." Buddhist monks traditionally spread a sitting cloth (*zagu*) onto the ground or floor in front of them before making prostrations, to protect their monastic robes (*kesa*) from being soiled, in both a literal and a figurative sense. In every case, prostrations are made "to" or "before" some person or being, whether in the flesh, in the form of an image (statue or painting), a stupa or mortuary tablet, or just imagined. When there is a physical frame of reference, i.e., when the object of respect (a person or an image) is visible, the prostration generally begins and ends in a standing position facing that object.

In Dōgen's writings, as in the Chinese Buddhist monastic rules he followed, basically two types of prostrations are frequently mentioned: (1) prostrations made to buddhas, bodhisattvas, ancestral teachers, protecting deities, and other figures enshrined on altars or just mentally conjured; and (2) those made by monks to other living monks, either in ritual settings that specify the type and number of prostrations to be made, or spontaneously in connection with individual requests for assistance or benefits and personal expressions of gratitude for things received. Again, there are far too many occurrences of both these types of prostration in Dōgen's works on monastic discipline to cite them all here, so I shall just give a few representative examples.

In his "Chiji shingi," Dōgen stipulates that the monk serving as garden manager (*enju*) should never fail to join the main assembly of monks when they engage in sutra chanting (*fugin*), recitation services (*nenju*), and other major ceremonies.[9] Moreover, "At the vegetable garden, mornings and evenings, he should never neglect to burn incense (*shōkō*), make prostrations (*raihai*), and recite buddha names (*nenju*), dedicating the merit (*ekō*) [produced by those activities] to the rain god (*ryūten*) and earth spirit (*doji*)."[10] Here Dōgen actually enjoins the strict observation of three of the practices that he names as unnecessary in *Bendōwa*: (1) burning incense as an offering before an altar; (2) making prostrations to a deity as an expression of reverence and/or an act of supplication; and (3) reciting buddha names (*nenju*), which is a form of "buddha-mindfulness" (*nenbutsu*) practice.

In "Ango," Dōgen discusses the formal salutations (*ninji*, literally "human affairs") that marked the beginning and end of the summer retreat (*ge ango*). The procedure, as he explains it, is as follows:

> "Salutations" (*ninji*) are mutual "prostrations" (*ai raihai*). For example, fellows from the same home district, some tens of people, may pick a convenient place, such as the illuminated hall (*shōdō*) or a corridor (*rōka*), and there make prostrations to one another, expressing felicitations on account of spending the same retreat together. . . . When dharma relatives (*hakken*) make prostrations to the abbot, this calls for spreading the cloth twice and making three prostrations (*ryōten sanpai*), or they may just fully spread the sitting cloth and make three prostrations (*daiten sanpai*). . . . Neighbors on the platform (*rintan*) and people in adjacent positions (*rinken*) all get prostrations. Acquaintances (*sōshiki*) and old friends (*dōkyū*) make prostrations together. As for the kind of people who reside in individual quarters (*tanryō*), including the head seat (*shuso*), secretary (*shoki*), canon prefect (*zōsu*), guest prefect (*shika*), bath manager (*yokusu*), and the like, one must go to their quarters and make congratulatory prostrations (*tōryō haiga*).[11]

As this passage indicates, different relations in the bureaucracy and social hierarchy of a monastery called for different levels of formality in making prostrations. In this chapter, Dōgen mentions a number of forms: "abbreviated three prostrations" (*sokurei sanpai*), "fully spreading the sitting cloth and making three prostrations" (*daiten sanpai*), "spreading the cloth twice and making three prostrations" (*ryōten sanpai*), "nine prostrations" (*kyūhai*), and "twelve prostrations" (*jūni hai*). He also explains the protocol for "prostrations in reply" (*tōhai*), in which senior monks politely acknowledge the obeisances paid them by juniors. The formal salutations (*ninji*) that Dōgen describes were also called for in connection with other major events on the monastic calendar, such as the New Year's celebration.

In "Jukai," Dōgen writes:

> One must burn incense and make prostrations (*shōkō raihai*) before the ancestral teachers (*soshi*) and ask [a living teacher] to receive the bodhisattva precepts (*bosatsu kai*). Having received permission, one should bathe and purify oneself, and don new clean robes. Or, one should thoroughly wash one's existing robes, scatter flowers, burn incense, make prostrations (*raihai*) and pay homage, and with that body don them. One should broadly make prostrations to graven images, make prostrations to the three treasures, and make prostrations to venerable monks of the abbot class (*sonshuku*), thereby removing all hindrances and purifying (*seijō*) body and mind.[12]

Here, burning incense and making prostrations are both presented as means of purification. Smoke, of course, can act as a disinfectant and preserving agent; also, incense smoke gets rid of bad smells. Prostrations cleanse one of the pride and arrogance that would hinder reception of precepts. Also, the merit produced by these acts is understood by Dōgen as an agent for counteracting karmic hindrances.

As an example of the somewhat less formal, essentially spontaneous occasions on which prostrations might be made, we have an account of Dōgen's own personal experience, found in "Shisho." Here, Dōgen reports that when he was in China, he got the chance to see an inheritance certificate that had been written by Chan Master Fozhao (*Busshō zenji*) and was currently in the possession of an abbot named Reverend Wuji (*Musai oshō*): "When I first saw it, how great was my feeling of joy! Surely this was thanks to the hidden influence of the buddhas and ancestors. I burned incense and made prostrations (*shōkō raihai*), then unrolled and examined it."[13] Later, he says, "I went to the abbot's quarters, burned incense and made prostrations, and thanked Reverend Wuji,"[14] for it was Wuji who had allowed him to see a document that was ordinarily kept hidden. The first act of burning incense and making prostrations mentioned here was Dōgen's way of showing reverence for the Chan lineage, as represented in a document that traced Fozhao's line of dharma inheritance back to the Buddha Sakyamuni. It was a mode of ritual so ingrained in the young foreign monk by that time that he seems to have performed it spontaneously. The second was performed as a way of expressing his gratitude to the abbot Wuji. Finally, quite apart from the formal adherence to norms of monastic etiquette, Dōgen argues in "Raihai tokuzui" that making prostrations (*raihai*) to spiritual guides is a practice that helps pave the way to one's own awakening.

Buddha-Mindfulness

In Japanese Buddhism, the expression "buddha-mindfulness" (*nenbutsu*) most often refers to the practice of invoking the Buddha Amitabha, using the formula "Adorations to Amida Buddha" (*namu Amidabu*), as taught in the Pure Land (*Jōdo*) and True Pure Land (*Jōdo shin*) schools that take Hōnen and Shinran as their founders. In the Buddhist monastic institution that Dōgen experienced in Song China and strove to replicate in Kamakura period Japan, however, "buddha-mindfulness" had a broader meaning that included, but was not limited to, the invocation of Amitabha in hopes of gaining rebirth in his pure buddha land, the western paradise. In Song Chinese monasteries, Amitābha was enshrined in the infirmary—a facility called the "life-prolonging hall" (*enjudō*) or, since many monks died there, the "nirvana hall" (*nehandō*)—and services for the newly deceased were designed to facilitate their rebirth in his pure land. In addition, as a matter of routine religious practice, the monks chanted a verse known as the *Ten Buddha Names* (*Jūbutsumyō*), and this too was a form of buddha-mindfulness. The verse was intoned as part of the daily mealtime ritual and as a merit-making device in the recitation services (*nenju*) that were performed on the 3rd, 8th, 13th, 18th, 23rd, and 28th day of every month.

That Dōgen endorsed and taught the recitation (*nenju*) of the *Ten Buddha Names* as a form of buddha-mindfulness used to invoke the figures named and to generate merit for dedication in support of specific prayers is clear from a number of his writings on monastic discipline. In the first place, his "Fushukuhanpō" contains a version of the *Ten Buddha Names* that is to be recited by the rector (*ino*) and great assembly of monks (*daishu*) before the midday meal:[15] "Birushana Buddha, pure dharma body./Rushana Buddha, complete enjoyment body./Shakamuni Buddha, of trillions of transformation bodies./Miroku Buddha, of future birth./All buddhas of the ten directions and three times./Mahayana *Sutra of the Lotus of the Wondrous Dharma*./Monjushiri Bodhisattva, of great sagacity./Fugen Bodhisattva, of the great vehicle./Kanzeon Bodhisattva, of great compassion./All honored bodhisattvas, those great beings./Great perfection of wisdom." A slightly different version of this formula (one that omits the *Lotus Sutra*) also appears in "Ango,"[16] where recitation (*nenju*) of it is used to produce merit (*kudoku*) for dedication (*ekō*) to "the dragon spirit of the earth (*doji ryūjin*) who is a protector of the true dharma (*goji shōbō*),"[17] in support of the following prayer: "We humbly pray that his spiritual luminosity will aid us; that he will widely extend his beneficial protection; that this monastery shall flourish; and that he shall long confer his selfless blessings."[18] The recitation of "buddha names" in this latter rite has a twofold aim: to invoke the buddhas and bodhisattvas as witnesses to the retreat, and to make a special appeal to the earth spirit (*dojijin*) for protection of the monastery during the three months of the retreat.

As noted above, Dōgen also calls for recitations (*nenju*) in conjunction with offerings to the earth spirit in "Chiji shingi." We know from that text, moreover, that he was familiar with the Chinese custom of holding so-called "three- and eight-day recitations" (*sanpachi nenju*) in the sangha hall (*sōdō*).[19] It is most likely, but not certain, that Dōgen implemented that practice at the Daibutsu Monastery (*Daibutsuji*), later known as Eihei Monastery (*Eiheiji*).

Repentance

The term used by Dōgen in *Bendōwa* that I translate as "repentances" (*shusan*) can be rendered more literally as the "cultivation" or "practice" (*shu*) of "regret," "remorse," "confession," or "repentance" (*san*). In East Asian Buddhism, that practice is more commonly referred to as *sange*, which can be glossed either as "confession/repentance (*san*) *and* remorse/regret (*ge*)," or the "confession/repentance (*san*) of transgressions (*ge*)." Buddhist rituals for effecting confession and the purification that it is said to bring about, moreover, are called "repentance procedures" (*senbō*) or "rites of repentance" (*sangeshiki*). Repentance rites and procedures were a ubiquitous feature of the Song Chinese monastic institution that Dōgen strove to replicate in Japan.

In the first place, according to the *Rules of Purity for Chan Monasteries*, the ordination (*jukai*) of novice monks (*shami*) in Song China called for repentances, which were brought about by reciting the following verse: "I now entirely repent/all the evil actions I have perpetrated in the past,/arising from beginningless greed, anger, and delusion,/and manifested through body, speech, and mind."[20] Sincere intonation of this verse, commonly known as the *Verse of Repentance* (*Sangemon*), is said in that text to "purify and heal (*jōji*) the karma (*gō*) of body, speech, and mind."[21] Secondly, there was in Chinese Buddhist monasteries a bimonthly ritual known as "confession" (*fusatsu*), which was based on the Indian Vinaya and entailed the gathering of the sangha to recite the *Pratimoksa* (*kaihon*), a list of moral precepts undertaken by individual monks at the time of ordination, and to solicit the public confession of any transgressions. In China, the *Pratimoksa* most often used was one associated with the *Four Part Vinaya* (*Shibun ritsu*); it contained 250 moral precepts for monks. Over time, however, there were efforts to replace the "Hinayana" *Pratimoksa* with a "Mahayana" version that could be used in rites of confession, such as the bodhisattva precepts (*bosatsu kai*) found in the *Sutra of Brahma's Net* (*Bonmōkyō*).

Dōgen was clearly knowledgeable about these Chinese precedents, and there is every reason to believe that he put them into effect in his own monastic community in Japan. In "Jukai," Dōgen begins by quoting the section of the *Rules of Purity for Chan Monasteries* called "Receiving the Precepts" (*jukai*). He does not specifically mention repentances in his own fascicle, probably because the section of the *Rules of Purity for Chan Monasteries* that he is commenting on does not broach the subject.[22] Nevertheless, it is evident from *Shōbōgenzō zuimonki*, a text traditionally attributed to his disciple Ejō (1198–1280), that Dōgen did endorse the practice of "reciting the precepts sutra" (*kaikyō*—i.e., the *Sutra of Brahma's Net*—"for the purpose of making repentances" (*sange no tame*) prior to receiving the precepts (*jukai*). He insisted, however, that there was no such thing as a violation of the precepts by a person who had not yet formally received them. Once the precepts were received, Dōgen said, any violation of them should be repented. That repentance would wipe out the sin, and the precepts could be administered again. We may infer, therefore, that he embraced the bimonthly rite of "confession" (*fusatsu*), although it is not explicitly called for in any of his extant writings.

The work in which Dōgen most directly states his faith in the power of repentance to mitigate the effects of bad karma is "Sanjigō": "The retribution for that evil karma of the three times will certainly be felt. Nevertheless, when one acts in a repentant (*sange*) manner, its heavy effects will be turned into light ones. Moreover, that [repentance] will extinguish one's sins (*metsuzai*) and cause one to be purified (*seijō*)."[23] In a somewhat different version of same text we find: "As the World Honored One has indicated, good and evil karma, once it has been produced, does not fade away even in a hundred, thousand, or ten thousand kalpas. When the causes and conditions (*innen*) are right, its results will certainly be felt. Nevertheless, if one repents (*sange*), one's evil karma will be extinguished, or its heavy effects will be turned into light ones." As Dōgen understands the dynamic of repentance, it is in itself a good deed that produces merit (*kudoku*) that counteracts, through a process of "purification" (*seijō*) or "extinguishing sins" (*metsuzai*), the otherwise inevitable negative results of bad deeds performed in the past.

Dōgen takes the practice of repentances (*shusan*) to be effective in two ways: (1) as an antidote to evil karma produced in past lives, which most people have no conscious memory of but which manifests itself nonetheless in difficulties that are experienced vividly here and now; and (2) as an immediate remedy to wrong actions that a person has recently committed and is fully aware of:

Dōgen recommends repentance of the first type in "Kesa kudoku":

> Thus, those who receive and hold a *kesa* should rejoice in their good karma from previous lives and should not doubt that there has been an accumulation of meritorious deeds and a piling up of virtue (*shakku ruitoku*). Those who have not yet been able to get [a *kesa*] should endeavor, quickly in this present life, to begin to sow the seeds [of good deeds]. Those have [karmic] obstructions and are unable to receive and hold [a *kesa*] should

feel ashamed (*zangi*) and repent (*sange*) to all buddhas—i.e., the tathagatas, and to the three treasures—buddha, dharma, and sangha.[24]

In other words, the good fortune of being able to receive a *kesa* (i.e., to become a monk) in one's present life is palpable evidence that one has performed good deeds in past lives and is cause for rejoicing. Conversely, an inability to receive a *kesa* in the present life is a sure sign of bad deeds done in past lives, which should make one feel ashamed and prompt one to make repentances before the buddhas and three treasures.

A good example of the second type of repentance is found in "Jūundōshiki": "One should not come into the [sangha] hall under the influence of sake. If one forgets this injunction and wishes to make amends, one should make prostrations (*raihai*) and repent (*sange*)."[25] Here we see repentance, coupled with prostrations (employed in this instance as a form of apology and a sign of submission to authority), being recommended by Dōgen as a means of making amends for a simple act of rule-breaking. In a similar vein, in "Den'e" he states: "If a feeling of loathing arises when one sees or hears about a *kesa*, realizing that this will lead to one's own rebirth in evil destinies (*akudō*), one should give rise to a mind of compassion (*hishin*); one should feel ashamed (*zangi*) and repent (*sange*)."[26] Here, the bad deed committed is a mental one. It is not a physical or a verbal act that is evident to others or overtly breaks any rule of monastic discipline, but it is something of which the person himself is aware, and thus it calls for immediate repentance.

One other aspect of Dōgen's understanding of repentance that is worth considering is the notion that repentances should be made "to," "before," or "in the presence of" buddhas and the three treasures. The idea here seems to be that repentance involves confession, and that confession requires a witness or audience if it is to be fully effective. In "Keisei sanshiki", Dōgen states: "Moreover, when one feels lazy in mind or in flesh, or experiences a lack of faith, one should make repent (*sange*) to past buddhas. When we act in this way, the power of the merit (*kudoku*) of repentances to past buddhas saves us and brings about purification (*seijō*). This merit gives rise to unobstructed pure faith (*jōshin*) and vigor (*shōjin*)."[27] And, somewhat later in the same chapter, he continues: "If one repents (*sange*) in this way, there is sure to be hidden assistance from the buddhas and ancestors (*busso*). With a reflective mind (*shinnen*) and properly deported body (*shingi*), one should confess (*hatsurō*) and tell all to Buddha. The power of confession takes the roots of evil (*zaikon*) and causes them to die out."[28] Here, Dōgen argues that repentance "to" (*ni* に) buddhas of the past, in addition to what might be called the "natural" or "automatic" good effect it produces in accordance with the law of karmic retribution, has the added benefit of enlisting the sympathy of the buddhas and ancestors of the Zen lineage, who will assist the penitent in mysterious and wonderful ways.

Sutra Reading

The term I translate as "sutra reading" (*kankin*) means to "look at," "read," or "think about" (*kan*) "sutras" (*kyō, kin*). Most Japanese Buddhist dictionaries draw a distinction between reading scriptures quietly, for the purpose of understanding the meaning, and reading scriptures aloud, for the purpose of generating merit for subsequent dedication in an offering ritual. However, there is nothing in Dōgen's use of the term "sutra reading" to suggest that he distinguished between the "intellectual" (reading quietly for meaning) and the "ritualistic" (reading aloud to generate merit) aspects of sutra chanting.

In the *Rules of Purity for Chan Monasteries* and other monastic rules dating from Song China, and in Chan biographies and discourse records contemporaneous with those texts, the term "sutra reading" (*kankin*) often refers to formal rites in which a group of monks chants scriptures aloud and the resulting merit is dedicated in support of specific prayers. Sutra reading, in those texts, also includes the practice of "revolving reading" (*tendoku*), which entails "turning" (*ten*) through the pages of sutra books at a speed too fast for actual reading (whether aloud or silently), and to "turning" or rotating the revolving stacks (*rinzō*) in a sutra library, both of which were understood as powerful merit-making devices. Those same texts also make it clear that, at designated times, monks could engage in sutra reading at their individual places in a common quarters (*shuryō*); in a sutra repository (*kyōzō*) or sutra hall (*kyōdō*); in a sutra reading hall (*kankindō*); or in an illuminated hall (*shōdō*), a building outfitted with desks and skylights that was located behind the sangha hall. In those settings, individual monks could select their own reading matter from the bookshelves and were expected to read quietly so as not to disturb their fellows. The range of meanings of "sutra reading" given in modern dictionaries is thus well attested in primary sources dating from Dōgen's day, but it is far from certain that anyone at the time drew such a sharp distinction between "reading quietly for meaning" and "reading aloud to generate merit." For all we know, monks who engaged in merit-making rituals also contemplated the meaning of the sutras they chanted, and monks who read sutras silently on their own also conceived that activity as one that would bring karmic reward.

In "Kankin" (Sutra Readings), Dōgen takes all of those meanings of the term for granted and gives detailed instructions for how the various rites are to be performed. I quote parts of those instructions here in order to show just how invested Dōgen actually was in merit-making rituals performed for the benefit of lay patrons and rulers, whose donations and political support sustained the monastic institution in both China and Japan. It is also worth noting how integral the practices of burning incense and making prostrations are to the rites of sutra reading prescribed and explained by Dōgen. The following is a translation of relevant sections of "Kankin":

In present day assemblies of the buddhas and ancestors (*busso no e*), there are many types of ceremonial procedures (*gisoku*) for sutra reading (*kankin*). Examples include: donors (*seshu*) visiting a monastery and requesting that the monks of the great assembly read sutras; sutra reading in which monks are requested to engage in perpetual revolving (*jōten*); sutra reading initiated by monks of the assembly on their own accord; and so on. In addition, there is sutra chanting performed by the great assembly on behalf of a deceased monk.

In the case of donors visiting a monastery and requesting that the monks of the great assembly read sutras . . . the head seat (*shuso*) and monks of the great assembly don *kesas*, enter the cloud hall,[29] go to their assigned places, and sit facing forward. Next, the abbot enters the hall, faces the Sacred Monk, bows in gassho, burns incense (*shōkō*), and when finished sits at his place. Then, have young postulants (*zunnan*) hand out sutras. . . .

The monks of the great assembly, having received sutras, immediately open them and read. At this point, the guest prefect (*shika*) at once enters the cloud hall leading the donor. . . .

The donor goes in before the sacred monk, burns a pinch of incense, and makes three prostrations (*sanpai*). . . .

Next, the sutra-reading money (*kankin sen*) is distributed. The amount of money accords with the wishes of the donor. In some cases, goods such as cloth or fans are distributed instead. The donor himself makes the distribution, or a steward (*chiji*) makes the distribution. Or, a postulant makes the distribution. The procedure for distribution is to place the item in front of the monk, not to put it directly into the monk's hands. When an allotment of money is placed in front of each individual monk of the assembly, they receive it with a gassho. Allotments of money, alternatively, may be distributed at the main meal time on the day of the sutra reading. . . .

The aim of the donor's dedication of merit (*seshu ekō*) is written on a sheet of paper, which is pasted to the left pillar of the Sacred Monk's altar. . . .

There is something called the imperial holiday (*shōsetsu*) sutra reading. If, for example, the current emperor's birthday is the 15th day of the first month, then the imperial holiday sutra reading begins from the 15th day of the preceding 12th month. . . .

From the opening day on, an "establishing ritual site for imperial prayers" placard (*ken shukushin dōjō no hai*) is hung under the eaves on the east side of the front of the buddha hall. . . . Sutra reading in this manner is continued up until the imperial birthday, when the abbot ascends to the dharma hall and performs prayers for the emperor. This has been the custom from ancient times, and even now it is not out of fashion.

Moreover, there is sutra reading that monks engage in of their own accord. Monasteries have always had communal sutra reading halls (*kankindō*). Sutra reading is done in those halls. The ritual procedures for that are as given in current rules of purity (*shingi*).[30]

Given these instructions, and the many similar passages that are found throughout Dōgen's writings on monastic discipline, it is remarkable that modern Japanese scholars have depicted him as a master of "pure Zen" (*junsui zen*) who rejected the "superstitious" (*meishinteki*) practice of merit-making, the "worldly" (*sekenteki*) concern with patronage, and the "overly intellectual" (*rikutsuppoi*) engagement with sutra literature, all of which they take as signs of the "degeneration" of Zen in Song dynasty China. The vision of a "pure," "original" Zen that informs this view is largely the product of wishful thinking on the part of academic apologists for the Zen schools of modern Japan. The projection of that ideal onto the figure of Dōgen is scarcely defensible, but the aforementioned passage from *Bendōwa* does give it some measure of credibility.

Dōgen's Interpretations of Rujing's Dictum

As noted above, Dōgen's admonition to "have no recourse whatsoever to burning incense, prostrations, buddha-mindfulness, repentances, or sutra reading" is voiced in Japanese in *Bendōwa*, but a very similar statement, written in classical Chinese and almost always attributed to Tiantong Rujing, occurs seven other times in his extant writings. In the following pages, I analyze each of the eight occurrences under the heading of the text in which it appears. I treat the texts in question in chronological order, based on the dates given in colophons and other indications of when they were written or recorded. In each case, I pay attention to Dōgen's reasons (stated or implicit) for citing Rujing, because his comments on his teacher's saying must be understood within those contexts.

Hōkyōki

The evidence of this text is especially useful for the purposes of this chapter because it opens a window on what Dōgen thought when he first encountered Rujing's dictum. The "Hōkyō Era" referred to in the title is the Baoqing (*Hōkyō*) era of the reign of emperor Lizong of the Song, which corresponds to the years 1225–1228.[31] Modern scholars have questioned whether the text as we now have it was actually written at that time, or whether it was redacted later by Dōgen or subsequent editors. Despite these uncertainties, I am inclined to accept the passage that deals with Rujing's dictum as a veritable record of Dōgen's initial reaction to it, for as we shall see, it does seem to represent an immature point of view that differs considerably from his subsequent comments. The setting, presumably, was in the abbot's quarters of the Tiantong Monastery, where the young Japanese disciple had been given the privilege of "entering the room" (*nisshitsu*) of the master:

> The reverend abbot (*dōchō oshō*) said, "Studying Zen (*sanzen*) is body and mind sloughed off (*shinjin datsuraku*). Make no use (*fuyō*) of burning incense (*shōkō*), prostrations (*raihai*), buddha-mindfulness (*nenbutsu*), repentances (*shusan*), or sutra reading (*kankin*). Just (*shikan*) sit (*taza*) and that is all."
>
> I respectfully enquired (*haimon*),[32] "What is 'body and mind sloughed off'?" The reverend abbot said, "Body and mind sloughed off is seated meditation (*zazen*). When one just (*shikan*) sits in meditation (*zazen*), one is separated from the five desires (*goyoku*) and rid of the five obstructions (*gogai*)."
>
> I respectfully enquired, "If you speak of being separated from the five desires and rid of the five obstructions, then that is the same as what the Teachings schools (*kyōke*) talk about.[33] Isn't that [what is taught] for the sake of practitioners of the two vehicles, great and small (*daishō ryōjō*)?" The reverend abbot said, "Descendants of the ancestral teachers (*soshi no jison*) do not stubbornly reject what is taught by the two vehicles,[34] great and small. If a practitioner turns his back on the sagely teachings of the Tathagata (*nyorai no shōgyō*), how could he possibly claim to be a descendant of the ancestral teachers?"
>
> I respectfully enquired, "Doubters these days say that the three poisons (*sandoku*) are the buddha-dharma (*buppō*) and the five desires are the way of the ancestors (*sodō*). If you eliminate those things, then that is selecting and rejecting, which is reverting to the same position as the Hinayana (*shōjō*)." The reverend abbot said, "If you do not reject the three poisons, five desires, and the like, then you are the same as those followers of alien paths (*gedō*) in the land of King Bimbasara and the land of Ajatasatru. As for us descendants of the buddhas and ancestors, if we eliminate even one obstruction or one desire, then we benefit greatly. That is precisely the moment when we encounter (*shōken*) the buddhas and ancestors."[35]

Here, Rujing describes "body and mind sloughed off" as a state of trance, achieved in seated meditation, in which the practitioner is free from desires associated with objects of the five senses and rid of the "five obstacles" to wisdom: lust, anger, torpor, agitation, and doubt. As the young Dōgen notes in his follow-up question, those are traditional formulae found in both Hinayana and Mahayana sutras, and the idea that transic meditation (*zen*) should be used to suppress such mental afflictions was often criticized in the Zen tradition as a "Hinayana" approach. Rujing chastises his disciple for doubting the value of any Buddhist sutras and emphatically affirms the value of suppressing harmful states of mind by means of meditation.

In this context, Rujing appears to be a conservative Buddhist monk whose admonition to "just sit and that is all" could reflect a view that burning incense, making prostrations, buddha-mindfulness, and repentances are frills that distract one from the all-important practice of seated meditation. Is it possible, then, that Rujing was a purist who held up the "single practice" of zazen as the end-all and be-all of Buddhist cultivation? No, for in the same exchange with Dōgen he stressed the importance of studying the teachings of the Buddha (*bukkyō*), as found in both the Mahayana and the Hinayana sutras.

Elsewhere in *Hōkyōki*, Rujing criticized the exclusive practice of meditation:

> [I, Dōgen] respectfully enquired, "If the great way of the buddhas and ancestors cannot be confined to a single pigeonhole, why do people insist on calling it the 'Zen lineage' (*zenshū*)?" The reverend abbot said, "One should not refer to the great way of the buddhas and ancestors with a vulgar designation like 'Zen lineage.' The designation 'Zen lineage' is a false expression, one-sided and perfidious. It is a name coined by bald-headed little beasts. This was known by all the ancient men of virtue. It was well known in the past. Have you ever read *Shimen's Record of the Monastic Groves* (Ch. *Shimen linjian lu*, Jp. *Sekimon rinkanroku*)?" [Dōgen] replied, "I have not read that scripture." The reverend abbot said, "You would do well to read through it once. That record explains the matter correctly."

The expression "buddhas and ancestors" (*busso*) was, in Song Chan usage, a synonym for the lineage of Bodhidharma, including the seven buddhas of the past, the 28 Indian ancestors, and the six ancestors in China. Rujing's point was that it is false to characterize Bodhidharma's lineage as one consisting of "practitioners of *dhyana*" (*shūzen*). This is not entirely clear from his dialogue with Dōgen, but it is certain when we consider his remarks in conjunction with the explanation given in *Shimen's Record of the Monastic Groves*,[36] which he endorsed.

Dōgen did, in fact, follow Rujing's advice to read that text, for he quoted it in "Butsudō":

> Those who are ignorant of this principle carelessly and erroneously speak of "the treasury of the true dharma eye (*shōbōgenzō*) that is directly transmitted by the buddhas and ancestors (*busso*), and is the wonderful mind of nirvana (*nehan myōshin*)," recklessly calling this the "Zen lineage"

(*zenshū*). They call the ancestral teachers (*soshi*) "Zen ancestors" (*zenso*). They give the name "Zen follower" (*zensu*) to trainees or call them "Zen monks" (*zennasu*). Or, they call themselves the "Zen family tradition" (*zenke ryū*). All of these [names] are branches and leaves that are wrongly viewed as the main roots. Those who recklessly refer to themselves as the "Zen lineage," when in fact that designation has never been used in India or China from ancient times down to the present, are devils who destroy Buddhism. They are enemies who incur the wrath of the buddhas and ancestors. *Shimen's Record of the Monastic Groves* says: "When Bodhidharma first went from Liang to Wei, he traveled to the base of Mount Song and took up residence in the Shaolin Monastery, where he did nothing but sit peacefully facing a wall (*menpeki*). This was not the practice of *dhyana* (*chan*). People long ago could not fathom his purpose, so they called Bodhidharma a practitioner of *dhyana* (*shūzen*). Now, *dhyāna* (*zenna*) is but one of the various practices: how could it alone be sufficient to become a holy man (*shōnin*)? Nevertheless, people of that day took it that way. The historian also followed along, placing [Bodhidharma's] biography together with [biographies of] other *dhyāna* practitioners, putting him a class with those who tried to make themselves like lifeless wood and dead ashes. But the holy man does not stop with *dhyana* (*zenna*), nor does he distance himself from *dhyana*."[37]

The "historian" referred to here is Daoxuan, compiler of the *Additional Biographies of Eminent Monks* (*Xu gaoseng zhuan*), who included a biography of the Indian monk Bodhidharma under the heading of "practitioners of *dhyana*." The thrust of Juefan Huihong's complaint in *Shimen's Record of the Monastic Groves* is that Bodhidharma was not merely a meditation master (*zenji*), but the ancestral teacher who transmitted the awakening of the Buddha Sakyamuni from India to China and became the founder of the Chan lineage in that eastern land—a story that Daoxuan did not mention.

In any case, it would appear from his endorsement of the passage from *Shimen's Record of the Monastic Groves* that Dōgen did not interpret Rujing's "just sitting" as an activity that excluded other Buddhist practices. On the contrary, he subscribed to Huihong's claim that the essence of Bodhidharma's practice was *not* sitting in meditation, although people of the day mistakenly came to that conclusion when they saw the first ancestor "sitting peacefully facing a wall." What Huihong meant was that the dharma transmitted by Bodhidharma was not any particular mode of cultivation, but the "buddha-mind" (*busshin*) itself—the awakening of the Buddha Sakyamuni. This raises the possibility that, for Dōgen, "just sitting" does not refer to any particular practice, but rather to an ideal state of mind with which any practice should be engaged.

Bendōwa

This work, composed in 1231, was one of the first pieces written by Dōgen after his return from China in 1227. Dōgen's aim in *Bendōwa* was to promote the practice of zazen, which he extolled as the "dharma gate [i.e., the mode of practice] that is easy and joyful" (*anraku no hōmon*) and described as the "marvelous means" (*myōjutsu*) used by all the buddhas and ancestors to "open awakening" (*kaigo*). Dōgen believed that zazen was essential to the true buddha-dharma that had been transmitted from India to China and that it had been neglected by the schools of Buddhism (mainly Tendai and Shingon) that were well established in the Japan of his day. In any case, when modern scholars hold up Dōgen's instruction to "just sit" as the essence of his teaching, it is this text that they generally cite: "From the start (*hajime yori*) of your consultation (*sanken*) with a wise teacher (*chishiki*), have no recourse (*mochiizu*) whatsoever (*sarani*) to burning incense (*shōkō*), prostrations (*raihai*), buddha-mindfulness (*nenbutsu*), repentances (*shusan*), or sutra reading (*kankin*). Just (*tadashi*) sit (*taza*) and attain the sloughing off of mind and body (*shinjin datsuraku suru koto wo eyo*)."[38] *Bendōwa* is one of only two extant texts in which Dōgen cites Rujing's dictum without attribution to his teacher, and the only instance in which he translates the dictum into Japanese. Nevertheless, for reasons that I explain below, it seems clear that he had his earlier conversations with Rujing in mind when he wrote this text.

Following the passage in which he translates Rujing's dictum, Dōgen responds to a number of questions from dubious or antagonistic interlocutors that directly challenge his admonition to "just sit."[39] In the words of one such question, "Chanting sutras (*dokkyō*) and buddha-mindfulness are in themselves the causes and conditions (*innen*) of satori; how could simply sitting idling, accomplish that?"[40] Dōgen's reply is harsh: "That you regard the samadhi of all the buddhas—the supreme great dharma—as sitting idly, makes you a slanderer of the Mahayana."[41] Moreover, he says:

> You do not understand the merit (*kudoku*) that one gets by practicing sutra chanting, buddha-mindfulness, and the like, do you? To think that simply flapping the tongue and raising one's voice is a meritorious Buddhist act is utter fantasy. As an approximation of the buddha-dharma, it is far off the mark and headed in the wrong direction. As for opening the sutra books, if you clearly understand what the Buddha taught about the procedures of sudden and gradual practice, and if you practice in accordance with those teachings, you will certainly attain realization. Squandering your time in thinking (*shiryō*) and calculation (*nendo*) cannot compare to the merit that results in bodhi. To try to gain the

buddha-way by idiotically piling up a thousand or ten thousand repetitions of verbal deeds is like pointing the tow-bars of an oxcart north while intending to head for the kingdom of Yue [in the south]. Or, it is like trying to put a square peg into a round hole. To be in the dark about the way of practice while perusing [Buddhist] scriptures is like a person who forgets to take some medicine because he is reading the doctor's instructions for it: there is no benefit at all. To voice words incessantly, like frogs who croak day and night in the paddy fields in spring, is also without benefit.[42]

Although the criticisms of sutra chanting and buddha-mindfulness—i.e., repeatedly calling the name of Amida or other buddhas—found in this passage are certainly harsh and even mocking in tone, what Dōgen condemns are not those practices per se, but rather the misguided pursuit of them under the influence of deluded thinking (*shiryō*) and calculation (*nendo*). What is idiotic, he says, is the recitation of sutras in the belief that this will lead, in some automatic or mechanical way, to a piling up of merit that will result in awakening. If, on the other hand, one grasps the true meaning of the sutras and practices accordingly, one will reap a genuine benefit.

The distinction that Dōgen draws between engaging in conventional Buddhist practices with a deluded mind that is greedy for imagined benefits and engaging in those same practices with a mind that is free from such "thinking and calculation" is clear and compelling, but it does create a problem for his overall argument in *Bendōwa*: Is not the practice of zazen, too, equally idiotic and pointless if undertaken with a deluded mind that expects to gain some imagined satori or counts up the hours spent sitting as if they were cash deposits in some spiritual bank? Dōgen implicitly concedes that point in his response to another question, which reads as follows:

> [I now see that] people who have not yet realized and understood (*shōe*) buddha-dharma may pursue the way in seated meditation (*zazen bendō*) and be able thereby to attain realization (*shō*). But what can those who have already clarified the true dharma of Buddha expect to gain through zazen?[43]

Dōgen's rejoinder is that anyone who engages in zazen as a means to gain awakening (in which case, having reached that goal, the practice of zazen would no longer be necessary) is laboring under the deluded view of a non-Buddhist (*gedō no ken*). The correct understanding, he says, is that practice and realization (*shushō*) are identical (*ittō*): even a beginner's pursuit of the way is the complete embodiment of innate realization (*honshō*), so the right attitude with which to engage in practice is not to expect any sort of realization to occur that is anything other than practice itself.[44] With these remarks, Dōgen concedes that zazen, just like any other Buddhist practice, can be approached in a misguided way that renders it ineffectual or even counter-productive.

If that is the case, however, then what makes zazen different from, or preferable to, any other practice? Any mode of Buddhist cultivation, it would seem, could be an embodiment of innate realization if it was undertaken with the correct understanding, and could be like "trying to put a square peg into a round hole" if it was not.

Elsewhere in *Bendōwa*, Dōgen is at pains to argue that the zazen he is calling for is not the same as the concentration (*jō*) that is the second of the three modes of training (*sangaku*), nor the same as the perfection of meditation (*zendo*) that is the fifth of the six perfections (*rokudo*).[45] Although he does not mention Rujing or *Shimen's Record of the Monastic Groves* in this context, it is clear that he is again echoing Juefan Huihong's (a.k.a., Shimen's) point that Bodhidharma was no mere practitioner of meditation, that being but one of the six perfections, but was the transmitter to China of the "unsurpassed great dharma (*mujō no daihō*), the treasury of the true dharma eye (*shōbōgenzō*), which is the single great matter (*ichi daiji*) of the Tathagata."[46] Here, Dōgen wants to claim that the zazen transmitted by the so-called Zen lineage of ancestral teachers is *not* one the six practices of a bodhisattva, any one of which can in principle be undertaken with either a correct or an incorrect understanding of the relationship between practice and realization, but rather a name for the awakened buddha-mind itself, which by definition is never caught up in delusion. This claim does distinguish zazen from all conventional Buddhist practices (including the practice of meditation itself), but it puts Dōgen in the position of contradicting himself, for "sitting" in this abstract sense is not really a "dharma gate" (a mode of practice) or a "marvelous means" at all.

Eihei kōroku, Volume 9.85

Volume 9 of the *Eihei kōroku* is a collection of Dōgen's verse commentaries on old cases (*juko*), which seem to have been composed up until 1236. Here, we find Rujing's dictum held up as an "old precedent" (*kosoku kōan*) that Dōgen commented on with a poem written in four phrases of seven Chinese characters each:

> Reverend Tiantong said, "Here in my place (*gakori*), make no use of burning incense (*shōkō*), prostrations (*raihai*), buddha-mindfulness (*nenbutsu*), repentances (*shusan*), or sutra reading (*kankin*). Just (*shikan*) sit (*taza*); only then will you get it." Dōgen said,

The turtle keeps hands and head to himself, but he is not unable to pick things up;/ "Of," "?," "this," and "is" are lost and later gained./When dragons and snakes are mixed up together, they still look like dragons and snakes; /although they sit together with coiled bodies, from the beginning [dragons have] wings.

Because the verse by Dōgen is presented as a commentary, in principle it tells us what he thinks about Tiantong Rujing's saying, but being a poem its message is hidden in a skein of metaphors that need to be unraveled if we are to make any sense of it.

In India, the image of a turtle with head and limbs drawn into its shell was a symbol of meditative trance, in which the five sense are entirely "pulled in" or disconnected from sense objects. The Chinese characters that I translate as "of" (*shi*), "?" (*ko*), "this" (*sha*), and "is" (*ya*) represent parts of speech and grammatical markers that are crucial for discursive thinking and writing. What Dōgen is saying in the first pair of lines, therefore, is that his teacher Tiantong Rujing was a master of transic meditation who withdrew into a realm beyond the reach of verbal representation, but who was able nevertheless to deal effectively with the world around him and to communicate skillfully using language. The second pair of lines evokes the image of a group of monks sitting in rows on the platforms in a meditation hall. Some are "dragons"—a standard metaphor for awakened masters, while others are "snakes"—impostors who pretend to have an understanding that they actually lack. The mere sight of a group of monks practicing zazen, all of them presumably deep in meditative trance, would not give the observer any clue as to which were awakened and which still caught up in delusion. Dōgen, nevertheless, says it is clear which are which, because the dragons have wings while the snakes do not. The presence or absence of "wings," in this context, must be something that is judged by how the monks act and communicate when they emerge from trance or "come out of their shells." One point of Dōgen's verse is that Rujing's dictum shows him to be a true dragon among a multitude of snakes.

Beyond that, does the verse tell us what Dōgen thinks Rujing's dictum means? That is far from certain, but I will hazard an interpretation. The image of "a turtle keeping hands and head to himself" while nevertheless being "able to pick things up" may represent an attitude of mental detachment in which one makes use of conceptual thought (or language) without being caught up in the delusion that the things (*hō*) named in language actually exist as discrete, independent entities. Dōgen could be comparing Rujing's admonition to "just sit" to the restrained mental posture of the "turtle," in which case the injunction against burning incense, prostrations, etc., is not to be taken literally as a rejection of those practices, but only as a caution not to engage in them in a deluded manner.

Eihei kōroku, Volume 1.33

The following passage is the first part of a sermon that Dōgen delivered from the abbot's high seat in the dharma hall during a convocation (*jōdō*) held at Kōshōji in 1240.

> Those who understand the buddha-dharma and attain spiritual powers (*jinzū*) are the ancient buddhas and ancestors (*busso*). To become a buddha and make oneself into an ancestor (*jōbutsu sakuso*) is not attained easily. However, those who attain spiritual powers are called experienced and venerable (*rōrō*), and those who understand the buddha-dharma are called accomplished and great (*daidai*). The only basis for understanding greatness and attaining venerability is investigation of the principle (*kyūri*) in pursuit of the way (*bendō*). Zhaozhou said, "Brethren, just investigate the principle, sit and see (*kyūri zakan*). If, in 30 or 20 years, you do not understand the way, then take this old monk's head and use it as a ladle for excrement and urine." That old buddha explained things in this way, and at present people practice in this way. Why would one ever neglect it? It is only due to the cognition of sounds and sights and ceaseless mental calculation that one is not yet able to gain liberation. How pitiable! What such a person gets as a result is only suffering as they come and go in the defiled world of sights and sounds. But now you have come to a time when you have an opportunity [to practice]. Dispense with (*hōkyaku*) burning incense (*shōkō*), prostrations (*raihai*), buddha-mindfulness (*nenbutsu*), repentances (*shusan*), and sutra reading (*kankin*), and just (*shikan*) sit (*taza*).

In this sermon, Dōgen quotes Rujing's dictum in the original Chinese. Together with his Japanese translation of the dictum in *Bendōwa*, this is one of the two instances in which Dōgen uses it without attribution to his teacher. In the present context, he seems to recommend zazen as the best way to break free from the defiled realm of the "cognition of sounds and sights and ceaseless mental calculation," which is to say, the world as ordinary unawakened people experience it. The practices of burning incense, making prostrations, reciting buddha names, repenting, and reading sutras, it would seem, are less likely to facilitate such a break because they all require the practitioner to pay attention to "sights and sounds" (as well as other sense data) and, in the case of sutra study, to engage in conceptual thought. The practice of zazen, because it does not entail focusing on objects of the six senses, offers a direct path to "sloughing off body and mind." Once that is attained, presumably, the practitioner (like the turtle of the metaphor discussed above) can engage in all the various conventional Buddhist practices and activities of daily life without danger of deluded attachment to sense objects.

Shōbōgenzō "Gyōji"

In the second of the two fascicles entitled "Gyōji" written in 1242, Dōgen quotes his "former master, Reverend Tiantong" (*senshi Tendō oshō*) as having said: "Studying Zen (*sanzen*) is body and mind sloughed off (*shinjin datsuraku*). Make no use (*fuyō*) of burning incense (*shōkō*), prostrations (*raihai*), buddha-mindfulness (*nenbutsu*), repentances (*shusan*), or sutra reading (*kankin*). Just (*shikan*) sit (*taza*); only then will you get it (*shitoku*)."[47] The context of the quotation in this text is a series of citations that Dōgen culled from the traditional biographies of ancestral teachers in the Zen lineage to exemplify the true "practice" (*gyō*) and "preservation" (*ji*) of the buddha-dharma. The stories that Dōgen selected feature key figures in the lineage whose indomitable way-seeking mind (*gudōshin*) gave rise to heroic extremes of exertion and ascetic practice. For example, Dōgen extols the second ancestor in China [Huike], who was so intent on having Bodhidharma accept him as a disciple that he stood outside the latter's dwelling all night long in the bitter cold, and then, when standing, cut off his own left arm with a knife and set it before the master, who "thus realized that he was a vessel of the dharma (*hōki*)."[48]

Other stories of ancestral teachers that Dōgen cites stress their dedication to communal manual labor (*fushin samu*)[49]; their disregard for creature comforts, as exemplified by their use of dilapidated and poorly equipped monasteries[50]; and their assiduous practice of sitting meditation (*zazen*).[51] Two themes that Dōgen stresses throughout "Gyōji" are the renunciation of fame and profit (*myōri*), attachment to which is the antithesis of the way-seeking mind, and not wasting any precious time on idle amusements or relaxation.

Rujing is the last of the ancestral teachers held up by Dōgen as a model of single-minded devotion to practice. Dōgen tells of one instance in which Rujing was offered a "purple robe and [Chan] master title" (*shie shigō*) by the Jiading emperor but did not accept it.[52] In another instance, he reports, Rujing declined a donation of 10,000 silver coins from Supervisor Zhao, a grandson of the Jiading emperor and minister of agriculture in the Prefecture of Mingzhou, at whose invitation he had gone to the prefectural capital, given a sermon, and dedicated the merit to the deceased emperor.[53] To clarify Rujing's motive in turning down the purple robe, Dōgen quotes Rujing as instructing his monks: "In studying Zen and practicing the way (*sanzen gakudō*), the primary thing is the way-seeking mind (*dōshin*). That is the starting point of practicing the way."[54] Rujing elaborated on that statement, Dōgen says, by raising the negative example of Guang Fozhao,[55] abbot of Jingshan monastery at the time when Rujing enrolled there as a young trainee, who "failed to supervise practice in the sangha hall, neglected his own disciples among the assembled monks in training, just entertained officials who came to the monastery, went off to visit them in turn, and . . . knew nothing of the workings of the buddha-dharma, but only desired fame and loved profit."[56]

It is at this point in the text of "Gyōji" that Dōgen holds up his teacher's dictum: "Studying Zen is body and mind sloughed off. . . . Just sit; only then will you get it." In this context, the quotation works to underscore the strength of Rujing's way-seeking mind, in contrast to abbots who "lack the mind of the way" (*mu dōshin*), such as the disciples of Guang Fozhao. Dōgen then states that among all the heirs to the ancestral lineage in China who call themselves students of Zen, who number not merely one or two hundred but are as common as "rice, hemp, bamboo, and reeds," his teacher Rujing was the only one who "encouraged sitting (*taza*) by sitting [himself]." He goes on to paraphrase Rujing's autobiographical account of his unceasing dedication to the practice of zazen, never missing a day or night of sitting on his cushion for the past 46 years, even when the flesh of his buttocks became injured and inflamed. It is clear from this that Rujing's approach to the practice of zazen had a strong ascetic dimension to it, and that Dōgen held that up as proof of his teacher's way-seeking mind.

Dōgen approved of the emphasis that Rujing placed on zazen, but in this chapter, too, he quoted the passage from *Shimen's Record of the Monastic Groves* in which meditation is described as "just one of many practices" necessary to become a holy man.[57]

Shōbōgenzō "Bukkyō" (Buddhist Sutras)

In the "Bukkyō" (Buddhist Sutras) fascicle written in 1243, Dōgen raises a kōan that pertains to the practice of sutra reading:

> The 27th ancestor, the Venerable Prajnatara (*Hannyatara sonja*) of Eastern India, happened to be invited to a maigre feast (*sai*) by the king of Eastern India. At that time, the king enquired of him: "Many people exhaustively revolve sutras (*tenkin*); why is it that only you, Venerable One, do not revolve them?" The ancestor said, "When this humble monk breathes out he does not follow along with conditions; when he breathes in he does not settle down in aggregates and elements. The perpetually revolved (*jōten*) sutra of suchness (*nyoze kyō*) has hundreds of thousands of myriads of millions of scrolls, not merely one scroll or two scrolls."[58]

Dōgen then comments on the kōan as follows:

> You should understand that when you hear such words of the ancestral teachers, the sutras are being turned at the very place where you are breathing out and breathing in. When you know the turning of sutras in this way, you will surely know the place where the sutras exist. Because it is

a matter of turning and being turned, turning sutras and sutras turning, you will know everything and see everything.

My former master always said, "In my place here, make no use (*fuyō*) of burning incense (*shōkō*), prostrations (*raihai*), buddha-mindfulness (*nenbutsu*), repentances (*shusan*), or sutra reading (*kankin*). Just (*shikan*) sit (*taza*), make a concentrated effort to pursue the way (*bendō kufū*), and body and mind will be sloughed off (*shinjin datsuraku*)."

Those who understand such words are rare. Why is that? Because if one reads the words "sutra reading" (*kankin*) and takes them to mean sutra reading (*kankin*), one butts one's head (*shoku su*) against them, but if one reads them and does not take them to mean sutra reading, one turns ones back (*somuku*) on them.[59] "You must not have anything to say, and you must not lack anything to say. Speak quickly! Speak quickly!"[60] You should investigate this principle. It is due to this essential point that a man of old said, "For reading sutras (*kankin*) one must be equipped with the eye for reading sutras (*kankingen*)."[61] You should know that if there were no sutras in the past or in the present there could be no words such as these. You should investigate the fact that there is "sloughed off sutra reading" (*datsuraku no kankin*) and there is "sutra reading of which one makes no use" (*fuyō no kankin*).[62]

In this commentary, Dōgen makes it clear that he does not take Rujing's admonition to "make no use" (*fuyō*) of sutra reading as a literal rejection of that practice, but rather as advice concerning the proper outlook or "eye" with which sutras should be read. "Sloughed off sutra reading," presumably, takes place when one understands the words but "makes no use" of them; i.e., does not reify the names and concepts found in them or cling to those as really existing things.

Shōbōgenzō "Zanmai Ō Zanmai"

In "Zanmai ō zanmai" written in 1244, Dōgen says: "My former master, the old buddha (*senshi kobutsu*) said: 'Studying Zen (*sanzen*) is body and mind sloughed off (*shinjin datsuraku*). Just (*shikan*) sit (*taza*); only then will you get it (*shitoku*). You do not need (*fuyō*) to burn incense (*shōkō*), make prostrations (*raihai*), recollect buddhas (*nenbutsu*), practice repentance (*shusan*), or read sutras (*kankin*).'"[63] Dōgen comments on Rujing's dictum as follows:

Clearly, for the last four or five hundred years, my former master is the only one who has plucked out (*kesshutsu*) the eye (*ganzei*) of the buddhas and ancestors, who sits within the eye (*ganzeiri*) of the buddhas and ancestors. There are few of equal stature in the land of China. It is rare to have clarified that sitting (*taza*) is the buddha-dharma (*buppō*), that the buddha-dharma is sitting. Even if [some] realize sitting as the buddha-dharma, they have not understood sitting as sitting—let alone maintained the buddha-dharma as the buddha-dharma. This being the case, there is the sitting of the mind (*kokoro no taza*), which is not the same as the sitting of the body (*mi no taza*). There is the sitting of the body, which is not the same as the sitting of the mind. There is the sitting of the body and mind sloughed off (*shinjin datsuraku no taza*), which is not the same as the sitting of the body and mind sloughed off. To be like this is the accordance of practice and understanding of the buddhas and ancestors. We should maintain this thought, idea, and perception; we should investigate this mind, mentation, and consciousness.[64]

In this commentary, Dōgen praises Rujing for clarifying that "sitting is the buddha-dharma," but he also indicates that "sitting" (*taza*) is an expression that has a number of different meanings. What Dōgen calls the "sitting of the body," presumably, is the physical posture of zazen. In contrast to that, we may infer, "mental" sitting is a kind of concentration or state of mind that can be cultivated in any posture, whatever the practitioner is doing. When "body and mind are sloughed off," the practitioner is no longer attached to any physical or mental phenomena, and that liberated or awakened state is also referred to—metaphorically, of course—as "sitting." This "sitting of the body and mind sloughed off," however, is "not the same" as the "sitting of the body and mind sloughed off," for in the latter and highest kind of "sitting," all such designations are cast aside as ultimately false.

In this context, therefore, it would seem that Dōgen does not take Rujing's "just sit" (*shikan taza*) literally as an admonition to dedicate oneself exclusively to the practice of zazen, but interprets it rather as advice to "just attain awakening." Rujing's dictum, interpreted in this manner, could be restated as follows: "In studying Zen, the essential thing is awakening, not dedication to any particular practices such as burning incense, making prostrations, recollecting buddhas, practicing repentances, or reading sutras." Indeed, insofar as Dōgen equates the highest form of "sitting" with liberation itself, which transcends any and all practices, he might just as well have added meditation—i.e., physical (*shin*) and mental (*shin*) sitting (*taza*)—to the list of conventional Buddhist practices that Rujing deemed "unnecessary" (*fuyō*).

Eihei kōroku, Volume 6.432

The following passage comes from a sermon that Dōgen delivered from the abbot's high seat in the dharma hall during a convocation (*jōdō*) held at Eiheiji in 1251:

The signature approach of buddha after buddha and ancestor after ancestor is pursuing the way in seated meditation (*zazen bendō*). My former master Tiantong [Rujing] said:

Cross-legged sitting (*kafuza*) is indeed the method of the old buddhas (*kobutsu hō*). Studying Zen (*sanzen*) is body and mind sloughed off (*shinjin datsuraku*). Make no use (*fuyō*) of burning incense (*shōkō*), prostrations (*raihai*), buddha-mindfulness (*nenbutsu*), repentances (*shusan*), or sutra reading (*kankin*). Just (*shikan*) sit (*taza*); only then will you get it (*shitoku*).

Now, in zazen, the most important thing is not to fall asleep, even for an instant. In every moment, ardor and vigor are essential.

Following this, Dōgen told two stories that were well known in the Buddhist tradition. The first is that of a young hermit who practiced zazen alone in the forest, became inattentive and lazy, repeatedly fell asleep while sitting, and was spurred on to become an arhat by a spirit, also a disciple of the buddha, who appeared to the hermit in the form of a zombie (a singing and dancing corpse) and then as a terrifying fire-breathing demon with ten heads. The second story is the parable of the poisoned arrow, in which the Buddha instructed a monk on the futility of pondering metaphysical questions about the nature of reality, and that monk attained arhatship. For the remainder of the sermon, Dōgen speaks in his own voice:

Nowadays, we are far removed from those times of the sages. How sad and lamentable it is that, more than 2,000 years after the Tathagata's nirvana, there is no one to remove arrows, nor any forest spirits who are disciples of the Buddha who would motivate and encourage us in our malaise. What can be done about this? Although our situation is indeed like this, we should not vainly pass the days and nights of our present time. Must we not pursue the way in seated meditation (*zazen bendō*), as urgently as if rescuing our own heads from fire? The primary thing is the zazen that buddha after buddha and ancestor after ancestor (*butsubutsu soso*) have conferred face-to-face in unbroken succession (*tekiteki menju*). Because of this, the World-Honored One spent six years sitting upright (*tanza*), pursuing the way (*bendō*). Day after day, night after night, he first sat in meditation (*zazen*); only later did he preach the dharma (*seppō*). The ancient ancestor on Mt. Song [Bodhidharma] faced a wall (*menpeki*) [in zazen] for nine years, and now his descendants have spread throughout the world. The great way of the buddhas and ancestors (*busso daidō*) transmitted to this monastery [Eiheiji] is our time's good luck, and people's good fortune. How could we fail to practice it?

Zazen is mind and body sloughed off (*shinjin datsuraku*). It is not the four formless trances (*shimushiki*) and it is not the four stages of dhyana (*shizen*). Even the former sages did not know this; how could ordinary people possibly conceive it? If anyone asks, "What does Eihei [Dōgen] mean by this?," I would just look at them and say, "At the beginning of summer, there is a lotus that blossoms facing the sun."[65] If that person says, "This is what one attains through practice on the long platforms [in the sangha hall]. What about that which goes beyond the buddhas and ancestors?" *After a long pause, [Dōgen] said*: The nose is aligned with the navel; the ears line up with the shoulders.[66]

Dōgen makes three main points in this sermon. The first is the primacy of zazen as the essential "method of the old buddhas." Just as Sakyamuni spent six years sitting upright before he began to preach the dharma, Dōgen argues, the people of his day should at the outset set aside practices such as burning incense, making prostrations, etc., and concentrate only (*shikan*) on sitting (*taza*). The implication here is that all other conventional Buddhist practices are a distraction at the outset of one's training, but that there may be a place for them later, after one has attained awakening or at least gained a firm foundation in zazen.

The second point is the necessity of making an intense effort in one's practice of zazen, as if struggling to escape terrifying demons or frantically rushing to douse a fire on one's own head. It is clear from this that Dōgen regards zazen as a method (*hō*)—a practice that serves as the means to a specific end—and not merely as a manifestation of original awakening (*hongaku* or *honshō*) or a symbolic assumption of buddhahood by taking the seated posture of a buddha image. In this connection, it is noteworthy that he says, "In zazen, the most important thing is not to fall asleep, even for an instant." This remark was not an incidental one for Dōgen, for as he relates in his colophon to the *Discourse Record of Chan Master Rujing of Jingde Monastery on Mount Tiantong*, written in 1242, it was just that admonition, spoken by his teacher Rujing, that triggered his own awakening:

Once the master [Rujing], upon entering the [sangha] hall, chastised the patch-robed monks for sleeping while sitting (*zasui*), saying: "Now, studying Zen (*sanzen*) is body and mind sloughed off (*shinjin datsuraku*). Why are you just sleeping (*shikan tasui*)?" When I [Dōgen] heard those words, I opened up with a great awakening (*daigo*). Going up to the abbot's quarters, I burned incense and made prostrations (*shōkō raihai*). The master said, "What is the meaning of these prostrations?" I said, "I come with body and mind sloughed off." The master said, "Body and mind are sloughed off; slough off body and mind." I said, "This is a temporary skill. Your Reverence must not give me your seal of approval recklessly." The master said, "I am not reckless in my approval of you." I said, "How can it be that you are not reckless in approving this matter?" The master said, "Sloughed off. Sloughed off." I then rested easy.[67]

It is clear from this colophon that, for Dōgen, the expression "body and mind sloughed off" was synonymous with "great awakening." In this telling, Dōgen was indeed practicing zazen in the sangha hall (*sōdō*) of Tiantong monastery when he experienced the sloughing off of mind and body, but his awakening was actually triggered by his teacher's words.

The third main point of the sermon cited above is that zazen is not the practice of meditation (*zen*) as that is traditionally explained in the formulas of the four stages of dhyāna (*shizen*) and the four formless trances (*shimushikijō*) or states of equanimity (*sanmapattei*).[68] Rather, Dōgen insists, "Zazen is mind and body sloughed off," which is to say, zazen is awakening itself. This statement echoes similar ones he attributes to Rujing in *Hōkyōki* and elsewhere. It also restates the point that Dōgen himself made in *Bendōwa*, where he denies that the zazen transmitted by Bodhidharma is the same as the meditation traditionally listed as the second of the three modes of training (*sangaku*) and the fifth of the six perfections. The problem with this position, as I noted above, is that Dōgen describes zazen as an indispensable means to an end that must be vigorously engaged until the goal is achieved (at which point one may "rest easy"), while simultaneously denying that it is a practice (i.e., meditation) or a method of gaining awakening at all.

Dōgen implicitly acknowledges this contradiction at the end of the sermon quoted above when he says, "Even the former sages did not know this [i.e., that zazen is mind and body sloughed off]; how could ordinary people possibly conceive it?" He does not shrink from the contradiction, but holds it up as a kind of kōan that appears impenetrable but can be resolved through the practice of sitting itself. When the nose is aligned with the navel and the ears line up with the shoulders, he wants to say, the round peg slides easily (though, in retrospect, pointlessly) through the round hole, and the cart finds itself already in the kingdom of Yue.

Conclusion

I have demonstrated that it is impossible to take Rujing's dictum, interpreted as it is by Dōgen in *Bendōwa* and elsewhere, as an admonition to literally cease the conventional Buddhist practices of burning incense, prostrations, buddha-mindfulness, repentances, and sutra reading. The evidence of Dōgen's own writings shows that he enthusiastically embraced all of those practices and taught them to his followers. Those practices were not mere formalities for Dōgen, but heartfelt expressions of his Buddhist faith. Thus, as he reports in his account of his own awakening, the first thing that occurred to him upon attaining that breakthrough was to rush to Rujing's room, "burn incense and make prostrations," and seek his teacher's confirmation of his understanding. When Rujing asked him why he was making prostrations, he replied that it was *because* he had sloughed off body and mind. For Dōgen, clearly, there was nothing about awakening that precluded or mitigated against such conventional practices.

Moreover, when Dōgen echoed Rujing in recommending "just sitting," he obviously did not mean that the practice of zazen should be undertaken in an intellectual vacuum, apart from the teachings of the Buddha as contained in the sutras, the discourse records (*goroku*) of ancestral teachers in the Zen lineage, or the immediate instruction and guidance of a living teacher. As he says in *Bendōwa*, the practitioner should practice upright sitting "from the start (*hajime yori*) of his/her consultation with a wise teacher (*chishiki*)," not before finding such a teacher. Indeed, the very idea of "just sitting" was something that Dōgen first heard from his teacher, struggled to comprehend, worked to put into practice, and finally came to understand not only through zazen itself, but through the words of Rujing, when the latter chastised his disciples for "just sleeping." That Dōgen gave extensive verbal instruction to his followers over the course of his career as an abbot also shows that he did not expect them to "just sit" in any literal sense, but to listen to his teachings and practice zazen with the proper understanding that he strove to instill in them.

So, what did Dōgen mean when he endorsed Rujing's admonition to "just sit" (*shikan taza*)? Scholars belonging to the Sōtō Zen tradition have glossed the expression *shikan taza* in a variety of ways, but one common view is that it refers to sitting "single-mindedly" (*hitasura ni*), "without regard for" (*kamawazu ni*) anything else. As the *Large Dictionary of Zen Studies* (*Zengaku daijiten*) puts it, *shikan taza* means: "Not to seek any meaning or conditions in zazen, but to engage in the actual practice of zazen straightforwardly, from the standpoint of 'nothing to be gained' (*mushotoku*) and 'no attainment of awakening' (*mush-ogo*)." That interpretation may be consistent with what Dōgen has to say about the identity (*ittō*) of practice and realization (*shushō*) in *Bendōwa*, in which he states that anyone who engages in zazen as a means to gain awakening is laboring under the deluded view of a non-Buddhist (*gedō no ken*). As we have seen, however, there are several other places in Dōgen's writings where he makes it clear that the practitioner should strive energetically in zazen to "slough off body and mind," which is to say, to break out of the web of sense data and conceptual thinking that ensnares the ordinary person. Moreover, he says, a strong aspiration to attain the way (*gudōshin*) is an essential motivating force in the practice of zazen.

In my view, there is no good philological evidence for glossing the adverb *shikan* in Rujing's dictum as "single-mindedly." In *Bendōwa*, Dōgen himself translates that colloquial Chinese expression as *tadashi*, which in classical Japanese is an emphatic way of saying "just" [do such-and-such] or "only" [do such-and-such, and nothing else]. Moreover, when Rujing rebukes the monks sitting in the sangha hall for "just sleeping" (*shikan tasui*), there is no way to interpret that as "single-minded sleeping." In short, Rujing's "just sit" means: practice zazen, not anything else.

As I see it, there are but two interpretations of Dōgen's admonition to "just sit" that are consistent with all the textual evidence reviewed above. The first is that he used Rujing's dictum to stress the importance of zazen relative to other practices, especially for beginners on the Buddhist path or those who had just begun to practice under a Zen master. As we have seen, Dōgen viewed zazen as the easiest way to cut attachment to conceptual thinking (*shiryō*) because, as he states in his *Fukanzazengi*, it is an approach that "is not thinking" (*hishiryō*). If we accept this interpretation, then what Dōgen meant was that practitioners should concentrate mainly on zazen, at least until they achieved some sort of initial breakthrough, at which point the danger of being led astray by other conventional Buddhist practices would be lessened considerably. As he says in "Bukkyō," there is a kind of misguided sutra reading that only serves to mire one further in delusion, and then there is "sloughed off sutra reading" (*datsuraku no kankin*) or "sutra reading of which one makes no use" (*fuyō no kankin*), which is to say, a mode of reading which gets the meaning without becoming attached to the entities (dharmas) named.

The other possible resolution to the apparent contradiction between Dōgen's citation of Rujing's dictum and his advocacy of the very practices rejected therein is that he intended the advice he gave in the passage from *Bendōwa* to be interpreted metaphorically, not taken literally as a guide to cultivating the way. In this reading, what Dōgen meant by "just sitting" was not an exclusive focus on the practice of zazen, but rather a deep-seated, unshakable insight into the emptiness (*kū*) of dharmas (*hō*)—that is, an awareness of the ultimately fictive nature of all mental constructs (*hō*)—which is the proper frame of mind for engaging in all Buddhist practices if one is to avoid the trap of deluded attachment to them. This interpretation gains credence from the passage in "Zanmai ō zanmai," quoted above, in which Dōgen speaks of different kinds of sitting—that of the body, that of the mind, and that of body and mind sloughed off. It is also consistent with his repeated claim that the zazen he recommends is not the practice of meditation, but rather "body and mind sloughed off"—awakening itself.

In the final analysis, these two interpretations are not mutually exclusive. On the level of conventional truth, which is to say, the conceptual realm in which a variety of Buddhist practices exist, Dōgen extolled zazen as the first among equals. At the same time, he was acutely aware that, from the standpoint of ultimate truth, there are no "practices" as such, and no "goals" of practice, either. That he chose to name that awareness "just sitting," "zazen," and "body and mind sloughed off" was his own peculiar skillful means.

4

A Day in the Life

DŌGEN'S VIEW OF CHAN/ZEN LINEAGE IN SHŌBŌGENZŌ "GYŌJI"

Steven Heine

> In a hundred thousand kalpas encompassing the cycles of
> life and death, a single day of sustained practice is a bright
> pearl in a topknot or an ancient mirror that lives and dies in
> conjunction [with buddhas], and is a joyous day reflecting
> the joyful effort of sustained practice itself.   *"Gyōji"*

Thematic Tensions within "Gyōji"

The "Gyōji" fascicle of the *Shōbōgenzō*[1] provides Dōgen's listing and exposition of
the significance of the ancestors (Ch. *zushi*, Jp. *soshi*), known for their recorded
sayings (Ch. *yulu*, Jp. *goroku*) that he considers to be the most pertinent for his
inheritance of the Chan/Zen lineage. This is the closest his writings come to the
approach taken by the transmission of the lamp records (Ch. *chuandeng lu*; Jp.
dentōroku) that document the hagiographies of leading masters. This text by Sōtō
Zen's founder (or *kōso*) also resembles the *Denkōroku* by Keizan, the eminent
fourth ancestor (also known as *taiso*), which is a collection of essays on the sect's
52 ancestors, including Dōgen and his main disciple Ejō as the final representatives. However, "Gyōji" is somewhat less systematic in structure and lengthy in
substance than is Keizan's work. A two-part composition that was, according to
the colophon, first recorded as a sermon on the fifth day of the fourth month of
1242 and edited by Ejō on the eighteenth day of the first month of 1243, it appears
as a single fascicle in the 95-fascicle edition (no. 30; see Table 4.1) and the
75-fascicle edition (no. 16) of the *Shōbōgenzō*. It also is included as two separate
units in the 60-fascicle edition (nos. 16 and 17).

   "Gyōji" offers a hagiographical discussion of 32 ancestors in 35 sections—
Mazu (5–33) and Yunju (7–18) are both treated twice, and the list also includes

Emperor Xuanzong from the ninth century who was a strong Buddhist sup-
porter. The ancestors range from Indian Buddhist figures Sakyamuni (1), Mahakasyapa (2), and Parsva (3), discussed at the beginning of Part I, to first Chinese
ancestor Bodhidharma (25) cited in Part II and other leaders, culminating in
Caodong (Jp. Sōtō) master Furong Daokai (32) (Jp. Fūyū Dōkai) and Dōgen's
mentor Tiantong Rujing (35) (Jp. Tendō Nyojō). Rujing's role is highlighted in
three paragraphs at the penultimate section of the fascicle's second division for
espousing a form of training that is superior in authenticity and efficacy to all others. The list of masters is somewhat mysteriously nonsequential and seemingly
erratic or out of order in some cases, but in the final analysis, the majority of these
figures represent either Mazu's Hongzhou school, which gave rise to the various
Linji (Jp. Rinzai) branches, or the Shitou lineage that eventually led to the development of the Caodong school. Thus, a wide variety of Chan leaders who reflect
the major historical streams of lineal affiliation are portrayed in "Gyōji," although
it is clear that the Caodong lineage gets favored treatment, particularly toward
the end of Part II.

This text is one of several *Shōbōgenzō* fascicles that are unique in varying ways.
The majority of fascicles focus on Mahayana Buddhist doctrines explicated in
terms of Zen kōan literature, which Dōgen often radically reinterprets, and
"Gyōji" does contain some of this element. In contrast to the generally thematic-
based nature of the great majority of Dōgen's works, this fascicle is centered on
the authenticity of daily life rather than the rhetoric of explicating doctrine. The
opening passage presents an abstract philosophical discourse on the meaning of
practice as related to the metaphysics of temporality in a way that is contiguous
with some of Dōgen's writings like the "Uji" fascicle. For the most part, however,
"Gyōji" uses concrete examples representing diverse streams of Chan from its origins to through the Song dynasty to show why the ancestors deserve to be vener-
ated. The masters are selected and recognized not for espousing high-minded
ideas or sophisticated literary styles, but for displaying spiritual ideals. This is evident in their unrelenting commitment to the strict regimen of everyday religious
practice (*gyōji*) carried out in all aspects of their behavior over the course of an
entire career.

This 760-year old text received special scholarly attention in the first decade
of the 21st century through the publication of the two major works that deal with
the distinctive fascicle in complementary ways. The first is a two-volume modern
Japanese translation (*gendaigoyaku*) with commentary by prominent literary
critic Yasuraoka Kōsaku, who has published extensively on Kamakura-era Buddhist works such as *Heike monogatari* and Chōmei's *Hōjōki*.[2] The other important study is a detailed examination of the fascicle's contents by the noted scholar
of Chan history, Ishii Shūdō, who has authored many works on Dōgen and who
was inspired to undertake the massive study in part by Yasuraoka's work.[3] Taken

together, these books emphasize that "Gyōji" plays a crucial role in articulating Dōgen's views—and the tensions carried within them—concerning lineal identity in relation to Chinese Chan and the establishment of the Sōtō sect in Japan.

As Yasuraoka and Ishii both show, some of the questions that arise in examining "Gyōji" concern the reasons for the division of the fascicle into two parts and the relation between these sections, along with the sources Dōgen cites regarding the lives and teachings of the ancestors, as seen in connection with materials and resources he evokes in other writings. Although it seems different from other Dōgen writings, "Gyōji" cannot be examined in isolation, but must be looked at in terms of whether it supports and/or counters the approach expressed elsewhere in his corpus. One of the main aims of studying the sections and sources of the fascicle is to understand how Dōgen endorses both a universal pan-sectarianism that embraces all streams and includes many elements of the Linji/Rinzai school and a highly polemical pro-sectarian standpoint linked to a harsh criticism of rival outlooks in support of Caodong/Sōtō. In the final analysis, as I will show, Dōgen's main interest lies in exhorting his band of followers with the *carpe diem* spirit of Zen practice in the midst of fleeting existence, regardless of labels and divisions, based on the significance of the notion of *gyōji dōkan*, or unbroken continuing practice forming the "circle of the Way."

Functions of Chan Lineage

To clarify the significance of lineage in Dōgen's appropriation of Chinese Chan sources applied to the formation of Japanese Zen, it must be noted that several prominent figures in traditional lineage charts play a dual role in serving as receivers who culminate a lineal transmission and as founders of a new legacy in a different land or realm.[4] For example, Sakyamuni is listed as the last of the seven primordial buddhas, as well as the first ancestor of the historical process of transmitting the teaching beginning in the sixth century BCE. Coming a millennium later, Bodhidharma is considered the 28th and final example of the ancestors in India who became the founder of the Chan school after he traveled and propagated his teaching and practice in China. Similarly, Dōgen, who established Eiheiji as the first head temple of the Sōtō sect, was the successor of the Chinese Caodong lineage, which he brought back to his native country through ordination bequeathed by mentor Rujing, at Mount Tiantong monastery, near what is now the city of Ningbo (traditionally Mingzhou) in Zhejiang Province. According to the *Denkōroku* by Keizan,

> Just as Bodhidharma, the 28th Indian ancestor, entered China and became the first Chinese ancestor, so Dōgen became the 51st Chinese ancestor [of Caodong] and the first ancestor [of Sōtō] in Japan. Thus, Dōgen is revered

as the founding ancestor of our school. Although China was full of authentic teachers, if Dōgen had not met a true master and penetrated his study, how could we have unfolded and clarified his treasury of the true Dharma-eye?[5]

Modern historians note that Dōgen actually received three different transmissions during the formative years of his career. The other two instances include his induction into Japanese Tendai, which took place when he was first ordained as a monk in 1213, on Mount Hiei, by receiving the bodhisattva precepts; and his ordination in the Huanglong (Jp. Ōryū) stream of the Rinzai Zen lineage, which was established by Eisai and developed by his disciple Myōzen at Kenninji temple in Kyoto. After leaving Mount Hiei because of his doubt concerning the consistency of the notion of original enlightenment (*hongaku shisō*), which seemed to preclude the need for meditation, Dōgen again received the bodhisattva precepts when he began training at Kenninji for about six years, before accompanying Myōzen on a pilgrimage to China in 1223.[6]

However, it is the tutelage under Rujing and, in particular, the breakthrough insight of casting off body–mind (*shinjin datsuraku*) gained during a prolonged session of zazen during the summer retreat of 1225 that are most important as the experiences shaping Dōgen's ideology and determining the substance and style of his distinctive approach to Zen theory and practice. Dōgen's role as founder and transmitter of Sōtō Zen was based on his reception of face-to-face (*menju*) transmission from Rujing, as depicted in *Hōkyōki*, a collection of dialogues between master and disciple, and a number of passages in other sources, including *Shōbōgenzō* (especially "Menju"), *Eihei kōroku* (especially 1.48), and *Shōbōgenzō zuimonki*, along with the traditional biographies, *Denkōroku* and *Kenzeiki*.

Despite the overwhelming emphasis on the importance of the Caodong transmission received from Rujing, and perhaps because of his ecumenical and trans-sectarian background, Dōgen's writings exhibit a complex and seemingly contradictory view of the meaning and significance of the transmission of Zen lineage as something he at once adamantly rejects or repudiates and firmly supports or defends. On the one hand, from an idealistic and universalistic perspective, in several writings, Dōgen dismisses sectarianism and discards the labeling of the Zen sect altogether in favor of a pan-Buddhist view of the spread of the Dharma. This standpoint, which rejects those who cling to the term Zen as "scoundrels," is forcefully expressed in the "Butsudō" fascicle, as well as in the "Gyōji" section on Bodhidharma and in fascicle seven of *Eihei kōroku*. Focusing on the role of any autonomous sect, school, or stream goes against the grain and will ultimately have a deleterious effect on the Buddha's teachings. In that context, Dōgen endorses zazen practice not because it is unique to Zen but because it was always practiced by all buddhas since the time of Sakyamuni's enlightenment.

Furthermore, it is not clear if Dōgen's fledgling movement was designated with the term "sect" (*shū*) during his lifetime. Perhaps the moniker was derived from later developments, particularly through the dissemination of Sōtō by Keizan, who established the second main temple at Sōjiji, which became the center of a wide network of expansionism through the conversion of existing Tendai and Shingon temples. At the same time, from a more pragmatic and localized standpoint, Dōgen was very much concerned with championing the legacy of his lineage stemming from Rujing, especially in seeking to promote his movement in the face of obstacles and opponents within the highly competitive religious environment of the early Kamakura period. He is even more scathing about the "ignorant skin-bags" who are too worthless to know enough to admire and respect Rujing's method of teaching than he is about supporters of the Zen sect.

The 13th century in Japan was a dynamic historical era in which a variety of new Buddhist schools were forming quickly, including Zen, Pure Land, and Nichiren, among others, with each emphasizing a distinctive approach to ritual practice and the theology of salvation. However, the schools were challenged and at times threatened by complex sociopolitical circumstances and critics, both within and outside of the mainstream Tendai Buddhist church, which was rapidly fading in power and prestige. All of the new sects had to be approved and registered by the government, and could be punished with proscription or exile if they fell out of favor, including the early Zen-based Daruma-shū movement developed by Dainichi Nōnin, which was attacked for antinomian tendencies by Eisai in the 1190s and prohibited and disbanded by the government in 1228.

The key phase of Dōgen's at times fierce defense of sectarianism was the period in the early 1240s, which led to his moving from the capital to the remote mountains of Echizen province in the summer of 1243. During this stage, several different developments seemed to cause him to champion the Sōtō school as superior and to highlight Rujing while denigrating apparent rivals or opponents. First, he inherited a number of followers from the Daruma-shū. Dainichi himself had never been to China, but sent a couple of disciples who received transmission from Deguang of the Linji branch linked to the famed 12th-century monk, Dahui. This may have led to Dōgen's focus on face-to-face experience as the only valid method of transmission, as well as his harsh criticism of Dahui and his followers. Ejō was from the Daruma-shū and became Dōgen's disciple in 1234, and the other erstwhile members of this movement who joined Dōgen at Kōshōji in Kyoto in 1241 had been occupying a temple in Echizen that was not far from where Eiheiji was going to be established just a couple of years later.

At this time, Dōgen may have felt vulnerable when Enni, who studied at the Linji school's head temple of Mount Jing in China for six years, returned to Japan and was favored by the authorities, especially Emperor Go-Saga, with a large new temple constructed for him at Tōfukuji. This was just up the road in southeast

Kyoto from, and it dwarfed, Dōgen's temple at Kōshōji. Dōgen was also starting to become largely dependent on the patronage of Hatano Yoshishige, who owned land in Echizen and may have sought to have the Zen master distinguish his movement from that of rival schools, in part to gain favor with the Hōjō shogunate, which invited Dōgen to preach in the new capital at Kamakura. Finally, on the fifth day of the eighth month of 1242, Dōgen received a copy of the recorded sayings of Rujing (Ch. *Rujing yulu*, Jp. *Nyojō goroku*), which he may have thought was not fully representative of the greatness of his mentor's teachings. Reading over this text may have instigated Dōgen to stress in his own writings the unique flavor of Rujing's approach, which he had experienced first-hand in China but was not captured in the official record. This also probably caused Dōgen to begin to focus, in addition to Furong, on the role of Hongzhi, the eminent Caodong monk and rival of Dahui, who preceded Rujing by two generations as a long-term abbot of Mount Tiantong.[7]

Why Two Parts?

As Yasuraoka shows, there are 13 main editions of the "Gyōji" fascicle originally held in various Sōtō temples, including four editions of the 75-fascicle *Shōbōgenzō* text version, two editions of the 60-fascicle text version, and one edition of the 95-fascicle text version. In addition, there are two editions of a lesser-known 83-fascicle version and one each of 84-fascicle, 78-fascicle, 96-fascicle, and 89-fascicle versions.[8] Whether it is counted as one or two fascicles, "Gyōji" is always divided into two parts, with the first section containing masters 1–24 and the second section masters 25–35 in a total of 42 paragraphs. This total includes multiple paragraphs for certain ancestors and additional writings on the meaning of *gyōji*, especially at the beginning (paragraphs 1–5) and middle (19–20) of Part I and at the very end of Part II (42).

What is the relation between the two divisions of "Gyōji"? In considering this question, it is important to note that one of the characteristics of both parts of the text is that, while chronological sequence is followed at first, there are quite a few notable exceptions. For example, Huangbo (22) appears after his disciple Linji (21) and Mazu, who is included in both parts, appears after Furong in the second division. It is difficult to understand the reasons for this breach of chronology as, at first read, it does not seem to be a case—otherwise typical of Dōgen's approach to appropriating Chinese sources—of taking poetic license with convention in order to make a specific ideological point. Perhaps Dōgen was preemptive of modern historical criticism of the fanciful elements of Chan transmission records by showing that he could avoid the "string of pearls" fallacy in his utilizing, but without being wedded to, the traditional narrative of generation-to-generation lineage. In this way, his aim was to accomplish for Japanese Buddhism what Eisai had not done, which is the extraction of the Zen element from the fourfold formula of Tendai's approach, namely, the Perfect Teaching-Esotericism-Meditation-Precepts (*en-mitsu-zen-kai*).

Because of ambiguities and inconsistencies in the traditional dating of events, the history of the formation of "Gyōji" is difficult to determine. Ishii speculates for reasons internal to the text that Part II was the original draft completed on the fifth day of the first month of 1242, prior to the composition of Part I, which was written subsequently, and that Ejō finalized the editing of the entire scroll on the eighteenth day of the first month of 1243. In doing so, Ejō apparently decided to place the section that was composed later as the first of the two parts, and it is safe to assume that Dōgen consented or even suggested this since he was very much involved in editing the *Shōbōgenzō*. In other words, the former date does not refer to the composition of the two sections, as is often understood, so that the latter date refers to the time when the sequence of the sections was set. In between the two dates was the time of the reception of Rujing's record, which no doubt greatly affected Dōgen's standpoint in regards to "Gyōji" and probably motivated him to revise and perhaps expand the section in Part II dealing with his mentor.

Ishii feels that the second division's introductory discussion of bringing the Dharma to the "remote outpost" of Japan—much as Bodhidharma once courageously brought it to China—as well as its emphasis on the Caodong lineage stretching from Shitou (27) to Furong and Rujing indicate that this was the initial draft. Afterward, Ishii argues, Dōgen must have decided to provide additional background, as well as praise and commentary for a wider variety of masters without regard to lineage. Since this section begins with introductory comments leading up to the role of Sakyamuni, Ejō placed it first. Dōgen also probably felt that the founder of the Caodong school, Dongshan (17), whose entry is very short compared to Zhaozhou's, for example, along with prominent Song dynasty master Hongzhi (15), a second-generation successor to Furong, was neglected and needed to be included. The only other Song figure Dōgen cites in Part I is Wuzu Fayan (14) in the Rinzai-Yangqi lineage, and both of these masters are for some reason treated before predecessors Dongshan and Yunju (7 and 18), among others.

Sources

"Gyōji" is unique because it deals with so many different Chan masters in a single fascicle, but at the same time, it shows the trend found in different ways throughout the *Shōbōgenzō* to reference directly or indirectly and to interpret creatively a tremendous diversity of sources. The remarkable richness of Dōgen's writings is seen in the way they are open to multiple texts and perspectives from

Sino-Japanese Buddhist literature. The studies of Yasuraoka highlight the extraordinary level of intertextuality infusing Dōgen's works with Chinese Chan and Japanese literary citations and allusions, as well as the extensive intratextual function within Dōgen's corpus of referring back and forth to the sources.

The approaches of Yasuraoka and Ishii are overlapping yet complementary in that they use Dōgen's writings as a window by which to view the flow of textual predecessors, antecedents, influences, and parallels. Both scholars highlight the impact of the *Lotus Sutra* and the seminal transmission of the lamp text, the *Jingde chuandeng lu*, which is the primary source for many of the anecdotes of the ancestors, in addition to Chinese sources like the *Zhuangzi*. But, for the most part, the two scholars pursue different directions. Yasuraoka naturally focuses on Japanese literary and linguistic elements and Ishii on Chan texts that Dōgen had studied in China and was importing and introducing to his native country.

Yasuraoka's opening statement in the preface to the first volume is the disclaimer, "I am not a Buddhist studies scholar. I am not a religious studies scholar. I am not a Zen Buddhist practitioner."[9] Influenced by his mentor Nishio Minoru, who wrote a frequently cited book dealing with Dōgen and Zeami,[10] in looking for influences on Dōgen, Yasuraoka explores such writings that were created at the same time as Dōgen's, such as *Hōjōki* by Chōmei and *Heike monogatari*, as well as concepts such as *yūgen* (mysterious depth) expressed in many kinds of early Kamakura-era writings. Of particular interest in Yaruraoka's approach is his linguistics expertise in identifying, for passage after passage throughout the fascicle, the innovative ways that Dōgen transforms Chan's Chinese literary style into Japanese vernacular. It is well known that one of Dōgen's main skills was in adapting the Chan sources to particular Japanese pronunciation and syntax patterns, and Yasuraoka does an outstanding job in documenting and explicating the complex linguistic process evident in this text.

Ishii's strength, on the other hand, lies in identifying the Chan sources from among the transmission of the lamp, kōan collection, and recorded sayings records for Dōgen's citations. He says in the postscript that undertaking this study gave him the opportunity to explore more extensively diverse Song Chan sources, much as his book on the *Mana Shōbōgenzō*, published over two decades ago,[11] which was similarly derived from a lecture series and released by the same publisher, focused on Tang dynasty masters and sources.[12] In considering the roots of Dōgen's notion of *gyōji dōkan*, Ishii, who finds resonances with the "Zenki" fascicle, turns inventively to Buddhist sources such as the *Congrong lu* (Jp. *Shōyōroku*), which in case 77 deals with "Yangshan's Swastika."[13] In this kōan record, a rival monk draws a circle around Yangshan's mystic symbol, and Hongzhi's verse commentary suggests, "The void of the circle of the Way is never filled."[14]

Question of Sectarianism

Ishii points out that, in Part I, and to a large extent in the second part as well, Dōgen generally avoids the sectarian partisanship that affects some of the discourse from this crucial transitional stage of his career, when he came to be highly critical in numerous *Shōbōgenzō* fascicles of rival lineages. Dōgen gives relatively equal weight to all factions of Chan, especially the multiple streams from the Tang dynasty, with the one relatively minor exception that in the discussion of Linji, who is greatly praised here, Dōgen criticizes Deshan as an inferior mind who "could not be Linji's equal."[15]

One way of getting a sense of how the approach toward lineage is taken in "Gyōji" in relation to Dōgen's other writings is to compare the list of masters in the fascicle in Table 4.1 with Table 4.2 that illustrates the ancestors most frequently cited by Dōgen throughout all of his major works. The table was compiled and catalogued based on my reading of the scholarship of Ishii Shūdō, as well as that of Kagamishima Genryū,[16] and it shows how many times Dōgen cites those ancestors who are most prominent for him. According to this table, the pre-Song masters who are key for Dōgen more generally and who are also mentioned in "Gyōji" are derived from both Mazu's Hongzhou school, which gave rise to the Linji branches, and Shitou's followers, among whom there was Dongshan, in addition to leaders of other streams. The Mazu-based ancestors include Nanyue, Baizhang, Huangbo, Zhaozhou, Linji, and Xiangyan, and Shitou's followers include such figures as Xuefeng, Yunju, and Xuansha. However, somewhat surprisingly, ancestors from the Shitou lineage, including Caoshan, considered the co-founder of Caodong, in addition to Yunmen, Fayan, and Xuedou (all of whom Dōgen does cite extensively in other writings) are not mentioned in "Gyōji."

This is a sign of pan-sectarianism. But Table 4.2 also shows that it is when Dōgen appropriates the teachings of Song dynasty masters that he reveals his sectarian colors by citing so extensively both Hongzhi (primarily in the *Eihei kōroku* from the mid-1240s) and Rujing (in both *Shōbōgenzō* and *Eihei kōroku* throughout the middle and late phases of his career). This is in a way that far surpasses any other master cited in his collected writings. Even so, it is not until the end of the second part of "Gyōji," in which Dōgen lavishes praise on Rujing and dismisses his opponents, that pro-sectarianism comes to the fore as the major agenda of the fascicle. At this stage of the text, it is abundantly clear that Dōgen favors the Caodong lineage as transmitted through his own mentor and indirectly rejects the Dahui–Dainichi axis through his attack on Deguang. While eulogizing Rujing, Dōgen takes the opportunity to assail Deguang, the Dahui follower who had given transmission to Dainichi Nōnin's Daruma-shū disciples. According to Dōgen's presentation of the matter, unlike the spiritually-committed Furong and

Rujing, both of whom would routinely turn down gifts from the rich and power-ful while embracing followers who were of lowly status in their fold, Deguang was not a genuinely enlightened master. Rather, he was nothing but a charlatan of sorts who merely sought fame and fortune by entertaining dignitaries who visited his temple.

During 1242, Dōgen composed 16 fascicles, his most productive period except for 1243, which was the year of his move from Kyoto to Echizen, when 22 fascicles were composed, 18 of these in mountain retreats before the new temple (later renamed Eiheiji) was opened. Dōgen's teacher receives the most attention and praise in three culminating paragraphs of "Gyōji," which presages three fascicles written, in the last two months of 1243, at Echizen hermitage that are almost entirely based on Rujing citations, including "Bustsudō," "Ganzei," and "Kajō," which have seven or eight citations each, many of them not included in Rujing's recorded sayings. Although most of the other masters are treated in "Gyōji" in a single paragraph of varying length, Bodhidharma is given three paragraphs, whereas second patriarch Huike along with Furong Daokai get two each. Ishii notes that the attention given to the latter, who was known for his fierce spirit of autonomy in declining an offer of the imperial robe and who figures prominently in the "Sansuikyō" fascicle and is also cited at the beginning of "Kajō," is signifi-cant as he represents an important link in the Chinese Chan Caodong lineage.

Exhortative Perspectives

It is clear that there is a basic tension in the two divisions of "Gyōji" between pro-sectarianism and pan-sectarianism, or highlighting the Caodong/Sōtō lineal transmission received exclusively via Rujing and appreciating the merit of nearly all other Chan/Zen teachers and sources. Is there a perspective embedded in the fascicle's interrelated though provisionally separable philosophical and hagio-graphical writings that transcends this sense of institutional polarity?[17] The com-bined impact of the emphasis on the metaphysics of daily, sustained practice based on the notion of *gyōji dōkan* in several key passages, as well as on the authenticity of lifelong training by evoking the ancestors in the remainder of the text, is to create an intense focus in "Gyōji" on the exhortative dimension of reli-gious rhetoric. Dōgen is true to his sacred vision (apparently first experienced with the early death of his mother, when he saw the smoke of incense wafting in midair and renewed by his doubt about Tendai doctrine) of the overwhelming importance of impermanence in shaping the spiritual endeavor. Life is short, he maintains repeatedly, and there is not an instant to spare or any moment to waste in order to pursue and sustain the goal of attaining enlightenment. Therefore, it is necessary to seize the twinkling of the eternal now while also maintaining and prolonging such an effort over the course of a lifetime of dedicated practice.[18]

Metaphysics of the Moment

As Ishii shows, there are fundamental affinities between "Gyōji" and other Dōgen texts that treat similar topics regarding the theory of practice, such as *Shōbōgenzō zuimonki* and *Eihei kōroku*. In addition, he highlights the modern Sōtō compilation that targets a lay audience based on passages selected from the *Shōbōgenzō*, the *Shushōgi*, which contains three consecutive paragraphs selected from Parts I and II of the "Gyōji" fascicle near the end of the text's fifth and final section on the role of practice. To cite some of this section:

> Our daily life should be spent constantly in selfless activity with no waste of time whatsoever. Time flies faster than an arrow and life passes with greater transience than the dew. However skillful you may be, you cannot ever bring back a single day of the past. Should you live for a hundred years just wasting your time means that every single passing day will be filled with sorrow. Should you drift as the slave of your senses for a hundred years and yet train in Buddhist mediation for only so much as a single day, you will, in that one day, not only live a hundred years of life but also gain a hundred years of your next life. The life lived this one day, in this very moment, is invaluable. . . . [19]

In addition, the assertion in "Gyōji" that "a single day of sustained practice is worth more than many lives lasting vast kalpas" can be considered to combine the features of "Uji," which explores the metaphysics of temporality, with the short exhortative text *Gakudōyōjinshū*, which similarly highlights the transient quality of existence but from the standpoint of emphasizing sustained training. According to the doctrine of the unending circle of the Way, the eternal now encompasses past, present, and future, yet is not merely a container or shell but a cosmological principle of understanding that supports selfless, renewable praxis of all ancestors at all times. *Gyōji dōkan* also includes positive and negative aspects of life, including flowers at once blooming and falling, as well as mirrors both reflecting and breaking, a sentiment also expressed in the "Hōshō" fascicle.

As also discussed in *Bendōwa*, Dōgen emphasizes the unity of practice and attainment (*shushō ittō*) here and now. His overall *carpe diem*-oriented reading of the lives of the patriarchs sends a clear message that an attitude of dedication affirmed through continuous practice in the eternal present moment during this fleeting life is an avenue for attaining the Dharma that is superior to conventional forms of training, such as following external guidelines for conduct like the precepts or monastic institutional regulations. Although transcending the path of orthodox activity in his exhortations, Dōgen's approach also avoids the pitfall of ethical antinomianism.

Authenticity of Praxis

The term *gyōji* 行持 can be translated in various ways, but the first kanji, *gyō* 行, indicates the discipline of practice and the second kanji, *ji* 持, suggests maintaining the resolve for the unrelenting continuation of this effort or exertion extended over a prolonged period. Practice in this sense is a broader category of training than *zazen*, although the two terms are inseparable in that, as Ishii explained it to me during an office interview (June 2007), *gyōji* is an attitude or state of mind of supreme dedication driving the commitment to ongoing meditation. In philosophical passages, Dōgen depicts *gyōji* as a cosmic power that upholds buddhas and beings, life and death, and right and wrong in each and every moment. It is an all-encompassing principle that embraces its opposite in that, "since all activity is a manifestation of dedicated practice, to attempt to avoid dedicated practice is an impossible evasion, for the attempt itself is a form of dedicated practice."[20]

Although "Gyōji" reflects Dōgen's particular interest in stressing the importance of *zazen* or sitting meditation,[21] it is not a text that advocates "just sitting" (*shikan taza*) in a way that is akin to the *Fukanzazengi* or *Shōbōgenzō* "Zazenshin," which both offer specific admonitions and instructions on how to meditate. Instead, as Yasuraoka and Ishii both show, "Gyōji" expresses a broad vision of how strict adherence to various forms of discipline underlies and is the necessary condition for meditation. The forms of discipline include the austerities of the 12 *dhuta* or severe ascetic practices (Jp. *zuda* or *zudagyō*) amid a life of constant wandering, or a commitment to spiritual independence and integrity while living in thatched huts on remote peaks to abandon worldly temptations, as frequently evidenced through the supernatural power to overcome indigenous spirits.[22]

To cite a few examples, Dōgen admires Sakyamuni because he did not replace his robe and did not stay alone for a single hour or single day, and he praises Mahakasyapa, not for receiving Sakyamuni's flower as in the prototypical Zen narrative, but for being an extraordinary representative of *dhuta*-based asceticism, as portrayed in early (pre-Chan) Buddhist literature. His emaciated state was disdained by other monks but was highly valued by Sakyamuni, who made him the senior member of his order. The lengthy entry on Parvsva, the tenth ancestor in India, stresses that he never used a bed (and slept in irregular quarters every night due to constant itinerancy) or wasted a single moment, and instead single-mindedly and unrelentingly kept his vows. Huineng (4) left his mother in pursuit of Dharma, making a greater sacrifice than Huike's cutting off an arm, and after enlightenment he remained humble and pure. Whereas Yunju from the Shitou lineage did not use a bed for 40 years of training, Mazu never neglected zazen. His disciple Baizhang (8) made such an effort that his legacy became synonymous with the injunction, "A day without work is a day without eating," and he turned down food when his disciples hid his tools one day to test his dedication and he was not able to labor in the fields.

Furthermore, Dōgen sums up the merit of several masters, such as Yunju Daoying (7), Jingqing Daofu (9), Sanping Yichong (10), and Changqing Daan (11), based on their supranormal skill in being able to dispense with the need to be served food or even to be seen by local gods who were eager to accommodate the Zen practitioners. The moral of these supernatural stories is that the capacity for selfless practice outweighs and transcends conventional divisions between gods and humans, now and then, or—despite indicators that may suggest otherwise—sectarian and pan-sectarian concerns. In that sense, the brevity, frailty, vulnerability, and uncertainty of evanescent existence is redeemed by being transformed from a weakness to strength in becoming the steady fulfillment of a majestic self-realization that supports all beings.

Table 4.1 Ancestors in *Shōbōgenzō* "Gyōji"

	Lineage	Para. No.	Page*
Part I			
Sustained Practice	--------	1–5	145
Buddhas and Patriarchs	--------		
1. Sakyamuni	First Patriarch	6	147
2. Mahakasyapa	Second Patriarch	7	147
3. Parsva	Tenth Patriarch	8	147
4. Dajian Huineng	Sixth Patriarch	9	151
5. Mazu Daoyi	pre-Linji (Hongzhou)	10	151
6. Yunyan Tansheng	pre-Caodong (Shitou)	11	151
7. Yunju Daoying	Caodong	11	152
8. Baizhang Huaihai	pre-Linji (Hongzhou)	12	152
9. Jingqing Daofu	non-affil. (Xuefeng)	13	152
10. Sanping Yichong	pre-Caodong (Shitou)	13	153
11. Changqing Daan	pre-Linji (Hongzhou)	13	153
12. Zhaozhou Congshen	pre-Linji (Hongzhou)	14	153
13. Damei Fachang	pre-Linji (Hongzhou)	15	155
14. Wuzu Fayan	Linji (Yangqi)	16	157
15. Hongzhi Zhengjue	Caodong	17	160
16. Daci Huanchong	pre-Linji (Hongzhou)	18	161
17. Dongshan Liangjie	Caodong	18	162
18. Yunju Daoying (Repr.)	Caodong	18	162

(continued)

Table 4.1 *(continued)*

	Lineage	Para. No.	Page*
Daily Practice	-------	19	162
Buddhas and Ancestors	-------	20	162
19. Nanyue Huairang	non-affil. (Huineng)	20	164
20. Xiangyan Zhixian	pre-Linji (Hongzhou)	21	165
21. Linji Yixuan	Linji	22	165
22. Huangbo Xiyun	pre-Linji (Hongzhou)	23	166
23. Xuanzong (Emperor)		23	167
24. Xuefeng Yicun	non-affil. (Shitou)	24	169
Part II			
25. Bodhidharma	1st Patriarch	25–27	171
26. Dazu Huike	2nd Patriarch	28–29	181
27. Shitou Xiqian	pre-Caodong	30	185
28. Dayi Daoxin	4th Patriarch	31	185
29. Xuansha Shibei	Fayan	32	187
30. Changqing Huileng	non-affil. (Xuefeng)	33	188
31. Guishan Lingyou	Guiyang	34	189
32. Furong Daokai	Caodong	35–36	190
33. Mazu Daoyi (Repr.)	pre-Linji (Hongzhou)	37	195
34. Damon Hongren	5th Patriarch	38	196
35. Tiantong Rujing	Caodong	39–41	196
Manifestation	-------	42	201

* In DZZ I, pp. 145–201.

Table 4.2 Chan/Zen Ancestors By Lineage as Cited in Dōgen's Works

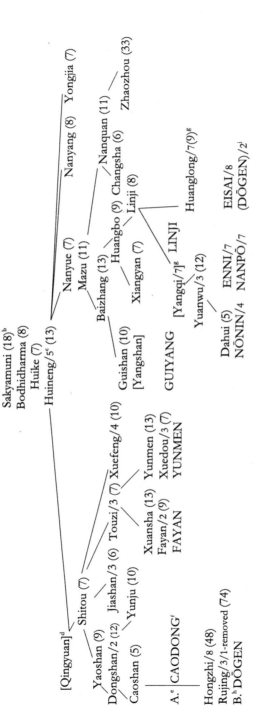

Notes:

[a] A total of at least 33 Chan masters are cited by Dōgen five or more times; based on 95-fascicle *Shōbōgenzō* in addition to other works such as *Eihei kōroku*.

[b] No. in parenthesis indicates citations.

[c] No. after slash indicates lineal generations.

[d] Brackets indicates not a significant source of citations for Dōgen.

[e] A. : Chinese Chan "Five Schools"; only Caodong and Linji continue in Japan.

[f] Caps indicate major streams in Chan/Zen.

[g] Yangqi and Huanglong are two main streams of the Linji School in China and Japan.

[h] B. : Zen masters transmitting Chan to Japan; only Nōnin did not travel to China.

[i] Dōgen received transmission from Eisai's disciple Myōzen (as well as Japanese Tendai) in addition to Rujing.

5

Dōgen's Approach to Training in Eihei kōroku

Taigen Dan Leighton

Introduction to Eihei kōroku

Dōgen's *Shōbōgenzō* is rightly celebrated for its playful, elaborate essays, with their intricate poetic wordplay and evocative philosophical expressions. Dōgen's other major and massive work, *Eihei kōroku*, has been less well known. The first seven of the ten volumes of *Eihei kōroku* consist of 531 usually brief *jōdō* (literally "ascending the hall"), which are referred to here as *Dharma hall discourses*. These short, formal talks were given traditionally in the Dharma hall, with the monks standing, and despite this formal context are highly revealing of Dōgen's humor and personality. In addition, volume 8 of *Eihei kōroku* includes 20 somewhat longer *shōsan*, or informal talks, all given at Eiheiji after 1245; and 14 *hōgo*, or Dharma words, most based on letters to students, some identified, all from before Dōgen moved away from the capital city of Kyoto in 1243 to the remote mountains in the northern province of Echizen. Volume 8 also includes a 1242 revised version of Dōgen's renowned early essay *Fukanzazengi*, a version of which is also sometimes included in editions of *Shōbōgenzō*. Volume 9 of *Eihei kōroku* is a collection of 90 kōan cases selected by Dōgen with his own verse comments, and volume 10 is a collection of Dōgen's Chinese poetry dating back from his four years of study in China, beginning in 1223, through his last years of teaching at Eiheiji before his death in 1253.

Except for the first volume of *Eihei kōroku*, from talks prior to his departure from Kyoto in 1243, the Dharma hall discourses in *Eihei kōroku* are the primary source for Dōgen's teaching at Eiheiji. These *jōdō* talks seem to be the genre of teaching he preferred at Eiheiji after he had finished writing the vast majority of the longer essays included in *Shōbōgenzō*, although he apparently continued editing some of those and also penned some new essays. The *Eihei kōroku* Dharma hall discourses are presented almost exclusively in chronological order, compiled by three of his leading disciples, including Senne, the author of the main commentary on the 75-fascicle edition of the *Shōbōgenzō*; his primary successor Ejō; and Gien, who later was abbot of Eiheiji. Although often based on Chinese Chan sources, Dōgen's talks to his cadre of disciples at Eiheiji show the development of his later teaching and reveal his own style of presentation.

Following Dōgen's death, the seven major disciples present at Eiheiji, together with their disciples over the next several generations, managed to spread the Sōtō lineage and teaching widely in the Japanese countryside. Thus, Sōtō became one of the most prominent schools of Japanese Buddhism (second only to the Pure Land Jōdō Shinshū in number of parishioners). As just one notable example of the spread, Dōgen's immediate disciple Kangan Gi'in returned home to the southern island of Kyushu, where he initiated a Sōtō lineage that persisted to modern times.[1]

Although not my main focus, it is worth mentioning that one major aspect of Dōgen's career is his comprehensive introduction of the Chan gong'an (Jp. kōan) literature to Japan. His writings reveal an extraordinary mastery of a wide breadth of this material. In the *Shōbōgenzō* essays, he comments on kōans in an original manner, with panoramic elaboration on particular stories in what has been called the "scenic route."[2] In *Eihei kōroku*, on the other hand, we can see Dōgen experimenting freely with variations on different traditional genres of kōan commentary from the *jōdō* in the Chinese Chan recorded sayings literature.

A comprehensive analysis of Dōgen's training methods as portrayed in the whole *Eihei kōroku* is far beyond the scope of this chapter, but I will consider several of the Dharma hall discourses that reveal key aspects of Dōgen's approach. In particular, I will focus on a detailed reading of one talk from 1248, which provides insight into how Dōgen saw major aspects of his own evolving teaching methods and their intended effects on his students. The selection of other Dharma hall discourses that I will briefly consider in chronological order express additional significant features of Dōgen's teaching approach. These qualities include his emphasis on practice in everyday activity, the importance of ethical conduct, the bodhisattva context for his teaching, the unified mind developed in zazen, and the importance of the ongoing renewal of practice.

The Courage of Patch-robed Monks

Dharma hall discourse 239 was delivered at Eiheiji in the late spring of 1247, and presents an insight into a primary context of Dōgen's training intention:

> Entering the water without avoiding deep-sea dragons is the courage of a
> fisherman. Traveling the earth without avoiding tigers is the courage of a

hunter. Facing the drawn sword before you, and seeing death as just like life, is the courage of a general. What is the courage of patch-robed monks?

After a pause Dōgen said: Spread out your bedding and sleep; set out your bowls and eat rice; exhale through your nostrils; radiate light from your eyes. Do you know there is something that goes beyond? With vitality, eat lots of rice and then use the toilet. Transcend your personal prediction of future buddhahood from Gautama.[3]

This talk exemplifies Dōgen's emphasis on practice in ordinary everyday activity, including even using the toilet. We can also note his whimsical humor in comparing the courage of monks to that of fishermen, hunters, and samurai in combat. In encouraging his disciples, Dōgen cites their daily monastic rituals at Eiheiji, including sleeping in the monks' hall in the same place where they each sit in meditation and formally take their meals. Yet, he adds the intriguing phrase, "radiate light from your eyes," which is not how we usually conceive of vision as a merely passive perception. However, it is not uncommon to recognize when one is being stared at that looking at someone or something can be an example of the active, even intrusive, potential of vision. Primarily in this text, Dōgen is inspiring his monks to bring dynamic responsibility and attentive caring to all their experience. "Radiating light" implies that vigorous insight and illumination should be applied in each routine activity.

Furthermore, Dōgen here exemplifies his primary teaching of the oneness of practice-awakening, or *shushō no itto*. For Dōgen, enlightenment is not something to await or hope for in the future, but is implicit and presently available in all daily activity. The last line, "transcend your personal prediction of future buddhahood from Gautama," references the Buddha's predictions of awakening in the *Lotus Sutra*, first for his various disciples, but ultimately for all those who find joy in hearing the sutra.[4] Dōgen is telling his disciples to forget aspirations for the future, as they are responsible to fully engage what is in front of them in their everyday lives.

A Mountain Homecoming from Kamakura

Later that year, on the third day of the eighth month of 1247, Dōgen left the remote mountains of Eiheiji and traveled to Kamakura, the capital of the military government established in the late 12th century. Most likely, his main patron, Hatano Yoshishige, arranged the visit, presumably to promote Dōgen's teaching. We do not know what actually happened there, except from what Dōgen said when he returned to Eiheiji after more than seven months. His Dharma hall discourse 251 was given on the 14th day of the third month of 1248, the day he returned:

On the third day of the eighth month of last year, this mountain monk departed from this mountain and went to the Kamakura District of Sagami Prefecture to expound the Dharma for patrons and lay students. On this month of this year, just last night, I came home to this temple, and this morning I have ascended this seat. Some people may have some questions about this affair. After traversing many mountains and rivers, I did expound the Dharma for the sake of lay students, which may sound like I value worldly people and take lightly monks. Moreover, some may ask whether I presented some Dharma that I never before expounded, and that they have not heard. However, there was no Dharma at all that I have never previously expounded, or that you have not heard. I merely explained to them that people who practice virtue improve; that those who produce unwholesomeness degenerate; that they should practice the cause and experience the results; and should throw away the tile and only take up the jewel. Because of these, this single matter is what this old man Eihei has been able to clarify, express, trust, and practice. Does the great assembly want to understand this truth?

After a pause, Dōgen said: I cannot stand that my tongue has no means to express the cause and the result. How many mistakes I have made in my effort to cultivate the way. Today, how pitiful it is that I have become a water buffalo. This is the phrase for expounding Dharma. How shall I utter a phrase for returning home to the mountains? This mountain monk has been gone for more than half a year. I was like a solitary wheel placed in vast space. Today, I have returned to the mountains, and the clouds are feeling joyful. My great love for the mountains has magnified since before.[5]

William Bodiford interprets this talk as reflecting the Eiheiji monks' strong disapproval of Dōgen's trip to Kamakura.[6] Some of the monks at least had "some question about this affair," and thought that Dōgen might "value worldly people and take lightly monks." Dōgen indeed seems defensive, claiming he had not taught anything in Kamakura that he had not also taught his monks at Eiheiji. In several of his *Shōbōgenzō* essays in the early years after leaving Kyoto, while establishing Eiheiji, Dōgen had tried to encourage his monks in their challenging, austere temple site by talking about the importance of monastic practice, as opposed to that of lay practitioners, for transmitting the Dharma. Although he did have lay students attend his talks at Eiheiji, his travels to teach powerful donors at the capital in Kamakura for so long might have felt like a betrayal to some his monks, who remained committed to the rigorous life at Eiheiji.

In late 1246, in Dharma hall discourse 200, Dōgen had apologized, "I'm sorry that the master [Dōgen] does not readily attend to others by disposition."[7] He acknowledges, "This temple in the remote mountains and deep valleys is not easy to reach, and people arrive only after sailing over oceans and climbing mountains." Yet he encourages his monks that, based on their commitment of the "Mind of the Way," or *bodhicitta*, the mountains are highly conducive to spiritual development.

Returning to his homecoming to Eiheiji from Kamakura, recorded in Dharma hall discourse 251, in regard to the teaching of karma and its ethical implications stressed therein, to practice virtue and not unwholesomeness is an emphasis found in much of Dōgen's later teaching. This increased accent is perhaps the greatest, or perhaps even the only, major shift in Dōgen's later teaching, as reflected in his shifting views of the celebrated fox kōan about not ignoring cause and effect. This issue has been discussed comprehensively in Steven Heine's book, *Shifting Shape, Shaping Text: Philosophy and Folklore in the Fox Kōan*.[8] The spread of Sōtō Zen in the medieval period by Dōgen's successors was helped by the performance of large lay ordination bodhisattva precept ceremonies, which had been initiated by Dōgen and provided the populace with both ethical guidance and a spiritual connection to the Zen lineage.[9] Significantly, Dōgen, upon his return to Eiheiji from Kamakura, proclaims the centrality of these ethical concerns for both monks and laypeople.

Demonstrations of Practice Clarified in the Dawn Wind

Later in 1248, a few months after returning from Kamakura, in Dharma hall discourse 266, Dōgen presents a brilliant description of his training program with a five-part typology of zazen practice in relation to his style of teaching. This incisive talk reveals a remarkable awareness by Dōgen of his pedagogical methods. I will suggest interpretations of these modes of teaching and their implications for understanding Dōgen's overall approach to practice:

> Sometimes I, Eihei, enter the ultimate state and offer profound discussion, simply wishing for you all to be steadily intimate in your mind field. Sometimes, within the gates and gardens of the monastery, I offer my own style of practical instruction, simply wishing you all to disport and play freely with spiritual penetration. Sometimes I spring quickly leaving no trace, simply wishing you all to drop off body and mind. Sometimes I enter the samadhi of self-fulfillment, simply wishing you all to trust what your hands can hold.
>
> Suppose someone suddenly came forth and asked this mountain monk, "What would go beyond these [kinds of teaching]?"
>
> I would simply say to him: Scrubbed clean by the dawn wind, the night mist clears. Dimly seen, the blue mountains form a single line.[10]

Dōgen describes four teaching modes and their intended impact on his students, with his capping verse indicating a fifth mode. These are not presented as a sequential training program or as stages of progression or development. In many places in his writings, including in *Eihei kōroku*, Dōgen clearly affirms the strong repudiation within the Caodong tradition of practice that involves any system of stages and instead declares that practice is based on immediate awareness and active engagement. As just one example, in Dharma hall discourse 301 from 1248, Dōgen says, "Not accompanied by the ten thousand things, what stages could there be?"[11]

These four, or perhaps five, characteristics of his teaching approach appear to be useful in varied circumstances as appropriate to the teaching issue at hand. They are explicitly related to varied realms of practice, including practice amid everyday activities, but also all might pertain to the activity of zazen, or sitting meditation, which Dōgen had at times described as the samadhi of self-fulfillment or as dropping body and mind that is mentioned in two of the first four characteristics. But all five modes may readily be seen as meditation instructions, as well as directions for mindful, constructive awareness during all of his disciples' conduct.

Dōgen's first line, "Sometimes I enter the ultimate state and offer profound discussion, simply wishing for you all to be steadily intimate in your mind field," reveals a major aspect of the zazen practice he promotes. This "ultimate state" is a rendering of *ri* (Ch. *li*), literally "principle" or "truth," commonly used in Chinese Buddhist discourse to denote awareness of the ultimate or universal aspect of reality as opposed to particular aspects of conventional, phenomenal reality. Dōgen's desired effect involves practitioners developing steadiness and intimacy with their field of mind. In his celebrated essay "Genjōkōan," Dōgen says, "To study the Buddha Way is to study the self."[12] Key to Dōgen's zazen praxis is just settling, not getting rid of thoughts and feelings, but finding some space of steadiness in oneself. Intimacy develops with the whole field of awareness, which includes everything, including all sense objects, even as new thoughts arise.

Dōgen says he wishes all beings, and especially his audience of disciples, to be intimate in their own mind field. This intimacy includes becoming familiar and friendly with habits of thinking, the particular modes of constructing this mind field that is thought of as "mine." Beneath the constructed identity lies the realm of awareness that Dōgen recommends to practitioners as a vital aspect of zazen—becoming familiar with habits of thinking, grasping, desire, and aversion, and resulting patterns of reaction, but also awareness of the underlying deep interconnectedness of mind and environment.

Dōgen says that the teaching he does to encourage this intimacy for his students is that he *himself* enters the ultimate state and offers profound discussion. He sees his own deep settling in connection with ultimate universal awareness and openness as encouraging his students to settle. Developing this steadiness includes gratitude and appreciation for the mind field of awareness, which has its own shifting patterns.

For his second training mode, Dōgen says, "Sometimes, within the gates and gardens of the monastery, I offer my own style of practical instruction, simply wishing you all to disport and play freely with spiritual penetration." Such practical instruction, "within the gates and gardens of the monastery," refers to Dōgen's various instructions for monastic procedures. Such material can be found in various places in *Shōbōgenzō*, as well as in *Eihei kōroku*, but most of this material, Dōgen's major writings about standards for the Zen monastic community written in Chinese, is collected in *Eihei shingi*, which was collected several centuries after Dōgen.[13] The many Zen monastic forms may function as a latticework for ethical conduct, with rules upheld and consequences enforced, and might be seen as rigid proscriptions or restrictive, hierarchical regulations. For example, *Eihei shingi* includes a short essay with 62 items on the proper etiquette to be taken when interacting with monastic seniors.[14] Although Dōgen does offer in *Eihei shingi* detailed procedural instructions, often borrowed from the Vinaya or previous monastic regulations, his clear emphasis is attitudinal instruction and the psychology of spiritually beneficial community interaction. Zen monastic regulations for Dōgen function as helpful guidelines to support awareness.

In "Chiji shingi," the final essay, which takes up nearly half of the full text of *Eihei shingi*, it is remarkable how many of Dōgen's exemplary figures from Chan lore (as contained in ten of the 20 stories cited) are involved in rule-breaking or at least rule-bending, sometimes even resulting in temporary expulsion from the monastery.[15] Monastic regulations and precepts are clearly at the service of Dōgen's priorities of total dedication to the spiritual investigation of reality and of commitment to caring for the practice community's well-being.

What Dōgen says he is encouraging with his practical instruction is not merely following rules, but "simply wishing you to sport and play freely with spiritual penetration." Spiritual penetration or insight requires paying close attention. These instructions concern the sangha, or the community of practitioners, and also support individual zazen, with forms for moving around the meditation hall, for sitting, and for performing ceremonies. But Dōgen says that the point is to play freely. Even for zazen, or sitting while facing the wall and assuming an upright posture and mudra, Dōgen's practical instructions are aimed at supporting the playfulness of his practitioners. He is encouraging his students to play freely both mentally in zazen, as well as in engagement with everyday life, while supporting detailed attention, caring, and spiritual penetration.

For the third aspect of his teaching, Dōgen says, "Sometimes I spring quickly leaving no trace, simply wishing you all to drop off body and mind." This phrase, dropping off body and mind, or *shinjin datsuraku*, is another synonym Dōgen often uses for zazen, but also to express total enlightenment. Such dropping of mind and body is not equal to discarding intelligence, or self-mutilation, or suicide. This dropping body and mind is just letting go. In his "Song of the Grass Hut Hermitage," an eighth-century teacher honored by Dōgen, Shitou (Jp. Sekitō) says, "Let go of hundreds of years and relax completely."[16] This is another way to say drop off body and mind. This is fully accomplished by totally letting go, and it does not indicate not paying attention or failing to take care of body and mind. Dōgen's sometimes abrupt exclamations or enactments recorded in *Eihei kōroku*, such as throwing down his fly-whisk or just stepping down from his teaching seat to end the talk, are demonstrations of his "springing quickly" to spark such immediate release.

The fourth kind of teaching Dōgen offers is a little more intricate. He says, "Sometimes I enter the samadhi of self-fulfillment, simply wishing you all to trust what your hands can hold." This samadhi of self-fulfillment is a technical term, yet another of Dōgen's names for zazen. This practice is discussed in one of his earliest essays, *Bendōwa.*[17] This samadhi of self-fulfillment, self-enjoyment, or self-realization, *jijūyū zanmai*, is another way in which Dōgen elaborates the meaning of zazen in his teaching approach. Dōgen designates this samadhi of self-fulfillment as the criterion for zazen.[18] He wishes his students to enjoy, realize, and fulfill their constructed self, connected beyond limited self-identity to the totality of self, and thereby sometimes called nonself.

The three Chinese characters for self-fulfillment are pronounced in Sino-Japanese as *ji-jū-yū. Ji* means self, and *jūyū* as a compound means enjoyment or fulfillment, but *jū* and *yū* read separately mean literally to accept one's function. These two characters might be interpreted as taking on one's place or role in life. Dōgen indicates in this phrase that when the practitioner accepts his life, his potential and qualities, and enjoys these, that he thereby discovers self-realization and fulfillment. This is not mere passive acceptance, but actively taking on and finding one's own way of responding, feeling, and accepting the current situation with its difficulties and richness.

Dōgen says he enters the samadhi of self-fulfillment so his followers can "trust what your hands can hold." Part of zazen is simply learning to actually take hold of who one is and the tools available, and to trust that. Trust might be rendered as faith, or simply as confidence. Dōgen wants his students to trust their own qualities and ability to engage practice. The image of what is held in the hands is reminiscent of the implements held in the many hands of Kanzeon, or Avalokiteshvara, the bodhisattva of compassion, and evokes the practice of skillful means or using whatever is handy to help relieve suffering and awaken beings. Dōgen's samadhi of self-fulfillment as he describes it here can thus be seen as intending to provoke faith and skillful means in his students.

Dōgen has quite impressively provided four primary aspects of practice and of his teaching strategy or pedagogy. Their aims might serve as a typology of

practice: to be steadily intimate in one's mind field, to disport and play freely
with spiritual awareness, to drop off body and mind, and then to trust what
one's hands can hold. These modes are inherent aspects of zazen practice. I
know of no other Zen writing that has described zazen directly in this manner,
but these are all aspects of the practitioner's intimate awareness of breath and
of her own upright posture, also applicable in engagement in everyday activity.

It is noteworthy that each of these four modes is introduced with a term translated in this context as "sometimes." The word Dōgen uses here for "sometimes"
is *uji*, which also the title of a highly celebrated essay from *Shōbōgenzō* that has
often been translated as "Being Time."[19] In this essay, Dōgen presents a teaching
about the multidimensional flowing of time as existence itself, which has been
analyzed by modern commentators, including those in the Kyoto School of Japanese philosophy, as a unique philosophy of temporality. For Dōgen, Zen practice
engages the present particular temporal situation of causes and conditions, not
some abstracted eternal present. Dōgen sees the temporal condition as moving in
many directions that are not reducible to linear clock-time, although that also is
being time. Time does not exist as some external, objective container, but time is
exactly the current dynamic activity and awareness. The four aspects of zazen and
teaching described in this 1248 Dharma hall discourse need not be seen in terms
of Dōgen's teaching about being time as presented in the *Shōbōgenzō* essay from
1240. However, the overtones of his using this term cannot be ignored. Thus, we
might also see these four practices as four aspects of the function and attentive
practice of being time, or *uji*.

Concluding this Dharma hall discourse, Dōgen offers a fifth response, not
introduced with the term "sometimes," and which might be seen as going beyond
any particular being time while still invoking the specific occasion of dawn.
Together, these five approaches might perhaps be correlated to the Sōtō Zen
teaching of the five ranks or degrees. The five-ranks teaching first attributed to
Dongshan Liangjie (Jp. Tōzan Ryōkai), founder of the Chinese Caodong (Sōtō)
school, was initially expressed in his "Song of the Precious Mirror Samadhi."
These are five interrelationships between the real and apparent aspects of life and
practice. The two sides can also be rendered as the ultimate and phenomenal, or
universal and particular, respectively. Their five interactions have been designated
in various ways, with one version being the apparent within the real, the real
within the apparent, coming from within the real, going within both apparent
and real, and arriving within both together.[20] The first, the particular within the
universal, might be seen in the students' intimacy with their mind field from wit-
nessing Dōgen expressing the ultimate state. The second, the universal within the
particular, may be seen in the students' realizing spiritual penetration from following monastic procedures. The third, coming from within the universal, might
be represented by Dōgen "springing quickly," prompting immediate dropping of

body–mind. The fourth, going within both particular and universal, may be exemplified by trusting what is handy while in the samadhi of self-fulfillment. And the fifth, arriving together within both particular and universal, might be recognized in the foreground and background of the blue mountains forming a single line, as discussed next. However, as appealing as such an interpretation might be, the five modes of practice described by Dōgen in this 1248 Dharma hall discourse should not be reduced to a mere expression of that five-ranks system, as they are much richer than this or any other formulation or system.

After presenting the first four aspects Dōgen adds, "Suppose someone suddenly came forth and asked this mountain monk, 'What would go beyond these kinds of teaching?'" Dōgen often uses the phrase "Buddha going beyond Buddha" to indicate the practice of ongoing awareness or awakening. This dynamic process is not something to be calculated or grasped, but is an organic engagement of going beyond. However well or poorly practitioners may feel they are playing freely with spiritual awareness, an endless unfolding of all of these approaches is possible. Having presented a vision of the fourfold heart of zazen, Dōgen is ever ready to further develop his awakening.

Dōgen imagines one of his students coming forward and asking, what would go beyond those teachings? He responds with a poetic capping verse to his four approaches, "Scrubbed clean by the dawn wind, the night mist clears. Dimly seen, the blue mountains form a single line." Saying "scrubbed clean by the dawn wind," Dōgen is concerned not simply with one time of day, but with the sense of freshness available in any inhale or exhale. "Scrubbed clean by the dawn wind, the night mist clears" speaks to the process of bringing oneself back to attention and awareness, waking up and realizing the immediate presence of body and mind. He encourages experiencing this every morning and realizing that this occurs breath after breath as well. "The night mist clears," sometimes hanging around for a while and sometimes suddenly dissipating. Either way one might feel "scrubbed clean by the dawn wind." Wind also serves as a customary Zen metaphor for the teaching and the flavor of awareness.

Dōgen adds, "Dimly seen, the blue mountains form a single line." This evokes the concrete image of distant mountains. The intervening space between and around mountains, as seen for example in the empty space of Japanese ink-brush landscape paintings, is significant here, evoking the spaciousness of awareness accessible in zazen. But since teachers are known by their mountain names, this image may also refer to the lineage formed by the Zen teachers who kept the practice alive before Dōgen. He might as well have said, "Dimly seen, the Zen monks form a single line," as in a row of meditators in the monks' hall, or on begging rounds. This concerns each mountain, each molehill, each situation, each problem, each master, each practitioner, or each aspect of the mind field, seen dimly, as they all form a single horizon. It might be envisioned as just this oneness, the single horizontal line for the kanji one, or the single line seen as a circle. This describes wholeness or totality. All diverse aspects of practice, of life, of the difficulties of the world, or of perplexity at how to respond may be forming a single circle or a single line in Dōgen's poetic capping verse. Such a sense of wholeness is the fifth aspect of zazen, including all the others in some way.

The single line acts as a metaphor for interconnectedness. But why does Dōgen say "dimly" of the insight into interconnectedness? The "dimly" here suggests the oscillation between seeing each particular mountain and then seeing the single line. They are foreground and background, both in the same image. Sitting zazen formally, facing the wall, one keeps eyes open with a soft gaze, and one can be open to what is in front and around, just as with ears open. Thus, one might see only dimly, balancing between the sharpness of one's particular life and the more amorphous background wholeness.

This brief but illuminating Dharma hall discourse can be seen as an amazingly concise account of Dōgen's training program related to zazen, everyday practice, and his conveying of the Dharma. He reveals a lucid awareness not only of his own teaching modes, but of the results he seeks to inculcate in his disciples from employing each of these approaches.

The Moon Shining on All Beings and Oneself

A later brief Dharma hall discourse, number 434, from spring 1251, provides a reminder of the significant bodhisattva background for Dōgen's teaching:

> The family style of all buddhas and ancestors is to first arouse the vow to save all living beings by removing suffering and providing joy. Only this family style is inexhaustibly bright and clear. In the lofty mountains, we see the moon for a long time. As clouds clear, we first recognize the sky. Cast loose down the precipice, [the moonlight] shares itself within the ten thousand forms. Even when climbing up the bird's path, taking good care of yourself is spiritual power.[21]

Dōgen evokes the bodhisattvic background of his teaching. The first priority is to "arouse the vow to save all living beings by removing suffering and providing joy." This Mahayana context and "family style" is sometimes easy to ignore in Zen studies amid all of the colorful kōan discourse and its dharma combat rhetoric. In a later Dharma hall discourse, number 483 from early 1252, the last year for which there are recorded jōdō before Dōgen's final illness, Dōgen tells his monks that true home-leavers must "carry out their own family property to benefit and relieve all the abandoned and destitute."[22] His emphasis on relieving suffering is clearly not trivial.

Returning to Dharma hall discourse 434, after reminding of their bodhisattva mission, Dōgen provides important instructions and a praxis paradigm for his monks by first saying, "In the lofty mountains, we see the moon for a long time. As clouds clear, we first recognize the sky." This poetically evokes that the purpose of their monastic training in the mountains of Eiheiji is to spend a long time immersed in meditatively communing with and examining the wholeness of the moon and finally recognizing the spaciousness, a synonym for the sky, of unconditioned awareness. But such well-honed realization is not sufficient. After such training, monks must depart their monastic enclosure, "cast loose down the precipice," and share this with all beings, the 10,000 forms. The image he cites for awakened practice, "the bird's path," is an image used in varied modes by the Caodong founder Dongshan, so Dōgen here invokes the style of his practice lineage. Dōgen closes with a friendly reminder to his monks to "take good care of yourself," which is a necessary element for the use of spiritual power.

The Endless Shoots of Zazen

Dōgen's final 165 Dharma hall discourses delivered during his last three years of teaching, from 1250 to 1252, explicitly reference his fundamental praxis of zazen 20 times, while often otherwise addressing zazen indirectly.[23] This demonstrates the continuity of his practice teaching, as his earliest writings also focus on zazen. Much of Dōgen's attitudes to zazen practice are revealed in his brief Dharma hall discourse 449 from late in 1251:

> What is called zazen is to sit, cutting through the smoke and clouds without seeking merit. Just become unified, never reaching the end. In dropping off body and mind, what are the body and limbs? How can it be transmitted from within the bones and marrow? Already such, how can we penetrate it?
>
> Snatching Gautama's hands and legs, one punch knocks over empty space. Karmic consciousness is boundless, without roots. The grasses shoot up and bring forth the wind [of the buddha way].[24]

Dōgen's practice of zazen he also sometimes calls "just sitting," or *shikan taza.* Here, he describes just sitting as cutting through the confusing smoke and clouds of delusive thinking and attachment. But he emphasizes not seeking merit. This again refers to his value of not seeking some future result or accomplishment from one's practice, that any merit is in the activity and awareness itself and is not to be sought as personal benefit. In this and other talks, Dōgen encourages engagement in the ongoing, endless process of dropping off body and mind by referring to letting go of physical and mental attachments: "Just become unified, never reaching the end," echoes other teachings of Dōgen to fully engage the continuing process of zazen, and his frequently used expression of "going beyond Buddha." For example, near the beginning of the 1241 *Shōbōgenzō* essay, "Gyōbutsu igi," Dōgen says that active or practicing buddhas "fully experience the vital process on the path of going beyond buddha."[25] Dōgen's training promotes engagement in the active process of zazen and its awareness here and now, rather than some outcome or accomplishment anticipated in the future.

Further, in Dharma hall discourse 449, Dōgen says, "Already such, how can we penetrate it?" Frequently, in both *Shōbōgenzō* and *Eihei kōroku*, he urges his students to further penetrate or study his teachings or phrases from traditional kōans. Here, he says his audience is "already such," referring to the fundamental principle of Buddha-nature and the reality of suchness as already omnipresent, not a matter of acquisition, but of the realization of present reality. A little later in 1251, in Dharma hall discourse 474, Dōgen says, "The Buddha nature of time and season, cause and conditions, is perfectly complete in past and future, and in each moment."[26] Here, and elsewhere in *Eihei kōroku*, Dōgen refers to the teaching of the underlying reality of Buddha-nature, which he expounded on in "Busshō," the longest essay in *Shōbōgenzō.*[27]

Continuing in Dharma hall discourse 449, with dharma combat style of rhetoric characteristic of much of the traditional kōan literature and often emulated by Dōgen, he exultantly talks about snatching "Gautama's hands and legs," and punching out empty space. This might refer to fully realizing emptiness, or *sunyata*, but also to not being caught in blissful attachment to emptiness. Although karmic consciousness, the conditioned, discursive source of suffering, appears to be boundless, it is also "without roots" and is ultimately an illusion. Thus, Dōgen encourages his disciples to see through the obstacles of attachments that obstruct the dropping of body–mind.

Finally, using the evocative image of grasses shooting up, Dōgen suggests that the vitality emerging in zazen calls forth some appropriate helpful response from the "wind" or teaching of the process of awakening. This is a much later echo of the teaching about self-fulfilling samadhi from his early writing on the meaning of zazen in *Bendōwa*, in which he describes the mutual response between zazen practitioners and their environment in the following terms: "Because earth, grasses and trees, fences and walls, tiles and pebbles, all things in the dharma realm in ten directions, carry out Buddha work, therefore everyone receives the benefit . . . and all are imperceptibly helped by the wondrous and incomprehensible influence of Buddha to actualize the enlightenment at hand."[28] Dōgen is reinforcing for his students that this zazen practice is not a merely personal exercise, but an act involving the dynamic interconnection of all beings.

One of the days in the traditional Chinese monastic calendar that Dōgen observed at Eiheiji was the first day of the ninth month. In Chinese Chan, due to the summer heat, the meditation schedule was customarily lessened for the three months prior to that day, at which time the cushions were brought back out and the intensive meditation schedule resumed. At Eiheiji, Dōgen did not in fact decrease the summer zazen schedule but he nevertheless often used that date to give encouragements about zazen. Dōgen's Dharma hall discourse 523 from 1252 is the last such talk given on this occasion, in which he says in part:

> Do not seek externally for the lotus that blooms in the last month of the year. Body and mind that is dropped off is steadfast and immovable. Although the sitting cushions are old, they show new impressions.[29]

Again, Dōgen emphasizes the necessity for endless, ongoing practice. Further engagement in zazen leads to more insight, with new impressions in the mind, as well as increased physical pressure from sitting on the cushions.

Conclusion

The Dharma hall discourses of *Eihei kōroku* reveal how Dōgen trained his monks in his final decade of teaching at Eiheiji, including how he understood the function of this training. Apparent are aspects of Dōgen's personality, his sense of his own limitations, his humor and warmth, and his deep commitment to teaching. My analysis offers just a slight peek into the richness of the source materials. But this selection of Dharma hall discourses demonstrates Dōgen's emphasis on practice in everyday activity; the essential role of precepts and ethical conduct; the importance of bodhisattva intention and practices; the sense of wholeness available in zazen; and a focus on sustainable, continuous practice. Furthermore, a profound five-part pedagogy of Zen training is depicted in the Dharma hall discourse 266 from 1248.

Historical Studies

6

Dōgen Zen and Song Dynasty China

Ishii Shūdō

(Translated by Albert Welter)[1]

The Development of Dōgen Zen in Japan

In the first year of the Baoqing era (1225), Dōgen returned again to Mount Tiantong from his travels in order to visit the abbot, the venerable elder Rujing.[2] As is well known, Dōgen's study with Rujing initiated a new development in the history of Zen in Japan during the Kamakura period. In the opening lines of the record of Dōgen's travels in China, the *Hōkyōki*,[3] Dōgen proclaims:

> When I, Dōgen, initiated the aspiration for enlightenment in my youth, I sought out teachings from various masters in my own country (Japan), and became aware to some extent of the principle of cause and effect, [namely, the effectiveness of Buddhist cultivation for precipitating enlightenment].[4] Even though I strove in this manner, I had not yet realized the true goal of [the three treasures]—the Buddha, Dharma, and Sangha—and became meaninglessly ensnared in the realm of name and form. Later, I entered the room of Zen master Senkō (Eisai or Yōsai), where I first learned of Rinzai (Ch. Linji) style teaching. [As a result], I then accompanied Master [Myō]zen and visited Song China. I sailed a great distance across the sea, entrusting my ephemeral existence to the billowing waves, eventually arriving in the great state of Song, where I was allowed to take a seat [in the monastery] of the Reverend [Rujing]. It was, perhaps, a blessing granted me from a previous life.[5]

In *Bendōwa* as well, Dōgen exhibits a strong self-awareness that the starting point of Dōgen Zen was indeed the meeting with Rujing: "Eventually, I visited

Chan Master [Ru]jing on Great White Peak (i.e., Mount Tiantong). I resolved the great event of my lifelong practice with him there."[6] And in the "Menju" fascicle of the *Shōbōgenzō*, when Rujing confirmed his awakening: "You have realized the Dharma Gate which Buddha after Buddha and patriarch after patriarch have conferred through face-to-face transmission," Dōgen relates how joyful he was at meeting Rujing, and comments:

> This is none other than the flower [which the Buddha] held up on Vulture Peak, the marrow [that Huike] realized on Mount Song, the robe transmitted [to Huineng] in Huangmei, or the face-to-face transmission conferred by Dongshan. This is the Eye-Treasure that the Buddhas and patriarchs conferred through face-to-face transmission. It exists only within our monastic family and is something that others have not yet encountered even in their dreams.[7]

Dōgen Zen was publicly established in the sermon delivered by Dōgen at the Kippō Vihara in Echizen recorded in "Menju" in the tenth month of the first year of the Kangen era (1243).[8] It is certain that Dōgen brought authentic Zen with him to Japan from his statement that "In Zen practice, body and mind are cast off" during his face-to-face meeting with Rujing, when transmission was granted. This is known from Dōgen's account in the *Fukanzazengi*, his first composition upon returning to Japan. The arrival of the continental Zen (i.e., Chan) of China to Japan is also attested to in various places in the *Eihei kōroku* written by Dōgen, as follows:

1. "Now when I, the Great Buddha, became a disciple of Tiantong [Rujing], I also gave informal lectures in the evening. This was the beginning of [Zen practice] in our country [Japan]."[9]

2. "I, the Great Buddha, was the first to transmit the procedures for the Chief Cook (Ch. *tianzuo*, Jp. *tenzō*) to monasteries and cloisters in the country of Japan. They did not exist prior to this."[10]

3. "This monastery is the first to have a Monk's Hall (Ch. *sengtang*, Jp. *sōdō*); it is the first one heard of in the country of Japan. It is the first one seen, the first one entered, and the first one used for seated meditation. It is a blessing for students of Buddhism."[11]

4. "The first time the people of Japan heard "Ascending the Hall" (Ch. *shangtang*, Jp. *jōdō*) lectures was by me, Eihei."[12]

5. "Former periods in the country of Japan have already spoken of holding the Ceremony of the Buddha's Birthday (*busshō e*) and the Ceremony of the Buddha's Decease (*butsu nehan e*). However, there is no mention of holding the Ceremony of the Buddha's Enlightenment (*butsu jōdō e*). It has already been

20 years since [such ceremonies] were first held by me, Eihei. From now on, [this ceremony] will continue to be held into the distant future."[13]

As a recipient of transmission from Rujing, Dōgen tried to implement pure Zen in Japan and was enthusiastic about doing so. According to the *Uji Kannondōri-in sōdō kanjin sho* compiled in the 12th month of the first year of the Katei era (1235) and contained in the *Kenzeiki*, Dōgen was the first to build a seven-alcove Monk's Hall. Even though it was not large compared with the 14-alcove Monk's Hall of Hongzhi Zhengjue mentioned in the *Sengtangji*, the fact that Dōgen's hall was modeled on the monastic regulations for constructing meditation platforms governing continental Chan institutions was pointed out by Mujū Ichien (1226–1312) in fascicle 8 of the *Zōdanshū*.[14] The evaluation of Dōgen in this source captures the special character of Dōgen Zen [as an attempt to establish the institutions and protocols prevalent at continental Chan monasteries].[15]

In Chapter 5 of his book on Buddhism in the Song Dynasty, Takao Giken outlines the characteristics of Song Dynasty Chan as: the establishment of "no dependence on words and letters," the completion of ideas emphasizing transmission, the opposition between Kōan-Introspection and Silent Illumination Chan, the flourishing of Chan literature, and the popularization of the monastic rules.[16] Such appraisals are not limited to Takao. Many scholars seize on the currents of Chan thought during the Song dynasty in terms of the opposition between "Kōan-Introspection" (Ch. *kanhua*, Jp. *kanna*) and "Silent Illumination" (Ch. *mozhao*, Jp. *mokoshō*) Chan. Silent Illumination Chan is the teaching of Hongzhi Zhengjue, a fellow student with Zhenxie Qingliao of Danxia Zichun, and a member of the same Caodong lineage that Tiantong Rujing belonged to. On the other hand, Kōan-Introspection is the teaching of Dahui, fiercely criticized by Dōgen.

In what follows, I explore the characteristics of Kōan-Introspection and Silent Illumination Chan in the Song Dynasty, with an aim toward determining what kind of connections these had with the Zen that Dōgen brought to Japan. I reflect on the unique character of Dōgen Zen when considered in the context of the currents of Song Dynasty Chan history.

The Chan Teaching of Dahui Zonggao

Dahui Zonggao was born in the Xuancheng district of Anhui province in the fourth year of the Yuanyou era (1089). His family name was Xi. He conducted his religious practice primarily in Jiangxi province, especially under the direction of Letan Wenzhun. After Wenzhun passed away, Dahui experienced awakening under Yuanwu Keqin, at the age of 37, in the fifth month of the Xuanhe era (1125), at Tianning monastery in Dongjing. After passing through Yangzhou, he was active in Jiangxi. At the age of 46, he went to Fujian province, where he attacked the teachings of the faction led by Zhenxie Qingliao, who was active on Mount Xuefeng at that time. This was an attack on the teachings of Silent Illumination Chan. At the age of 49, he lived on Mount Jing, but was exiled four years later for being entangled in the attack. He spent ten years in Hengyang in Hunan province, and eventually moved to Meizhou in Guangdong province. At the age of 68, he returned to monastic life, moving to Mount Ayuwang at the encouragement of Hongzhi Zhengjue. At the age of 70, he returned again to live on Mount Jing. He passed away in the Hall of the Bright Moon (*mingyue tang*) on Mount Jing, in the eighth month of the first year of the Longxing era (1163), at the age of 75. His thought is known through his 30-fascicle *yulu* (Jp. *goroku*, Recorded Sayings)—the first *yulu* of an individual master to be included in the Song edition of the Buddhist canon—as well as through such other works as the four-fascicle *Pushuo* (Public Sermons), the *Zongmen wuku* (Arsenal of the Chan Lineage), and the three-fascicle *Zheng fayan zang* (Jp. *Shōbōgenzō*, Treasury of the True Dharma Eye).[17]

Dahui's Chan, referred to as Kōan-Introspection, is described in Dahui's *Da Fu Fengmi* (*Response to Fu Fengmi*) in the *Dahui shu* (Dahui's Letters), as follows:

> Simply take the mind of fanciful delusions, the mind of analytical thought, the mind that cherishes life and abhors death, the mind that perceives and understands, the mind that revels in silence and detests upheaval, and settle it for a moment. Once it is settled, investigate the "critical phrase" (*huatou*, Jp. *watō*): "A monk asked Zhaozhou, "Does even a dog have the Buddha-nature?" Zhaozhou answered: "No!" (*wu*, Jp. *mu*). This one word is none other than the tool capable of extracting evil knowledge and evil awakening itself. Do not try to create an understanding of it [based on notions of] existence and nonexistence (*youwu*). Do not try to create an understanding [based on] logic (*daoli*). Do not try to form baseless presumptions about it and speculate on the basis of them. Do not try to understand it in the moment it takes to raise an eyebrow or blink an eye. Do not devise a plan for your life based on verbal explanations. Do not become attached to a state of doing nothing (*wushi*). Do not try to handle it in the time it takes to open your fist. Do not try to verify it by citing words and letters. Then, all of a sudden you will surely realize it. [It is as if] the affairs of an entire province with a territory of 1,000 square *li* were all governed without any interference whatsoever.[18]

In other words, to deal with the mind of false thoughts and delusions, take up Zhaozhou's word "No!" kōan, and all of life's dispositions are eliminated; from that point, no matter what one does or where one does it, one will realize an awakening that is free of discriminative thought. One may employ other kōan cases, but it is a unique feature of Dahui's Kōan-Introspection that he often used Zhaozhou's word "No!" kōan to recommend to officials as the "critical phrase." This letter to Fu Fengmi was written in the eighth year of the Shaoxing era (1138), when Dahui was 50 years of age.[19]

In any case, Dahui's Kōan-Introspection had the character of an effective method for overcoming "Chan maladies" (Ch. *chanbing*, Jp. *zenbyō*). In a Dharma Talk for Wang Tongban (*Shi Wang Tongban daren*) attached to the fourth fascicle of Dahui's four-fascicle *Pushuo*, he says:

> When ministers study the Way, they do not depart from two kinds of paths. One is called "emotional detachment" (*wanghuai*). The other is called "attachment to concepts" (*zhuoyi*). The one called "attachment to concepts" is what unreliable elder's refer to as "watchful control" (*guandai*). "Emotional detachment" is what unreliable elders refer to as "Silent Illumination" (*mozhao*). "Watchful control" and "Silent Illumination" are two kinds of illnesses, and if you do not eliminate them, you will not be able to escape birth and death.[20]

Dahui frequently points out that if one does not subdue the two kinds of Chan maladies, exemplified as "emotional detachment" and "Silent Illumination" on the one hand, and "attachment to concepts" and "watchful control" on the other, one will be unable to overcome the confusion resulting from the karmic consequences of birth and death.[21] Whenever one distinguishes between the realm of birth and death and the realm of liberation, there is no way to overcome the realm of birth and death. Birth and death and liberation are both provisional concepts. When birth and death itself is perceived as liberation, there is a way to escape from delusion. This must be accomplished through one's effort in the normal activities of everyday life. Dahui's Dharma Talk to Wang Tongban continues:

> Long ago, Bodhidharma said to the second patriarch [Huike]: "You only externally cut off circumstances, internally your mind is unaffected (does not gasp for breath); mind is like wall-contemplation (*biguan*), enter the Way (i.e., attain awakening) through it." The second patriarch over and over again spoke about mind and spoke about nature, and even though he cited words and letters for verification, none of them hit the mark. When mind is concentrated internally, it will of its own accord be indistinguishable from wall contemplation.[22]

According to the explanation of "wall-contemplation" provided in Guifeng Zongmi's *Chan Preface* (*Chanyuan zhuquanji duxu*), the conception of eliminating the two kinds of Chan maladies came from Bodhidharma.[23] For Dahui, it serves as a concrete method to overcome these Chan maladies using Kōan-Introspection as well.

In addition, Dahui's Chan teaching possesses a special character known as "Chan practice devoted to enlightenment" (*daiwu chan*), as strictly limited to the pursuit of awakening. Yet, in a later part of the Dharma talk to Wang Tongban,[24] Dahui clearly contradicts this with the phrase, "exerting the mind in anticipation of enlightenment" (*jiangxin dengwu*). When Dahui uses the phrase "lump of doubt" (*yiduan*), he is referring to one's entire body as representing the delusion of birth and death itself. To overcome it, there is none other than the "one-word 'No!' kōan." "Kōan-Introspection" is the effort exerted, without interruption, when "walking, standing, sitting, or lying down"; when obstructed by delusional thoughts, Dahui instructs one to focus on the word "No!" while engaged in sitting meditation (Ch. *zuochan*, Jp. *zazen*). By penetrating the critical phrase (*hua*) of the word "No!," samadhi that transcends karmic retribution is achieved. At that moment, Chan maladies are also said to disappear.

A general explanation of Kōan-Introspection is provided in both Dahui's letter to Fu Fengmi and his Dharma Talk to Wang Tongban, but questions pertaining to when, where, and why Dahui promoted Kōan-Introspection remain to be considered. Dahui makes an interesting observation regarding this in fascicle 3, in a public sermon requested by Fang Shuwen (*Fang Shuwen qing pushuo*) contained in the *Pushuo*:

> Recently, I stayed at the Yangyu Hermitage where, from the fifth day until the 21st day of the third month 13 people participated in an intensive meditation session together. One 84-year-old elderly monk was included among them, referred to as Great Compassionate Elder (*dabei zhanglao*). I asked him: "Who is not a companion of myriad good deeds?" He replied: "No one comes to mind." I then asked him: "Who is it that no one comes to mind to? Speak! Speak!" All of a sudden he was enlightened. His whole back was drenched in sweat. Throughout his life, he refused to believe in the possibility of awakening, but experienced awakening suddenly, in an instant. From this point on, I began using "critical phrases," employing them as individually suitable to each practitioner. Chan monks and lay practitioners, if there actually exists in you an inclination to attain something, this is nothing more than brick polishing. It will, in the end, turn against you. There is an official who claims that when one nourishes the seeds of joy and happiness, it is as if one were totally absorbed in the matter at hand.[25] If only it were true [for you]! If you do not yet have your own individual access point, I will exert every effort to provide it to you.[26]

According to this passage, Dahui first used the "critical phrase" method while staying at Yangyu Hermitage, to guide to enlightenment a practitioner who did not believe in enlightenment. This episode is also recorded in Dahui's tomb inscription, the *Dahui pujue chanshi taming*, compiled by Zhang Jun.[27] It is described in the chronological record of Dahui's life, the *Dahui nianpu*, in an entry under the fourth year of the Shaoxing era (1134) concerning the events at Yangyu Hermitage in Fujian province.[28]

As a result, we can understand that Kōan-Introspection was formulated in the fourth year of the Shaoxing era in the process of criticizing Silent Illumination Chan.[29] Yet, we must also try to look at why the critique was so insistent. Dahui criticized Chan practices in various places around this time. For example, a representative critique can be found in a lecture to the assembly contained in the final fascicle of the *Zheng fayan zang* (Jp. *Shōbōgenzō*, Treasury of the True Dharma Eye),[30] in which Dahui likens the pursuit of enlightenment engaged in by Chan monks as "building bird's nests" (*cheng kejiu*), in other words, engaging in purposeful effort to construct an artifice, to no avail. Noting the use of the phrase by Reverend Yantou, Dahui accuses Chan practitioners of passing the time unproductively, content in their conventions, relying on words, sitting in meditation, taking inspiration from scriptural teachings and from the "public cases" (Ch. *gong'an*, Jp. kōan) of the ancients, or in phrases like "the tripartite realm is only mind" (*sanjie weixin*) and "myriad phenomena are merely consciousness" (*wanfa weishi*). Those who take inspiration in freedom from words and verbalization, absorbed in tranquility, rely on artifices like shutting their eyes, blocking out sight, and meditating in a dark mountain on the state of the world before the appearance of the first Buddha.[31] By erroneously accepting purposeful effort as the work of the Buddha-nature, those who take inspiration from these things create bird's nests in the instant it takes to spark a flint-stone or for lightning to flash. Based on what they hold in esteem, practitioners conceive of laudable ideas, concepts of the profound, notions of tranquility, concepts of the ultimate, and notions of liberation. But, Dahui pointedly asks, "How will the Buddha ever appear to those of you who create notions such as these?," noting that the teachings themselves refer to this as the delusions of simpletons and fools. Only when one frees oneself of such impulses and is not dependent on anything will one move freely through phenomena.

Taken from one perspective, we should not overlook the emphasis on the spontaneous, free Chan that Chan masters often refer to. In order to realize spontaneity and freedom, Dahui emphasizes the experience of awakening (Ch. *wu*, Jp. *satori*). In another sermon (*Fangwai daoyou qing pushuo*), in fascicle 2 of the *Pushuo*, Dahui provides examples of Chan masters who must be criticized for reasons similar to those above:

None of you talk about the gateway to awakening (*wumen*). You tell people to sit in silent meditation (*qingzuo*), and as a result, fail to talk about awakening. Even though you talk about mind (*xin*) and talk about nature (*xing*), you fail to talk about awakening. Even though you emphasize reflection (*gushi*), you fail to talk about awakening. Even though you [talk about the instant it takes to] spark a flint-stone or lightning to flash, you fail to talk about awakening. Even though you assess public cases from the past and present, you fail to talk about awakening. In contrast to this, I, at times, focus completely on awakening, and emphasize pursuing it quickly and effectively.[32]

Regardless of what is taught, Dahui insists that one must "consider awakening as the goal" (*yi wu wei ze*) born out of Dahui's own belief in his instruction techniques used in the formation of Kōan-Introspection at Yangyu Hermitage.

As a result, where should we search for the meaning of how Kōan-Introspection was formed? Dahui's critique of Silent Illumination Chan played a large role. This can be understood from his assigning Silent Illumination Chan the lowest rank in the "Response to Li Langzhong" (*Da Li Langzhong*), in the *Dahui shu*:

Those who hold the better kinds of perverse views lump together what they see and hear, perceive and understand, and regard it as their own self, and regard the realm of objects that appears before them as the "gateway to the phenomena of the mind-ground" (*xindi famen*). Those with worse [kind of perverse views], play around at exerting themselves, regarding this as the entryway to awakening. They boast about themselves, and discuss how profound and marvelous [the teaching is]. Those with the worst [kinds of perverse views] wildly talk [about the teaching] nonstop, blabber on—whether in Chinese or a foreign tongue—without thinking, pointing to one thing while depicting another. Those with worse than the worst [kinds of perverse views] practice "Silent Illumination" without uttering a word, remaining empty and quiet. Sequestering themselves in the caves of the deceased, they seek ultimate bliss. Their remaining types of perverse views can be understood without articulating them:[33]

From this example, we can understand the extent to which Dahui contrasted Silent Illumination Chan with Kōan-Introspection. Because many of the letters in the *Dahui shu* are devoted to converting officials who have received instruction in Silent Illumination Chan to Kōan-Introspection, we can infer that Silent Illumination Chan had a very large contingent of followers, most of whom emphasized Silent Illumination and quiet sitting in meditation. Kōan-Introspection urges us to counter this emphasis and consider deeply that Chan not revert back to Hinayana types of meditation practices.

Another intention of Dahui's teaching is to rescue imitators of "doing nothing Chan" (*wushi chan* Jp. *muji zen*), introduced in the *Linji lu*, where followers of the Way are told that the Buddha-Dharma has no special activity to engage in and that they should simply go about their business everyday with nothing to do, and to make themselves Lord over all circumstances, wherever they are.[34] Although the *Linji lu* promotes a notion of Chan in which there is "nothing to do" (*wushi*), Dahui often spoke against practitioners succumbing to an imitative "doing nothing Chan" in which they affirm the world of delusion just as it is.

In fascicle 3 of the *Pushuo*, the "Public Lecture [delivered] at the request of two great masters Zhao and Chao" (Ch. *Zhao Chao erdashi qing pushuo*), Dahui distinguishes between true "doing nothing Chan" and imitative "doing nothing Chan," criticizing those who talk of a "matter of fact Chan" (*pingshi chan*), and exhaust themselves going off to create "doing nothing assemblies" (*wushi hui*) and becoming skilled in the art of "matter of factness." They engage *ad naseum* in "matter of fact" discussions, mistaking playful banter for authentic dialogues. Focusing exclusively on the matter at hand (*zhiguan*), they simply make "matter of factness" their objective. Although their statements, says Dahui, are, on the one hand, completely accurate, they are utterly wrong on the other. They never mention awakening (*wu*).[35] As such, Dahui emphasizes the contrast between "the state of true awakening" (*zhenshi wuchu*) and "never mentioning awakening" (*bu zeng wu*).[36]

Yanagida Seizan indicated the significance of Dahui's formation of Kōan-Introspection as follows: "Chinese Zen is a faction of Mahayana Buddhism, and it is self-evident that it was based on the doctrine of inherent enlightenment (*hongaku mon*). However, Zen being what it is, it somehow destroyed the doctrine of inherent enlightenment, and developed into a doctrine of the actualization of enlightenment (*shigaku mon*) type Kōan-Introspection technique."[37] As Kagamishima Genryū has stated, "Kōans were born out of the conflicting perspectives on Zen as a 'special transmission outside the teachings' (*kyōge betsuden*) and 'harmony between Zen and the teachings' (*kyōzen itchi*), and the historical significance of kōan probably lies in the aim to unify these two perspectives."[38] Kōan-Introspection was constructed through Dahui's critique of contemporary Chan, particularly Silent Illumination Chan and imitative "do nothing" Chan. We can refer to this as a religious movement, epoch-making in the history of Chinese thought, for prompting a surge of influence among secular officials.[39]

The Chan Teaching of Hongzhi Zhengjue

Hongzhi Zhengjue was two years younger than Dahui, born in the sixth year of the Yuanyou era (1091) in Xi district, Shanxi province. His family name was Li, and the family had connections to Chan dating from his grandfather's generation. At 11 years of age, he was inducted into the Buddhist precepts, and at age 14, received full ordination. At 18 years of age, he went travelling, going to Henan province to study with Kumu Facheng. At 23 years of age, he studied with Zichun at Mount Danxia, where he experienced awakening and inherited the Dharma. He remained a follower of Zichun until Zichun's death in the third month of the seventh year of the Zhenghe era (1117), on Mount Dahong in Hubei province; later, he became chief monk (*shouzuo*) on Mount Dahong in the third year of the Xuanhe era (1121). Already by this time, he had attracted talented students.

The following year, at the age of 32, a split occurred among the brethren at Yuantong Monastery on Mount Lu between Hongzhi and his Dharma-uncle Chanti Weizhao, and he took over teaching duties. The following year, when Hongzhi was 33, his elder Dharma-brother, Zhenxie Qingliao, became abbot at Zhanglu, and at the request of Zhenxie, Hongzhi became head monk. At the age of 34, Hongzhi took over Puzhao Monastery in Sizhou. At age 37, he resided at the Taiping Xingguo Cloister in Shuzhou, followed by residence at the Yuantong Chongsheng Chan Cloister on Mount Lu in Jiangzhou; the following year, he went to reside at Nengren Chan Monastery. He left Nengren Chan Monastery and visited Yuanwu Keqin at Mount Yunju after the conclusion of the summer retreat in the second year of Jianyan (1128). At the urging of Keqin and Zhao Lingjin, he entered the Zhanglu Chongfu Chan Cloister in Zhenzhou in the ninth month, as the position of abbot became vacant.

In the tenth month of this year, Dahui Zonggao visited Yuanwu Keqin again at the Yunju Zhenru Chan Cloister, following his enlightenment experience, but this was after Hongzhi had already left for Zhanglu. After Hongzhi left Zhanglu, he visited the sacred sites associated with Guanyin on Mount Butuoluo, where Zhenxie Qingliao resided. With the abbot's position vacant on Mount Tiantong, Hongzhi was invited to ascend the hall (*shangtang*, i.e., become abbot) in the 11th month of the Jianyan era (1129). Until his death at the age of 67 in the tenth month of the Shaoxing era (1157), for a period of nearly 30 years, Hongzhi devoted himself to the revival of Mount Tiantong. Except for a period of one month at the age of 48 when Hongzhi resided at the Lingyin Monastery (in Hangzhou) at imperial request, Mount Tiantong remained the center of his activity.

Hongzhi and Dahui had a complicated relationship. As stated previously, soon after Dahui lived on Mount Jing for the first time at the age of 49, Hongzhi was criticized by him as an opponent for a period of 15 years, from the time Dahui was 53 until he was 68. Yet, Dahui officiated at Hongzhi's funeral service, and Dahui would often say such things about Hongzhi as: "When I, a mountain monk, set out to travel, Reverend Tiantong is already established as a monk. His is the best residence for honorable monks [to practice at] at the present time."[40] Regarding the sources for studying Hongzhi Zhengjue's thought, they are all included in the six-volume Song edition of the *Hongzhi lu* (Record of Hongzhi).[41]

First of all, we need to consider the question of what Silent Illumination Chan is, and when and where Hongzhi promoted it. The passage that expresses Hongzhi's thinking regarding Silent Illumination Chan most clearly is the section entitled *Inscription on Silent Illumination* (*Mozhao ming*), contained in fascicle 1 of the *Hongzhi lu*.[42] In it, Hongzhi exhorts us not to rely on words and discriminatory thinking. Seated meditation (*zuochan*) transcends all distinctions, and this alone is the realm where practice and realization are nondual. He tells us that silent, seated meditation, just as it is, is illumination, awakening revealed in a single flash.

Regarding seated meditation, Hongzhi also describes it in the *Zuochan zhen* (Instructions on Seated Meditation) as "The essential component of the buddhas; the component essential to the patriarchs (*fofo yaoji, zuzu jiyao*). Know without interfering in affairs; illuminate without opposing conditions,"[43] it is not the heterodox seated meditation practice of the two vehicles. As the seated meditation practice of the buddhas and patriarchs, it was also the motivation for Dōgen's compilation of the *Shōbōgenzō* "Zazenshin." Hongzhi provided instruction on seated meditation in a preface to an informal lecture (*xiaocan*) compiled by Feng Wenshu in the seventh year of the Shaoxing era (1137):

> At the end of the Jianyan era (1127–1130), I, Hongzhi, supplied a place that met the needs and we put up an abode and quietly meditated (*anchan*). Students attending the meetings regularly numbered a thousand. The master [Hongzhi] instructed the congregation to practice stillness and to sit erect like withered tree trunks.[44]

This occurred after Hongzhi assumed his position as abbot on Mount Tiantong. If, when instructed by Hongzhi on how to master a state of tranquility, one practices seated meditation such that one sits erect like a dead stump, one may also be subjected to criticism as a follower of "dead ashes and withered trees."

Hongzhi himself compiled an entry, the *Sengtang ji*, regarding the Monk's hall (Ch. *sengtang*) that he initiated as a construction project in the winter of the second year of the Shaoxing era (1132) and that was completed in the spring of the fourth year (1134). In it, he says:

> In winter, it is warm; in summer, cool. During the day, [it smells of] incense; at night, lamps [burn]. [The monks] open their bowls and eat, wash their feet and sit; they till [the soil] or feed [the livestock]. I instruct on how to achieve tranquility. In autumn, water immerses the old well; in spring, everything is engulfed in change. In the depth of solitude, silence is achieved; as we radiate forth, our activity is dazzling.[45]

This clearly indicates that Hongzhi instructed his students on how to achieve tranquility and silence (Jp. *jimo*).[46] For practitioners, the monks' hall is where all of their practice takes place. It is probably the most noteworthy aspect of the revival of Mount Tiantong as a meditation center. We can thus consider that Mount Tiantong became a center for the practice of seated meditation, and even though Hongzhi never used the technical term "Silent Illumination" at this time, it is quite reasonable to assume that there were aspects in Hongzhi's teaching style that could be referred to as Silent Illumination Chan prior to Dahui's attack in the spring of the fourth year of the Shaoxing era. But, when is it that the phrase "Silent Illumination Chan" can be verified in writing? In fascicle 3 of the *Hongzhi lu*, there is a sermon in which Hongzhi is first invited to lecture by his elder Dharma-brother, Zhenxie Qingliao.[47] Later in the same year, the fourth year of the Jianyan era (1130), Hongzhi composed Zhenxie's tomb inscription.[48] That same year, Hongzhi delivered a lecture in which Silent Illumination Chan is referred to for the first time:

> The master [Hongzhi] then said: "Virtuous Chan practitioners, you are inherently perfect and inherently enlightened, inherently tranquil and inherently sacred. From the beginningless past, you have had the seed [of enlightenment]. Though embroiled in the great void, you are without form. Our family teaching of 'beyond the eon' is serene and simple. The 'land in the jar' is completely at peace. . . .[49] Clouds harbor the potential for thunder; cranes dream of far off places. Heaven creates the colors of autumn; geese fly off to the nether regions. Just be completely silent and self-illuminating, immersed in dew, pure and pristine.[50]

Among the many Dharma-lectures delivered by Hongzhi, the phrase "just be completely silent and self-illuminating" (Ch. *wei momo er zizhao*) expresses well his Chan teaching. It includes the Chan teaching "beyond the eon" (Ch. *jiewai*), emphasized by Hongzhi's teacher Danjia Zichun, and can also be traced to Song dynasty Caodong Chan teachings that predate Zichun. The family tradition of "beyond the eon" is serenity and simplicity, not a world informed by rigid concepts and sensory perceptions. It is the principal teaching of clear and pure Silent Illumination Chan, in which Chan meditation does not get bogged down in either the emotions or wisdom, and is without a trace of clinging. Moreover, this is the Chan that possesses the special quality in which one is "inherently perfect and inherently enlightened, inherently tranquil and inherently sacred."

In determining the date when Hongzhi commenced his teaching about Silent Illumination Chan, it is useful to consider when the lectures that discuss it were first delivered. The above lecture dates from the end of the summer of the fourth year of the Jianyan era (1130), and as I concluded previously in my examination of the *Hongzhi guanglu*,[51] the *Inscription on Silent Illumination* (*Mozhao ming*) is contained in fascicle 1 of the *Hongzhi lu*, which has a preface attached by Fu Zhi-rou dated the tenth month of the first year of the Shaoxing era (1131). Moreover, the *Sengtang ji* was written at the completion of the Monk's Hall in the fourth year of Shaoxing (1134). Because there is no mention of "Silent Illumination" in any records of Hongzhi's teachings prior to this, we can conclude that the first mention of it dates from the *Inscription on Silent Illumination*, and that his Chan teaching on Silent Illumination dates from the early period of his tenure on Mount Tiantong.

In Dahui's critique of Silent Illumination Chan, there is the phrase "being silent and constantly illuminating" (*mo er chang zhao*) in the *Letters of Dahui*:

> In recent years, the Way of Chan and the Buddha Dharma have seriously declined. Some irresponsible elder monks [hold the position that] since essentially there is nothing one awakens to, and since exerting oneself end-lessly is essentially useless, there is ultimately nothing to rely on. Nor do they have any real ability to attract students. They instruct all people as if they were similar to each other, painting them all with the same stroke [as without any distinctions]. They have them close their eyes tight, referring to it as "being silent and constantly illuminating."[52]

The phrase "being silent and constantly illuminating" refers to the Chan teaching "be completely silent and self-illuminating" mentioned in the above Dharma-lecture by Hongzhi. His use of the term "Silent Illumination" is also confirmed in another Dharma-lecture delivered prior to the conclusion of the summer retreat in the first year of the Shaoxing era.[53]

Until now, the received opinion has been that Hongzhi compiled the *Inscription on Silent Illumination* later in his life, following Dahui's critique,[54] but as stated earlier, contrary to this general view, Dahui launched his attack against Silent Illumination Chan following Hongzhi's completion of the *Inscription*. This being so, we must ask ourselves what prompted Hongzhi to initiate the notion of Silent Illumination? In the first place, it derives from the teachings of Hongzhi's master, Danxia Zichun. The *Danxia Zichun songgu* provides a repre-sentative view of sitting meditation practice in the Song dynasty Caodong line-age, when it speaks of such things as Vimalakirti remaining speechless at the gate on nonduality, Bodhidharma sitting facing a wall for nine years, and sitting silently at Shaolin.[55] As understood from this view by Dayang Jingxuan, an emphasis on sitting mediation practice was a special feature of the Chan teaching of the Song dynasty Caodong lineage. But beyond that, we need to consider ear-lier precedents for the use of the term *mozhao* (Silent Illumination).[56] To start with, we need to consider the influence of Sengzhao's *Zhaolun*. In the *Tendō*

Shōkaku oshō geju shinmeiki monge, Fuzan Gentotsu claims, "The two words 'Silent Illumination' appear in Dharma master Sengzhao's treatise, 'Prajna Has No Knowing' (*Panro wuzhi lun*)."[57] Beginning with the use of the term "Silent Illumination" in the *Baozang lun*, where it was borrowed from Sengzhao,[58] the influence of the *Zhaolun* on terminology used by Hongzhi was great.[59]

Besides this, the concept of Silent Illumination appears similar to a phrase used by the third patriarch Sengcan, in "Remarks on Believing Mind" (*Xinxin ming*), "Void luminosity is self-illuminating, and does not rely on the exertion of the mind. With nothing to think of, consciousness and emotion are difficult to engage in."[60] The phrases "void luminosity" (*xuming*) and "self-illuminating" (*zizhao*) are phrases frequently cited by Hongzhi.[61] Moreover, Zhenxie Qingliao compiled the *Xinxin ming niangu*, and the purpose of his compilation according to Yiyuan is as follows:

> During the Shaoxing era (1131–1162), Miaoxi [Dahui] was in the legitimate lineage of the East Mountain [of Wuzu Fayan], and he slandered Silent Illumination (*mozhao*). Ji'an [Qingliao] [then] raised this [commentary]; one might say that he went into his room and took up his spear, grabbed his lance, and beat his shield. Readers should be able to get [the meaning] themselves.[62]

As understood from this, the *Inscription on Believing Mind*, on its own, was thought to contain allegations in support of Silent Illumination Chan.

The above references provide background for usages of the term "Silent Illumination." Considering that many of the terms employed by Hongzhi first appear in the *Zhuangzi*, the formation of Hongzhi's Chan teaching will require detailed investigation in future. Nevertheless, it suggests that the formation of Hongzhi's Chan teaching was concretely formed in accordance with the provisos stipulated here, and confirmed by Sakyamuni's enlightenment and Bodhidharma's wall-gazing practice.

I turn next to the special features of Silent Illumination Chan, as seen in an informal lecture (*xiaocan*) recorded in fascicle 4 of the *Hongzhi lu*:

> The realm of enlightenment of all the Buddhas and patriarchs is exactly the same realm of enlightenment for you monks. If you create a head full of Buddhas and patriarchs, how will you ever get to see what is your own? If you see what is your own, there is no longer any need to rely on Buddhas, any need to rely on patriarchs, any need to rely on others, any need to rely on the Dharma. You are at once in a state of void tranquility, thoroughly realizing everything. As soon as you let go of these, it is exclusively yours alone. So, why talk of becoming a Buddha, or becoming a

patriarch? A patriarch is not someone else; Buddha is numinousness, pure awakening. This is the true reality for you monks, the opportunity for self-realization.[63]

By affirming that the enlightenment of Buddhas and patriarchs is the same as the enlightenment of monks, that neither Buddhas nor patriarchs are external to oneself, it becomes unnecessary to refer to the realization of one's own enlightenment in terms of becoming a Buddha or becoming a patriarch for one who realizes enlightenment is not distinguishable as monk or layperson.

Those who become Buddhas and patriarchs originally are neither monks nor laypeople. They are simply people who have achieved realization, and are in a state of having truly attained enlightenment in their own person.[64]

In addition, Hongzhi claims "The true state of monks is necessarily [revealed] in actual practice."[65] Since the true nature of the self is revealed during cultivation, cultivation is essential. Cultivation is revealed as: "There is no difference in the enlightenment [realized] by the Buddhas and the patriarchs. Together, they arrive at the state of stillness. The triple realm is cut off, the myriad activities tranquil. At that very moment, not even the minutest particle will be in opposition."[66]

As expected, the content of cultivation centers on seated meditation practice, but it is substantiated by the experience of true awakening: "They do not cultivate enlightenment, they are endowed with it from the beginning. They are not impure, they are completely pure from the outset."[67] In this state of cultivating enlightenment while not impure, Hongzhi cautions that good intentions alone are not effective: "Moreover, there was a fellow with a boat. He cut notches on the bow, unlimited in number, to mark his accomplishments. [This is like] cutting a notch to remember where the sword [has fallen into the water]."[68]

Even though Hongzhi's Chan is often reduced to the teaching of Silent Illumination alone and understood only in terms to its connection to seated meditation, this is a one-dimensional perspective on Hongzhi's Chan. To be more precise, Hongzhi states in an entry, the *Inscription on the Ultimate Playfulness Hermitage (Zhiyou an ming)*:

The ultimate playfulness of students of the Way! Tread on edge of the void; preserve exquisite luminosity; Drink true, unadulterated liquid; Dwell in a pure, clean abode. Losing footing on a steep bluff, your body tumbles into the empty eon. You happen to gain an exquisite place to remain. Death's grip awaits you. You appear naturally, with no particular aim, like an echo in a valley or the moon [reflected in] water. Not even the slightest of things hinders you; your thoughts are in a state of complete harmony (*xinxin ruyi*). Self and other are both forgotten; right and wrong disappear therein. The myriads and myriads of things are of varying sizes; viewed clearly, there is no difference among them. If you are able to be like this, whatever realm you enter, you tacitly authenticate the enjoyment samadhi (*youhu sanmei*). This can be referred to as "ultimate playfulness" (*zhiyou*). It is the place where monks dwell. What need is there to confine yourself to a hut, folding thatch? Alone, you rise above the world.[69]

As stated here, Hongzhi stressed the aspect of "Chan as ultimate playfulness" (*zhiyou chan*), which tacitly authenticates the enjoyment samadhi (*youhu sanmei*) while immersed directly in the afflictions of everyday life. In understanding Hongzhi's Chan teaching in terms of "a teaching style for monks where one enters samadhi wherever they find themselves,"[70] it is useful to note Hongzhi's lecture in which he talks of how this samadhi was initiated by Sakyamuni and transmitted from patriarch to patriarch. In this samadhi, the sound of knowledge (*zhiyin*) is the capacity to reflect all things (*jian*); Silent Illumination is miraculous spiritual activity (*shen*). When the Way (*dao*) is tacitly joined to the center of the jade disk (*huan*, i.e., the sacred essence), one has the wisdom to play freely; one's words (*yan*) fill the world, but one commits no transgressions of the mouth. If one is able to do this unfailingly, one straightaway knows that the truth is independent of words and letters (*wenzi*), eliminating any need for oral speech (*yanyu*). Since one is pure and exquisitely luminous, one is fundamentally free to act however one pleases (*youjian*).[71] The "jade disk of the Way" (*daohuan*) referred to here can be viewed as the communicative nature of all enlightened activity. Moreover, it can also be referred to as the nondual world of words and silence, the nonduality of words and enlightenment, and the nonduality of silence and enlightenment.

When the aspect of Chan as ultimate playfulness (*zhiyouchan*) is factored into the consideration of Silent Illumination, the special character of Hongzhi's Chan teaching seems clearer. Yet, where does the significance of Hongzhi's Chan teaching lie? We can determine this by looking to fascicle 4 of Dahui's *Pushuo*, in which Dahui comments on the work of the statesman and Chan devotee Zhang Shangying:[72]

[Zhang Shangying's text] also says: "When the actualization of enlightenment (*shijue*) merges with inherent enlightenment (*benjue*), this is called 'Buddha.'" That is to say, by actualizing enlightenment now, one merges with inherent enlightenment. Followers of Silent Illumination often say that wordless silence is the actualization of enlightenment, while [the instant before] the first Buddha [appeared] is inherent enlightenment.[73] This is impossible. Since it is impossible, what kind of enlightenment is it?

If everything is enlightenment, how can there still be delusion? If you claim there is no delusion, how on earth, then, did that old Sakyamuni become suddenly awakened when the morning star appeared, and understood his own essential nature had existed from the very beginning? That is why it is said that with the actualization of enlightenment, one merges with inherent enlightenment. It is exactly the same principle when practitioners suddenly find their own noses. What's more, there is not a single person for whom this matter is not already complete.[74]

This is, of course, Dahui's critique of Silent Illumination Chan, and in it we can see the special character of Dahui and Hongzhi's Chan teaching. Borrowing Kagamishima Genryū's depiction,[75] even though Dahui's claim "there is not a single person for whom this matter is not already complete," establishes the teaching of inherent enlightenment from the perspective of principle (*li*), his statements "by actualizing enlightenment now, one merges with inherent enlightenment," and "with the actualization of enlightenment, one merges with inherent enlightenment," establish the actualization of enlightenment from the perspective of phenomena (*shi*). This view of cultivating enlightenment largely dominates the Chinese Chan school.[76] The main current in the history of Chan in the Song dynasty, the view "everything is enlightened" (*quan shi jue*), in other words, the standpoint that the actualization of enlightenment (speechless and silent) is at once inherent enlightenment (the first Buddha, Bhishmagarjitasvara), is the main characteristic of the Chan teaching adopted by Hongzhi.

Although it concurs with the Chan teaching of Heze Shenhui and with Guifeng Zongmi's view of harmony between Chan and the Teachings (*jiaochan yizhi*), the main current in Chan was Hongzhou Chan. Zongmi criticized Hongzhou Chan for claiming that everything is true, for affirming that things had only conditional existence, and for denying the significance of impermanence. He pointed out that, by claiming that whatever one said or did was all the complete functioning of the Buddha-nature, Hongzhou Chan teaching degenerated into the heterodox teaching of naturalism.[77] The significance of Hongzhi's Chan teaching, as understood from its chief characteristic, lies in its acceptance of the main current of Chan thought, especially its emphasis on cultivation, through connecting the meaning of inherent enlightenment to the practice of seated meditation. It is easy to say that the view characterizing the actualization of enlightenment in terms of phenomena, which completely sweeps away such teachings as the doctrine of inherent enlightenment in the Japanese Tendai school, is largely based on the words of Hongzhi. We should also add that the significance of Hongzhi's Chan teaching rests, in any case, on the development of Silent Illumination Chan, which is based on a perspective on the cultivation of awakening in terms of the doctrine of inherent enlightenment, something that Dahui criticized in terms of both principle and phenomena.

Kōan-Introspection, Silent Illumination Chan, and Dōgen Zen

Because the formation of Dōgen Zen originated from the face-to-face meeting with Rujing, it makes sense to consider the differences and similarities between the Zen teaching of Dōgen and the Chan teaching of Rujing. Based on the research previously conducted by Kagamishima Genryū, I will consider what kind of connection Dōgen has with the two streams of Song dynasty Chan: Kōan-Introspection and Silent Illumination Chan. In particular, I consider a special aspect of Dōgen Zen through a comparison with the representatives of these two streams of Chan teaching, Dahui and Hongzhi. My aim is, through this comparison, to assign the place that Dōgen Zen occupies. Dogen's estimation of these two representatives of Song Chan is clearly revealed in the following passage from the "Ōsaku sendaba" fascicle of the *Shōbōgenzō*:

> When the old Buddha who was my former Master (i.e., Rujing) was giving sermons in the Dharma Hall, he would customarily refer to "the old Buddha Hongzhi." Even so, only the old Buddha who was my late master personally encountered the old Buddha Hongzhi as an old Buddha. In Hongzhi's time, there was a certain Zonggao, Chan Master Dahui of Mount Jing, who supposedly was a distant descendant of Nanyue. [Everyone in] the whole realm of Great Song China thinks Dahui is the equal of Hongzhi, and some even think him a person who surpassed Hongzhi. This error arose because both monks and laity in Great Song China are negligent in their learning, and their eye for the truth is not yet clear; they are not clear about knowing others, and they have no ability to know themselves.[78]

Because Rujing refers to Hongzhi as "the old Buddha" in the "Kobusshin" fascicle of the *Shōbōgenzō* and the *Hōkyōki*, we can say that, in Dōgen's appraisal, Rujing possessed the true dharma eye. Examples of Dōgen's disavowal of Dahui and praise for Hongzhi are found throughout his writings. His criticism of Dahui is found in the "Jishō zammai," "Sesshin sesshō," and "Jinshin inga" fascicles of the *Shōbōgenzō*, and his high estimation of Hongzhi is referred to often, beginning with "Zazenshin."

Next, I consider whether Dōgen's criticism of Dahui extended to his entire teaching. Dōgen's criticism of Dahui is fiercest in the "Jishō zammai" fascicle. The object of his criticism is constructed around the *Dahui Zongmen wuku* and the *Tomb Inscription* (*taming*) for Dahui composed by Zhang Jun, and the biography of Dahui drawn up by Dōgen. It is generally held that Dōgen claimed Dahui did not achieve awakening, but actually, in fascicle 17 of the Dialogue Records of Chan master Dahui Jue (*Dahui Jue chanshi yulu*), there is a sermon in which Dahui's awakening experience is described in detail.[79] It is explained in fascicle 15 of the *Universal Lamp Record* (*Pudeng lu*), which Dōgen certainly read. Dahui's enlightenment at the hands of Yuanwu is attested to in an extract in the *Linji zhengzongji* (Record of the Correct Lineage of the Linji Faction), although Dōgen was probably unfamiliar with this work. The four-fascicle Pushuo frequently speaks of Dahui's enlightenment as well.[80] Even so, Dōgen criticized Dahui as achieving enlightenment through his own efforts, equating it with heterodox explanations of naturalism based on emotional perceptions. At the same time, as noted previously, considering that Dōgen praised the special character of Dahui's Chan, and especially Dahui's conduct, as described in the *Shōbōgenzō zuimonki*,[81] it suggests that this esteem for Dahui by Dōgen extended to Dahui overall.

In considering Dōgen's estimation of Dahui's Chan, there is the following statement regarding Dahui recorded in the "Sesshin sesshō" fascicle of the *Shōbōgenzō*:

> Of late, there was a certain Zonggao, the Chan Master Dahui of Jingshan, who said, People today, because they like "talking about mind and talking about nature" or "discussing the dark and discussing the subtle," are slow to realize the Way. You must simply cast off both "mind" and "nature" and forget about both the "dark" and "subtle"; when dualities do not arise, your tacit agreement (i.e., awakening) will become a reality.[82]

Dōgen's source for Dahui's statement here is unclear. It is from this passage onward that Dōgen's critique of Dahui Chan begins, and I agree, on the whole, with Ichikawa Hakugen's assessment that Dahui's criticism of Silent Illumination and Dōgen's criticism of Dahui share a common ground.[83] In this regard, Dōgen explains his view of *sesshin sesshō* (talking about mind and talking about nature) in fascicle 8 of the *Eihei kōroku* in a way that differs from what he says in "Sesshin sesshō":

> Truly, the point of the singular transmission between the Buddha and patriarchs, the implicit truth of direct understanding beyond words, is not confined to the kōans of the former wise ones or the entryways to enlightenment of the ancient worthies. It is not confined to commentaries and appraisals in words and phrases or to question-and-answer exchanges; it is not confined to intellectual understanding or to mental calculations; it is not confined to discussions about abstruse mysteries and discussions

about miraculous wonders or to talking about mind and talking about nature. Only when one lets go of these handles, without retaining even a glimpse of them, [the point of the singular transmission and the implicit truth of direct understanding] is perfectly complete right here, and is able to fill one's eyes.[84]

This Dharma-lecture is reminiscent of points insisted upon by Dahui. Dōgen makes fun of those who use the phrase, *sesshin sesshō*, in the same way as Dahui. The two examples cited here are intended as direct criticisms of Dahui, and it was a critique raised time and again by Dōgen, directed at the evil cadre of followers of Dahui's Chan teaching.

The unique character of Dōgen Zen is especially found in the notion of "the nonduality of cultivation and realization" (*shushō funi*), found at the beginning of the *Fukanzazengi* (General Advice on the Principles of Seated Meditation): "The Way is inherently perfect and all pervasive. Why rely on cultivation and realization? The vehicle of implicit truth is spontaneously free. Why expend effort on it?"[85] The notion of "the nonduality of cultivation and realization" is explained more precisely in the *Bendōwa*, as follows:

> Now, to think that cultivation and realization are separate from each other is a heterodox view. In Buddhism, cultivation and realization are one and the same. Since even at this very moment cultivation is based on realization, the diligent pursuit of the Way (*bendō*) that springs forth from our initial resolve (*shoshin*) is, in itself, inherent realization in its entirety.[86]

Because the position that cultivation and realization are one and the same is not something found in the teachings of Dahui, Dōgen criticized him as follows:

> This sitting in meditation [practice] (*zazen*) is what the Buddhas transmit to each other and what the patriarchs directly point to. It is the only practice from which true successors to the Zen lineage are born. Even though other practitioners use its name, theirs is not the same as the sitting in meditation [practice] of the Buddhas and patriarchs. Why is this? The sitting in meditation practiced in other factions makes the anticipation of awakening the rationale [for the practice]. By analogy, it is like using a boat with oars to cross a great sea. They teach that once you cross the sea, you must discard the boat. The sitting in meditation practiced by our Buddhas and patriarchs is not like this, it is the practice of the Buddha.[87]

Since the standpoint "to make the anticipation of awakening the rationale" (Ch. *daiwu wei ze*, Jp. *taigo isoku*) is Dahui's Chan teaching—when wayward thoughts occur, practice seated mediation for inspecting the "critical phrase," calm your spirit and when you have done so, concentrate on the "critical phrase" with all your might—in the Dharma talk to Wang Tongban (*Shi Wang Tongban daren*) related previously, it goes without saying that it differed substantially from Dōgen's view of sitting meditation practice. Regarding Dahui's view of seated mediation practice, the following passages are representative:

> At the present time, there are some types of unreliable fellows who, even though they sit themselves in cross-legged positions without a firm grasp of what they are doing, they command others (i.e., practitioners) to control their minds and sit in silence, and while sitting, halt their breathing. Such types of people are truly pitiable.[88]
>
> It is like the practitioners of Silent Illumination who simply teach others to be silent. In a square hut, they remain [seated] deep into the night for lengthy periods. This is a really mistaken view. How will they ever rid themselves of [such] expedient practices?[89]

Because Dahui's view of this sitting in mediation practice is regarded as purposeful effort "in a demon's cave on a dark mountain," ranked only as non-Buddhist or Hinayana meditation, it is not something one would expect ever to associate with Dōgen. Moreover, in Dahui, there is the idea of the unification of the three teachings (*sankyō itchi shisō*, Ch. *sanjiao yizhi sixiang*) and an emphasis on the *Surangama Sutra*, and so on, notions that Dōgen rejected.[90] The difference in Dōgen's view of sitting meditation practice is related in a Dharma hall discourse recorded in fascicle 7 of the *Eihei kōroku*,[91] which begins with a quote attributed to the patriarchal master Nagarjuna, claiming that sitting in meditation is none other than the Dharma of all the Buddhas. Even though non-Buddhists also practice sitting in meditation, they do so erroneously, tying it their own inclinations and thus being subject to charges of holding false views; their practice is not the same as the sitting in meditation practice of the Buddhas and bodhisattvas. The sravakas- and pratyeka-Buddhas of the two vehicles also practice sitting in meditation, but they do so bent on controlling their own minds, and have a tendency to seek after nirvana. This is also not the same as the sitting in meditation practice of the Buddhas and bodhisattvas.[92]

Commenting on Nagarjuna's statement, Dōgen claims that even though practitioners of the two vehicles and non-Buddhists name their practice "sitting in meditation," same as the Buddhas and bodhisattvas, it is not the same practice. In the monasteries of Song dynasty China, he continues, unreliable elders and others do not understand Nagarjuna's rationale, and are undoubtedly contributing to the deterioration of the Buddha Dharma. Even though there was sitting practice based on textual explanations in China since the Eihei era of the Later Han dynasty,[93] it was completely lacking the proper technique. Only with the arrival of Bodhidharma was the true vein of the Buddha Dharma, wall-facing sitting in meditation practice, transmitted.[94]

If one inquires into where this sitting in meditation practice of Dōgen is from, it is none other than from Rujing. There is a passage explaining this in the *Hōkyōki*:

> Reverend [Rujing] once addressed [the assembly]: "Even though the seated meditation practice of the arhats and pratyeka-buddhas is free of attachments, it lacks great compassion. Because of this, it is not the same as the sitting in meditation practice of the Buddhas and patriarchs who, by making great compassion a priority, vow to save all sentient beings. Non-Buddhists in India also practice seated meditation. But even though they do so, they are still bound by the three evils, in other words, attachment, perverse views, and arrogance. As a result, theirs is forever different from the seated meditation practice of the Buddhas and patriarchs. Moreover, there is also seated meditation practice among the sravakas. But even though they do so, sravakas are weak in their compassion. Even with their keen [power of] perception focused on phenomena, they do not penetrate thoroughly the true character of phenomena, and by only improving themselves, destroy the seeds of Buddhahood. As a result, theirs is forever different from the seated meditation practice of the Buddhas and patriarchs. What is meant by the seated meditation practice of the Buddhas and patriarchs is the aspiration, from the initial yearning for enlightenment, to absorb the teachings of all the Buddhas, and as a consequence of this, neither forgetting sentient beings nor abandoning sentient beings, even insects, in the practice of seated meditation, always enjoining thoughts of compassion and vowing to save them, transferring all meritorious virtues to them whenever possible."[95]

Dōgen, who thought of sitting mediation practice as an end in itself and whose position on cultivation and realization based in the doctrine of inherent enlightenment gave the initial starting point of cultivation the status of enlightenment, can be seen as having a position completely different from that of Dahui, who regarded sitting meditation practice as a means to an end.

The next thing to consider is the case of Hongzhi.[96] The seated mediation practice Dōgen inherited from Rujing was, according to Dōgen, the seated mediation practice of the Buddhas and patriarchs.[97] The seated mediation practice of the Buddhas and patriarchs, also adhered to by Dōgen, is clearly "the essential component of the Buddhas; the component essential to the patriarchs" (*fofo yaoji, zuzu jiyao*) of Hongzhi in the *Zuochan zhen*. Since Dōgen borrowed this terminology in his *Zazenshin*, he regarded Hongzhi's *Zuochan zhen* as "the way awakening is realized." The reason why Dōgen did not concur with the rituals of seated meditation, seated mediation inscriptions, or instructions on seated meditation of any other Zen master, is because he admired Hongzhi alone. Moreover, Dōgen emphasized cultivation and realization in terms of the nonduality of cultivation and realization and in forsaking impurity, seen previously as special characteristics of Hongzhi's Chan teaching, founded on the notion of inherent enlightenment, in which enlightenment is inherently realized and practice wondrously cultivated. As a result, the question to consider is whether Hongzhi's Chan and Dōgen's Zen are identical. In fascicle 2 of the *Eihei kōroku*, Dōgen briefly cites words from Hongzhi, as follows:

> When the old Buddha Hongzhi was residing at Mount Tiantong, at a winter solstice Dharma hall discourse he said: "When *yin* reaches its peak and *yang* [begins to] arise, our strength is depleted and our state of being changes. A green dragon rushes off when it forsakes its bones.[98] A black cat is transformed when it is clothed in mist. Without fail, take the skulls of the Buddhas of the three times and thread them into a single stringed rosary. Do not talk of bright heads or dark heads; they are truly sun face and moon face.[99] Even if your measuring cup is full and the balance scale is level, in transactions I sell high and buy cheap. Zen worthies, do you understand yet? In a bowl, the luminous pearl rolls on its own without prodding.
>
> [Hongzhi continued], raising [the following case]. "Xuefeng asked a monk, 'Where are you off to?' "The monk said, 'I'm off to do community work.' "Xuefeng said, 'Go.' "Yunmen commented, 'Xuefeng understands people through their words.' Hongzhi commented, "Don't move. If you move I'll give you 30 blows. Why is this so? A luminous pearl without flaw; inscribe words on it and deprive it of its virtue."
>
> The master [Dōgen] said, "Although these three venerable ones spoke this way, I, the old man Great Buddha, do not agree. Great assembly, listen carefully and consider this well. A luminous pearl without flaw; polish it and it shines even brighter. This month's first [arising of] *yang* is an auspicious occasion; a noble person reaches maturity. Although this is an auspicious occasion for lay people, it is truly a magnificent benefit to the Buddhas and patriarchs."[100]

Here, Dōgen rephrased Hongzhi's "a luminous pearl without flaw; inscribe words on it and deprive it of its virtue" to "a luminous pearl without flaw; polish it and it shines even brighter." Because the first part, "a luminous pearl without flaw," is exactly the same, even if the position of inherent realization in which one has awakened to one's original enlightened nature is not understood, Dōgen, by rejecting "inscribe words on it and deprive it of its virtue" as purposeful activity and embracing the risky proposition of sticking to nonpurposeful spontaneity, advocated the nonduality of cultivation and realization through making it shine even more through grinding and polishing it. Precisely because of this, the practice of cultivation for Dōgen became wondrous cultivation. Later, in the same sermon, Dōgen changed Hongzhi's "in a bowl, the luminous pearl rolls on its own without prodding," cited above, to "in a bowl, the luminous pearl rolls on its own by prodding it oneself."[101] This alteration from "without prodding" to "prodding it oneself" is the same as in the previous example. Adopting the position "without prodding" runs the risk of becoming an imitator, a practitioner of "doing nothing Zen." The unique character of Dōgen consists in this "prodding it oneself," which refers to discovering the point when cultivation and practice underscore inherent realization is discovered. The unique character of revealing (*gen*) and actualizing (*jō*) Buddhist teaching for oneself is clearly revealed in Dōgen's *Zazen shin*, where he transforms Hongzhi's phrasing in the *Zuochan zhen*, "it knows without touching things; it illumines without facing objects," into "it is revealed without thinking; it is actualized without interacting."[102]

In addition, I find one more difference between Dōgen and Hongzhi. There is the following informal lecture in fascicle 4 of the *Hongzhi lu*:

> The Master [Hongzhi] then said: "Mind is the root; phenomena are dust. Together, both are like stains on a mirror. Once the dust has been removed, the light (i.e., its reflecting capacity) begins to appear. When mind and phenomena are both forgotten, nature is true. When you reach that moment, everything is cast off and you begin to realize. When it has been properly cast off, neither self nor other has anywhere to grasp onto."[103]

Hongzhi's notion of "casting off" (Ch. *tuoluo*, Jp. *datsuraku*) is taken directly from the reference to casting off of mind and phenomena, or root and dust, in the *Zhengdao ge* (Song on Realizing the Way): "Mind is the root; phenomena are dust. Together, both are like stains on a mirror. Once the dust has been removed, the light (i.e., its reflecting capacity) begins to appear. When mind and phenomena are both forgotten, nature is true."[104] The phrase "mind and dust are cast off" is not a reference to the dust of the mind, but casting off both mind (as sense organ) and dust (as sense object).[105] Therefore, it is naturally not intended as the dust-wiping method found in Hinayana meditation practice or Northern school Zen.

In fascicle 3 of the *Hongzhi lu*, Hongzhi uses the phrase "mind and body are entirely cast off" in a sermon delivered at the end of the summer retreat.[106] In it, the dualities of seated meditation practice and pilgrimage wandering, activity and stillness, and body and mind are transcended through abiding in the mental state of nonabiding and assuming external forms that are noncontrived. As a result, Hongzhi's sermon can be seen as explaining that cultivation and realization are one and the same. We can compare Hongzhi's teaching here to "practicing Zen by casting off body and mind" that Dōgen inherited from Rujing.[107] After citing Hongzhi's sermon delivered at the conclusion of the summer retreat, Dōgen says further:

> Even though the old Buddha Hongzhi joined with the Tathagata, he did not practice in the same way as the Tathagata. I, Eihei, here today join with Hongzhi and perform the same practices as the Tathagata.[108]

Although Dōgen's teaching is not essentially different from Hongzhi's, and both emphasize "unification with the Tathagata" (inherent realization), Dōgen changes the priority to "performing the same practice as the Tathagata" (wondrous cultivation). In Hongzhi, the phrases "casting off mind and dust" and "entirely cast off body and mind" indicate "inherent realization." Even though Dōgen also adopted the notion of "inherent realization," he emphasized the practice of "wondrous cultivation" in "casting off body and mind." When Hongzhi used the phrase "casting off mind and dust," he used it frequently in the context of developing the realm of complete perfection. When Dōgen used the phrase "casting off body and mind," he emphasized nature as an unending process of cultivation and realization that refrains from the notion of complete perfection.

The position of Dōgen Zen as inherent realization and wondrous cultivation, and as undefiled cultivation and realization is completely different from the view of cultivation and realization in Dahui's Chan teaching. Although Hongzhi's Chan teaching is based on the same view of cultivation and realization as Dōgen's, the difference lies in Dōgen's stress on wondrous cultivation. Dōgen realized that Silent Illumination Zen was not found in the opposition between examining the "critical phrase" (Ch. *Kanhua,* Jp. *Kanna*) and practicing Silent Illumination, and even though he cited the words of Hongzhi often, he never once characterized his own position as Silent Illumination Zen. In paying scrupulous care to sitting meditation practice, he never used the words "Silent Illumination," and fundamentally rejected the concept. This is also the case with the notion of the "five ranks" in the Caodong/Sōtō faction.[109] We can say that these were not something Dahui emphasized either.[110]

Whether one emphasizes a non-Buddhist naturalism to which Silent Illumination Chan easily succumbs or Kōan-Introspection's exclusive concern for stimulating awakening, one will end up in a cave with common people who easily succumb to "irrational dialogue" Zen (in the words of Dōgen in the *Sansui kyō*).[111] The meditation practice of the Buddhas and patriarchs, in other words,

"to take up sitting is the treasure of the true Dharma eye, the wondrous mind of nirvana,"[112] establishes the Zen teaching of the "True Dharma" (Jp. *shōbō*) that is never biased.

Conclusion Chinese Chan and Dōgen Zen

We have seen that, after Dōgen entered Song China, he established a Zen teaching that differed from Dahui's, but according to Dōgen's *Tenzokyōkun*, he was greatly influenced by two elderly cooks. One was a Chan monk he met on the boat after first arriving in China, whom he met again later on Mount Tiantong. The other was a cook on Mount Tiantong by the name of Yong, who noted the words of his predecessor, "Know words and letters; exhaustively pursue the Way." These two elder cooks were teachers who studied under Guyun Daoquan and Wuji Liaopai, disciples of Fozhao Deguang (1121–1203) of the Dahui faction. Not to be overlooked here is that the real-life factors leading to Dōgen Zen transcended continental Chan factionalism.

Before Dōgen Zen arrived in Japan, the Zen teachings of Dainichi Nōnin's Japanese Daruma shū (Bodhidharma school) and that of Eisai (a.k.a., Yōsai) flourished in Japan.[113] Both had a direct impact on Dōgen, and both were greatly influenced by continental Chan. The people who supported Dōgen's initial Sōtō order of monks were members of the Japanese Daruma shū. The original character of Zen in Japan was due to the foundation provided by Eisai's disciple, Myōzen. Here, I would like to touch on an aspect of the unique character of Dōgen Zen by looking at the connection between Dōgen and Nōnin, and Dōgen and Eisai.

Dainichi Nōnin achieved awakening on his own, without the aid of a teacher, and because he was criticized by people of the time for not belonging to a lineage, he dispatched his students Renchū and Shōben to China to present Fozhao Deguang with his enlightenment verse and received verification of his realization. The two disciples returned with such articles as a Dharma robe and a portrait of Bodhidharma with an attached verse in the 16th year of the Chunxi era (1189), the fifth year of the Bunji era in Japan. In contrast to this, Dōgen Zen is seen as markedly different. Dōgen insists on meeting a true (i.e., genuine) master. In the *Gakudōyōjinshū* (Employing the Mind to Study the Way), Dōgen writes: "To practice Zen and study the Way, you must seek out a true master."[114] And in the *Shōbōgenzō Hotsubodaishin* fascicle, he comments: "If you don't meet a true master, you will not hear the true Dharma. If you do not hear the true Dharma, odds are you will never develop the causes and conditions that precipitate enlightenment, you will never experience liberation, you will never realize the three treasures, and you will never manage the phenomena of the tripartite realm, and so on."[115] As stated above, Dōgen commented on how deeply moved he was on meeting Rujing face to face.

The details of Dainichi Nōnin's thought are unclear, but it appears that he believed "mind is Buddha," and following the trend of the Japanese Tendai doctrine of inherent enlightenment, held the position that cultivation and practice were unnecessary owing to our original enlightened nature. He also had the standpoint that even precept practice was unnecessary. Eisai, being a strict traditionalist who advocated the combined practice of both the Mahayana and Hinayana precepts, was critical of this position. Furthermore, as Dōgen states in fascicle 5 of the *Eihei kōroku*, "It is neither the case that it is not limited to the greater or lesser vehicles, nor that it is not different from the greater or lesser vehicles,"[116] he writes of leaping out of the confines of both the Mahayana and Hinayana precepts and establishing a style of Zen in which one achieves purity through constant practice and attention to minute detail.

Moreover, the syncretism based on "unity between Chan and the Teaching" found in Yongming Yanshou's 100-fascicle *Zongjing lu* represents a major trend in continental Chan. Dainichi Nōnin and Eisai both were influenced by the *Zongjing lu*. Nōnin was inclined toward the naturalistic, non-Buddhist Zen teaching based on the proposition "mind is Buddha." Eisai, by adopting Yanshou's traditionalism based on strict adherence to the precepts, developed a new combined practice of Tendai, Mikkyō, and Zen, centered in Kyōto and Kamakura, and aimed to revive Buddhist practice on Mount Hiei. This was also a tradition inherited in the Huanglong faction to which Eisai's teacher, Xu'an Huaibi belonged. Dōgen ignored the *Zongjing lu* and denied both the proposition of "unity between Chan and the Teaching" and "a special transmission outside the Teaching," advocating following the Buddha Dharma in its entirety. In fascicle 7 of the *Eihei kōroku*, Dōgen states:

> How sad! How sad! The fact that evil demons and spirits, wild beasts and domesticated animals irresponsibly call themselves the "Zen School" and mistakenly champion its merits in comparison to the *Lotus* and *Huayan* schools shows that there are no [true] people in this degenerate age. What the Buddhas and patriarchs exclusively transmit is simply the True Dharma (*shōbō*) of our Buddha, Sakyamuni, annutara samyaksambodhi (i.e., supreme enlightenment). As a result, we should understand that the Buddha Dharma is contained in the *Lotus*, *Huayan*, and other teachings.[117]

As detailed in the *Butsudō* fascicle of the *Shōbōgenzō*, Dōgen strictly prohibited naming his own position the "Zen School." In the sermon here, Dōgen holds a view of which we must make special note. What the Buddhas and patriarchs transmitted is the True Dharma. Within Buddhism are the teachings of sutras like the *Lotus* and *Huayan*, but at the same time, the Buddhism contained in the teachings of the *Lotus* and *Huayan* is not the teaching in its entirety. The Buddhism of sutras like the *Lotus* and *Huayan* are entirely what the patriarchs transmitted, and there is no Way of the patriarchs other than the Buddhist teaching contained in sutras like the *Lotus* and *Huayan*. Elsewhere, Dōgen explains that what the patriarchs transmitted is the True Dharma; it is Buddhist teaching in its entirety. Like the ruler of a country, there is nothing else to compare it to. Moreover, seated meditation practice is the main gateway to Buddhism. In the family of Buddhists, there are no arguments over which teaching is superior and inferior, and no distinguishing of methods as superficial or profound. The only important thing to know is how to distinguish between authentic and inauthentic cultivation and practice.[118]

We can say that the role Dōgen played in establishing the teachings of Song Dynasty Chan in Japan—the failings of Song Dynasty Chan that Dōgen observed, coupled with the joy of meeting Rujing, and his evaluation of the forms of continental Chan that had already appeared in Japan—represented a new development. Even though Dahui and Hongzhi, who I have made topics of discussion here, did not meet Dōgen directly, their influence remains in the structure of Dōgen Zen and in Dōgen's aspiration for liberation.[119] Even compared to the question of how Dōgen incorporated Dahui and Hongzhi, there are issues regarding Dahui and Hongzhi's Chan teachings in the history of Chinese Chan. Chinese Chan, which recognized meditation as a form of practice in everyday life, releasing the practitioner from the strictures of sitting, developed an antagonism between Kōan-Introspection and Silent Illumination Chan. This antagonism was based fundamentally on Dahui's emphasis on "wisdom" and Hongzhi's emphasis on "meditation." Although Dōgen refuted Dahui directly, the foundations of Dōgen Zen teaching favor neither Dahui nor Hongzhi.

7

Zen Syncretism

AN EXAMINATION OF DŌGEN'S ZEN THOUGHT IN LIGHT OF YONGMING YANSHOU'S CHAN TEACHING IN THE *ZONGJING LU*

Albert Welter

Zen Buddhism on a Song–Kamakura Continuum

Scholars of Zen Buddhism have often been pained to explain the alleged emergence of "pure Zen" (*junsui zen*) out of the degraded condition of "syncretic" Song Chan. The trope of "purity" was accorded normative status in Zen circles, and the notions of "true Zen" and "pure Zen" became synonymous. In this interpretation, true Zen represents the heroic exploits of Tang Chan masters of an alleged "golden age," who established the patterns and customs of classical Chan, replete with the shouting and beating, iconoclastic and antinomian practices for which the school is well known. As is now well established, the exploits of these iconic Tang Chan figures were largely the construct of Song advocates, a retrospective and creative imagining of Chan, or a historical fiction largely inspired by Song Chan proponents.[1] This revelation has rendered moot and untenable the supposition that Tang Chan was somehow "pure," and that Song Chan descended into complacency and syncretic compromises that represented a degradation of the earlier Tang Chan idea.

In an earlier work, focusing on the Zen thought of Eisai expressed in his *Kōzen gokokuron*, I concluded that our understanding of Eisai was poisoned by normative categories privileging "pure Zen" over Zen syncretism, that modern Zen ideology was constructed on a basis that privileged Zen as an "outsider" tradition connecting Tang Chan iconoclasts with their Tokugawa Zen compatriots (a "Tang–Tokugawa alliance" linking Mazu Daoyi, Baizhang Huaihai, Huangbo Xiyun, Linji Yixuan, etc., with Bankei and Hakuin), and that Eisai's Zen syncretism should be understood in terms of a Song–Kamakura continuum.[2] Griffith

Foulk has clarified in detail the extent to which the presuppositions of Japanese scholars have determined the ways in which the relationship between Song Chan and Japanese Zen have been (mis)read.[3] The story of the relationship between Song Chan and Kamakura Zen is not a tale of the emergence, against all odds, of "pure Zen" in Japan, but the transmission of Chan syncretism to Japanese soil. This is true of the monastic institution, as Foulk has shown, which embraced a wide array of Buddhist practices and ceremonies with little or no connection to an allegedly independent Chan or Zen tradition. It is also true of Chan and Zen intellectually and ideologically. Making use of the normative categories of pure Zen, which characterizes itself as "a separate transmission outside the teachings" versus Zen syncretism's notion of "harmony or agreement between Zen and the teachings," I argue that the transmission of Zen to Kamakura Japan needs to be understood in terms of the latter as well as (even more so than) the former, and rather than cede normative status to the former, we should acknowledge the ubiquitous presence of the latter in the transmission of Chan to Japan as Zen.

When the presence of syncretism is acknowledged and validated, several features of the relationship between Song Chan and Kamakura Zen begin to appear. Zen syncretism is no longer an aberration to be apologized for, but a legitimate mainstream position in the Zen tradition. The contours of Song Chan syncretism, although in need of further study, begin to emerge. We also begin to see how Chan and Zen syncretism, united in the value accorded Buddhist scriptures and the doctrines and practices they authorize, is not a monolithic category, but demands careful attention to the nuances that inform particular syncretic arrangements. Likewise, it is also incumbent to recognize that Zen as "a separate transmission outside the teachings" may be understood in varying ways, on a scale mandating (at least rhetorically) total renunciation of scriptural teachings and the practices they mandate to varying degrees of tolerance toward scriptural teachings and practices. Those who acknowledged Zen as a separate transmission did not necessarily renounce scriptures, only the priority they were given and how they were appropriated. Those who acknowledged harmony between Zen and the scriptures also acknowledged the validity, even the necessity of a separate Zen factional identity, although this was not always the case. The point is that while categories like Zen as a separate transmission and Zen syncretism should not be privileged as normative, they retain utility as descriptive concepts that inform our understanding of Song Chan Buddhism as it was transmitted to Kamakura Japan.

The question broached in this essay concerns the impact that Song Chan syncretism had on the thought of the founder of the Japanese Sōtō faction, Eihei Dōgen (1200–1252). As is well known, Dōgen spent several years studying in China, visiting and practicing at prominent Chan institutions. Although all agree that Dōgen's experience at Song Chan institutions was formative, there has been great reluctance to acknowledge the essentially syncretic structure of Dōgen's thought. Following the paradigm of modern Japanese Zen orthodoxy, noted above, Dōgen was cast as a quintessential representative of "pure" Zen, who somehow rejected the literati pretensions and syncretic doctrines that characterized Song Chan in favor of a supposedly pure Chan, practiced by the likes of Tang masters like Mazu, Baizhang, and Linji.[4] In the current essay, I demonstrate that not only does Dōgen not fit the "pure" Zen model, but that his thought is contiguous with the major presuppositions of Song Chan syncretism. My analysis is undertaken through a comparison of Dōgen's views with the major representative of Song Chan syncretism, Yongming Yanshou (904–975). Rather than vindicate the notion that Dōgen managed to see through the supposed degradations of Song Chan and return to the hallowed verities of Tang Chan, I argue here that Dōgen rested securely in the syncretic doctrines that perpetrated the Song–Kamakura Chan–Zen continuum.

Before embarking on an analysis of the syncretic basis of Kamakura Zen and Song Chan thought, as exhibited in patterns of agreement between Dōgen and Yongming Yanshou, I take a few moments to comment on the nature of syncretism and the troubled history its usage as a concept has encountered. It is in part a symptom of the negative connotations that the notion of syncretism has evoked that Chan and Zen syncretism has been so poorly regarded.

The Uses and Abuses of Syncretism

The term *syncretism* derives from the Greek *synkretismos* (Latin *syncretismus*), where it was used by Plutarch to refer to the "Cretan federation" that withdrew differences separating them to form an alliance when faced with external dangers.[5] Prior to the modern period, the most common use of the notion of syncretism was found in Christian theological circles, where it was used to accuse those who accommodated non-Christian principles and practices, thereby adulterating an otherwise "pure" Christian faith. This tendency, in fact, was not the monopoly of Christianity or other Abrahamic traditions that mandated exclusive allegiance to a one true God as a pretext for salvation, but is characteristic of any ideology demanding an exclusivist approach. In point of fact, it is difficult to maintain a purist approach, except hypothetically, as human societies and the individuals who comprise them are constantly exposed to change, necessitating an ongoing process of adaptation (i.e., synthesizing) to external forces in both expected and unexpected ways. In light of this, notions regarding the "purity" of a tradition are not descriptions of nascent concepts rooted in the tradition, but ideological propositions rooted in a particular place and time that tell us more about a tradition's aspirations regarding its identity, as framed by the demands for orthodoxy, than about the allegedly incipient universal teachings of the tradition.

Given the Christian predispositions over the study of religion in the West, syncretism was frequently used as a tool or analytic category in the service of "comparative religions" to highlight the syncretic nature of other traditions as opposed to Christianity (in spite of Christianity's obvious borrowings from Judaism and Platonic philosophy). Although couched in "objective" methodologies and promoted as "universal," Christianity was regarded as the normative standard in the comparative religious enterprise against which the other traditions were measured.[6] In this regard, Asian religious and intellectual traditions, as the products of an intense sharing and borrowing across ideological "boundaries" indicative of pluralistic, multiethnic, and multi-ideological societies, lacked the kind of ideological purity that normative Christianity presupposed as the model. In response to this, the "isms" of world religions were comprised, at least in part, to service the needs of a world order predicated on the building blocks of discreet and readily identifiable cultural and religious traditions. The fact that China, and East Asia in general, did not readily succumb to the discreet "isms" model (although in large part it did) was because its syncretic tendencies were so endemic that they could not be ignored. Judith Berling, in her book *The Syncretic Religion of Lin Chao-en*, laid down the gauntlet, so to speak, by challenging the inherently biased appraisals against syncretism that had infiltrated academic treatments and calling attention to the intrinsically syncretic nature of virtually anything having to do with Chinese thought.[7]

Yet, the enterprise to revive syncretism as a valid mode of analysis and descriptive term free of ideological bias is hampered by the ambiguous notion of syncretism itself. The basic question is whether syncretism is seen in terms of a final, conclusive product, a new "ism" that incorporates disparate elements, or simply as a progression of syncretic tendencies that defy neat and definitive packaging.[8] Those who hold the former view reduce syncretism to a teleological system in which hitherto heterogeneous propositions are reestablished in a new system of harmonious cohabitation that is in principle untenable,[9] on the one hand, but has the potential to lead to a new world theology, on the other.[10] As such, syncretism is either an invalid category as logically suspect (Baird), or a theological proposition with the potential for a new world ideology (Martin). Those who hold a second view, who see syncretism in terms of a "syncretic process," refrain from grand "isms" in favor of a more mundane, if significant view of the influence and ubiquity of syncretic forces in our social and cultural lives. In this case, one applies the notion of syncretic forces not as ideology, but as a descriptive category that informs the plurality of forces that influence cultural phenomena, specifically how they interact with each other. In this regard, one sees the application of the notion of syncretism to specific ritual or phenomena, as a means to understand the complex, heterogeneous elements operating within it and the relationships between them.[11] Still, there is a danger that such a conceptual tool becomes too vague and unwieldy to be of much utility, or that it is too universal and common-place to be of any service as a descriptive tool.[12]

In spite of the difficulties associated with defining syncretism, its impreciseness, and the problems incumbent in its application as a conceptual tool in the study of religion and ideological traditions, I am reluctant to abandon it. The notion of syncretism has a functional utility even in the general and common-place sense with which it is often used—as an attempt to reconcile contrary beliefs, melding practices of various schools of thought. Although it may be particularly useful in discussing East Asian traditions that are often predicated on asserting an underlying unity allowing for inclusiveness and tolerance, one must not lose sight of the intentionality that animates such inclusiveness and tolerance. Syncretic systems do not treat all parts equally, but order them hierarchically in ways that predetermine places of priority within the hierarchy, so that even though all are included, certain ideas and practices take precedent over others.

In this study, definitions of syncretism and the question of whether syncretism serves an end or is a process are secondary to the hierarchical arrangements a particular syncretism, or a syncretic process, intends to validate. Syncretism was a fact of Song and Kamakura Buddhist life, if it can be allowed that the attempt to resolve inter-Buddhist factional rivalries and ideological discrepancies and tensions is worthy of the name "syncretism" in the first place. These tensions, be they over lineage claims, what constitutes awakening, or essential ideological orientation, are what animate discussions associated with Zen as it was transmitted to Kamakura Japan from Song China. Particularly heated was the debate, which was inherited from Chinese Chan, over Zen's relationship with the Buddhist scriptural tradition. According to Linji orthodoxy, Chan represented "a separate transmission outside the teachings," a view that found a vocal critic in Dōgen.

"The World Cannot Have Two Buddha Dharmas": The Truth of Universal Mind as Embodied in Buddhist Scriptures

Section two of Dōgen's record of travels and experiences in Song China, the *Hōkyōki*,[13] begins with a question by Dōgen posed to his master Rujing:

> At present, it is everywhere claimed that there is "a separate transmission outside the teachings," and that this was the principal intention of the patriarch [Bodhidharma] when he came from the west. What does this mean? Rujing replied: "Why concern yourself over whether the great Way of the Buddhas and patriarchs is inside or outside [the teachings]? Even so, the phrase 'a separate transmission outside the teachings' simply refers to what was transmitted in addition to [the scriptures] that such people as Mateng brought [to China]. When the patriarch [Bodhidharma] came

from the west and arrived in the eastern land [of China], he personally transmitted the Way and bestowed his method of practice. Because of this, it is referred to as 'a separate transmission outside the teachings.' The world cannot have two Buddha Dharmas. Before the patriarch [Bodhidharma] arrived in the eastern land [of China], there were travelers with baggage in the eastern land but no one to lead them. As soon as the patriarch [Bodhidharma] arrived, it was as if the people had a ruler. And at that time, the land, the treasures, and the people of the country were all the possessions of the ruler."[14]

As the opening section of the *Hōkyōki* is limited to a biographical synopsis of Dōgen's life leading to his journey to Song China and meeting with Rujing, the above passage represents the initial foray into the main content of the work, the alleged conversations and dialogues between Dōgen and Rujing.[15] The fact that Dōgen chose to begin with the question of Zen as "a separate transmission outside the teachings" underscores both the impact that this view had on him and its prevalence in the Song China in which he had landed. This was a new and novel understanding of Buddhism for Dōgen, virtually unknown in Japan, and one that surely caught his attention.

The passage relates to several aspects of Dōgen's understanding of Zen. Although the teaching is attributed to Rujing here, there can be no doubt that the views expressed are Dōgen's.[16] Mateng refers to Jiashe Mateng (Kasyapa Matanga), who allegedly was a leading member of the first Buddhist envoy to China, along with Zhu Falan (Dharmaraksha), in the tenth year of the Yongping era (67 CE), during the reign of Emperor Ming of the Latter Han dynasty. In Chinese records, this event marks the initial transmission of Buddhist teaching to China, and although it is specifically associated with the *Scripture in Forty-Two Sections* (*Sishierbu jing*), it is taken symbolically to refer to the general introduction and spread of Buddhist scriptural teachings in China. The point made here is that the phrase "a separate transmission outside the teachings" (*kyōge betsuden*) not be understood as an independent transmission, separate from scriptural teachings, but as an essential complement to the teachings, to indicate their meaning and purpose. In essence, this is an affirmation of the understanding of Chan and its relationship to doctrinal teachings proffered by Tang master Guifeng Zongmi (780–841), who famously characterized the scriptures (*jing/kyō*) as the word of the Buddha (*foyu*) and meditation (*chan/zen*) as the thought of the Buddha (*foyi*), and that what the buddhas uttered with their mouths and thought in their minds was in no way different.[17] Rujing's understanding, as characterized by Dōgen here, is essentially a development of Zongmi's position and is an important strain running through Song dynasty Chan masters as well.

The Chinese era, Yongping, when the initial transmission of Buddhism to China allegedly occurred, was a significant designation for Dōgen as well. The Japanese pronunciation, *eihei*, became the preferred name for Dōgen's monastery, Eiheiji, after he changed it from Daibutsuji (Monastery of the Great Buddha) in 1244. Although it may be the case that Dōgen adopted the name simply for its literal meaning, "eternal peace,"[18] it is also likely, as James Kodera suggests, that he wanted his monastery to be recognized as the true beginning of Buddhism in Japan.[19] If this is the case, it is important to acknowledge its connection with the transmission of the scriptural teaching to China, not the method of practice allegedly introduced by Bodhidharma centuries later. By inference, the real beginning of "Chan" (or "Zen"), if such a designation is allowed, occurred through the transmission of Buddhist scriptures, regardless of the importance accorded Bodhidharma's later initiatives. This is affirmed in a later section of the *Hōkyōki*, when Dōgen asks Rujing if single-minded, intense sitting (*shikan zazen*) leading to the elimination of desires and defilements does not make Zen teaching indistinguishable from the discussions of the scripturalists, and Zen practitioners the same as Mahayanists and Hinayanists. Rujing declares, "The descendants of the patriarch [Bodhidharma] should not reject the explanations of Mahayana or Hinayana. As students, if you turn your back on the sacred teachings of the tathagatas, how can you call yourself a descendent of the buddhas and patriarchs?"[20]

The fact that Dōgen valued the Buddhist scriptures and disparaged those who professed independence from them is amply evident in the "Bukkyō" (Buddhist Teaching) fascicle of the *Shōbōgenzō*, in which Dōgen cites a statement from an unidentified fellow claiming to represent the "truth" of universal mind as "a separate transmission outside the teachings," against the partial understanding revealed in scriptural teachings.

> Some fellow has said, "Old Man Sakyamuni, besides expounding scriptural teaching throughout his life, also directly transmitted to Mahakasyapa the supreme vehicle's Dharma of universal mind, and it has been passed down one individual at a time from successor to successor. As a result, the teachings are meaningless discussions catering to the capacities of listeners; mind is the essential true reality. This authentically transmitted universal mind is referred to as 'a separate transmission outside the teachings.' It should not be compared to anything discussed in the three vehicles or 12 divisions of the teaching. Because of the supreme vehicle of universal mind, we speak of 'direct pointing to the human mind' and 'seeing nature and becoming a Buddha.'"[21]

Dōgen comments on this statement as follows:

This expression ['a separate transmission outside the teachings'] is not about the actual performance of the Buddha Dharma.[22] It offers no vital path for transcending the self, nor any model of how one should act to transform oneself. Even though fellows like this have proclaimed themselves to be leading authorities for hundreds or even a thousand years, we should understand that when they explain things in this way, the Buddha Dharma is not made clear, and the Way of the Buddha is not made comprehensible. Why not? Because they do not know the Buddha; they do not know the teaching; they do not know mind; and they do not know what is essential versus what is extraneous.[23] The reason they do not know is that they have not actually heard the Buddha Dharma. . . . When they say that they directly transmit universal mind exclusively, and do not directly transmit the Buddha's teaching, they do not know the Buddha Dharma. They do not know that universal mind [is contained] in the Buddha's teaching, and have not heard the Buddha's teaching of universal mind. They say that the Buddha's teaching is outside of (i.e., extraneous to) universal mind. The universal mind that they speak of is not [true] universal mind. When they say universal mind is outside of the Buddha's teachings, the Buddha's teachings they speak of are not the Buddha's teachings. Even though they pass on the fallacy of "a separate transmission outside the teachings," because they do not know how to distinguish between what is essential and what is extraneous, the logic in what they say is not consistent.[24]

Dōgen affirms the message attributed to Rujing, above, that "the world cannot have two Buddha Dharmas," that the transmission of universal mind by the patriarchs is essentially the same as the teachings of the Buddha recorded in the scriptures. Anyone who authentically transmits universal mind does so in the knowledge that the Buddha's teaching on universal mind is embodied in the scriptures of the supreme vehicle and is not something that exists independently of them. As Dōgen's statement attests, this position on the compatibility between the truth of universal mind and the teachings of the scriptures ran counter to powerful forces that rallied behind the slogan of "a separate transmission outside the teachings" and understood the transmission of universal mind as at odds with the decidedly inferior teachings of the scriptures. I explore Dōgen's arguments against those who rallied around the slogan "a separate transmission outside the teachings" in more detail below, but prior to that, I turn to an examination of the major proponent of the Buddha's teaching on universal mind as embodied in the scriptures and not independent of them, the early Song Chan master, Yongming Yanshou.

Yongming Yanshou's Influence: Universal Mind in the Zongjing lu

The notion of Chan as "a separate transmission outside the teaching" pervaded Song China. Proponents of the Linji (Jp. Rinzai) faction seized upon this saying in the early Song and made it a hallmark of their teaching.[25] It functioned as the raison d'etre for many classic Chan works compiled in the Song, notably lamp records like the *Jingde Chuandeng lu* (Jingde era Transmission of the Lamp Record) and *Tiansheng Guangdeng lu* (Tiansheng era Expanded Lamp Record), gong'an (kōan) collections like the *Wumenguan* (Gateless Barrier) and *Biyan lu* (Blue Cliff Record), and figured prominently in the dialogue records (Ch. *yulu*, Jp. *goroku*) of individual masters. Widely identified as inseparable from the "classic" Chan position, "a separate transmission outside the teaching" figures prominently in the modern understanding of Zen, especially as fostered by Rinzai orthodoxy.

Where did Dōgen (and allegedly, Rujing) come up with his opposition to the notion of Chan as "a separate transmission outside the teaching"? In actuality, the notion of Chan as an independent tradition was strongly contested in Song China.[26] The position ascribed to Rujing by Dōgen, and that of Dōgen himself, was not unique, but represented a continuous line of thinking about the compatibility of Chan and scriptural teachings that originated as far back as Zongmi, and as we shall see later, arguably farther. Zongmi's position was adapted and furthered in the early Song by Yongming Yanshou, and it is to Yanshou's vision of the compatibility between Chan and scriptural teachings that Rujing and Dōgen are especially indebted.

Although it is true that Dōgen ignored Yanshou's writings, namely the *Zongjing lu* (Records of the Source-Mirror), and denied the proposition of "unity between Chan and the Teaching" as well as "a special transmission outside the Teaching,"[27] it is inaccurate to deny that Yanshou had influence over Dōgen. In the first place, there is the recognition of Yanshou's influence upon the pioneers of the Zen school in Japan, Dainichi Nōnin and Eisai.[28] Given this influence, it is certain that Dōgen was aware of Yanshou and the *Zongjing lu*. Although some may read into Dōgen's failure to make reference to Yanshou's writings as a pointed critique, by omission, of Yanshou's ideas, it is clear that Dōgen was an admirer of Yanshou. In the *Shōbōgenzō Zuimonki*, Dōgen recounts an episode from Yanshou's life extolling his devotion and willingness to sacrifice his life for Buddhism:

> There is a story about how a man known as Zen master Zhijue [Yanshou] long ago developed a mind intent on enlightenment and left household life [to become a monk]. This master was originally a government official. He had a high reputation for honesty and intelligence. Once, when he was

serving in a government office, he appropriated government money and used it to save [living beings]. An associate reported it to the emperor. When the emperor learned of it, he was really astonished and puzzled over it; his ministers were all puzzled as well. As the crime was not an insignificant one, it was determined that the death penalty be carried out.

At the time, the emperor discussed [the situation] with his ministers, saying: "This official is talented and wise, yet he now deliberately commits a crime such as this. Perhaps he had a deep inner motive for doing so. If he appears remorseful when his neck is about to be severed, sever it quickly. If he has no such expression, [it is because] he has a deep inner motive. Don't sever his head."

When the judicial commissioner brought out [Yanshou] to have his neck severed, he bore no expression of remorse whatsoever. To the contrary, he appeared joyful, and said to himself, "I dedicated my life in this incarnation to saving all sentient beings." The commissioner, surprised and puzzled, returned to report it to the emperor. [Upon hearing of it], the emperor said, "It is as I thought, he definitely had a deep inner motive. As he acted in this way, [his deep inner motive] was present all along." Accordingly, the emperor asked [Yanshou] his reason [for doing what he did].

The master [Yanshou] said: "I thought that by leaving my post [as a government official] and sacrificing my life, carrying out actions to save [others] and feeling deep empathy with sentient beings, I would be reborn as a Buddhist monk in my next life and devote myself to practicing Buddhism." The emperor was moved and allowed him to become a monk. Thereupon, he granted him the name Prolonged Life (Yanshou) as a reminder of his reprieve from execution.

You monks today should develop a resolve like this at some point in your lives. You should develop a deep feeling of compassion toward living beings [to the point that you are ready] to sacrifice your life, and develop the resolve to relinquish your life for Buddhism. If you exhibit this resolve beforehand for even an instant, you will be protected from [later] harm. Unless you can develop a resolve like this at some point, it will be impossible for you to awaken to the Buddha Dharma.[29]

Based on this, Dōgen's admiration for Yanshou's alleged devotion to Buddhism is indisputable. The deep inner motive that rendered Yanshou imperturbable in the face of death was held up as a model by Dōgen for others to emulate. Still, critics may reasonably assert that even though Dōgen admired Yanshou for his example of devoted practice, he found Yanshou's actual thought as expressed in his writings wanting. There is some truth to this contention.

Whereas I argue here that Yanshou's thought had a profound influence over Song Chan and Dōgen, this does not mean that Yanshou and Dōgen were in complete agreement.

A case in point is Yanshou's willing adoption of the name "Chan School" (*chan zong*) for his affiliation. Dōgen had no tolerance for any such factional distinctions for Buddhist teaching, but advocated following the Buddha Dharma in its entirety. In fascicle 7 of the *Eihei kōroku*, Dōgen laments in the strongest of terms those who irresponsibly call themselves the "Zen School" and champion its merits in comparison to the *Lotus* and *Huayan* schools. He contends that what the Buddhas and patriarchs transmit is simply the True Dharma (*shōbō*) of the Buddha, Sakyamuni, or supreme enlightenment. The Buddha Dharma contained in the *Lotus, Huayan*, and other teachings is not unique to them, as if there were individual Buddha Dharma teachings in each of them. The Dharma treasures found in the *Lotus, Huayan*, and other teachings are precisely what the Buddhas and patriarchs transmitted. There is no separate way of the patriarchs outside of the *Lotus, Huayan*, and other teachings. People who pursue supreme enlightenment should never designate the True Dharma of the Buddhas and patriarchs as the "Zen School."[30]

This point is also elaborated by Dōgen in the "Butsudō" fascicle of the *Shōbōgenzō*, in which he harshly condemns calling his own position the "Zen School." The True Dharma, Dōgen repeats, is what the Buddhas and patriarchs transmitted. Buddhism includes the teachings of scriptures, like the *Lotus* and *Huayan Sutras*, and even though these teachings, taken individually, are not Buddhist teaching in its entirety, they are in complete concord with what the patriarchs transmitted. There is no Way of the patriarchs other than the Buddhist teaching contained in scriptures like the *Lotus* and *Huayan Sutras*. He also takes to task those who hold that there are "five houses" in the Zen school, with distinctive ways of training and teaching, claiming, as above, that there is only one "way of the Buddha," not a "Zen school" or "five houses." Although he acknowledges that there are various lineages, he insists these lineages all share an underlying "way of the Buddha" and are not unique or separate from it.[31]

The point for Dōgen is that what the patriarchs transmitted is not reducible to factional designation, but is Buddhist teaching in its entirety. To designate it otherwise is to concede that it is something different or separate, or has some quality or characteristic that marks it as such. The designation itself reveals the tendency to redeem a perspective on Buddhism in terms that distinguish it from Buddhist teaching. This is a false presumption. It is on this point that Dōgen and Yanshou part ways.

And yet, the difference between Dōgen and Yanshou is not as great as it appears. Although Yanshou adopted the designation "Chan" for his affiliation, he has markedly ambivalent feelings about Chan factionalism, and, arguably, factionalism in general. He also holds views on the "way of the Buddha" as a singular teaching that knows no divisions that are remarkably similar to those adopted by Dōgen and attributed by Dōgen to his master, Rujing. Consider the following remarks by Yanshou in the *Zongjing lu*:[32]

> The Buddha said: "In these 49 years I have not added one word to the Dharma which all the Buddhas of the past, present, and future preach. Therefore, know that you can arrive at the truth (*dao*) through the gate of universal mind (*yixin*). When those with superior abilities enter it directly, they will never rely on other methods. For those of average and inferior abilities who have not entered [the gate of universal mind], I have devised various paths as expedients." Consequently, the patriarchs and Buddhas together point to the profound ultimate [truth] of worthies and sages. Even though the names [by which they refer to it] differ, the essence is the same. In other words, circumstances distinguish [their teachings], but they are harmonious by nature. The *Prajna Sutra* simply speak of nonduality. The *Lotus Sutra* only talks of the one-vehicle. According to the *Vimalakirti Sutra*, there is no place where one does not practice. In the *Nirvana Sutra*, everything ends in the secret storehouse. Tiantai teaching focuses exclusively on the three contemplations (*sanguan*). Jiangxi proposes the essence as the truth in its entirety. For Mazu, mind is Buddha. Heze directly pointed to knowing and seeing.

Moreover, the teaching is explained in two ways. The first is through explicit explanations. The second is through implicit explanations. Explicit explanations are sutras like the *Lankavatara* and *Miyan*, and treatises like the *Awakening of Faith* and *Consciousness-Only*. Implicit explanations establish their unique character according to the implicit truth (*zong*) taught in individual scriptures. For example, the *Vimalakirti Sutra* regards miraculousness as the implicit truth. The *Diamond Sutra* regards nonabiding as the implicit truth. The *Huayan Sutra* regards the dharma-realm as the implicit truth. The *Nirvana Sutra* regards Buddha-nature as the implicit truth. By relying on these, one establishes a thousand pathways. All of them are different aspects of universal mind.[33]

According to Yanshou, the principle of unity within apparent diversity is sanctioned here by none other than the Buddha himself, who posited "universal mind" (*yixin*) as the orchestrating principle of Buddhist teaching and the means for "arriving at the truth." Allowing for different articulations based on individual temporal circumstances, "universal mind" is rendered variously in unique but consistent ways. In spite of the apparent diversity, the essence (*ti*) is the same. Yanshou here invokes a common pattern in Chinese thought for explaining the relationship between a principle's noumenal essence (*li/ti*) and its phenomenal functionality (*shi/yong*). Yanshou provides specific examples demonstrating how this is evident in different representations of Buddhist teaching, using a conventional shorthand that pairs well-known scriptures, schools, and masters with their commonly designated teachings. In this way, the *Lotus Sutra* (*Fahua jing*) is paired with the teaching of the "one-vehicle," the *Prajna Sutra* (*Panro jing*) with the teaching of "nonduality," and so on. Tiantai teaching is designated by its focus on the "three contemplations," a reference to the emphasis in Tiantai meditation practice on regarding phenomena in each of three ways, as "empty" or devoid of reality (*kong*), as nonsubstantial but existing provisionally as temporal phenomena (*jia*), and as "existing" in their true state between these two alternatives (*zhong*). The teachings of Chan master Jiangxi, Mazu Daoyi, and Heze Shenhui are similarly rendered according to the principal teachings associated with them: proposing the essence as the entire truth (Jiangxi), maintaining that mind itself is Buddha (Mazu), and directly pointing to knowing and seeing (Shenhui).[34] All of the above cases point to examples in their respective areas (scriptures, schools, and masters) that can be extended throughout the entire corpus of Buddhist teaching, embracing all Buddhist discourse within a comprehensive framework.

Extending his methodology still further, Yanshou introduces the distinction between explicit and implicit explanations of Buddhist teaching. Explicit explanations, according to Yanshou, are the literal teachings contained in the countless scriptures and treatises of the Buddhist tradition. Implicit explanations, by contrast, are based on the unique character of individual teachings, which Yanshou terms their *zong*, their basic or implicit message. As examples, Yanshou gives the *zong* (or implicit message) of the *Vimalakirti Sutra* as "miraculousness," an apparent reference to the miraculous activities of Vimalakirti described therein. The *zong* of the *Diamond Sutra* is given as its teaching on "nonabiding." The *zong* of the *Huayan Sutra* is its teaching on "the dharma-realm," and the *zong* of the *Nirvana Sutra* is its teaching on "Buddha-nature." For Yanshou, the concept *zong* indicates an exegetical method through which the implicit, underlying message of a teaching, its fundamental meaning as opposed to its explicit depiction, is determined. The method parallels the essence–function (*ti/yong*), noumena–phenomena (*li/shi*) dichotomy introduced earlier to explain the inherent unity of Buddhist teaching amidst its apparent diversity (even contradiction).

At this stage, however, we are still left with an apparent diversity. The sundry teachings of a particular scripture or school may be reduced to a common underlying message, but an array of different messages, the *zong* of individual scriptures or schools, remains. Yanshou refers to these as the "thousand pathways," the expedients for approaching the truth. For the truth itself, Yanshou posits a supraordinating *zong*, universal or all-encompassing mind (*yixin*). The individual *zong* of the various scriptural teachings are but different aspects of this overriding, unifying principle. Universal mind as the "great *zong*," the grand progenitor, represents the source of all truth, articulated through the individual *zong* of scriptures, schools, and teachings.

For Yanshou, the ultimate meaning of *zong* is the underlying or implicit truth of universal mind. Universal mind constitutes the fundamental principle of all truth; however, it is depicted in different renditions of Buddhist teaching. This principle is all encompassing and transcends sectarian bounds. Through it, the doctrinal differences of Buddhist schools are all resolved. Even non-Buddhist teachings like Confucianism and Daoism may be incorporated within this framework, as partial representations of truth implicit in the principle of universal mind.[35]

As a result of what I call the "deep structure" of Yanshou's concept of mind—understanding truth as implicit in the principle of universal mind—Yanshou refers to mind alternately as "the deep abode of myriad good deeds" (*wanshan*), "the profound source of all wisdom," "the precious ruler of all existence," or "the primordial ancestor of the multitude of spiritual beings."[36] In Yanshou's interpretation, the deep structure of mind resolves apparent contradictions in Buddhist teaching, including the heralded division in Chan circles between the gradual and sudden teachings of the Northern and Southern school factions. It is the abode of myriad good deeds *and* the source of all wisdom, a shorthand reference to practitioners bound for enlightenment through the accumulation of merit and those whose awakening is based on discerning insight. It functions as the ruler over existence and the progenitor of spiritual beings.

Although Dōgen strongly opposed any notion of unity or harmony between the three teachings—Buddhism, Daoism, and Confucianism[37]—he advocated a universality of Buddhist truth that extended to all manner of things, including phenomenon of the natural world like plants, trees, mountains, rivers, and all species of inanimate objects (see below). Such a view has strong resonances in the thought of Yanshou, who posited mind as the spiritual abode of all living beings and imbuing all phenomena with meaning and truth:

> [The mind] is constantly changing in unpredictable ways, expanding and contracting with unimpeded spontaneity. It manifests traces as conditions warrant, and names are formed according to the things [manifested]. When Buddhas realize the [mind-essence], it is called complete enlightenment. When bodhisattvas cultivate it, it is known as the practice of the six perfections. Transformed by "ocean-wisdom," it becomes water. Offered by dragon maidens, it becomes a pearl. Scattered by heavenly maidens, it becomes petals that do not stick to one. Sought after by good friends, it becomes a treasure that is granted as one pleases. Awakened to by pratyeka-buddhas, it becomes the 12 links of causal arising. Attained by sravaka-buddhas, it becomes the four noble truths and the emptiness of

self-nature. Apprehended on non-Buddhist paths, it becomes a river of erroneous views. Grasped by common people, it becomes the sea of birth and death. Discussed in terms of its essence, it is in subtle harmony with principle (*li*). Considered in terms of phenomena (*shi*), it is in tacit agreement with the conditioned nature of existence as properly understood [according to Buddhist teaching].[38]

Mind, according to Yanshou, accounts for the variations that occur in different renditions of Buddhist teaching, as well as the varied nature of phenomenal existence. It is the implicit meaning and truth (*yizong*) of the myriad dharmas.[39] As the "deep structure" of existence, mind accounts for the diversity encountered in both the abstract realm of mental constructs and the concrete realm of physical objects. It is but a step in application to get from Yanshou's notion of mind as the spiritual abode of all existence to Dōgen's view of the role nature may play in preaching the Dharma and inspiring awakening.

In *Bendōwa*, his earliest writing after returning from China, Dōgen comments, "everything in the dharma-realm in [all] ten directions—soil and earth, grass and trees, fences and walls, tiles and pebbles—performs the work of the Buddha."[40] A little later in the same work, Dōgen further states that these phenomena (grass and trees, soil and earth), possessing the ability of the Buddha's transformative influence, all radiate great brightness and preach the profound and exquisite Dharma without end.[41] Ultimately, according to Dōgen, each and every single thing is endowed with an implicit impulse for cultivation and practice (*hon shugyō*) as an implicit aspect of its existence (*hon menmoku*).[42]

This is a theme repeated throughout Dōgen's writings. The "Sansuikyō" (Mountains and Water Sutra) fascicle of the *Shōbōgenzō* begins by inferring that the natural landscape we now see before us, the "mountains and waters," are but "the expression of the former Buddhas."[43] In the "Keisei sanshiki" (Sound of the Valley Stream, Form of the Mountain) fascicle, Dōgen extols the potency of nature for occasioning awakening, personifying the physical world in terms of Buddha-nature, citing a verse by the Song dynasty poet, Su Dongbo (or Su Shi), "The sound of the valley stream is the long, broad tongue [of the Buddha]. The form of the mountain is nothing but his immaculate body."[44] The implication is that by living in the world, one is exposed constantly to an ever-present Buddha-nature, revealed through natural phenomena.

On Agreement Between Chan and the Scriptures

Although Dōgen disagreed with Yanshou on the notion of unification of the three teachings (Ch. *sanjiao yizhi*, Jp. *sankyō itchi*), in keeping with their critique of Chan/Zen as a "a separate transmission outside the teachings (Ch. *jiaowai biechuan*, Jp. *kyōge betsuden*), Dōgen was in fundamental agreement with Yan-shou's notion of agreement or harmony between Chan and scriptural teachings (Ch. *jiaochan yizhi*, Jp. *kyōzen itchi*). Dōgen's attitude toward Buddhist scriptures as the core of Buddhist teaching is highly reminiscent of Yanshou, as was seen above. In addition, Yanshou expressly stipulated that the teachings of the Chan patriarchs in no way deviate from these scriptural teachings:

> All [the patriarchs] are descendants of the Buddha . . . [They] know the implicit truth [of Buddhism] (*zong*) through reading the Dharma, do not rush around searching for it elsewhere; personally realize the Buddha's in-tention . . . [W]hat contradiction is there between the scriptural teachings and the message of Chan patriarchs? In the case of the 28 patriarchs of former ages in India, the six patriarchs in this land . . . all of them perfectly awakened to their own minds through thorough knowledge of the scrip-tures and treatises. Whenever they preached to their followers, they always referred to real documented evidence. They never speculated beyond what was in their own heart, or expounded on the basis of false presuppo-sitions (*wangyu*). Consequently, even as the years pass uninterrupted, the winds of truth do not abate. By regarding the words of the sage (the Bud-dha) (*shengyan*) as the true measure, you will not be deceived by perverse and false claims. By using scriptural teachings (*jiao*) as your guide, you will have something to rely on.[45]

The sentiments expressed here by Yanshou on the need to regard the words of the Buddha as the true measure and scriptural teachings as the guide pervade Dōgen's writings. In the "Bukkyō" (Buddhist Scriptures) fascicle of the *Shōbōgenzō*, Dōgen stipulates that the Dharma taught to bodhisattvas and the Dharma taught to Buddhas, whether in the western regions or the lands of the East knows no discrepancy whatsoever—all follow the same process of initiating the aspiration for enlightenment, cultivation, and practice, and the experience of realization. In every case, initiating the aspiration for enlightenment, cultivation, and practice, and the experience of realization is accomplished by relying on scriptural teach-ings and knowledgeable guides, and that knowledgeable guides are, above all, thoroughly versed in the scriptures. They see the scriptures as means for establish-ing the teaching for others.[46] Moreover, the phraseology employed by Dōgen here, "the Dharma taught to bodhisattvas" (*kyō bosatsu bō*), is taken from the *Lotus Sutra*, where it is used in reference to Mahayana scriptures, specifically one called "Infinite Meanings" (Sk. *Mahanirdesa*, Ch. *Wuliang yi*) as well as the *Lotus Sutra* (*Miaofa lianhua*).[47]

It comes as no surprise that the *Lotus Sutra* figured prominently in Dōgen's conception of Buddhism. Yanagida Seizan emphasizes the huge impact that the

Lotus Sutra and Tendai thought and practice had over Dōgen (as well as all the Kamakura era Buddhist reformers).[48] Kagamishima Genryū has demonstrated that the *Lotus Sutra* was the most cited scripture (51 times) by Dōgen throughout his works. In addition, Dōgen cited frequently from the prominent Tang dynasty Tiantai work, *Zhiguan fuxing chuan guangjue* by Zhanran (24 times), as well as from other works prized in the Tendai school— the *Nirvana Sutra* (10 times), the *Da zhidu lun* (16 times), and various *Perfection of Wisdom* scriptures (11 times).[49] This has led Yanagida to conclude that, along with Rujing, the *Lotus Sutra* constitutes one of the twin pillars upon which Dōgen's thought was constructed.[50]

The *Lotus Sutra* and Tiantai doctrines and practices also loomed large in the thought of Yongming Yanshou. Yanshou hailed from the Wuyue region during the Five dynasties period, when Mount Tiantai experienced a major revival as a training center through the efforts of Yanshou's master, Tiantai Deshao, and the support he received from the Wuyue ruling family, particularly the ruler Zhongyi, himself a student of Deshao.[51] Ikeda Rosan has called attention to the role that Tiantai played in Yanshou's doctrines.[52] Next to the *Huayan Sutra* and its commentaries, the *Lotus Sutra*, its commentaries, and works associated with the Tiantai school are the most frequently cited sources in Yanshou's major writings, the *Zongjing lu* and *Wanshan tonggui ji*.[53] One instructive way to look at the *Wanshan tonggui ji*, for example, is to understand it in terms of the structure of *li* (noumena or principle) and *shi* (phenomena or activity), whereby *Huayan* thought provides the theoretical basis for *li*, while Tiantai doctrine provides the practical application as provided by *shi*.[54]

In short, both Yanshou and Dōgen authorized scriptural study as an essential component for the actualization of Buddhist understanding and practice. Moreover, the *Lotus Sutra* and Tiantai doctrine loomed large in the background of that understanding and practice for both. As a result of their shared interests and concerns regarding the essential role the scriptures play in the study of Buddhism, Yanshou and Dōgen concurred on which Chan and Zen perspectives they criticized.

Critique of Linji Chan (Rinzai Zen)

Dōgen had personal acquaintance with Rinzai Zen teachings, having trained at a Rinzai monastery in Japan before departing for China and having visited a number of Linji monasteries while in China. In *Bendōwa*, Dōgen reflected on this:

> After I initiated the aspiration to pursue the Dharma, I visited knowledgeable instructors throughout our country. In that pursuit, I met Myōzen of Kennin [monastery]. Nine seasons of frosts and flowers swiftly passed in this manner. [During this period], I learned a little of the customs of the

Rinzai lineage. Myōzen was the top student of the patriarchal master, venerable Eisai, and the only one to receive direct transmission of the supreme Buddha Dharma. None of the other students could compare with him. I then went to the great kingdom of Song, visiting knowledgeable instructors in the Zhejiang regions, learning the customs of the five lineages.[55]

Linji Chan was the most vibrant form of Buddhism practiced during the Song dynasty, and Dōgen would have encountered it at every turn as he made the rounds of prominent Chan monasteries and masters during his visit there. Dōgen's experience with Linji Chan teachers prominently appear in his writings. Although Dōgen often mentioned well-known episodes from the life of Linji in a positive manner,[56] it is clear that he was highly critical of Linji Chan, especially as he witnessed its practice in Song China. The reason for Dōgen's critical attitude toward Linji Chan teachers pertains to their disdain for Buddhist scriptures. In the "Bukkyō" (Buddhist Scriptures) fascicle of the *Shōbōgenzō*, Dōgen states:

> [E]very one or half a one who trains and studies inevitably transmits and upholds the Buddhist sutras and becomes a disciple of the Buddha. . . . Because the Treasury of the True Dharma Eye realized right here and now is none other than the Buddhist scriptures, all Buddhist scriptures are the Treasury of the True Dharma Eye . . . never recklessly say that the Buddhist scriptures are not the Buddha Dharma . . . never insult the Buddhist sutras in your disbelief.
>
> Be that as it may, over the last century or two and more in the great kingdom of Song, all sorts of unreliable stinking skin bags have said, "There is no need to keep in mind the sayings of the ancestral masters, even less so to read at length the teachings of the scriptures and rely on them. Only make your bodies and minds like withered trees and dead ashes, or like broken wooden ladles and bottomless tubs." People who are like this have for no good reason become a bunch of non-Buddhist demons. They rely on seeking after what cannot be relied on, and consequently, turn the Dharma of the Buddhist patriarchs into a meaningless, perverse teaching. . . . Those who say that the Buddhist scriptures are not the Buddha Dharma have not looked into the occasions where Buddhist patriarchs rely on the scriptures, have not investigated the occasions when Buddhist patriarchs have revealed [their enlightened natures] by following the scriptures, and do not know the degree of intimacy between Buddhist patriarchs and Buddhist scriptures.[57]

Although Dōgen acknowledged Linji and even cited his example favorably on many occasions, it is also clear that he found Linji and his teaching wanting.

The "unreliable stinking skin bags" and other epithets Dōgen uses to refer to those who abandon the teachings in the scriptures for some false, imaginary notion of a truth transmitted independently of them, is a broadside aimed against the perpetrators of it in Song China, largely adherents of the Linji school. But it is not the contemporary advocates of Linji Chan alone who are at blame; the teachings of Linji (and his co-conspirator Yunmen) are decidedly lacking in Dōgen's view:[58]

> In truth, Linji was a late-comer to Huangbo's congregation. He received 60 blows of [Huangbo's] staff, and eventually [went] to study with Dayu. After [Dayu] informed him that [Huangbo] had the mind of a [kindly] old woman, he reflected on his former conduct and returned once again to Huangbo. Because this account spread like pealing thunder, it is thought that Huangbo's Buddha Dharma was transmitted to Linji alone. And what is more, it is even thought that Linji surpassed Huangbo. This is patently not so. Even though we can say that Linji stayed a short while in the congregation of Huangbo and practiced along with the assembly, when Venerable Chen encouraged him [to put questions to Huangbo], he responded, "I don't know what to ask." When someone has not clarified the great matter (i.e., experienced awakening), how could they, as a serious monk devoted to study, stand at a [master's] place learning the Dharma and be dumbstruck like that? Understand that he is not of the highest abilities.
>
> Moreover, Linji did not have the spirit of his celebrated master, and we never hear sayings [of Linji] that surpass those of his master. . . . Linji does not have such excellence of spirit. Why? [Because] he never uttered anything that had not been expressed before, not even in his dreams. . . . How could there be the taste of truth in such notions as "the four evaluations," and how could these serve as guides for learning the Dharma?[59]

Dōgen goes on to characterize Linji and Yunmen as deplorable branch lineages, in which proper Buddhist conduct has not been transmitted. The standard for proper Buddhist conduct predated Linji (and Yunmen), and setting up Linji's (and Yunmen's) teachings as the standard is unwarranted. Lacking the proper standards for Buddhist teaching, people recklessly promote outlandish explanations and ridicule Buddhist scriptures. Dōgen cautions strongly against falling victim to these erroneous attitudes.[60]

In the "Jishō zanmai" fascicle, Dōgen extends his critique of Linji Chan to Dahui Zonggao, the faction's leading proponent in the Song dynasty, and his followers. After relating Dahui's repeated attempts to gain enlightenment under different masters, Dōgen asserts that, contrary to his own claim, Dahui never received sanction. Dahui tries time and again to initiate awakening, but in the end fails to experience the one event (i.e., enlightenment). Dōgen chides Dahui for brazenly requesting the enlightenment certificate, an affront against all those who have attained legitimate certification before him.[61] He accuses Dahui of a lack of decorum and aptitude for the truth, of being motivated merely out of greed for fame and love of profit. Chroniclers attribute a "spiritual awakening" to Dahui and write that he "attained the Dharma of great peace and joy."

He wanted to break into the inner sanctum of the Buddhist patriarchs, but according to Dōgen, he experienced no such thing. In spite of his reputation, Dōgen cautions against taking him seriously, saying that he is not worthy of the respect accorded other legitimate masters, even though there are those who regard Dahui as superior, and that the words Dahui has left behind do not come even close to the Dharma (i.e., the truth). As a result of this great deception, Dōgen writes, there are many in the great kingdom of Song who claim themselves to be descendants of the Buddhas and patriarchs, but few who have studied the truth and few who teach the truth. And although this was true in the Shaoxing era (when Dahui lived), the situation, according to Dōgen, is far worse today.[62]

Dogen's low regard for Dahui in comparison to Rujing and Hongzhi is readily evident from his comments in the "Ōsaku sendaba" fascicle of the *Shōbōgenzō*:

> When the old Buddha who was my former Master (i.e., Rujing) was giving sermons in the Dharma hall, he would customarily refer to "the old Buddha Hongzhi." Even so, only the old Buddha who was my late master personally encountered the old Buddha Hongzhi as an old Buddha. In Hongzhi's time, there was a certain Zonggao, Chan Master Dahui of Mount Jing, who supposedly was a distant descendant of Nanyue. [Everyone in] the whole realm of Great Song China thinks Dahui is the equal of Hongzhi, and some even think him a person who surpassed Hongzhi. This error arose because both monks and laity in Great Song China are negligent in their learning, and their eye for the truth is not yet clear; they are not clear about knowing others, and they have no ability to know themselves.[63]

Although Yanshou lived well before Dahui, it is clear from his writings that he held reservations similar to Dōgen's toward Linji-style Chan. For a variety of reasons, Yanshou's comments are no way near as pointed as were Dōgen's. For example, Dōgen was dealing with a congregation that included the recent arrival of members of the proscribed Daruma faction, whose founder, Dainichi Nōnin, championed antinomian views and the suspension of Vinaya precepts and other practices in ways validated by Linji Chan teachings. In the relative privacy of his congregation, Dōgen addressed a number of matters that concerned the members of his assembly in the direct style of a sermonizing abbot. Yanshou's writings were more public in nature, and although he also addressed matters of concern to the Buddhism of his day, he did so within the polite conventions of Chinese literati society. In addition, although the positions of Linji Chan were of rising concern to the likes of Yanshou, they did not have the overwhelming popularity they would later enjoy, bolstered by the support they received by prominent literati figures at the Song court.[64] In short, although Yanshou expresses concerns about positions that are identifiable with the Linji faction (and possibly others), he writes with the confidence of one who has the support of the Buddhist and ruling establishment of Wuyue.

A question posed in the *Zongjing lu*, for example, challenges directly the need to cite scriptures in order to attain the insights revealed by Chan patriarchs:

> If you want to clarify the inherent truth [of Buddhist teaching] (*zong*), you need only promote the message of the patriarchs. What use is there in combining it with citations from the oral teachings (*yanjiao*) of the Buddhas and bodhisattvas, taking these as a guide? The reason why members of Chan lineages (*zongmen*) claim "by availing oneself of the eyes of a snake, one will not distinguish things for oneself,"[65] is that one only becomes a sage of words and letters (*wenzi*) [by following the scriptures], but does not enter the ranks of the patriarchs.[66]

In response, Yanshou counters that claims like this are not intended to prohibit reading the scriptural teachings (*jiao*). If people do not know the words of the Buddha (*foyu*) and develop understanding through the corpus of Buddhist writings, they will be negligent of the Buddha's message. The scriptures lead one to precisely the insight that mind and the realm of objects are not a duality, and to direct realization of Buddha-mind.[67] Later, Yanshou contends further:

> In other words, the distinctive explanations [contained in the scriptures] do not amount to different paths. When you divulge it (i.e., *zong*), it covers the entire dharma-realm . . . it is simply universal mind (*yixin*). When the root is unfurled and the branches divulged, everything is included in the same reality. In the final analysis, there are no inappropriate doctrines [in Buddhism] that block one from access to what is implicitly true (*zong*). They all address [the state of] emotional confusion that recklessly leads to [feelings of] attachment or renunciation. When one only sees black words and letters on a page, they often close the book in disgust. Obsessed with tranquility and nonoral (*wuyan*) [communication], they delight in paring the teaching down to its essentials. They thoroughly confuse their minds by acquiescing to the realm of objects. They turn their

backs on awakening and are captivated by the dusty impurities [of the world]. They do not seek out the implicit origin of activity and silence. They do not try to comprehend the state where [the distinction between] the one and the many arises (i.e., nonduality).[68]

According to Yanshou, stubborn students with limited points of view are simply afraid of learning too much, like students of the lesser vehicle were when the Buddha introduced Mahayana teachings (in the *Lotus Sutra*) regarding the emptiness of phenomena. Because they do not understand the real, true nature of phenomena, Yanshou asserts, they are absorbed by the various transformations phenomenal forms go through, and they fall into the trap of making qualitative distinctions regarding them (i.e., as "real" or "unreal").[69] Elsewhere, Yanshou stipulates that the pure dharma-realm is the wondrous mind of true suchness; it constitutes the basis for the vast sea of virtues that propels one to Buddhahood and forms the ground of true reality for living beings. Individual teachings represent different names that have been established for the implicit truth (*zong*), not separately existing essences.[70]

Although Yanshou nowhere refers specifically, by name, to those whom he is addressing here, it is clear from other sources that the Linji faction identified with the position of "a separate transmission outside the teachings" in the early Song, and that Yanshou's comments are directed against this position and associated practices and claims.[71]

Admiration for Nanyang Huizhong

Although Dōgen held strong reservations against Linji faction teachings, he was uniformly positive toward the Chan teaching of Linji's alleged master, Huangbo Xiyun. He acknowledged the lineal affiliations between Mazu Daoyi, Baizhang Huaihai, Haungbo Xiyun, and Linji Yixuan, and although he recognized Linji as an inheritor of the Dharma methods initiated by Mazu, Baizhang, and Huangbo,[72] it is clear that he held Huangbo in highest esteem. In the "Butsu kōjōji" fascicle, Dōgen claims that, whereas Ōbaku (Huangbo) is descended from Hyakujō (Baizhang), who is descended from Baso (Mazu), Ōbaku is the clear superior of the three and that, among the patriarchs of these three or four generations, none can compare with Ōbaku.[73]

Still, if one looks for an early advocate of compatibility between Zen and scriptural teaching in a manner reminiscent of Dōgen and one who Dōgen openly admired, there is Nanyang Huizhong (Jp. Nanyō Echū), Preceptor of State (Ch. *guoshi*, Jp. *kokushi*) and an alleged disciple of the sixth patriarch Huineng.[74] It is even possible to assert that the lineage Huizhong belonged to was the most prized by Dōgen after that of his own Sōtō lineage. After Caodong lineage masters, especially his own master, Rujing, one may say that Dōgen held Huangbo and Huizhong in highest esteem.[75]

Huizhong was a highly regarded Chan master in his day. He was personally acquainted with two Tang emperors, Suzong (r. 756–764) and Daizong (r. 765–779), and was appointed Preceptor of State, a role akin to national teacher, by each. He was noted for his nonsectarian and ecumenical approach to Chan as a movement within the larger tradition of Buddhism, a perspective that made him attractive to the likes of Dōgen.

In the "Sokushin zebutsu" fascicle, for example, Dōgen mentions National Preceptor Huizhong in connection to his discussion of the so-called "Senika controversy," the view that the soul or spirit is immortal whereas the body or physical forms are transient.[76] In this discussion, a monk from the south characterizes Buddhist teaching there in terms of "mind itself is Buddha," and Buddha in nothing other than self-awareness. Buddha-nature is fully endowed in sense perception—seeing and hearing; we are, by nature, fully aware and fully knowing. Every movement—the raising of the eyebrows, the wink of an eye—is the functioning of Buddha-nature. This "true, all pervading knowledge" is the Buddha; there is no other Buddha than this. The body is subject to birth and death, but the mind-nature (Buddha-nature) is permanent and never subject to birth and death. In response, Huizhong strongly criticizes this perspective as a heretical teaching. Noting that he had often encountered this view in his travels and that it had become very popular, Huizhong chastises those who characterize this as the essential message of Southern school teaching, accusing them of perverting the meaning of the *Platform Sutra* (*Tan jing*) and destroying the sage's intentions. He laments this as the undoing of the Chan school. Dōgen praises Huizhong as a true student of the old Buddha of Caoqi (i.e., Huineng), a good and wise counselor whose views should be heeded. None of the recent generations of masters who head monasteries in Song China can compare with Huineng, Dōgen claims, even though it is commonly held there that Linji and Deshan (Jp. Tokusan) are his equal.

The point for Dōgen, in enlisting Huizhong's support, is to challenge the view that "mind itself is Buddha" excuses one from earnest and strenuous practice on the pretext that, since we are enlightened by nature, no effort is necessary to assert this. For Dōgen, "mind itself is Buddha," properly understood, is the effort exerted by all the Buddhas to initiate the aspiration for enlightenment, cultivate and practice, experience awakening, and pass into nirvana. Without these, Dōgen insists, the teaching "mind itself is Buddha" is meaningless. Undergoing training to become a Buddha, in effect, is the teaching "mind itself is Buddha." The term "Buddha," therefore, does not refer to "self-awareness," but to Sakyamuni Buddha. It is to Sakyamuni Buddha that practitioners must look to as their model (not Linji or Deshan). When all the Buddhas of the past, present, and future become Buddhas, they inevitably become Sakyamuni Buddha. This is the meaning of "mind itself is Buddha."[77]

Huizhong's teaching was also instrumental for Dōgen in establishing that even nonsentient beings, a euphemism for all of nature—mountains, rivers, grass, trees, forests, etc.—preach the Dharma, an important proposition for Dōgen discussed previously. This is readily evident in the "Mujō seppō" fascicle, in which Dōgen comments extensively on a story about Huizhong as a proponent of this view.[78] Yongming Yanshou cites the same story in the *Zongjing lu*,[79] and this suggests that Yanshou and Dōgen were united in their admiration for the stance that Huizhong took. The reasons why Dōgen found Huizhong's teachings attractive are similarly noted in the writings of Yanshou, and Huizhong constitutes a model for correct Buddhist practice shared between them. In the *Zongjing lu*, Yanshou places Huizhong among an elite group of Chan masters for consideration in fascicle 1.[80] The following excerpt of Huizhong's teaching recorded in the *Zongjing lu* is reminiscent of Dōgen's and Yanshou's own teachings:

> Chan school teaching (*chanzong fa*) must follow the words of the Buddha (*foyu*), the perfect meaning (*liaoyi*) of the one-vehicle, and tacitly conform to the original mind-ground (*benyuan xindi*). What [members of the Chan school] transmit, in turn, to each other is the same as what the Buddha taught (*fodao*). It is not obtained by relying on presumptuous attitudes (*wangqing*). Moreover, when [members of the Chan school] do not understand [Chan through] doctrinal teachings (*yijiao*), they form wild views and opinions about it. In their uncertainty, they lead future students astray and deprive them of the advantages [the teaching offers]. If only they would trust a [true] master's skill, they would be inducted into the [true] aims of the Chan school (*zongzhi*). If they, through training with a master, understand the correspondence between [Chan] and doctrinal teaching, they should rely on practice. Without understanding [the correspondence between Chan and] doctrinal teaching, [a true master] will not allow their succession in the Chan lineage. They will be like insects on the body of a lion. Although feeding on the flesh of a lion's body is not [as bad as] the demonic way of Mara, it is able to destroy Buddhist teaching (*fofa*).[81]

Although Guifeng Zongmi is highly regarded as the instigator of compatibility between Chan and scriptural teachings, Nanyang Huizhong preceded him. His severe critiques of the perverted interpretations of Southern school Chan were largely ignored by the rising current of proponents, namely the Linji faction, who saw Chan as "a separate transmission." In spite of this, the view that insisted on not just the compatibility of Chan and the scriptures, but also that there could be no true Chan transmission without a thorough knowledge of the scriptures, was maintained. Irrespective of how directly Yanshou influenced Dōgen, it is clear that they drew from common sources of inspiration for views they shared in shared.

Conclusion

Syncretism was the main tradition of Zen adopted in Japan in the early Kamakura period. This is evident in the teachings of the two lineages transmitted to Japan, the Rinzai lineage teachings of Eisai and the Sōtō lineage teachings of Dōgen. Although the story of Zen in Japan has often been couched in the tropes of "pure Zen" and Japanese uniqueness, it is clear that Zen syncretism was the order of the day, and neither Eisai nor Dōgen pretended otherwise. The only purity that they concerned themselves with was moral purity, enacted through abiding by the vinaya precepts and dedication to one's practice, especially seated meditation. To become a Chan master and join the ranks of the patriarchs was to become the Buddha. The words of the Buddha, Buddhist teachings, were the only acceptable guide in this endeavor. To suggest otherwise was presumptuous heresy.

In Kamakura Japan, the question was not about pure Zen versus Zen syncretism, but about the degree and kind of Zen syncretism in which one engaged. Eisai's disciples, Gyōyū and Eichō, for example, practiced forms of Buddhist syncretism that hardly distinguished them as "Zen." As head of the Kongōzammai'in, Gyōyū was a devoted practitioner of Shingon ritual and the study of Zen. Eichō, too, lacked interest in an independent Zen tradition, and preferred to absorb Zen into the general structure of Mahayana Buddhism. He was especially devoted to Daimitsu, or Tendai esotericism. In addition, Enni Ben'en, who transmitted the Yangqi (Yōgi) Linji lineage to Japan, was an avid proponent of syncretic Zen, melding Tendai and Shingon rituals with Zen practice. He was an avid proponent of Yanshou's *Zongjing lu*, on which he often lectured, as his model for Zen syncretism. Although the Sōtō school generally regards the syncretistic process as initiated largely through the evangelical efforts of the fourth patriarch, Keizan, and his disciples, who readily assimilated Tendai and Shingon elements and folk religious customs, is clear that Sōtō Zen teaching in Japan was highly syncretic from the outset. The teachings of Dōgen, as seen above, were highly accommodating—even preferential—toward the scriptural tradition, as the "word of the Buddha."[82] Throughout Kamakura Zen, Zen teaching and practice were not conceived as something separate from, different from, or antagonistic toward scriptural teaching. If anything, Zen was regarded as the "value added" component that gave Buddhist practice an intensity and richness it otherwise may have lacked. This is essentially the same perspective that Yongming Yanshou held with regard to Chan, and it was this spirit that infiltrated and animated many of the practice halls of Song Chan monasteries. It was this spirit that was transmitted to Japan by Zen pioneers in the Kamakura period.

In studying the transmission of the Chan monastic institution from Song China to Kamakura Japan, Griffith Foulk has noted how Song Chan monasteries were remarkably eclectic in nature, accommodating a wide array of Buddhist practices in addition to Chan meditation, that all the elements of "syncretic" practice that were adopted in Kamakura Zen monasteries were commonly found in the public monasteries of the Southern Song, including those that bore the Chan name.[83] In spite of the urgings of Japanese Sōtō scholars to contrast Dōgen's "pure" Zen with Eisai and Enni's syncretism, Foulk argues that "Dōgen embraced Song Chinese Buddhist monastic practice in its entirety, in a manner that was scarcely distinguishable from that of Eisai or Enni."[84] In addition, I have argued here that Dōgen also embraced in strident terms an ideological position that placed him at odds with the "separate transmission outside the teachings" advocates who are usually aligned with the "pure" Zen camp. Dōgen was not isolated in this regard, but stood firmly within an alternate camp that strongly rejected separatist posturing in favor of open acknowledgment of Zen's indebtedness and complementarity with the scriptural tradition and the conventional array of practices it authorized. In this scenario, Dōgen belongs with a long line of syncretists, including Nanyang Huizhong, Guifeng Zongmi, Xuefeng Yicun, and Fayan Wenyi, in addition to Yongming Yanshou. Ultimately, these figures are prone to consider themselves simply as disciples of the Buddha, not of any particular Buddhist faction.[85]

8

Disarming the Superpowers

THE *ABHIJNA* IN EISAI AND DŌGEN[1]

Carl Bielefeldt

In his *Kudenshō*, the 14th-century Tendai author Tōkai tells the story of an encounter between Zhiyi and Bodhidharma.[2] In this story, the Chinese Tiantai scholar appears in the air over the Indian patriarch to challenge Bodhidharma's claim that he has "a special transmission outside the teachings" (*kyōge betsuden*). At issue here, of course, is the notorious Chan conceit that its form of Buddhism represents an esoteric tradition handed down from the Buddha himself, beyond what is recorded in scripture. Taken seriously, this claim seems to put Chan beyond the authority of scripture and the norms of orthodox Buddhist tradition based on scripture. By Tōkai's day, the claim had long been familiar in China and was not taken too seriously there; but in Tōkai's Japanese world, it was still problematic. His story of Zhiyi's challenge of Bodhidharma well symbolizes the reaction of the Tendai Buddhist establishment to the claim when Chan was introduced to medieval Japan.

For my purposes here, what is most interesting about Tōkai's story is the fact that Zhiyi defends the normative tradition while hovering in the air above his earth-bound opponent. Zhiyi, of course, is known more for his systematic thought than for his magical powers; Bodhidharma was not much of a thinker, but he rose from the grave after death. Yet here, the images of the two men seem reversed: the mysterious Indian patriarch is grounded; the orthodox scholar displays his *siddhi-pada* (*jinsoku*). The story reminds us that good Buddhists can fly. Zhiyi was not only a scholar but a master of *dhyana*; and, according to the scriptural tradition that Zhiyi is defending, masters of *dhyana* could acquire the psychic powers of the "higher knowledges" (*jinzū*). Although he spent nine years sitting in front of a wall and founded the *dhyana* school, Bodhidharma here seems to lack the signs of a master.

Good Buddhist masters of meditation, of course, could do much more than fly. According to scripture, they could appear and disappear at will, divide their bodies into multiple manifestations, pass through walls, sink into the earth, and walk on water. They could touch the sun and moon, or visit the heavens, or make the earth shake. They could, if they wanted to for some reason, emit water and fire from their bodies. They could see and hear everything going on everywhere; they could read minds, remember their past lives, and know the past and future of all beings. Such powers might be optional for most Buddhists, but for really good Buddhists—those who would claim the supreme, perfect enlightenment of a buddha—they were obligatory. In the course of his training, the bodhisattva was expected by scripture to acquire the six *abhijna*, the "three knowledges" (*sanmyō*), "three conjurings" (*san jigen* or *san jidō*), "five eyes" (*gogen*), "ten powers" (*jūriki*), and so forth. And, of course, he was supposed to develop a glorified body, graced with the 32 marks and 80 auspicious signs of a buddha.

The question of how Bodhidharma's Chan tradition dealt with the issue of these powers and attributes of the buddha has not attracted much attention in Zen studies. It has, however, received interesting treatment in two chapters of my colleague Bernard Faure's work, *The Rhetoric of Immediacy*, in which Professor Faure proposes a historical development of the image of the Chan master in China from wonder-working "thaumaturge" to "trickster" figure (and later to "bodhisattva").[3] From a sociological angle, such development appears to be a process of "taming," or "domestication," through which the potentially disruptive powers of the Chan master are neutralized, and—rather like the local gods and spirits—he is "converted" and "civilized" into a harmless, if still somewhat eccentric, member of the sangha. Yet, as our story of Bodhidharma and Zhiyi suggests, the situation is complicated by the fact that the sangha expected its exemplars to have supernormal powers. Hence, from what we might call a theological angle, the domestication of the Chan master introduces a heterodox type into the community—a new, powerless type of buddha that, in its own way, may be just as threatening to the normative Buddhist tradition as the untamed thaumaturge.

In what follows, I would like to explore this theological angle, by considering how two early Japanese authors, Eisai and Dōgen, dealt with the expectations of the normative tradition in their attempts to explain the new image of the Chan master to their Buddhist contemporaries. In the course of this consideration, I want to make three points: (1) that, although my two authors had recourse to earlier treatments of the issue of the powers in China, their own arguments are rather different from what we usually find in the Chinese Chan sources; (2) that, while they differ from the more popular Chinese approaches, they also differ sharply from each other, with Eisai taking a relatively cautious position, whereas Dōgen offers a much bolder treatment; and (3) that, although one is cautious and the other bold, both authors seem to be trying to neutralize the "trickster" image of the Chinese Chan master, to interpret him in terms more familiar to the Japanese Buddhist establishment and thus to overcome his alien, potentially disruptive character.

Chan Literature

As Bernard Faure has shown, the theological issue of the supernormal powers has a long history in the Chan literature. The issue derives primarily from the Chan masters' characteristic rhetoric of "sudden awakening" (*dunwu*) to buddhahood, or the claim that one could simply "see one's nature and become a buddha" (*jian xing cheng fo*). Since the depictions of a buddha in scripture regularly include descriptions of his supernormal attributes and powers, the question naturally arises whether the awakened Chan master also has such attributes and powers. In Song China, where the lineage of the masters had become an established institution and their claims to sudden awakening a familiar feature of the Buddhist rhetorical landscape, the question was no longer of much moment; but in Kamakura Japan, where the new Zen movement was still seen in some quarters of the Buddhist establishment as a foreign and potentially dangerous development, the claim to a powerless buddhahood could still the raise the eyebrows of those familiar with scriptural tradition. Thus, we see the question put quite clearly in an early Japanese Zen text like the *Zazen ron*, attributed to the 13th-century figure Enni.

Why is it that, although one who sees his nature and awakens to the way is immediately a buddha, he does not have the psychic powers and radiance (*kōmyō*) or, unlike ordinary people, show the marvelous functions (*myōyū*) [of a buddha]?[4]

Enni responds to the question with what appear to be three different sorts of answers. First, he claims that the buddha's supernormal attributes are not visible on the ordinary human body produced by past karma. Next, he dismisses interest in the psychic powers as the "way of Mara and the pagan paths" (*tenma gedō*) and points out that foxes may have magical powers but are hardly revered for that. Finally, he offers a "higher," metaphorical reading of the buddha's attributes and powers: his six psychic powers, are really just the six senses of the enlightened person; his marvelous functions are but the sudden awakening to the buddha nature; his glorious halo is simply a symbol of the radiant light of wisdom.[5]

These three answers provide a fairly good summary of the varied strategies already worked out in the Chinese Chan sources for dealing with the issue of the powers. Put crudely, they may be summarized as (1) we do not display our powers; (2) we dismiss the powers as trivial; and (3) we have a higher, esoteric understanding of the powers. In these answers, in fact, Enni is likely drawing on one of his favorite Chinese sources, the *Zongjing lu*, by the 10th-century figure Yongming Yanshou. This book contains a lengthy discussion of the supernormal powers, probably the most explicit in the Chinese Chan corpus. The discussion opens with the same sort of question that Enni poses: if the Chan masters are equivalent to the buddhas, "why are they not equipped with the psychic powers and functions (*shentong zuoyong*) of the buddhas?"[6]

Yanshou begins his answer by saying, "It is not that they are not equipped; it is simply that beings do not know it." He then goes on in his characteristic scholarly fashion to lay out a schema of five types of supernormal powers (*wuzhong tong*) that need to be taken into account when considering the issue. The five range from (1) the uncanny transformations of animal and nature spirits (*yaotong*); through (2) the preternatural acts of gods, demons, dragons, and such (*baotong*); and (3) the workings of talismans and magic potions (*yitong*); to (4) the traditional "higher knowledges" (Sk. *abhijna*, Ch. *shentong*) of the contemplative adept; and finally (5), what he calls *daotong*, the enlightened state in which one with "no mind" (*wuxin*) accords with all things, existing without subject (*wuzhu*) like the moon in the water or the flower in the sky.[7]

For all his scholarly analysis of the various levels of the powers, Yanshou opts in the end to dismiss the cultivation of the traditional *abhijna* as irrelevant to those concerned with the ultimate wisdom. In one sense, this position was nothing peculiar to Yanshou or Chan: Buddhist tradition had long held that acquisition of the *abhijna* was not intended for one's own understanding but for the sake of sentient beings, in order to better attract them to and teach them the dharma. When Yanshou is asked about this ethical obligation to cultivate the powers, he redefines the "true spiritual transformations" (*zhenshi shenbian*) as the teaching devoted solely to the one vehicle (*yisheng*) and the principle of nonarising (*wusheng*), such that every word accords with the Way.[8]

In effect, then, Yanshou is reducing the salvific techniques of a buddha to his revelation of the ultimate truth and the content of his powers to his philosophy. Indeed, when Yanshou gives his own definition of the term *shentong*, it turns out to be pure philosophy: "*shen* (spirit) means that the substance of wisdom (*zhiti*) is without shape or form, not constructing or producing, yet responding to the various things; *tong* (penetration) means that this wisdom extends throughout the ten directions, with neither object nor its cognition, neither sense organ nor its consciousness."[9]

Since the display of the powers is the teaching of the ultimate truth, in effect, the Chan masters, by the very act of teaching the higher meaning of the powers, are already displaying their powers. Thus, they have no need to fly about like mere magicians. Yanshou makes this clear in a story he tells about the early Chan master, Niutou Farong. This monk, held to have been a disciple of the Fourth Patriarch Daoxin, was well known as an ascetic contemplative with supernatural powers. The later masters used to say that, during his early years of training alone in the mountains, he became so saintly that the wild birds and beasts would bring him offerings, but that after his enlightenment under the Fourth Patriarch, they stopped coming.[10]

According to Yanshou, a certain King Peng Cheng once challenged Farong with the following proposition: "If you've verified the fruit (*zheng ke*) and become a holy man (*sheng*), would you please emit water from your left side and fire from your right side, fly up into the sky, send out a ray of light, and move the earth. Then, I'll bow to you and make you my teacher."

To this, Farong responded that for Peng Cheng to judge buddhahood the way he does would mean that "even magicians (*huanshi*) could be buddhas." The *Zongjing lu* text then goes on to point out that even the Buddha appeared as an ordinary monk, even the great bodhisattva Vimalakirti seemed an ordinary layman, even the great Mahayana teacher Srimaladevi retained her female form. In short, Yanshou concludes, we should understand that "verification" (*zheng*) has to do with the mind (*xin*), not with alterations of form (*xingqian*); awakening is a transformation of wisdom (*zhibian*) and has nothing to do with extraordinariness of appearance (*xiangyi*).[11]

Yanshou here echoes a theme that we find in one of our very first sources for the "sudden awakening" doctrine, the text, preserved at Dunhuang, supposed to record the debate between Shenhui and the Northern school dharma master Yuan. When Shenhui claims that, in his practice of the "sudden" teaching, he has fulfilled the ten *bhumis* of the bodhisattva path, his opponent quickly reminds him that a bodhisattva, even on the first *bhumi*, should be able to divide his body into 100 buddha lands and asks him if he would therefore please display a few of his spiritual transformations.

Shenhui replies by quoting a line from the *Mahaparinirvana Sutra*, in which the Buddha praises his lay disciple Cunda by saying, "Though you have the body of a human, your mind is like the mind of the buddha." From this, Shenhui seems able to conclude that it is possible to be a buddha in the mind while remaining a *prthagjana* (*fanfu*) in the body.[12] This claim, that one could be a buddha merely in the mind, through a purely epistemological transformation, became, in one version or another, a standard means by which the later Chan authors justified their doctrine of sudden awakening to buddhahood and fended off the traditional definitions of the buddha's powers. They could claim, in effect, to be a "buddha mind" school, as opposed to a "buddha body" school.

We find, for example, this kind of claim in a sermon by the famous Tang-period master Linji Yixuan. It opens with a quotation from a commentary on the *Diamond Sutra*, which describes the 32 marks and 80 signs of the buddha's perfected body as mere "empty talk" (*kongsheng*), intended to encourage the worldly, and then redefines the true feature of the buddha's "enlightened body" (*jueti*) as "no marks" (*wuxiang*). Linji proceeds to dismiss the traditional list of the six *abhijna* and distinguish them from the "buddha's six knowledges" (*fo liutong*). The latter are defined as the understanding that the six sense realms are all marked by emptiness (*kongxiang*), such that one can enter into these realms without being deluded by them. Such powers, he emphasizes, occur in the *sasrava* state of the five *skandhas* (*wuyun louzhi*), what he calls the "psychic powers of the grounded" (*dixing shentong*).[13]

Similarly, Baizhang Huaihai (749–814) identifies the six *abhijna* with the liberation of sensory experience—what he describes as "the six sense fields without traces" (*liuru wuji*), defined as nonobstruction by any dharma and non-reliance on any understanding. These are the powers of what he calls the "bodhisattva of no psychic powers" (*wu shentong pusa*), one who does not bother to maintain (*shou*) the powers. Baizhang describes such a being as a "person beyond the buddha" (*fo xiangshang ren*), "the most inconceivable person" (*zui bukesiyi ren*), who may not fly but who leaves no footprints (*zongji*) on earth.[14]

In this way, the Chan masters could celebrate their inability to fly as a sign that they had flown beyond the buddha—that is, had transcended the traditional definitions of buddhahood. Indeed, it was precisely their ordinary—if often highly eccentric—behavior that was the true sign of their powers. As the famous line by the Layman Pang put it, "The psychic powers and the marvelous functions: bearing water and carrying firewood."[15] Thus, in the hagiographic accounts of the masters, Dongshan could demonstrate his "psychic powers and marvelous functions" by paying respects to his teacher and leaving the room; and Guishan's students show powers exceeding those of Maudgalyayana when they bring the master a wash bowl and tea bowl.[16] In such stories, the buddha's powers, like the traditional understanding of buddhahood itself, have become a kind of in-house joke for the trickster Chan master.

Eisai and Dōgen on the Chan Texts

Such, in brief, was the sort of treatment of the supernormal powers that Eisai and Dōgen could read in the Chinese Chan sources. Now, let us see how our two Japanese authors chose to deal with this topic. Eisai takes up the issue in the third section of his *Kōzengokokuron*, devoted to "settling the doubts of the world" (*sejin ketsugi*) about the Zen teachings and their place in the Buddhist order of things. One of these doubts concerns the question of how Eisai himself, who seems to have no "extraordinary attributes" (*itoku*), could hope to represent the tradition of the ancient patriarchs, those legendary figures who were all supposed to be "great incarnate bodhisattvas" (*daigon satta*).[17]

In his somewhat rambling answer, Eisai employs two of the apologetic strategies we have already seen: (1) I cannot be expected to display any extraordinary attributes, and (2) I do not really care about such matters. Yet, if these general lines of argument are familiar from the Chinese texts, Eisai's way of filling them in is novel and takes him in a rather different direction from the Chan masters. In explaining, for example, why he does not manifest any special attributes, rather than invoke a Chan redefinition of the powers as purely internal states invisible to the observer, he turns to the monastic code and cites two well-known cautionary tales about disciples of the Buddha who were tempted to demonstrate their psychic powers.

The first concerns Maudgalyayana (*mokuren*), known, along with the nun Utpalavarna (*uhatsurashiki*) as the disciple preeminent in *abhijna*. In this story, Maudgalyayana kindly offers to fly over Mt. Sumeru to the northern continent of Uttarakuru (*hokkuru shū*) and bring back rice for the buddha's hungry monks. The Buddha, however, refuses to permit it, saying that the community should not rely on such unpredictable supernormal aid. In the second story, Maudgalyayana's friend Pindola is chastised by the Buddha for using his power of flight to retrieve a begging bowl placed by a lay donor atop a pole. Eisai does not actually retell this famous tale but only quotes Sakyamuni's caustic admonishment upon learning of the feat: "To show one's psychic powers to a donor for a meal," he said, "is like a prostitute showing her privates to a customer for cash."[18]

Notice here that Eisai seems content to leave the standard definitions of the psychic powers in place—and to leave the questioner wondering whether, were it not for the prohibition against it, Eisai himself might take flight. Indeed, he teases the questioner with the remark that it is, after all, not so easy to tell who does and does not have what he calls the "signs of sacrality" (*reiken*).[19]

Yet, in a second line of argument, Eisai makes it clear that he has no need for the powers. He reminds the questioner, through a series of metaphors, that the issue here is not the messenger but the message. The message of the Zen school is the Buddha's prime message of liberation (*do*) from samsara. Here, given what we have seen in Yanshou, Eisai seems on the verge of redefining the true display of powers as the act of teaching the saving truth. But instead, he takes a different turn. In the "Buddhism of the last age" (*matsudai buppō*), he says, many teachers have recognized that they must focus only on the primary issue of inner liberation—what he calls the "esoteric benefit" (*mitsuyaku*)—without pursuing the supernormal transformations (*hentsū*). Hence, he argues, he is hardly the only one in this age who lacks extraordinary attributes.[20]

One rarely encounters this argument from history in the Chinese Chan sources, but it was, of course, a popular one among the Pure Land movements of Eisai's Japanese contemporaries, which likewise emphasized the doctrine of the last age as justification for their own revisions of Buddhist soteriology. Like the Pure Land teachings, such an argument is a nice mix of spiritual humility and arrogance: as a Buddhist of the last age, Eisai cannot claim any special powers; but as a representative of the Zen school, he need not worry about such worldly matters because he has the key to liberation from the world.

Like the Pure Land teachings, the position is also a somewhat dangerous one: if Buddhists of the last age are to focus solely on liberation from the world and no longer follow the traditional practices of the bodhisattva path, why is this not a justification for ignoring the norms of the path that provide the basis for Buddhist ethics? This was in fact one of the charges being brought against the Pure Land teachings in Eisai's day. Hence, whatever it may have done to handle his immediate problem of the supernormal powers, as a defense of Zen, Eisai's reliance on the historical argument here seems an odd resort—one that might seem to undercut his first argument, from the precepts.

In fact, however, like some of his contemporaries in the *vinaya* movement, Eisai saw the spiritual difficulties of the last age as justification, not for abandoning the Buddhist precepts, but precisely for reemphasizing their strict observance. Indeed, his *Kōzengokokuron* was written in part to cast the Zen teachings in terms of the *vinaya* and distance them from their antinomian implications. Thus, he uses the precepts as a weapon against both radical factions (like the so-called Daruma school) within the Zen movement and opponents of Zen within the Buddhist establishment. An interesting example of this use occurs in our section of the text.

When criticized for presuming the spiritual qualifications to establish a new school of Zen in Japan, Eisai responds by invoking the rule against criticism of a fellow monk. He goes on to quote at length the story of the monk Upagupta, fourth patriarch in the Zen (and Tendai) lineage, who lived some 100 years after the death of Sakyamuni. Longing to hear a description of the Tathagata's own physical presence, the monk once visited an aged nun of 120 who had actually seen the Buddha in her youth. Upagupta was particularly eager to hear about the nimbus (*kōmyō*) said to surround the Tathagata's body, one of the 32 physical "marks" (*sō*) of his perfected spiritual state. The nun, however, took the opportunity to test the monk's own spiritual state by secretly placing a bowl full of oil just inside the door through which Upagupta would enter. Sure enough, when he opened the door, he spilled the oil. Then the nun chastised him, saying, "You may be an arhat, endowed with the six *abhijna* (*roku jinzū arakan*), but you are not the equal of the monks of the gang of six (*rokugun biku*)." Those six monks in the congregation of the Buddha, she explained, might be notorious for their evil ways, but "in walking, standing, sitting, and reclining, they never broke the rule; they could have opened the door without spilling the oil." Eisai then adds his own comment that, if even an arhat like Upagupta could be thus humbled, how much more should we in the final age (*matsudai*) respect every precept.[21]

The Upagupta story here is clearly doing double duty, protecting Eisai from criticism and contrasting his own concern for the precepts with his questioner's interest in the supernormal powers and attributes. Yet, here again, Eisai seems on dangerous ground. Although the passage is not quoted from Chan sources, in a structural sense, it is just the sort of story that appealed to the Chan masters. Like the tale of the illiterate wood cutter Hui-neng besting the esteemed monk Shen-hsiu in competition to become the sixth patriarch, or the account of the learned scholar of the *Diamond Sutra*, Deshan, being stumped by the questions of an old woman selling rice cakes, the defeat of the arhat by an old nun dramatizes the overturning of the Buddhist spiritual hierarchies implied by the sudden teaching.

In the usual Chan story, the competition has to do with the higher wisdom, and the winner is the one who demonstrates the greater freedom from the doctrinal categories and ethical assumptions of the tradition. In contrast, the Upagupta story focuses on practice, and the victor is the one with the greater fidelity to the rule. Because of this victory, Eisai may not have noticed that the story is a rather precarious perch for his conservative position. Not only does its plot suggest precisely the sort of questioning of religious authority that he wants to avoid, but its attitude toward the precepts is at best highly ambiguous: just as the nun's rebuke of the arhat breaks the very injunction against criticism that Eisai invokes, so her humiliating test of the arhat breaks the rule that even the most senior nuns are to show respect for even the most junior monks. It does not much help that the nun holds up the notorious "gang of six" as her exemplars of deportment.

In the end, it seems clear that Eisai finds the issue of the supernormal powers quite awkward. He wants somehow to justify the Chinese claim that the Chan master does not need the powers, without invoking the disturbing Chinese rhetoric of the trickster gone "beyond the buddha." Hence, throughout his treatment of the issue, he studiously avoids quotation from the sort of Chan literature we have seen above that mocks the doctrine of the buddha's *abhijna*, preferring to cite canonical texts accepted by the Japanese Buddhist community and to emphasize fidelity to the monastic rule governing the entire sangha.[22]

Dōgen and Sectarian Chan Literature

In sharp contrast to Eisai, it is precisely the sectarian Chan literature that attracts Dōgen, and precisely the literature's dismissal of the supernormal powers that appeals to him. Already in the *Fukanzazengi*, one of his earliest works, we see Dōgen celebrating the eccentric teaching practices of the masters and explicitly contrasting them with the powers. Furthermore, turning the opportunity with a finger, a pole, a needle, or a mallet, and verifying the accord with a whisk, a fist, a staff, or a shout—these are not to be understood through the discriminations of thinking; how could they be known through the practice and verification of the psychic powers?[23]

Dōgen returns to this theme in two fascicles of his *Shōbōgenzō*. In the *Tajinzū*, as its title indicates, he takes up the ability to read minds, one of the six traditional *abhijna*. The root text here is the famous story of a contest between the Chan master Nanyang Huizhong, disciple of the Sixth Patriarch, and an Indian pundit-styled Tripitaka Master Big Ears (Da'er Sanzang). Huizhong was known in some sources for his mind-reading powers, but in this case he has been assigned by the emperor to examine the powers claimed by the foreign visitor. As the story goes, Huizhong challenges Da'er three times to read his mind. On the first two tests, the Indian monk seems successful and expresses dismay that the Chan master's mind is completely taken up with the sensory world of ordinary pleasures, flying off to distant scenes of racing boats and sporting monkeys. On the third test, however, he is quite stumped and has nothing to say. Then the examiner rebukes him, saying, "What a fox spirit (*yehu jing*)!"[24]

The story neatly captures the Chan claim to enlightenment amidst the human defilements, showing the mind of the master at once completely at home flying about amidst the pleasures of the ordinary world and yet completely beyond all worlds. Meanwhile, the learned Indian monk, for all his supposed spiritual powers, cannot enter either of these states but remains stuck somewhere on the old Buddhist spiritual path "between" them.

Dōgen's commentary on this story is too long to review here.[25] Suffice it to say that he makes two major points. In very general terms, both can be seen as versions of the sort of argument we have already seen: that powers like mind-reading are trivial. Yet both introduce new elements that we have not yet seen. Dōgen begins with a striking claim. Mind-reading, he says, is simply a "local Indian custom" (*saitenjiku koku no dozoku*) that has no role on the Buddhist path. Not only this power, but all the five or six psychic powers talked about in India are quite useless, a waste of time, and therefore the Buddhists of East Asia (*shintan koku yori higashi*) have not bothered to cultivate them.[26]

This claim is remarkable on two counts: its odd denial of Chinese interest in the psychic powers, which flies in the face of much historical evidence to the contrary, and its unusual cultural argument, to the effect that East Asian Buddhists can do without the Indian understanding of the buddha's attributes. The argument reminds us a bit of Eisai's historical appeal to a "pared down" Buddhism for the final age, but the tone here is of course very different. Eisai's doctrine of historical decline gives him a certain humility in the face of ancient Indian tradition, such that he seems willing to admit that his Zen awakening may be but a "poor man's version" of enlightenment. Dōgen's argument goes in the opposite direction: his vision of the *Shōbōgenzō*, the sacred history of the patriarchate deriving from Sakyamuni himself, gives him a higher perspective on buddhahood, from which he can dismiss the Indian tradition as merely contingent cultural practice, irrelevant to the esoteric wisdom transmitted by the Chan masters. Clearly, then, Dōgen's dismissive attitude toward Indian tradition is not merely a matter of East Asian cultural chauvinism. In fact, in his second point, he goes on to dismiss the notion that Chan masters are like any other Buddhists, whether of India or China.

Huizhong's test of Big Ears was a famous story in Chan and collected many comments by later masters. Dōgen takes up several of the comments and dismisses them all, largely for their assumption that the Indian monk actually might have read the Chan master's mind on the first two tests. The body and mind of a Chan master like Huizhong, he says, even when it is at play in the world, is quite beyond the ken even of the most advanced bodhisattva.[27] In the end, Dōgen says, this was no contest. In fact, he says, Huizhong's test of the Indian monk had nothing to do with mind-reading: it was a test of the monk's understanding of the nature of the Chan master's mind, his understanding of the true buddha dharma (*buppō*).[28]

Here, as so often in his commentaries, we see Dōgen offering his own higher reading of the story, a reading that serves to sharpen the distinction between ordinary Buddhists and the fully enlightened Chan masters. Whatever else we may say about this style of reading, it is just the sort of exaggerated sectarian claim to buddhahood likely to annoy the Japanese Buddhist establishment. Still, notice that, so far, although dismissing the importance of the powers, like Eisai, Dōgen seems willing to leave their traditional definitions intact, without invoking a higher reading of their meaning. Elsewhere in the *Shōbōgenzō*, however, he also adopts this latter strategy, and here his higher reading may actually serve to soften the distinction between the Chan masters and the Buddhism of the Japanese establishment.

In his essay entitled "Jinzū," Dōgen takes up several of the Chan passages on the powers. Surprisingly enough from what we have seen so far, the essay opens with the strong assertion that the psychic powers are the very "tea and rice in the house of the buddha" (*bukke no sahan*)—that is, the everyday fare of the buddhas.[29] He warns us, however, that to understand this we must distinguish between what he calls "great powers" (*daijinzū*) and "small powers" (*shōjinzū*). Small powers are those, like the five or six *abhijna*, valued by the small vehicle (*shōjō*) and the pagan religions (*gedō*), plus all the various marvels attributed to the buddhas and advanced bodhisattvas by the Indian scholars of the sutras and *sastras* (*kyōshi* and *ronshi*)—tricks like absorbing the oceans in a single pore or putting Mt. Sumeru in a mustard seed.[30] Those who wish to know the great powers should ignore such things and study only the powers that have been handed down from the Buddha himself in the lineage of the Chan masters (*chaku chaku sōden seru jinzū chie*).[31] Dōgen then goes on to cite a half dozen examples of the great powers, drawn from the records of the Chinese masters—examples of the sort we have already seen in my brief review of the Chinese literature above.

Again, Dōgen's comments on these passages are too extended to examine here. For our purposes, what is most important to note is that, although his quotations all reflect the celebration of the Chan master's freedom from the powers, Dōgen seems to see the masters not just as free agents, acting spontaneously, but as agents, so to speak, of a higher power acting through them. In his comment on Layman Pang's famous verse, for example, he remarks that the great power of bearing water and carrying firewood operates whether or not we know it as such; whether or not we know it, this power is never extinguished; whether we know it or not, the power remains just as it is (*hōni*).[32]

In his comment on the story of Guishan Guishan and his disciples, mentioned above, he tells us that the great psychic powers of the characters in this story are manifest not only in the buddhas but beyond the buddhas (*butsukōjō*). Here, we may think that Dōgen is simply adopted the terminology of the Chan masters' claim to have gone "beyond the buddha," but in fact he introduces his own understanding of this claim. Such powers, he says, occur before the body of the buddhas, beyond their appearance in time; they are what make possible the spiritual life of the buddhas: their initial aspiration (*hosshin*), their practice (*shugyō*), their enlightenment (*bodai*), and their final nirvana (*nehan*). The true psychic powers beyond the buddha are in fact the "inexhaustible ocean of the *dharmadhatu*" (*mujin hokkai kai*).[33]

Far from reducing the buddha's powers to a purely mental, epistemological state, Dōgen here expands them to cosmic proportions—proportions he explicitly attributes to the body. "The one true body of the *sramana* (*shamon isshaku no shinjitsu tai*)," he says, is the entire world in the ten directions (*jin jippō kai*), covered by the powers above and below. Then, playing on the scriptural tradition that the bodhisattva can emit water from his body, Dōgen describes the water emitted from this body as "the eight oceans of our world system (*kyūsan hakkai*)," "the ocean of the [buddha] nature (*shōkai*)," "the ocean of omniscience (*sabanya kai*)," "the ocean of the *dharmadhatu* (*hokkai kai*)." From this body come not only water but all the physical elements of the world, the entire historical succession of the buddhas and patriarchs, and indeed all the incalculable eons of time (*muryō asōgi kō*).[34]

Whatever else we may say about his comments here, Dōgen is clearly taking the discussion of the supernormal powers to a level of metaphysical mystery beyond anything imagined by the Chinese masters in his stories. The masters here are no longer simply "tricksters," playing freely in a higher realm beyond the norms of buddhological law; they are being played by a higher law. Their powers are no Chan master's joke: they have become the fundamental animating forces of being itself. As such, these powers are not just something in the Chan masters' minds but something in their bodies. Yet, the Chan masters' bodies no longer belong to them: they have become, so to speak, the limbs of a cosmic buddha body.

However strange Dōgen's remarks here may seem to us, his redefinition of the supernormal powers as the properties of a cosmic buddha body may actually serve to make the Chan masters less strange to Dōgen's Japanese Buddhist audience. The redefinition seems to lift them out of the alien world of the Chinese Chan literature on "sudden awakening" (*dunwu*), with its focus on the epistemological leap to buddhahood and its celebration of the radically ordinary buddha, and drop them into the Japanese Buddhist theological world of "inherent enlightenment" (*hongaku*), where buddhahood is built into the very fabric of things, and the human expression of buddhahood is accomplished through the symbolic expression, or channeling, of its powers.

Chan Masters

Dōgen is often held up in our histories of Japanese Buddhism as a prime example of "pure Zen" (*junzen*)—that is, of a religious style that refused compromise with the Japanese Buddhist establishment and focused solely on the Chinese Chan of the Southern Song. In this, he is contrasted with a monk like Eisai, who remained within the establishment and sought to accommodate his Zen teachings to the norms and institutions of his Japanese contemporaries, in a style sometimes called "joint practice" (*kenshū*). Such a contrast might seem fair enough in what we have seen here of the two authors' treatments of the supernormal powers, both in the sorts of proof texts they use and in the ways that they use them. Yet, for all his devotion to the Chan masters and his aggressively sectarian claims for their higher status, there is a sense in which Dōgen's vision of the masters is no less a product of his Japanese context than Eisai's more circumspect efforts to keep them in the fold of familiar orthodoxy. There is also a sense in which Dōgen's metaphysical treatment of the masters is, in the end, no less a prophylactic against their alien powers than Eisai's more cautious ethical and historical arguments.

The powers of the Chan masters, what made them alien and dangerous to the established Buddhist community, were precisely their dismissal of the traditional powers and their refusal to play by the rules of standard buddhology. Eisai tried to downplay this danger by appealing to the circumstances of the final age and invoking the authority of monastic law. Dōgen handled the problem by reaffirming the Chan masters fidelity to orthodox esoteric buddhology and their consequent subjection to the higher metaphysical laws of the cosmic body. Eisai turned the Chan tricksters into sober vinaya specialists, meditating in their monasteries; through very different means but with rather similar effect, Dōgen seems to transform them into a new kind of ritual master, enacting the way of the buddha. Thus transformed, the Chan master could now become a familiar figure in the Japanese theological scene—somewhat eccentric, perhaps, in his style of ritual practice but hardly a threat to the established order.

In the context of the established order of Japanese esoteric theology, the charge that, by reason of their claim to be awakened buddhas, Zen masters ought to have the psychic powers of a buddha was, of course, patently unfair. The esoteric Buddhist *ajari* all claimed to represent a higher vehicle, beyond the traditional bodhisattva path, that offered "buddhahood in this body" (*sokushin jōbutsu*); yet no one seemed to nag them about their lack of a nimbus or challenge them to fly. No one nagged them because they represented the established church; no one challenged them because their exaggerated soteriological claims were part of a recognized theology of ritual practice, for the most part limited to the clerical community. But the Chinese Chan masters were different. They were outsiders who mocked the theological norms of the scholars and ritual practices of the clerics, and who not only claimed enlightenment for themselves but seemed eager to offer it to their lay followers.

No one in the Buddhist order really wanted the proponents of Zen to demonstrate their powers; they just wanted them to play by the rules of power, both theological and institutional. The representatives of the order might gladly invoke the normative soteriological definitions of enlightenment as a weapon against heresy, but no one wanted real buddhas and bodhisattvas wandering the streets of Japan. The transcendent saints and saviors that populated Buddhist lore were welcome enough in scholarly treatises and edifying miracle tales of the past; they might even be acceptable as isolated ascetics off in the mountains or ritual specialists praying for the state. But no one in power wanted wood cutters and water bearers imagining that they had the psychic powers and marvelous functions of a buddha. Eisai and Dōgen both knew this; and judging at least from what we have seen of them here, although they took very different paths toward it, both seem also to have known full well just where the real powers in Japan resided.

9

Remembering Dōgen

EIHEIJI AND DŌGEN HAGIOGRAPHY

William M. Bodiford

Today, Dōgen (1200–1253) is remembered as the founder of the Sōtō school of Buddhism. As such, he is afforded high status as one of the most significant Buddhists in Japanese history. His image adorns countless altars in temples and households affiliated to the Sōtō school. He is the subject of numerous biographies and studies. His works are available in multiple editions and translations. His ideas are taught in university classrooms, in and outside of Japan, as being representative of Japanese spirituality. In these respects, he exemplifies many aspects of founder worship, a practice widespread among sectarian religious organizations in Japan. The remembrance of Dōgen, the ways that his memory has been used and developed over time, illustrates not just the importance of founder worship in Japanese religious history but also the structures that give it life. However great his personal religious charisma while alive, Dōgen was never prominent. After his death, he soon faded into obscurity. He would have remained forgotten but for several specific ritual techniques that brought his memory back to life, imbued it with mythic qualities, and then exploited its power. The rural monastery of Eiheiji in particular aggrandized Dōgen to bolster its own authority vis-à-vis its institutional rivals within the Sōtō denomination. The power of ritual memory enabled Eiheiji to command tremendous respect and authority without actually possessing great wealth or power (analogous, somewhat, to Japan's royal house during the medieval period). In this chapter, I trace the history of the remembrance of Dōgen and the special importance it has held for Eiheiji, and for Eiheiji's status within the Sōtō Zen school, the religious order that looks to Dōgen as its founder.

Today, the Sōtō Zen school constitutes the largest single religious denomination in Japan. In this statement, one must emphasize the word "single." Pure Land Buddhism boasts a greater number of temples—about 30,000—but they are divided among some ten (or more) separate legal entities, the largest of which (Jōdo Shinshū Honganjiha) commands the allegiance of about 10,000 temples. Sōtō Zen, in contrast, consists of more than 14,000 temples and monasteries, all of which coexist within a single institutional structure.[1] Unlike every other Buddhist denomination in Japan, this single organization recognizes not just one, but two separate head temples: Eiheiji and Sōjiji.[2] Only one of these two temples, Eiheiji, owes its existence to Dōgen. Not only did Dōgen found the temple complex that evolved into Eiheiji, but after his death Dōgen's memory or, rather, the exploitation of that memory has ensured Eiheiji's survival and growth for more than 700 years. Without special efforts by Eiheiji's leaders to promote Eiheiji as the sacred locus for worship of Dōgen, it is doubtful if Eiheiji could have survived, much less thrived, as the head temple of the Sōtō school. To understand the precarious nature of Eiheiji's position, one need merely to examine the structure of temple economics within the Sōtō Zen denomination, as in Table 9.1.

During the Tokugawa period, the Sōtō denomination consisted of more than 17,500 temples. These temples were grouped into networks identified with the dharma lineages of prominent monks. Of these temples, the military government (shogunate) ordered temple factions affiliated with the dharma lines of the monks Giin (i.e., centered at Daijiji and Fusaiji monasteries) and Meihō Sotetsu (i.e., Daijōji monastery) to affiliate with Eiheiji. The addition of these two networks lines gave Eiheiji a total of about 1,300 affiliated temples. The approximate 16,200 remaining Sōtō temples were affiliated with Sōjiji.[3] Today, of the 14,000 Sōtō Zen temples in modern Japan, only 148 have direct ties to Eiheiji.[4] Of these 148, approximately one-third are minor temples located in Hokkaidō, where they were founded after the Meiji government began colonization of that island at the end of the 19th century. Of the temples outside of Hokkaidō, only five or six of them maintained any formal relationship to Eiheiji prior to the Tokugawa period reorganization of Sōtō temple relationships that was ordered by the military government.[5]

Table 9.1. Number of Japanese Sōtō Temples Affiliated to Each Head Institution

	Eiheiji	Sōjiji	Total Number of Temples
Tokugawa Period (ca. 1750)	1,300	16,200	17,500
Today (ca. 1980)	148	13,850	14,000

In other words, almost all Sōtō temples, directly or indirectly, are affiliated to Sōjiji, not to Eiheiji. Sōjiji is a true head temple (*honzan*) in the sense that it actually stands at the head of thousands of branch and sub-branch temples (*matsuji*). Eiheiji is a head temple in name only, without any institutional ties to the vast majority of Sōtō branch temples. Sōtō clerics sometimes describe this situation by saying that Sōjiji is "head of all Sōtō temple lineages" (*jitō no honzan*) whereas Eiheiji is "head of all Sōtō dharma lineages" (*hōtō no honzan*).[6]

This statement warrants closer examination. The assertion that Sōjiji is the "head of all Sōtō temple lineages" concerns like terms, in that it says that one particular religious institution (Sōjiji) enjoys special institutional relationships with other religious institutions. The statement that "Eiheiji is the head of all Sōtō dharma lineages," however, mixes unlike terms, in that it ties a physical institution to the abstract religious concept of dharma lineages. In this equation, Eiheiji itself acquires abstract symbolic significance by standing at the beginning of a religious interpretation of Sōtō history, in which all Sōtō priests inherit spiritual authority through a diachronic genealogy that can be traced back to Dōgen. Its symbolic power rests on a refusal to admit any distinction between this religious image of Dōgen as an ancient originator and Eiheiji's synchronic sovereignty over the ways that other institutions can use that image. Eiheiji thus has been able to maintain its status as head temple of the entire Sōtō order by portraying itself as the embodiment of that order's collective memory of Dōgen.

For the past 500 years or more, Eiheiji's leaders have employed a variety of strategies to exploit Dōgen's memory. They have sought the endorsement of the royal court, have demanded attendance at memorial services for Dōgen, have asserted that only Eiheiji maintained the traditional practices advocated by Dōgen, have placed their imprimatur on publications of Dōgen's writings, have organized celebrations of Dōgen's birth, and have promoted scholarship concerning Dōgen. Extant sources do not document every step in the evolution of these strategies, but they provide sufficient details to offer us a view of how the promotion of Dōgen served the institutional needs of Eiheiji. Even a brief examination of the development of these strategies will help us better understand how Dōgen and the concept of "Dōgen Zen" acquired such importance for Sōtō Zen teachings and such prominence in modern accounts of Japanese religious history.

Royal Endorsements

Of these various strategies, none was more important than currying favor with the royal court.[7] Eiheiji always has been poor, geographically isolated, without extensive land holdings or wealthy patrons. Nonetheless, according to entries in the diary of the court noble Nakamikado Nobutane (1442–1525), in 1507, the abbot of Eiheiji succeeded in having the court award his temple with calligraphy for a gate plaque that proclaimed Eiheiji to be the "Number One Training Center of Our Kingdom's Sōtō Lineage" (*honchō Sōtō daiichi dōjō*).[8] Receipt of this plaque constituted not just royal proclamation of Eiheiji's preeminence, but signified the establishment of new financial arrangements with the court. In the same way that the warrior government (*bakufu*) received payments for each inauguration of an honorary abbot at one of the official Five Mountains (*gozan*) Zen monasteries, henceforth the court received payment for each honorary abbot at Eiheiji.[9] This arrangement enriched Eiheiji as well, since it also collected fees for each honor. Monks who paid sufficient fees could receive not just the honorary title of "former abbot of Eiheiji" (*Eihei senju*), but also the prestigious purple robe (the royal color), as well as bestowal of a royal Zen master title (*zenji gō*). Eiheiji used the fees collected for these honors to erect new monastic buildings or to rebuild ones that had been damaged by winter snows or fires. Throughout the medieval period Eiheiji repeatedly sought to finance monastic construction projects by issuing solicitations for more Sōtō monks to seek honorary titles.[10]

Today, no records survive to tell us how Eiheiji won court recognition. We cannot know with certainty even the names of Eiheiji's leaders at that time. Our only clues concerning Eiheiji's relations with the court, therefore, are found in the wording of the royal proclamations by which the court awarded Zen master titles to abbots of Eiheiji.[11] These proclamations name the title itself, such as "Zen Master of Great Merit in the Legitimate Tradition" (*daikō shōden zenji*; awarded in 1509), as well as a brief statement praising the recipient of the award. These words of praise probably reflect the terminology suggested by Eiheiji, since the court would not have been familiar either with the honoree or the Zen vocabulary used to praise him. Significantly, many proclamations—especially the earliest ones—specifically praised the recipients as being the "legitimate descendants of Dōgen" (*Dōgen no tekison*). The repeated use of this phrase suggests that Eiheiji's status rested on its being recognized as Dōgen's monastery.[12]

Eiheiji subsequently cited its royal recognition whenever its status as head temple was threatened, both in its many struggles with Sōjiji and during the reorganizations of religious institutions that occurred under the Tokugawa and the Meiji regimes. Eiheiji's attempts to raise funds by granting honorary titles, however, suffered from one major weakness: payments for these titles had to come from outside of Eiheiji. In other words, it required the cooperation of monks from temples that were affiliated with other factions, such as Sōjiji. Naturally Sōjiji's leaders worked hard to ensure that cooperation would not be forthcoming. Sōjiji recruited monks many times more honorary abbots than Eiheiji, and it issued orders forbidding monks from its branch temples from seeking honors at Eiheiji. It even sought to prevent temples outside the Sōtō order from recognizing purple robes awarded at Eiheiji. Among Sōjiji's branch temples, only those affiliated with the Ryōan faction proved defiant and continued to seek honorary titles at Eiheiji. In exchange for their financial donations, though, the Ryōan leaders demanded that Eiheiji refuse to grant honors to monks from any rival factions.[13]

Memorial Services

The second most prominent strategy used to link Eiheiji to Dōgen's memory is memorial services. It is these services more than any other event that eventually came to emphasize Eiheiji's status as head of all Sōtō dharma lineages. In stark contrast to their subsequent importance, however, there is no evidence that Dōgen memorial services assumed a role of any importance during Eiheiji's early history. In fact, there is no documentary evidence for any Dōgen memorial service at all until after the passage of 350 years.

Surely, memorial services must have been observed. We know, for example, that the Eiheiji community observed memorial services for Dōgen's teacher Rujing (Jp. Nyojō; 1163–1227) during the years 1246 to 1252 while Dōgen was alive.[14] Likewise, the recorded sayings of the Sōtō monk Giun (n. d.), who became abbot of Eiheiji in 1314, include reference to the 33rd memorial service that he observed in 1331 for his teacher, Jakuen (1207–1299).[15] This reference is important because it demonstrates observance at Eiheiji of the standard Chinese sequence of memorial services on the 3rd, 7th, 13th, and 33rd years.[16] More important, a memorial hall specifically for Dōgen, the Jōyōan (since renamed Jōyōden), was erected at Eiheiji shortly after his death.[17] It is reasonable to assume, therefore, that regular memorial services for Dōgen were a standard part of Eiheiji's annual calendar of events even before the 350-year memorial.[18]

At the same time, we must also note that Dōgen's memorial hall, the Jōyōan, was not the only one found at Eiheiji during the medieval period. A memorial hall (called the Reibaiin) for Giun also existed. As mentioned above, Giun became abbot of Eiheiji in 1314. In so doing, he established control over Eiheiji by members of the Jakuen lineage.[19] According to a 1495 inventory of Eiheiji's endowment, the Reibaiin derived income from lands covering about two and a half times as much area as the lands of the Jōyōan. The inventory further reveals that whereas the Jōyōan's endowment consisted only of land donated immediately following Dōgen's death, the Reibaiin had repeatedly received donations of additional land over a period of many years.[20] Therefore, based on the lack of records concerning memorials for Dōgen and on the substantially greater wealth of Reibaiin, one can conclude that medieval period leaders at Eiheiji placed more emphasis on memorial services for Giun (i.e., for ancestors of their own Jakuen line) than for Dōgen.

About the same time that Giun served as abbot at Eiheiji, another Sōtō monk named Keizan Jōkin (1264–1324) strove to promote memorial services for Dōgen. Keizan's base of operations, however, was not Dōgen's Eiheiji, but at

Yōkōji, a new temple he had just founded in Noto Province. In 1323, Keizan erected a memorial hall (the Dentōin) at Yōkōji, in which he enshrined relics from the previous four ancestors of his lineage: Dōgen's teacher Rujing, Dōgen, Dōgen's disciple Ejō (1198–1280), and Ejō's disciple (i.e., Keizan's teacher) Gikai (1219–1309). Keizan ordered that all Sōtō monks must revere these ancestors and contribute to memorial services held in their honor at Yōkōji, so that Yōkōji might function as the new head temple of the Sōtō order.[21] The fact that mandatory attendance at memorial services figured so prominently in Keizan's plans for empowering Yōkōji should alert us to the ultimate significance of memorial halls. In Keizan's eyes, they sacralized a temple by giving concrete form to the abstract concept of dharma lineage, and in so doing they commanded support from other temples associated with monks in that same lineage. At this time in medieval Japan, many new religious orders coalesced around rites of shared worship at their founder's mausoleums. For example, among Pure Land devotees the gravesite of Hōnen at the Chion'in temple became the center of the new Jōdoshū and the gravesite of Shinran at the future Honganji temple became the center of the Jōdo Shinshū.[22] Keizan's ambitions for Yōkōji nonetheless failed. As mentioned above, it was not Yōkōji but Sōjiji that rose to power as the head temple of the Sōtō order.[23]

Keizan's activities at Yōkōji did produce one important result, however. They helped to popularize observation of memorial services for Dōgen throughout Japan. The written liturgical calendar that Keizan implemented at Yōkōji naturally included instructions for Dōgen memorials. This calendar, the *Tōkoku gyōji jijo* (later known as the *Keizan shingi*), eventually was widely imitated by monks at other Sōtō temples, both within and outside of Keizan's lineage. In this way, by the middle of the 16th century many, but certainly not all, Sōtō centers for monastic training observed annual memorial services for Dōgen.[24]

Monkaku (d. 1615) organized the first notable memorial service for Dōgen, which occurred in 1602, to mark the 350-year memorial. This service was noteworthy because Monkaku organized a fund-raising campaign to finance it and because he used these proceeds to rebuild Eiheiji's main gate (*sanmon*). Sometime during the 1570s, many of Eiheiji's building were destroyed or damaged by fire.[25] Since that time, many of them had been rebuilt by Monkaku's predecessors, who relied primarily on funds raised through the awarding of honorary titles. Monkaku also raised funds using that method: his first known act as abbot of Eiheiji was his 1599 appeal for temples to nominate more monks for titles, so that Eiheiji might be rebuilt.[26] Linking the rebuilding of Eiheiji to Dōgen's memorial, however, created a powerful new fund-raising tool. It provided a convenient deadline that encouraged other temples to donate funds sooner rather than later.

Monkaku's decision to emphasize the importance of Dōgen's memorial might very will be related to the fact that he was the first abbot at Eiheiji in 300 years who was not affiliated to the Jakuen line. Monkaku was an outsider from the Kantō region of Eastern Japan, originally affiliated to a temple network known as the Tenshin lineage faction. As an outsider, his only link to Eiheiji was through the fact that both the Tenshin lineage and the Jakuen lineage shared Dōgen as a common ancestor. Dōgen's memory provided the necessary link that provided Monkaku with the status to assume office at Eiheiji.[27]

After Monkaku, Dōgen's memorial services became a major source of revenue for Eiheiji. The memorial services observed at 50-year intervals in particular provided crucial opportunities for Eiheiji to assert itself and to rebuild itself. For this reason, the history of Eiheiji during the Tokugawa period can be told largely in terms of Eiheiji's observances of major memorials for Dōgen.[28] For example, in 1652, for Dōgen's 400th memorial, hundreds of monks gathered at Eiheiji for ten days of ceremonies. The sangha hall (*sōdō*), bath (*furo*), main gate along with its images of arhats (*rakan*) were either rebuilt or substantially repaired. Eiheiji also built a new scripture library (*kyōzō*) and received a copy of the recently printed Tō Eizan (i.e., Tenkai) edition of the Buddhist canon.[29] In 1702, for the 450th memorial, Eiheiji raised funds to rebuild its buddha hall (*butsuden*), its sangha hall, its corridors (*ryōrō*), its study hall (*sōryō*), its guest quarters (*hinkan*), and a new memorial hall (*tōin*) for Dōgen. In 1752, for the 500th memorial, 23,700 monks gathered at Eiheiji for the ceremonies. The main gate was rebuilt yet again.[30] In 1802, for the 550th memorial, Eiheiji rebuilt its sangha hall and its study hall. In 1852, for the 600th memorial, Eiheiji rebuilt its retired monks' dormitory (*furōkaku*) and its scripture library. It also cast a large bronze monastic bell (*daibonshō*). In 1902, for the 650th memorial, Eiheiji rebuilt its buddha hall, its sangha hall, and its infirmary (*chōjuin*). Major repairs were made to its kitchen office (*kuin*) and other buildings. Eiheiji again cast a large bronze monastic bell. The bell that had been cast 50 years earlier for the previous memorial service had disappeared for some undisclosed reason.[31] (Perhaps it had been confiscated by the government following the Meiji restoration of 1868.)

The 1092 memorial service was significant as the first major Dōgen memorial of the new Meiji period. Only about 300 monks participated in the actual memorial services, but over the course of the months leading up to the ceremonies and during the ceremonies themselves, about 30,000 lay people visited Eiheiji. Therefore, compared to previous occasions during the Tokugawa period (such as in 1752, when 23,700 monks are said to have participated), the number of monks in attendance had decreased dramatically, but the number of laypeople had increased exponentially.[32] The participation of a large numbers of laypeople in Dōgen memorial services had begun in the 1830s. Saian Urin (1768–1845), who served as Eiheiji's abbot from 1827 to 1844, actively encouraged the formation of lay fraternities (known as Kichijō kō) dedicated specifically to Dōgen's memory, throughout Japan. These fraternities existed for the purpose of sending representatives to Eiheiji every year to participate in Dōgen's memorial.[33] By 1902, therefore, the practice of lay pilgrimage to Eiheiji had become well established.

Dōgen memorials have continued down to the present. The 700th occurred in 1952, just seven years after the end of the Fifteen-years War (*jūgonen sensō*; i.e., 1931–1945). At that time, Japan still had not recovered economically from its wartime devastation and defeat. For this reason, major new building projects were out of the question. In place of buildings, Eiheiji decided to sponsor publications about Dōgen. They drew up a list of the types of works they wanted to publish: Dōgen's writings, commentaries on Dōgen's writings, academic books about Dōgen, a dictionary of Dōgen's vocabulary, and biographies of Dōgen. Ultimately, 16 monographs related to Dōgen were published.[34] The 750th memorial was commemorated by a newly commissioned kabuki play, "Dōgen's Moon" (*Dōgen no tsuki*, by Tatematsu Wahei), which was performed at theaters in many of major cities.

War has not been the only historical calamity that restricted Eiheiji's ability to stage memorials for Dōgen. Earlier, during the Tokugawa period, agricultural famines, government policies, and conflicts with its rival head temple, Sōjiji, had severely limited the scope of the 550th and 600th memorials in 1802 and 1852. Beginning in 1774, the Agency of Temples and Shrines began to restrict direct solicitations of donations by Buddhist temples because of the economic burdens they placed on the country's economy.[35] These restrictions applied to Eiheiji and to Sōjiji equally, of course, but hurt Eiheiji more because of its relatively small economic base. In 1788, Sōjiji, in order to preserve its own economic base, ordered that monks in Gasan's lineage (i.e., the lineage of all the temples affiliate with Sōjiji) could no longer seek monastic titles from Eiheiji. In other words, just when the government would no longer allow Eiheiji to solicit funds, its revenue from honorary titles also dried up.

Sōjiji's new policy had one more important implication. Until this time, the warrior government had appointed new abbots to Eiheiji from three Kantō area Sōtō temples (the so-called *Kan sansetsu*), which remained affiliated to Sōjiji. Therefore, after Sōjiji forbade its monks from receiving honors at Eiheiji none of the senior monks from those three Kantō temples would accept a government appointment to Eiheiji. As a result, Eiheiji's abbotship went vacant for three years between 1792 and 1795.[36] At the beginning of 1795, Eiheiji had no abbot, no fund raising campaign, and almost no income from honorary titles. Dōgen's 550th memorial would occur in 1802, just seven years away. In 1795, therefore, any neutral outside observer probably would have concluded that Eiheiji would be unable to afford any special events or special constructions.

Traditional Practices

Eiheiji escaped from this crisis by asserting that it alone preserved the traditional monastic practices that had been taught by Dōgen. In 1795, Gentō Sokuchū (1729–1807) assumed office as Eiheiji's new abbot. Sokuchū had been affiliated to the Meihō line (via Entsūji), a lineage whose members had fought against Sōjiji in the past. Once he entered Eiheiji, Sokuchū immediately began working to restore his new monastery's fund-raising capabilities. He wrote a series of long missives to the Agency of Temples and Shrines in which he argued three main points (summarized from the original documents):

1. Eiheiji must be recognized at the single, unequaled comprehensive head temple [*sō honzan*] of all Sōtō dharma lineages in Japan. This status had been granted to Eiheiji by the court in medieval times. Sōjiji is wrong to deny it. Therefore, Sōtō monks in Gasan's dharma lineage must be allowed to appear at Eiheiji for honorary titles.

2. In accordance with the regulations established by the Eastern Shining Divine Ruler [Tōshō shinkun; i.e., Tokugawa Ieyasu, 1542–1616], all Sōtō monks in Japan must adhere to Eiheiji's house rules [i.e., standards].[37] Recently, however, the monastic ceremonies performed by Japanese Sōtō monks have become corrupted by influences from "new styles of monastic regulations based on Chinese Ming-dynasty elaborations" [*Minchō karei no shinki*]. Japanese Sōtō monks have been turning their backs on Eihei's standards [*Eihei no kakun*; i.e., Dōgen's teachings]. In so doing, they are unfilial. This unfilial behavior must be reformed. Sōtō monks who refuse to adhere to Dōgen's old regulations [*koki*] should be punished by the government.

3. In order to reform Sōtō monks, it is absolutely necessary that Eiheiji be allowed to build a new sangha hall and study hall in accordance with Dōgen's old regulations. The new sangha hall and study hall must be ready in time for Dōgen's 550th memorial 1802. Dōgen wrote that he [i.e., Dōgen] had erected the first sangha hall ever built in Japan. Therefore, an old-style sangha hall constitutes the very basis of Dōgen's Buddhism. For these reasons [Sokuchū argued], Eiheiji must be permitted to raise funds for these important construction projects. Otherwise, Eiheiji will be unable either to uphold its court-recognized status or to adhere to the dictates of the divine ruler [Tokugawa Ieyasu].[38]

Gentō Sokuchū's arguments carried the day. In 1801, the Agency of Temples and Shrines authorized Eiheiji to implement Dōgen's old regulations by building a new sangha hall and study hall. Sokuchū immediately compiled new monastic regulations that would explain how ceremonies, including Dōgen's memorial services, were supposed to be performed in accordance with his so-called old standards. In 1803, he published these new regulations in three fascicles as *Eihei shō shingi* (Eihei's Little Regulations). The word "Eihei" in this title simultaneously refers to Eiheiji monastery and to Dōgen as the founder of that monastery. Moreover, the title as a whole alluded to a compilation of temple regulations attributed to Dōgen, popularly known as *Eihei shingi* (Dōgen's Regulations), which Sokuchū had published in 1799, during his negotiations with the government.[39] With these two publications, Sokuchū established Eiheiji's reputation as the center for ancient monastic traditions, which he identified as the ancient unchanging essence of Zen itself.

The timing of these events is very significant. Sokuchū's *Eihei shō shingi* was published in 1803, but the procedures it described had been implemented at Eiheiji in time for the 550th Dōgen memorial in 1802. One can easily imagine how the "old" procedures would have impressed visitors. Senior monks from Sōtō temples throughout Japan came to Eiheiji to participate in the memorial rites. In previous years, they had few occasions to think about Dōgen. Throughout this year, however, they had to work to raise money for the journey on behalf of Dōgen's memory. At Eiheiji, they experienced a new form of monastic practice, unlike what they performed at home. They found a new sangha hall and new study hall, both of which differed in many ways from what they had known at their home temples. The daily routine of ceremonies also differed. The memorial services also differed. These differences impressed upon them Eiheiji's unique status and Eiheiji's unique authority. The assertion that Eiheiji alone preserved the traditional monastic practices that had been taught by Dōgen was not just rhetoric. The visiting monks were made to experience it for themselves. Their eyes, ears, and bodies told them that Eiheiji was unique. They discovered in Dōgen's memory a new importance for his temple.

Eiheiji used these same tactics for the 600th Dōgen memorial in 1852. At that time, Gaun Dōryū (a.k.a., Kamimura Dōryū; 1796–1871) served as Eiheiji's abbot. In 1850, he sent a detailed missive to the Agency of Temples and Shrines in which he repeated the same assertions mentioned above, especially that all Sōtō monks in Japan must adhere to Eiheiji's house rules (*kakun*, i.e., standards) as dictated by the Eastern Shining Divine Ruler (i.e., Tokugawa Ieyasu). He also added a new twist. According to Dōryū, Eiheiji's house rules demand that all monks wear Buddhist "robes that accord with the dharma" (*nyohō e*). Of course, exactly what kind of robe accords with the dharma has never been exactly clear. At the very least, robes that accord with the dharma correspond to the kind worn at Eiheiji but not found at other Buddhist temples in Japan. Dōryū's request, therefore, that the Agency issue new regulations requiring Sōtō monks to observe this standard was an attempt to force all Sōtō monks to acknowledge Eiheiji's supremacy.

Unlike the previous case, however, on this occasion, the Agency of Temples and Shrines did not issue a ruling in favor of Eiheiji's position. Not waiting for the government to act, on the 11th day of the fifth moon of 1852, Gaun Dōryū sent a letter to Sōjiji notifying them that any monks who wore improper robes would not be permitted to enter Eiheiji. In other words, any temple representatives who came to Eiheiji to participate in the 600-year Dōgen memorial—just three months hence—would not be admitted unless they first changed into new robes acceptable to Eiheiji. The implications of this position should be crystal clear. Senior Sōtō monks from throughout Japan who came to Eiheiji for the 600-year Dōgen memorial would experience Eiheiji's authority—Eiheiji's ability to define Dōgen's memory—in concrete ways. They felt Eiheiji's power not just in its different kinds of buildings, not just in its different kinds of ceremonies, but also in their own new clothes.[40]

Birth Celebrations

After the Meiji restoration of 1868 and the new regime's anti-Buddhist policies severely reduced the nationwide population of ordained monks and nuns, Eiheiji enlisted Dōgen's memory to cement closer ties with laypeople. On the tenth day of the fifth month of 1899, a year corresponding to the 700th celebration of Dōgen's birth, Eiheiji organized its first lay ordination ceremony specifically tied to Dōgen's birth rather than his death. Laymen and -women were invited to spend seven days at Eiheiji to observe ceremonies, listen to Buddhist sermons, and to receive ordination with the Sōtō lineage's special version of the bodhisattva precepts. This event, officially called "Ordinations to Repay Kindness" (*hōon jukai e*) proved so successful that the following year (1900) it was made an annual event at Eiheiji. The date of the ceremony, however, had to be changed. May 10 was inconvenient for the monks at Eiheiji because it came too close to the start of the summer training period (*ango*; which begins on May 15 each year) and impractical for laypeople, most of whom were farmers, because it conflicted with the spring planting. In 1899, therefore, the ceremony was advanced one month to April 28.[41] Finally, in 1900, Sōtō leaders officially designated January 26 as Dōgen's birthday and ordered all Sōtō temples in Japan to celebrate it.[42] Of course, no one knows the actual day of Dōgen's birth. The "*Annotated Edition of Keizei's Chronicle*" (*Teiho Kenzeiki*), an extremely influential biography of Dōgen edited and annotated by Menzan Zuihō (1683–1769; regarding which, see below) gives the date of Dōgen's birth as the second day of the first moon of 1200. None of the earlier manuscript versions of this text, however, provide any evidence from which Menzan might have derived this date.[43]

Scholarship

Mention of Menzan's *Teiho Kenzeiki* brings us to the final component in Eiheiji's efforts to promote Dōgen's memory, the one that has exerted the greatest influence on ordinary people both inside and outside Japan whether affiliated to sectarian Sōtō institutions or not. I refer, of course, to scholarship. Documentary investigation into Dōgen's life and times began at Eiheiji during the 15th century when one of its abbots, a man named Kenzei compiled a chronological account of Dōgen's life, supplemented by copious quotations from Dōgen's own writings, letters, and other historical records. This work was originally titled "An Account of the Activities of Eiheiji's Founder" (*Eihei kaisan gogyōjō*) but is more widely known as "Kenzei's Chronicle" (*Kenzeiki*). It is, without a doubt, the single most influential biography of Dōgen ever written. Since 1452, when Kenzei finished his account down to the present day almost all biographies, histories, encyclopedia articles (etc.) that mention Dōgen repeat, either directly or indirectly, information found only in Kenzei's chronicle.

The year 1452, when Kenzei wrote his history, is significant because it corresponds to the 200th memorial of Dōgen's death. In his record, however, Kenzei never mentions memorial rituals and does not suggest that Dōgen's memory served as a motivation for his chronicle.[44] It is possible that Kenzei did not consciously choose 1452. After all, his chronicle does not end with Dōgen's death, but continues with the early history of Eiheiji down to about the year 1340.[45] Nonetheless, we can be certain that Dōgen memorial services played a major role in preserving the text for later generations. The most accurate extant manuscript version of Kenzei's chronicle (the so-called *Zuichō hon Kenzeiki*), for example, was copied in 1552 to commemorate Dōgen's 300th memorial.[46] It is reasonable to assume that Kenzei's scholarship had been motivated by a similar desire to memorialize Dōgen.

To commemorate Dōgen's 500th memorial in 1754, the Sōtō monk and scholar Menzan Zuihō published his annotated edition of Kenzei's chronicle, the aforementioned *Teiho Kenzeiki*.[47] In his version of the text, Menzan deleted anything not directly related to Dōgen. All events after Dōgen's death were eliminated. Moreover, Menzan added considerable amounts of new material concerning biography, such as Dōgen's parentage, Dōgen's training on Mt. Hiei, Dōgen's meeting with Eisai (a.k.a., Yōsai, 1141–1215), Dōgen's relations with his teacher Myōzen (1184–1225), Dōgen's trip to China and his travels there, Dōgen's move to Echizen, and Dōgen's trip to Kamakura, Dōgen's miracles, Dōgen's relationship to Sōtō medicinal products, and so forth. Menzan's deletions and additions narrowed the focus of Kenzei's chronicle and converted it more clearly into a hagiographic account of Dōgen's life and a comprehensive overview of Dōgen's environment. More importantly, they inserted Menzan's authorial voice into

Kenzei's chronicle in ways that are not always readily apparent and to a degree much greater than the title "Annotated Keizei's Chronicle" might suggest. This point is significant because, until 1975, Menzan's version of Kenzei's chronicle was the only one readily available.

Fifty years later, in celebration of the Dōgen's 550th memorial, Eiheiji published an illustrated version of Menzan's annotated chronicle, the *Teiho Kenzeiki zue* (preface dated 1806, but actually published 1817).[48] This illustrated edition was ideally suited for lecturing to an audience of laypeople since the lecturer could describe the contents of the illustrations without being confined by the words of the text. It played a key role, therefore, in encouraging laypeople to become more closely involved in Sōtō activities.[49] In 1828, for example, Saian Urin (1768–1845) instigated a new policy of encouraging the formation of lay fraternities (the Kichijō kō), the members of which would send representatives to Eiheiji every year to participate in memorials for Dōgen. Donations to Eiheiji by the members of these lay fraternities helped maintain the monastery through times of severe economic hardship, such as the Tenpō period (1830), when Japan suffered many famines. Without the illustrated version of Kenzei's chronicle to encourage lay devotion to Dōgen, it is questionable if Eiheiji would have been able to solicit finances from poor people.[50]

Publication of the illustrated *Teiho Kenzeiki zue* led to another tactic that Eiheiji used to encourage lay pilgrimages by members of Kichijō fraternities. By the middle of the 1800s, Eiheiji had begun erecting monuments (*kinen hai*) to commemorate the major events in Dōgen's life that are illustrated in the *Teiho Kenzeiki zue*. Of course, no one knew for sure where most of these events might have occurred—if in fact they did occur. Nonetheless the monuments were erected. Members of the Kichijō fraternities stopped off at these sites along their route to and from Eiheiji.[51] These monuments made the pilgrimage to Eiheiji more interesting and also provided incentive for some people to participate in the pilgrimage even if they could not travel the entire length of the route to Eiheiji.

The popularity of Kenzei's chronicle, along with Menzan's additions and the subsequent illustrations, among such a wide audience throughout all levels of Japanese society helped to firmly establish Dōgen as a familiar figure among Japan's eminent monks. Until 1975, all accounts of Dōgen's life, whether written for popular consumption or for scholarly consideration, were based almost entirely on Menzan's annotated version of Kenzei's chronicle. There simply were no other sources beyond the meager biographical details found in Dōgen's own writings. By 1952, for example, more than 21 separate biographies of Dōgen had been published. Most of these biographies were published during the years 1852, 1902, and 1952—corresponding to major Dōgen memorials—and all of them simply repeated or abridged the text of the Kenzei's chronicle or the captions to its illustrations.[52]

For this reason, our understanding of Dōgen's biography entered a new era when, in 1975, Kawamura Kōdō published a compilation of six early manuscript versions of Kenzei's chronicle. This book, the *Shohon taikō Eihei kaisan Dōgen zenji gyōjō Kenzei ki* (Collated editions of all the manuscripts of the Activities of Eiheiji's founder, the Zen master Dōgen, chronicled by Kenzei) reprints manuscripts that were originally copied as early as 1472 and that, therefore, much more closely adhere to Kenzei's own pen than Menzan's annotations had allowed. Examination of these early versions revealed for the first time just how extensively Menzan Zuihō had altered Kenzei's account. We now know that Menzan's version of Dōgen's biography cannot be trusted. In other words, since all previous biographies of Dōgen were based on Menzan's work, none of them can be trusted. Even the 1953 biography by Ōkubo Dōshū, his celebrated *Dōgen zenjiden no kenkyū* (Biographical Studies of Dōgen) must be used with caution. Since the full extent of Menzan's distortions was not immediately understood, many encyclopedia entries, reference works, and statements by Western and Japanese scholars published after 1975 repeated the erroneous accounts in Menzan's annotated version of Kenzei's chronicle. One cannot trust anything written about Dōgen's life, therefore, unless one first ascertains whether or not its author had made full use of Kawamura's early manuscripts.

Aside from publishing Dōgen's biography, the second major way that Eiheiji has influenced how we remember Dōgen is through its efforts to promote study of Dōgen's *Shōbōgenzō* (True Dharma Eye Collection)—now one of the most well-known religious books of Japan. Today, when someone remembers Dōgen or thinks of Sōtō Zen, most often that person automatically thinks of Dōgen's *Shōbōgenzō*. This kind of automatic association of Dōgen with his *Shōbōgenzō* is very much a modern development. By the end of the 15th century, most of Dōgen's writings had been hidden from view in temple vaults, where they became secret treasures.[53] Even after textual learning was revived during the early Tokugawa period, most Japanese Sōtō monks studied only well-known Chinese Buddhist scriptures or classic Chinese Zen texts.[54] Eventually, a few scholarly monks like Menzan Zuihō began to study Dōgen's writings, but they were the exceptions. Even when scholarly monks read Dōgen's writings, they usually did not lecture on them to their disciples. In fact, from 1722 until 1796, the government authorities actually prohibited the publication or dissemination of any part of Dōgen's *Shōbōgenzō*.[55]

The government ban on publication of the *Shōbōgenzō* was lifted as a result of petitions submitted by Gentō Sokuchū, the monk who assumed office as Eiheiji's new abbot in 1765 and whose efforts to implement Dōgen's "old regulations" at Eiheiji were summarized above. Upon accepting Eiheiji's abbotship, Sokuchū had vowed to publish Dōgen's *Shōbōgenzō* in time to commemorate Dōgen's 550th memorial in 1802. The exact wording that Sokuchū used to advance the case for publication has not survived, but he probably sounded arguments similar to those cited earlier. At least the same line of reasoning can be detected in the official order lifting the publication ban where it specifically recognized the *Shōbōgenzō* as constituting Dōgen's house rules (*kakun*), which must be followed all members of his Sōtō lineage.[56] Work on the publication project began immediately, so that two *Shōbōgenzō* chapters were printed in 1796. The task proved to be so onerous—collating variant manuscripts, editing texts, rearranging the order of chapters, insertion of unrelated works, retitling chapters, carving woodblocks, and raising money to finance publication—that the project was not completed until 1815, seven years after Sokuchū's death (see Table 9.2).[57] In spite of its numerous textual inaccuracies, the version of the *Shōbōgenzō* published by Eiheiji (known as the "Head Temple," *honzan*, edition) remains the one most widely read even today.[58]

Eiheiji not only published Dōgen's *Shōbōgenzō*, but also promoted its study by Sōtō monks and laypeople. Beginning in 1905, Eiheiji organized its first *Shōbōgenzō* conference (*Genzō e*). Academics, popular writers, interested laypeople, and monks attended a series of workshops in which they read and discussed specific *Shōbōgenzō* chapters. This first *Genzō e* was successful beyond all expectations. Since 1905, it has become an annual event at Eiheiji, and over time,

Table 9.2 Chronology of Eiheiji's *Honzan* edition of the *Shōbōgenzō*. Based on Kumagai, "Koki fukko to Gentō Sokuchū zenji," in Sakurai, ed., *Eiheijishi*, pp. 1086–1102

	Year	Number of *Shōbōgenzō* chapters published
	1796	2
	1797	14
	1798	11
	1799	9
	1800	22
	1801	14
	1802	5
	1803	8
	1804	1
	1805	3
	1811	1
	1815	boxed set of entire edition
Total	20 years	90 chapters

it gradually changed the direction of Sōtō Zen monastic education. In earlier generations, only one Zen teacher, Nishiari Bokusan (1821–1910), is known to have ever lectured (*teishō*) on how the *Shōbōgenzō* should be read and understood. One of Bokusan's disciples, Oka Sōtan (1890–1921), served as the first leader of the *Genzō e*. Sōtan's lectures provided a model that could be emulated by each of the other Zen monks who came to Eiheiji.[59] This model has become the norm, not the exception. Today, every Sōtō Zen teacher lectures on Dōgen's *Shōbōgenzō*.

Conclusion

Dōgen's memory has helped keep Eiheiji financially secure, in good repair, and filled with monks and lay pilgrims who look to Dōgen for religious inspiration. Eiheiji has become Dōgen's place, the temple where Dōgen is remembered, where Dōgen's Zen is practiced, where Dōgen's *Shōbōgenzō* is published, where Dōgen's *Shōbōgenzō* is read, and where one goes to learn Dōgen's Buddhism. As we remember Dōgen, we should also remember that remembrance is not value neutral. It cannot be a product of pure, objective scholarship. We should perhaps remind ourselves that the Dōgen we remember is a constructed image, an image constructed in large measure to serve the sectarian agendas of Eiheiji in its rivalry with Sōjiji. We should remember that the Dōgen of the *Shōbōgenzō*, the Dōgen who is held up as a profound religious philosopher, is a fairly recent innovation in the history of Dōgen remembrances. However important that modern Dōgen may be for our time, he might not be so important for Kamakura Buddhism or for medieval Buddhism or for most of Tokugawa-period Buddhism. Instead, it is the Dōgen of sectarian agendas, the Dōgen who stands above Keizan, the Dōgen who works miracles, and so forth, who commanded the memory of earlier generations of Japanese. As we remember Dōgen for the 21st century, we must not forget about these other, older images of Dōgen. Finally, in remembering Dōgen, the time is ripe for someone to write a new, more accurate biography of Dōgen, one that sorts out what can be known and what was only remembered or invented by Menzan Zuihō and the artists of the illustrated version of Kenzei's chronicle.

10

New Trends in Dōgen Studies in Japan

Ishii Seijun

There have been two major currents of the study of the teachings and institutional legacy of Zen Master Dōgen in modern Japan, called Sōtō Shūgaku in Japanese and referred to here as Sōtō Theology. The first is the traditionalistic approach undertaken within the Sōtō school, which began in the Edo period and was designed to construct the identity of Sōtō sectarian followers as legitimate successors to Dōgen's ideas and monastic style. The second major current of the study of Dōgen involves the emergence of a number of diverse methodological approaches, including philosophical commentary and the impact of Lay Buddhism, as well contemporary historical and linguistic criticism that highlights the role of Dōgen's citations of Chinese Chan Buddhist teachings, in addition to the social criticism of the method known as Hihan Shūgaku, or Critical Sōtō Theology. The Tables 10.1 and 10.2, respectively, help to provide an historical overview of the development of modern Sōtō Theology with a focus on key scholars and trends of both currents, and in this chapter I will go into detail regarding some of the more salient features in the development of these approaches.

Traditional Studies

The traditional approach began in the Edo period with two different types of content, Koki-fukko (revival of Dōgen's and Keizan's monastic regulations) and Shuto-fukko (revival of the legitimate transmission of Dōgen's Dharma). Koki-fukko is the movement to correct monastic regulations that had been inappropriately changed by acceptance of a new monastic style imported with the introduction of the Ōbaku (Ch. Huangbo) school from China in the middle of the 17th century. Within the Koki-fukko movement, all known monastic regulations of the Sōtō school were maintained. The most notable achievement of this movement is presumably the publication in a single volume known as the *Eihei shingi* of Dōgen's works on monastic regulations and rules that includes five short texts, "Tenzokyōkun," "Fushukuhanpō," "Chiji shingi," "Taidaikogogejarihō," and "Bendōhō," which had originally been transmitted as independent essays.

On the other hand, Shūtō-fukko was the attempt to correct the disorder of Dharma transmission of the Sōtō school. This effort did not proceed smoothly, however, since there was considerable controversy between two groups. One group insisted that the fundamental transmission system should be based on the enlightened state of the successor, and the other group insisted on constructing formalistic procedures for the transmission system. The chief representative of the former group was Menzan Zuihō, and the leader of the latter group was Tenkei Denson. Eventually, the Menzan group became considered mainstream, and Tenkei was relegated to an inferior position.[1]

Simultaneously, Menzan and Tenkei had another controversy on the approach to interpreting Dōgen's *Shōbōgenzō*. Menzan asserted that we should regard *Shōbōgenzō kikigakishō* (abbreviated *Goshō*), the oldest commentary based on the 75-fascicle version of the text written in the Kamakura period by Dōgen's disciple Senne and his follower Kyōgō, as the most important basis for interpreting the *Shōbōgenzō*. In contrast, Tenkei rejected the adoption of this text, which he considered inaccurate, and instead he advocated the 60-fascicle version edited by Giun in the mid-14th century. Tenkei was also bested in this controversy. This is the origin of the traditional method of relying on the *Goshō* to interpret the *Shōbōgenzō*.

After the Meiji Restoration, in his work *Shōbōgenzō keiteki* (1930), Nishiari Bokusan placed the major *Shōbōgenzō* commentaries in the following order of importance:

1. *Shōbōgenzō kikigakishō*, by Senne and Kyōgō, a disciple of Senne
2. *Shōbōgenzō monge*, by Menzan and Fuzan Gentotsu, a disciple of Menzan
3. *Shōbōgenzō naippō*, by Fuyō Rōran, a disciple of Tenkei
4. *Shōbōgenzō benchū*, by Tenkei

By the adoption of this ranking, the basic approach to the interpretation of the *Shōbōgenzō* was settled. However, I feel that modern Sōtō school academic scholars should "graduate" from this tendency and reconceptualize our approach to traditional commentaries by making use of the modern historical study of Zen thought and contemporary linguistic methods, including the study of colloquial Chinese and ancient Japanese literature.

Emergence of Modern Methodologies

The second major current of the study of the teachings and institutional legacy of Zen Master Dōgen began after the Meiji restoration of 1868, when the three main Japanese Zen schools all looked to intellectuals for assistance in the face of the government's policy of endorsing National Shintoism (Kokka Shinto). Tanabe Hajime and Akiyama Hanji, both of the Kyoto School of modern Japanese philosophy, were two of those who responded to this call. These philosophers did not try to interpret the *Shōbōgenzō* as a sacred canon of the Sōtō school, but rather as an ideological or philosophical work of universal significance. They also treated Dōgen as primarily a philosopher or thinker instead of the founder of a sect. That is, Dōgen's thought as indicated in *Shōbōgenzō* was separated from Sōtō Theology, and it became an independent academic subject.

In addition, in the late 19th century, Lay Buddhism prospered for various social and historical reasons. Ōuchi Seiran and Daidō Chōan were representative of lay-oriented Sōtō school leaders of the time. Ōuchi, in particular, established the Sōtō fushūkai, and he compiled a new canon for lay believers. Selecting eloquent and appropriate passages from the *Shōbōgenzō*, Ōuchi combined them into five chapters in one volume. Although Ōuchi initially compiled this just for lay believers, Sōtō Headquarters accepted his draft and published it in 1890, after additional editing by the abbots of both Eiheiji and Sōjiji. This new canon is called *Shushōgi*, and subsequently it has been used in most Sōtō school rituals. In this fashion, with the change of government policy and drastic modernization that occurred in the Meiji period, Dōgen studies have now come to have two faces, including theological studies for Sōtō school members and philosophical studies for intellectuals who are not necessarily affiliated with the sect.

These two major currents of Dōgen studies developed independently at first, but after World War II, their distinctive identities began to break down as new trends emerged in academic methods for studying Zen. In the remainder of this chapter, I will introduce the inception and unfolding of the trends of modern Sōtō Theology from the early 20th century on and, in particular, will highlight their relationship with the developing field of studies of Chinese Chan sources.

Taishō and Shōwa Periods

From the Taishō period to the early Shōwa, that is, the 1910s through the 1940s, a great number of works devoted to the historical study of Zen were published by leading scholars in Japan. Particularly notable among these are the following books: Kohō Chisan's *Zenshūshi* (1917), Nukariya Kaiten's *Zengaku shisōshi* (1924), Ui Hakuju's *Zenshūshi kenkyū* (1941), and Okada Gihō's *Nihon zenseki shiron* (1943). The main methodological tendency underlying these various works was to undertake the specialized study of Japanese Zen thought and history, not from a sectarian or doctrinal standpoint, but within the context of modern academic research dealing with the development of Buddhist thought and history more generally.

Dōgen studies also began to develop its particular style by importing the methods of academic studies. In fact, the very name of Sōtō Shūgaku emerged at this time. The name and conception of Shūgaku seems to have derived from the time when Etō Sokuō initiated a class named "Shūgaku Josetsu" at Komazawa University in 1932. Prior to this, stemming from the Edo period, Sōtō theologians had called their research subject "Shūjō," or Sōtō Vehicle.

Subsequently, in 1944, Etō published *Shūso to shite no Dōgen zenji* (Zen Master Dōgen as Founder of a Sect). His so-called "Kindai Shūgaku," or Modern Sōtō Theology merged the methodology of religious studies with the doctrinal study of other Buddhist schools, especially Kegon (Ch. Huayan) and Tendai (Ch. Tiantai). At around the same time, Nukariya published *Bukkyō no shinzui wo ha-aku seru Dōgen zenji no kyōgi* (The Doctrine of Zen Master Dōgen Who Grasped the Essence of Buddhism). This study had approximately the same motive as Etō's book. The publication of these two works constituted the academic debut of modern Sōtō Theology.

Post-World War II Studies

In 1970, Kurebayashi Kōdō proposed in his *Dōgen Zen no honryū* (The Mainstream of Dōgen Zen) that traditional Sōtō Theology should include the interpretation of the many citations of kōan (Ch. gong'an) cases in Dōgen's writings. On the one hand, Kurebayashi defines Dentō Shūgaku (Orthodox Sōtō Theology) as "a standpoint which respects the doctrine constructed by Senne, Dōgen's direct disciple, and Kyōgō, Dōgen's grand disciple, as supreme." On the other hand, he rejects the tradition by which the interpretation of kōan case records cited extensively by Dōgen was blindly excluded from the study of Sōtō doctrine, which derived solely from rivalry with the Kōan-Introspection Zen approach of the Japanese Rinzai school that originated in the Edo period when the shogunate charged each Buddhist school with the task of defining and justifying their basis in mutually exclusive ways.

In my opinion, Kurebayashi's proposal was influenced by Takahashi Masanobu's theory about the role of kōan as suggested in *Dōgen no jissen tetsugaku kōzō* (The Construction of Dōgen's Practical Philosophy). This work was of such epochal importance that a Sōtō school traditional theological scholar like Kurebayashi proposed to utilize Takahashi's approach within the Sōtō school. Naturally, there was a lot of opposition to doing this at the time. However, Kagamishima Genryū further adopted Kurebayashi's standpoint, influenced by Takahashi, in defining Dōgen's mode of citing kōans as the approach of *genjōkōan* (emergence of truth) and distinguishing this from the *kosoku-kōan* (ancient case) approach of Kōan-Introspection Zen. This was especially evident in his work, *Dogen no shisō* included in *Kōza Dōgen*. In contemporary Dōgen studies, Kurebayashi's proposal and Kagamishima's definitions are now generally accepted as the legitimate standard.[2]

Takasaki Jikidō's work originally produced with Umehara Takeshi in the late 1960s, *Kobutsu no Manebi; Dōgen* (Learning of an Ancient Buddha: Dōgen) is also an unforgettable book. Sōtō monks and theological scholars rejected it soon after publication. As a result, Takasaki, a specialist in Tathagatagarbha thought, has ceased writing about Dōgen. However, its contents have been reevaluated recently, and many scholars, including me, set a high value on it.

As we have seen, the Taishō period through the postwar period was a time of conflict within Dōgen studies and Sōtō studies between traditional (or older) methodologies and innovative ones. This conflict was true not only in previous years, but also applies to today's scholarship, as Dōgen studies seems to be in same situation as before. That is, because of the existence of the Sōtō school as a religious institution, Dōgen studies and Sōtō studies have developed in two identifiably different directions: one is the conservative attempt to protect the identity of the Sōtō school, and the other is an innovative exploration of Dōgen's most profound ideas. These two movements exist sometimes in harmony and sometimes in conflict. The recent situation that developed after the proposal of Critical Sōtō Studies (Hihan Shūgaku) is no exception.

A New Interpretation Based on Dōgen's Citation Style

The next generation of scholars after Kurebayashi proceeded from the assumption that Dōgen's ideas and identity should be defined on the basis of the historical development of Chinese Chan/Zen thought. Quickly becoming the mainstream of recent Sōtō school studies, this trend was established by Kagamishima Genryū and appeared initially in 1965, with his *Dōgen Zenji to in'yō kyōten-goroku no kenkyū* (A Study of the Scriptures and Recorded Sayings Cited by Zen Master Dōgen). Kagamishima's approach involved the following elements:

- Determining the sources, either in sutras or Chinese Chan texts, from which Dōgen quotes
- Examining the original contexts of the passages cited and comparing them with their use by Dōgen
- Analyzing how Dōgen, either intentionally or unintentionally, reinterpreted the passages in question

- Describing the differences between Dōgen's ideas and Chinese Chan conceptions, especially the Song dynasty attitudes that Dōgen critiques
- Clarifying the characteristics of Dōgen's thought by locating it within the historical development of Buddhist ideas

Twenty years later, Ishii Shūdō described the unique characteristics of the Chinese text version of Dōgen's writings, *Shinji* (or *Mana*) *Shōbōgenzō*, showing that of all Dōgen's works only the *Shinji Shōbōgenzō* uses the rather obscure 11th-century text, *Zongmen tongyao ji* (*Shūmon tōyōshū*) as the primary source of its citations involving the sayings of Chinese Chan monks. In response to Ishii's pioneering essay published in the journal *Shūgaku kenkyū* (1985), Kagamishima reconfirmed the sources of Dōgen's other citations and published his new results in 1995 as *Dōgen in'yō goroku no kenkyū* (A Study of the Recorded Sayings Texts Cited by Dōgen); note that this title deletes the word *kyōten* (sutras) from the title, thus emphasizing that it concentrates on *goroku* (Ch. *yulu*, Chan recorded sayings). Using this publication, Dōgen scholars could easily discover the seemingly trivial alternations occurring in Dōgen's citations of primary text passages. Kagamishima's study thus brings Dōgen scholars a new method, which is to clarify the originality of Dōgen's thought objectively by comparing it with the original sources (Song Chan texts) that he cites and sometimes changes or modifies, usually deliberately so.

For example, Dōgen cited Caodong ancestor Hongzhi Zhengjue's words in discourse 3.206 of his *Eihei kōroku*. Although Dōgen greatly respected Hongzhi, as is evident in the extent to which he cites his writings, he also inventively took the original phrase:

> [A] precious stone (our nature) has no scratch (is immaculate); if one tries to carve it (add any practice), all the virtue (all its qualities) will be lost, 皓玉無瑕、彫文喪徳.

and he altered it to read:

> [A] precious stone (our nature) has no scratch (is immaculate); if one tries to polish it (add any practice), this will increase its glitter, 皓玉無瑕、琢磨増輝.

Although only four characters are changed, it shows that Dōgen surreptitiously ignored Hongzhi's tendency toward obviating the need for meditative practice and changed the passage, so that it emphasizes the necessity of "polishing (practice)" to activate one's innate immaculate nature through continuing zazen training.[3]

There are dozens or hundreds of examples of this process throughout Dōgen's corpus. Influenced by the research methods of Kagamishima and Ishii, the approach of maintaining a close exegetical focus on philological research is continuing through the work of subsequent scholars up to the present. In these additional studies, important phrases that seem to indicate the essence of Dōgen's thought have been recognized and analyzed in terms of their relation to Chinese Chan sources.

Importing the Yanagida-Iriya Approach to Chinese Chan Studies

To clarify Dōgen's position and his originality, Sōtō scholars have also adopted the new style of analysis that arose in Chinese Chan studies established by Yanagida Seizan and Iriya Yoshitaka. In *Shoki Zenshūshi no kenkyū*, Yanagida helped to pioneer modern historical methodology in the field of Zen studies. This historical approach suspends belief in the hagiographical narratives about the lives of the ancestors as a matter of the propagation of faith, and instead examines critically the traditional transmission accounts. This approach was enhanced in large part by the discovery in Korea of the originally Chinese transmission text, the *Zutang ji* (*Sodōshū*) from 952, which was considered lost for many centuries and the discovery of which dramatically changed scholarly perspectives on the historical background of Zen. Also, in his *Zen no goroku*, Yanagida sought to discern the intellectual development of Chan literary records dealing with masters from the Tang dynasty.

In addition, Iriya's work helped to clarify the use and meaning of Chan phrases based on a detailed study of Chinese linguistics, including the role of vernacular locutions that reveal a sense of the vibrant forms of expression in Chan texts. Before this study, the elusive nature of Chan language was primarily interpreted for transcendental rather than sociohistorical contextual qualities. The results of Iriya's research team are published in *Zengo jiten* (Zen Phrase Dictionary). Furthermore, in recent research, the digitalization of Chinese Chan texts, enhanced by the capability for advanced searches through electronic files, makes possible an improved and more greatly nuanced understanding of Zen literary works.

Although a fuller account of the Yanagida-Iriya method, which has been analyzed by John McRae and others in the Western academy, is beyond the scope of this chapter, I will mention only that the appreciation of the role of colloquial Chinese language as used in Chan texts that was initiated by Iriya has led to important innovations in Sōtō studies as well. Ishii Shūdō's *Chūgoku zenshū shiwa: Shinji Shōbōgenzō ni manabu* (The Historical Stories of Chinese Chan: References to Kōan cases in the *Shinji Shōbōgenzō*) is one of the most notable results of the interaction between Chinese Chan studies and Sōtō studies.

Attention to Other Works by Dōgen

Simultaneous with the development just mentioned, some scholars have begun to pay careful attention to works by Dōgen other than his *Shōbōgenzō*, especially the *Eihei kōroku*, which mainly contains his Dharma hall discourses (*jōdō*) in the first seven of ten volumes, as well as the *Eihei shingi*, which contains the monastic regulations he constructed at Eiheiji temple. Scholars who study these works aim at the analysis of Dōgen's thought in more specialized fashion, so as to clarify the position of Dōgen's religious community as a social institution functioning in contemporary Japanese culture. My own essay (2002), "Concerning the Eiheiji Monastic System Indicated in Dōgen's Writings During the Eiheiji Period," which was published in *Dōgen Studies: Commemorating the 750th Anniversary of His Death*, belongs to this trend. Steven Heine, I note, cited this essay extensively in his recent book, *Did Dōgen Go to China?*

Influence of "Critical Buddhism" on Sōtō Theology

In 1997, Matsumoto Shirō asserted his position on Hihan Shūgaku or Critical Sōtō Theology in a lecture delivered at Komazawa University, as recorded in the journal *Shūgaku to gendai* and titled "Hihan Shūgaku no kanōsei" (The Possibility of Critical Sōtō Theology). With this lecture as catalyst, disputation concerning Sōtō Theology became very animated.[4] Matsumoto defined his Critical Sōtō Theology in eight articles as follows:

- Researching the correct doctrine of the Sōtō school, and never taking anything as an absolute or mystical state while always ignoring one's own individual position.
- "Anything" means any persons (including the founder), any sacred canons, any practice such as zazen, and any Buddhist doctrine such as causality.
- Therefore, Critical Sōtō Studies is the denial of esoteric Buddhism.
- Critical Sōtō Studies does not stand on the theory that the founder never makes any mistakes, and entirely excludes the cult of the guru.
- It aims at discerning what was the goal in Dōgen's view (authentic Buddhism), and admitting that Dōgen changed his ideas during his lifetime.
- Critical Sōtō Studies claims that the correct interpretation of Sōtō studies is that of causality, and its practice is zazen, with the mind of compassion that arises from causality.
- Critical Sōtō Studies basically must endorse an orientation toward promoting social reform issues, including human rights.
- The Sōtō school should cast away both original enlightenment thought and the esoteric mystical view of zazen, as indicated in Dōgen's *Bendōwa*, and proceed to heartily embrace causality and zazen with compassion, as indicated in Dōgen's works in his later years.[5]

ISHII Kiyozumi (Rev. Seijun)

Genealogical Table of Dogen Studies and Soto Theology

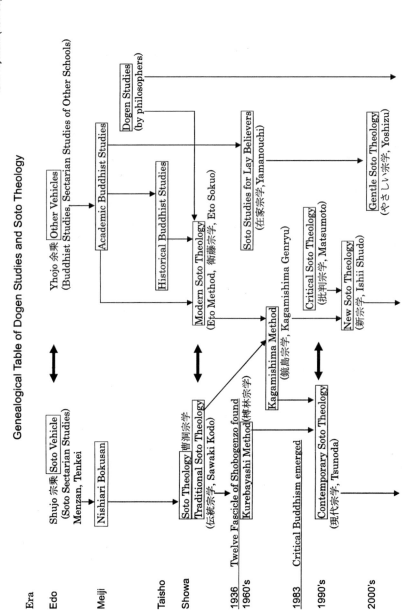

List of Scholars on Zen & Dogen Studies

Group	Scholar (with lifespan / notes)	氏名
Rinzai	SYAKU Soen — 58 ··· 70 ··· 19	釈 宗演
	SUZUKI Daisetsu — 70 ··· (Superintendent priest of Kenchoji Branch) ··· 66 (Matsugaoka Bunko)	鈴木大拙
Hanazono Univ.	IRIYA Yoshitaka — 10 ··· (Professor) ··· 98	大矢義高
	YANAGIDA Seizan — 22 ··· (Professor) ··· –06	柳田聖山
Soto	DESHIMARU Taisen — 14 ··· (Europe) ··· 82	弟子丸泰仙
	NISHIARI Bokusan — 21 ··· 10	西有穆山
	KISHIZAWA Ian — 65 ··· 55	岸澤惟安
	NUKARIYA Kaiten — 67 ··· 34	忽滑谷快天
Komazawa Univ.	KOHO Chisan — 79 ··· (Chancellor) ··· 67 (Sojiji 17th abbot)	孤峰智璨
	SAWAKI Kodo — 85 ··· 65 (Professor)	沢木興道
	UCHIYAMA Kosho — 12 ··· 98	内山興正
	UI Hakuju — 82 ··· 63 (Prof of Tokyo & Komazawa)	宇井伯壽
	OKADA Giho — 82 ··· (Professor) ··· 61 (Chancellor)	岡田宜法
	ETO Sokuo — 88 ··· 58 (Chancellor)	衛藤即応
	KUREBAYASHI Kodo — 93 ··· (Chancellor) ··· 87 (Chancellor)	榑林皓堂
	KAGAMISHIMA Genryu — 12 ··· (Professor) ··· 01	鏡島元隆
	SAKAI Tokugen — 12 ··· (Professor) ··· 96	酒井得元
	SUZUKI Kakuzen — 25 ··· 99	鈴木格禅
	TAKEUCHI Doyu — 22 ··· (Professor) ··· →	竹内道雄
Lay Budhists	OUCHI Seiran — 45 ··· 18 (Soto Fushu-kai)	大内青巒
	DAIDO Choan — 43 ··· 8 (Kyusei Kyo)	大道長安
Philosophers **Kyoto School**	NISHIDA Kitaro — 70 ··· 45	西田幾多郎
	TANABE Hajime — 85 ··· 63	田辺 元
	AKIYAMA Hanji — 93 ··· 80	秋山範二
	NISHITANI Keiji — 00 ··· 90	西谷啓治
Tokyo Univ.	WATSUJI Tetsuro — 89 ··· 60	和辻哲郎
	HASHIDA Kunihiko — 82 ··· 45 (Minister of Education)	橋田邦彦

Era / C.E.: ~1840 · 1850 · Meiji (60 70 80 90) · 1900 · Taisho (10 20 30) · Showa (40 50 60 70 80) · Heisei (90 2000)

In direct opposition to Matsumoto's position, Tsunoda Tairyū proposed a different approach, which he called Contemporary Sōtō Theology (*Gendai Shūgaku*). The point in dispute was whether or not to accept that Dōgen's ideas changed substantively from his Kyoto years to his Echizen period. Tsunoda's refutation is as follows:

- Affirm that the founder never made any mistakes.
- Do not select Dōgen's works based on one's own opinion of their merit; that is, do not regard Dōgen's later works as more important than earlier ones.
- Do not admit that Dōgen changed his ideas during his lifetime.
- Research Dōgen's thought using his works as objectively as possible.
- Do not draw conclusions regarding Dōgen's doctrine by relying on any extraneous idea such as causality, human rights, or so on.

We can see from the above articles that Tsunoda's standpoint is very protective of the traditional understanding of Dōgen's life and thought. The apparently diametrically opposed standpoints of Matsumoto and Tsunoda have generated much discussion regarding Dōgen studies.

In responding to this dispute, Ishii Shūdō proposed the adoption of a New Sōtō Theology, as discussed in "Shūgaku, Zenshūshi, to Shin Shūgaku" (Sōtō Theology, the Historical Study of Chan/Zen, and A New Sōtō Theology) published in the journal *Shūgaku to gendai* (1998). In this lecture, Ishii posited that Sōtō Theology should accept all available new methods and materials from both outside and inside the Sōtō school; hence the label "new" in the sense of renewed.

In addition, Yoshizu Yoshihide, a professor of Komazawa University who specializes in Kegon studies, proposed Yasashii Shūgaku or Gentle Sōtō Theology (2000). This proposal is based on the notion of Gentle Buddhism (Yasashii Bukkyō), which was also formulated by Yoshizu in opposition to Critical Buddhism and applied to research on Zen. Yoshizu arranges the Sōtō school (as an organization) and the self (as individuals) to be equal importance, which reflects his independent research style. The controversy regarding Sōtō Theology is ongoing, and contributions by scholars within and without the Sōtō School continue to appear on the scene, often reflecting many of the latest developments in Dōgen studies that have emerged on the basis of the epoch-making contributions enumerated above.

BIBLIOGRAPHY

Akiyama Hanji, *Dōgen no kenkyū*. Tokyo: Iwanami Shoten, 1935.
Etō Sokuō, *Shūso to shiteno Dōgen zenji*. Tokyo: Iwanami Shoten, 1944.
———, *Shōbōgenzō josetsu*. Tokyo: Iwanami Shoten, 1959.

Hashida Kunihiko, *Shōbōgenzō no sokumenkan.* Tokyo: Ninbun Shoin, 1936.

———, *Shōbōgenzō shakui*, 4 vols. Tokyo: Sankibō, 1939–1950.

Heine, Steven, *Did Dōgen Go to China?* New York: Oxford University Press, 2006.

Iriya Yoshitaka, *Gudō to etsuraku: Chūgoku no Zen to shi.* Tokyo: Iwanami Shoten, 1983.

———, *Jiko to chōetsu: Zen, hito, kotoba,* Tokyo: Iwanami Shoten, 1986.

———, and *Koga Hidehiko, Zengo jiten.* Kyoto: Shinbunkaku, 1991.

Ishii Seijun, "Dōgen zenji no sodan ni taisuru igi ni tsuite," *Komazawa Daigaku Bukkyōgakubu ronshū*, vol. 20 (1989).

———, "*Shinji Shōbōgenzō* no seiritsu ni kansuru—shiken," *Indogaku bukkyōgaku kenkyū*, vol. 43 (1994).

———, "Eiheiji ni okeru Dōgen zenji no sōrin-unei igi ni tsuite," *Nihon Bukkyō gakkai nenpō*, vol. 59 (1994).

———, "'Goshō' no Zengo kaishaku," *Indogaku Bukkyōgaku kenkyū*, vol. 47 (1998).

———, "Eiheiji ni senjutsu bunken miru Dōgen zenji no sōrin-unei," in Dōgen zenji kenkyū ronshū, Daihonzan Eiheiji Daionki Kyoku, ed. (Fukui-ken: Eiheiji, 2002).

Ishii Shūdō, "*Shūmon tōyōshu* to *Shinji Shōbōgenzō: Shinji Shōbōgenzō* no shūten no zenmenteki hosei," *Shūgaku kenkyū*, vol. 27 (1985).

———, *Sōdai Zenshūshi no kenkyū.* Tokyo: Daitō Shuppansha, 1987.

———, *Chūgoku Zenshū shiwa: Shinji Shōbōgenzō ni manabu.* Kyoto: Zen bunka kenkyūsho, 1988.

———, *Dōgen Zen no seiritsushiteki kenkyū.* Tokyo: Daizō Shuppan, 1991.

———, "Shūgaku, Zenshūshi to Shin Shūgaku," *Shūgaku to gendai*, vol. 2 (1998).

Kagamishima Genryū, *Dōgen Zenji to in'yō kyōten-goroku no kenkyū.* Tokyo: Mokuji-sha, 1965.

———, "Etō shūgaku ni tsuite," *Komazawa Daigaku Bukkyōgakubu ronshū*, vol. 8 (1977).

———, *Dogen no shisō*, in *Kōza Dōgen*, vol. 3. Tokyo: Shunjūsha, 1979.

———, *Dōgen in'yō goroku no kenkyū.* Tokyo: Shunjūsha, 1995.

———, *Shūshi to shūmon, Dōgen shisō taikei*, vol. 21. Kyoto: Dōhōsha, 1995.

Kinugawa Kenji, "Yanagida sensei no 'Sodōshū' kenkyū," *Zen bunka kenkyūsho kiyō*, vol. 30 (2009).

Kishizawa Ian, *Shōbōgenzō zenkō*, 25 vols. Tokyo, 1972–1974.

Kohō Chisan, *Zenshūshi: Indo, Shina, Nihon.* Tokyo: Kōyūkan, 1917.

Kurebayashi Kōdō, *Dōgen Zen no honryū.* Tokyo: Shunjūsha, 1970.

Kurita Isamu, *Dōgen no yomikata.* Tokyo: Shōden, 1984.

Maekawa Toru, "Chūgoku shisōshi kenkyū no tachiba kara mita Yanagida Seizan no ichi," *Zen bunka kenkyūsho kiyō*, vol. 30 (2009).

Matsumoto Shirō, "Dentō Shūgaku kara Hihan Shūgaku e," *Shūgaku kenkyū*, vol. 40 (1998).

———, "Hihan Shūgaku no kanōsei," *Shūgaku to gendai*, vol. 2 (1998).

———, "Dōgen to nyoraizō shisō: Hihan Shūgaku no kanōsei; jō," *Komazawa Daigaku Bukkyōgakubu kenkyū kiyō*, vol. 56 (1998).

————, "Dōgen to Hihan Shūgaku: Hihan Shūgaku no kanōsei; ge," *Komazawa Daigaku Zen kenkyūsho nenpō*, vol. 9 (1998).

Morimoto Kazuo, *Dōgen to Sartre*. Tokyo: Kōdansha, 1974.

————, *Shōbōgenzō nyūmon*. Tokyo: Mainichi Shinbunsha, 1985.

————, *Derrida kara Dōgen e*. Tokyo: Fukubu Shoten, 1989.

Nishiari Bokusan, *Shōbōgenzō keiteki*. Tokyo: Daihōrinkan, rpt. 1965.

Nishitani Keiji, "*Shōbōgenzō* kōwa," 28 parts, *Kyōdai*, vols. 131–192 (1966–1972).

Nukariya Kaiten, *Zengaku shisōshi*. Tokyo: Genkōsha, 1924.

————, *Bukkyō no shinzui wo ha-aku seru Dōgen zenji no kyōgi*. Tokyo: Kōyūkan, 1935.

Okada Gihō, *Nihon zenseki shiron*. Tokyo: Ida Shoten, 1943.

————, *Shōbōgenzō shisō taikei*, 8 vols. Tokyo: Hōsei Daigaku Shuppanbō, 1953–1955.

Ogawa Takashi, *Rinzai roku: Zen no goroku no kotoba to shisō*. Tokyo: Iwanami Shoten, 2008.

Ōuchi Seiran, ed., *Tōjō Zaike Shushōgi*. Tokyo, 1888.

Sawaki Kōdō, *Zendan*. Tokyo: Daihōrinkan, 1938.

Sōtōshū, ed., *Sōtō Kyōkai Shushōgi*. Tokyo, 1890.

Takahashi Masanobu, *Dōgen no jissen tetsugaku kōzō*. Tokyo: Sankibō, 1967.

————, "Genjōkōan no kōansei," *Sōtō shūgaku*, vol. 18 (1976).

Takasaki Jikidō and Umehara Takeshi, *Kobutsu no manebi: Dōgen*. Tokyo: Kadokawa Shoten, rpt. 1997 (1969).

Tanabe Hajime, *Shōbōgenzō no tetsugaku shikan*. Tokyo: Iwanami Shoten, 1939.

Terada Tōru, *Shōbōgenzō wo yomu*. Kyoto: Hōzō .

————, *Dōgen no gengo uchū*. Tokyo: Iwanami Shoten, 1974.

Tsuchiya Taisuke, "Yanagida Seizan sensei no gakujutsu gyōseki," *Zen bunka kenkyūsho kiyō*, vol. 30 (2009).

Tsunoda Tairyū, "Shūgaku kō," *Shūgaku kenkyū*, vol. 40 (1998).

————, "'Hihan Shūgaku' hihan," *Komazawa Tanki Daigaku kenkyū kiyō*, vol. 26 (1998).

————, "Shūgaku sankō," *Komazawa Tanki Daigaku kenkyū kiyō*, vol. 27 (1999).

Ui Hakuju, *Zenshūshi kenkyū*. Tokyo: Iwanami Shoten, 1941.

Washio Junkei, *Nihon zenshūshi no kenkyū*. Tokyo: Kyōten Shuppan, 1945.

Watsuji Tetsurō, *Shamon Dōgen*. Tokyo: Iwanami Shoten, 1925.

Yamanouchi Shun'yū, *Sōtōshū ni okeru zaike shūgaku no teishō*. Tokyo: Daizō Shuppan, 1990.

————, "Dōgen Zen no kindaika katei," *Shūgaku kenkyū*, vol. 40 (1998).

Yamaori Tetsuo, *Dōgen*. Tokyo: Shimizu, 1978.

Yanagida Seizan, "Goroku no rekishi," *Tōhō gakuhō*, vol. 57 (1985).

Yoshizu Yoshihide, "Shūshi no manebi ni tsuite," *Shūgaku kenkyū*, vol. 29 (1987).

————, "Dōgen ni okeru 'shū' ni tsuite," *Shūgaku kenkyū*, vol. 36 (1994).

————, "Gendai Bukkyō no kiki to shūgaku," *Shūgaku to gendai*, vol. 3 (2000).

Notes

DZZ   *Dōgen zenji zenshū*, ed. Kagamashima Genryū, et. al., (Tokyo: Shunjūsha, 1988–1993).

T   *Taishō shinshū daizōkyō* (Tokyo Daizōkyōkai, 1924–1935).

ZZ   *Zoku zōkyō* (Kyoto: Zōkyō shoin, 1905–1912).

CHAPTER 1

1. The commentary titled *Shōbōgenzō monge* (E-SBGZ-ST vol. 17) was written by Menzan's disciple Fusan Gentotsu and not, as previously thought, by Menzan Zuihō himself. The confusion over authorship derives in part from the fact that Menzan did author commentaries on three books of the *Shōbōgenzō*, namely, *Bendōwa monge*, *Genjō kōan monge*, and *Zanmai ō zanmai monge* (see the editorial notes in E-SBGZ-ST vol. 17).

2. It is common in English-language sources to refer to the individual books of the *Shōbōgenzō* as "fascicles." In this chapter, I wish to distinguish between "book" as the main literary division of a larger written work and "fascicle" as the physical groupings in which the work is copied or published. A literary work in ten books, for example, might be bound into one fascicle (of all ten books), two fascicles (of five books each), or three fascicles (of three, three, and four books).

CHAPTER 2

1. Because the term is so elusive and complex, translations of the title of the fascicle can vary tremendously from "The Way of Everyday Life" to "Actualizing the Fundamental Point," "Issue at Hand," and "Readily Apparent Kōan," among others. Like kōan (Ch. *gong'an*), the term was apparently derived from the Tang-Song Chinese legal system, in which the magistrate served all at once as detective, prosecutor, judge, and jury, to refer to an "open-and-shut" case. It was

adapted by Chan thinkers to indicate situations in which the puzzling and per-plexing quality of truth embedded in a kōan case was broken through and dis-played in a more overt fashion. Also, as indicated below, while "Genjōkōan" is used as the first section of the 75-fascicle edition of the *Shōbōgenzō* that was traditionally favored by most scholars in the Sōtō sect, it relinquishes this posi-tion to "Bendōwa" in the 95-fascicle edition that was created in the Edo period and is more commonly cited in the modern period ("Bendōwa," not included in the 75-fascicle version, is also considered separate from the 87-fascicle edition that combines the 75-fascicle and 12-fascicle *Shōbōgenzō* texts).

2. All citations of the fascicle are from the version in DZZ vol. 1, pp. 2–7.

3. Kurebayashi Kōdō, *Genjōkōan wo kataru: Ima wo ikiru Shōbōgenzō kōsan* (Tokyo: Daihōrinkan, 1992.

4. Nishiari Bokusan, *Shōbōgenzō keiteki* vol. 1, Tomiyama Soei, transc., and Kure-bayashi Kōdō, ed. (Tokyo: Daihōrinkan, 1965).

5. These include: Yoshizu Yoshihide, "'Ippō wo shōsuru toki wa ippō wa kurashi' no ikku no kaishaku nitsuite," *Shūgaku kenkyū* 35 (1993): 12–17; Ishii Seijun, "*Shōbōgenzō* 'Genjōkōan' no maki no shudai ni tsuite," *Komazawa Daigaku Bukkyō gakuburonshū* 28 (1997): 225–239; and Matsumoto Shirō, *Dōgen shisōron* (Tokyo: Daizō shuppan, 2000), pp. 191–258.

6. DZZ vol. 1, p. 7.

7. During the last years of his life, Dōgen was primarily devoted to producing the 12-fascicle *Shōbōgenzō* in addition *to Eihei kōroku* sermons in Sino-Japanese (*kanbun*) included in the comprehensive 95-fascicle edition, which means it is particularly interesting that he still was attending to the editing of "Genjōkōan."

8. Kurebayashi mentions this in his preface.

9. Another interesting trajectory is to contrast "Genjōkōan," written in 1233, with the last of his dated writings, "Hachidaingaku," composed as a final exhortation for disciples in 1253 and included in the 12-fascicle *Shōbōgenzō*; see Kuromaru Kanji, "'Genjōkōan' to 'Hachidaningaku,'" *Bukkyōgakubu ronshū* 31 (2000), pp. 23–36.

10. Norman Waddell and Masao Abe, *The Heart of Dōgen's Shōbōgenzō* (Albany, NY: State University of New York Press, 2002), p. 39.

11. Taizan Maezumi and John Daido Loori, *The Way of Everyday Life: Zen Master Dōgen's Genjokoan with Commentary by Hakuyu Taizan Maezumi* (Great East-ern Book Co., 1978); Hakuun Yasutani; *Flowers Fall: A Commentary on Dog-en's Genjokoan* (Boston: Shambala, 2001); and Shohaku Okumura, *Realizing Genjokoan: The Key to Dogen's Genjokoan* (Boston: Wisdom Publications, 2010).). Note that a new book, Eihei Dōgen Zenji, *Dōgen's Genjo Koan* (Berke-ley, CA: Counterpoint Press, 2011), which consists of commentaries by several

Zen teachers and practitioners, was not available when I was conducting research for this article.

12. The source for this was not found, but according to disciples of the late Loori Roshi, whom I queried, this was originally written as a promotional comment.

13. Dōgen had another lay disciple from Kyushu, referred to as Yakō, for whom he dedicated *Eihei kōroku* 8.5 (sermon) and 10.62 (Chinese verse); see Taigen Dan Leighton and Shohaku Okumura, trans., *Dōgen's Extensive Record: A Translation of the Eihei Kōroku* (Boston: Wisdom Publications, 2004), p. 26, for an explanation of the historical context, and for the passages see pp. 507–510 and 625. Other examples of epistles to lay disciples in the *Shōbōgenzō* include the "Zenki" and "Shōji" fascicles.

14. The source for this is the *Zongmen liandeng huiyao* (*Shūmon rentōeyō*) vol. 4.

15. Many examples of these are contained in Christopher Cleary, trans., *Swampland Flowers: The Letters and Lectures of Zen Master Ta Hui* (New York: Grove Press, 1977).

16. *Eihei kōroku* vol. 9, in DZZ IV, pp. 262–276, and Leighton and Okumura, trans., *Dōgen's Extensive Record*, pp. 610–625. Although Dōgen followed the model of Dahui in this and other regards, particularly in his collection of kōan cases, he is also known for his occasional severe criticism of the Chinese master, particularly in *Shōbōgenzō* "Jishō zammai."

17. Yoshizu, "'Ippō wo shōsuru,'" p. 12.

18. In addition to the three polarities that are mentioned in different ways in all three sentences, practice is a kind of wildcard in the passage and is referred to just one time in the first sentence. Could this be Dōgen's way of saying that the role of practice is important only on the first level of awareness, something that would seem to contradict his emphasis here and elsewhere throughout his career on the importance of zazen meditation in casting off body–mind?

19. See Ishii Shūdō, *Shōbōgenzō [Gyōji] ni manabu* (Kyoto: Zen Bunka Kenkyūjō, 2007), p. 535.

20. Waddell and Abe, *The Heart of the Dōgen's Shōbōgenzō*, p. 40. For *Goshō* and its followers, *genjō* signifies Dharma or *shōbōgenzō* (treasury of the true dharma-eye).

21. For an earlier work that makes this point, see Takahashi Masanobu, "Genjōkōan no kōansei," *Sōtō shūgaku*, vol. 18 (1976), which is cited in the chapter by Ishii Seijun in this volume.

22. Some of this discussion is drawn from Steven Heine, "Multiple Dimensions of Impermanence in Dōgen's 'Genjōkōan,'" *Journal of the International Association of Buddhist Studies*, vol. 4/2 (1983), pp. 42–62. Also, the three interpretive levels indicated in the fascicle's first paragraph's opening sentences can be

considered to correspond roughly to the following categories of the Japanese religio-aesthetic tradition, as analyzed by Kyoto school thinker Karaki Junzō: *hakanashi* (sensing the fleeting and fragile quality of life in everyday affairs), *mujō-kan* (emotional pain of impermanence in times of crisis or loss), and *mujō-kan* (clear, contemplative observation of impermanence as the unbridled truth of nonsubstantiality).

23. The number of paragraphs used in various versions is, in descending order, 25 in Waddell and Abe, 22 in Kurebayashi, 21 in Yasutani, 14 in *Goshō*, and 13 in Okumura; note that the last sentence comprises a separate paragraph in the translations of both Yasutani and Okumura.

24. Thomas Cleary, *Shōbōgenzō: Zen Essays By Dōgen* (Honolulu: University of Hawai'i Press, 1986), p. 32; yet, I disagree with his use of "whole body and mind."

25. William M. Bodiford, "The Fully Apparent Case," in *Sources of Japanese Tradition: Volume One, From Earliest Times to 1600*, William Theodore de Bary and Donald Keene, comp. (New York: Columbia University Press, 2002), p. 326. This rendering may be too active in that the second phrase referring to darkness or concealment is passive in the original.

26. However, in Keizan's *Denkōroku*, it is claimed that among Dōgen's closest disciples, it was only Ejō who was privy to the abbot's quarters on a regular basis and was able to hear and record/edit the teachings of Dōgen through private instruction; see T.82: 410b.

27. Another example of a doctrine closely associated with Dōgen by Sōtō sectarian followers but never explicitly articulated in his writings is *honshō-myōshū* (original enlightenment-wondrous practice).

28. This recalls the passage in "*Bendōwa*" that "even a single person sitting in zazen meditation for even a single instant joins with all beings in contemplation and with all moments of time"; see DZZ vol. 2, pp. 538–540.

29. "Kōmyō," in DZZ vol. 1, p. 142.

30. On original enlightenment thought, see Jacqueline Stone, *Original Enlightenment and the Transformation of Medieval Japanese Buddhism* (Honolulu: University of Hawai'i Press, 1997). For an insightful analysis of Dōgen's philosophical relation to Tendai thought, along with other Kamakura Buddhist thinkers, see the classic study by Tamura Yoshirō, *Kamakura shin Bukkyō shisō no kenkyū* (Kyoto: Heirakuji shoten, 1965).

31. Yasutani, *Flowers Fall*, p. 33.

32. Ibid., p. 34.

33. Okumura, *Realizing Genjokoan*, p. 72.

34. Ibid., p. 73.

35. I am grateful to Professor Matsumoto Shirō for helping to clarify the history of the publication process during conversations in the summer of 2010; yet, Matsumoto himself does not acknowledge or attribute much importance to Kurebayashi's work.

36. Conversations with Professor Yoshizu were held in his office during the summer of 2006.

37. T.48: 296b.

38. T.48: 294b.

39. According to the case's verse commentary, "When the screen is rolled up the great sky opens,/Yet the opening of the great sky does not mean that one has attained the truth of Zen./It is best to let go of the sky/And to realize deeply so that you are not blowing with the wind."

40. T.48:143b.

41. Yoshizu, "'Ippō wo shōsuru toki,'" p. 13.

42. Ibid., p. 14.

43. Matsumoto, *Dōgen shisōron*, pp. 215–216.

44. See Jamie Hubbard and Paul L. Swanson, eds., *Pruning the Bodhi Tree: The Storm Over Critical Buddhism* (Honolulu: University of Hawai'i Press, 1997).

45. According to Matsumoto, "Genjōkōan," written a couple of years later, marks a significant improvement over "Bendōwa," which is still wedded to Tendai panentheism.

46. Matsumoto, *Dōgen shisōron*, pp. 197 and 222.

47. Ibid., p. 217.

48. Ibid., p. 215.

49. Ibid., p. 197.

50. Ibid., p. 220.

51. These options seem preferable to other variations, including "you see nothing," "ocean with no mountains," or "ocean where there are no mountains."

52. Ishii, "*Shōbōgenzō* 'Genjōkōan' no maki," p. 234.

53. Ibid., p. 235.

54. A contrary modern example would be cases in which a driver or conductor crashes his or her vehicle because of overattention to text messaging at a critical moment that leads to an absence of thought and an accident.

55. The source is *Jingde chuandeng lu* (*Keitoku dentōroku*) vol. 11 in T.51: 283c, and also *Zongmen liandeng huiyao*, vol. 8.

56. Nishiari, *Shōbōgenzō keiteki*, pp. 310–312.

57. *Eihei kōroku* commentaries include 1.36 (Lingyun), 1.39 (Jingqing), 6.457 (Xiangyan and Lingyun), and 9.72 (Lingyun). For additional examples of enlightening perceptual moments cited by Dōgen, see *Mana Shōbōgenzō* cases

192, 230, 242, as well as *Shōbōgenzō* fascicles such as "Baige," "Gyōji" I, "Immo," 'Jishō zanmai," "Kokū," "Kokyō," "Makahannya haramitsu," "Muchū setsumu," and "Tenbōrin," among many other instances in these and other texts.

58. See Beata Grant, *Mount Lu Revisited: Buddhism in the Life and Writings of Su Shih* (Honolulu: University of Hawai'i Press, 1994), pp. 3, 124–126. Grant points out that non-Buddhists did not consider the poet to be a Chan practitioner and saw the verse as an example of generic literary pantheism.

59. Note John Daido Loori's modern capping verse on case 17 of the *Mana Shōbōgenzō* based on a "Genjōkōan" passage: "Hearing sounds with the body and mind and seeing forms with the whole body and mind/one understands them intimately," in *The True Dharma Eye: Zen Master Dōgen's Three Hundred Kōans*, Kazuaki Tanahashi and John Daido Loori, trans. (Boston: Shambhala, 2005), p. 24; see also p. 210 (Note 1 on case 155) for a similar example.

60. DZZ vol. 3, p. 28, and Leighton and Okumura, trans., *Dōgen's Extensive Record*, p. 104 (slightly altered).

61. DZZ vol. 7, p. 156, and Steven Heine, *A Blade of Grass: Japanese Poetry and Aesthetics in Dōgen Zen* (New York: Peter Lang, 1989), p. 93. Also, note the following poem on Xiangyan in DZZ vol. 7, p. 172, and Heine, *A Blade of Grass*, p. 115:

Koe zu kara	Just at the moment
Mimi no kikoyuru	Ear and sound
Toki sareba	Do not interfere—
Waga tomo naran	There is no voice,
Katarai zo naki	There is no speaker.

> A literal rendering is: "Because when the sound enters the ear naturally on its own, there is no conversation between friends." In some versions of the verse, the fourth line is a negation indicating, "there is no conversation and no friends." This poem alludes to case 46 of the *Biyanlu*, cited below, in which Zen master Jingqing more or less claims to not "hear" as a distinctive sensation—or perhaps does really hear—the sound of raindrops because his enlightened mind and body are at one with them.

62. DZZ vol. 7, p. 179, and Heine, *A Blade of Grass*, p. 124.

63. See especially *Shōbōgenzō* "Baige," as well as dozens of references to the symbolism of the plum blossom in *Eihei kōroku* sermons and verse comments.

64. T.48: 182b-183c.

65. Dōgen cites a Dongshan verse comment on a dialogue about whether insentient beings can hear the Dharma, which says that one must "hear sounds with the eyes," in *Eihei kōroku* 6.452 and 9.52, as well as *Shōbōgenzō* "Mujō seppō."

Loori comments on the value of synesthesia in his capping phrase on case 155 of the *Mana Shōbōgenzō*, in *The True Dharma Eye*, p. 210.

66. Kim, *Dōgen on Meditation and Thinking: A Reflection on His View of Zen* (Albany: State University of New York Press, 2006), pp. 1–2.

67. Kim, *Dōgen on Meditation and Thinking*, p. 3.

68. A similar point seems to be made in the 13th-century painting by Mu Qi, "Six Persimmons," in which the fruits at the center of the piece are filled in with color but the shading gradually recedes as the viewer's eye gazes over to the fruit standing on the sidelines, with the lack of color seeming to reflect the inability to perceive this area fully with one's peripheral vision.

69. DZZ vol. 3, p. 38, and Leighton and Okumura, trans., *Dōgen's Extensive Record*, p. 115 (slightly altered).

CHAPTER 3

1. See T. Griffith Foulk, "Rules of Purity in Japanese Zen," in Steven Heine and Dale S. Wright, eds., *Zen Classics: Formative Texts in the History of Zen Buddhism* (New York: Oxford University Press, 2006), pp. 138–146; and T. Griffith Foulk, "Ritual in Japanese Zen," in Steven Heine and Dale S. Wright, eds., *Zen Ritual* (New York: Oxford University Press, 2007), pp. 24–40.

2. T 82.15c28–16a1.

3. For a detailed introduction to this text, see T. Griffith Foulk, "*Chanyuan qingui* and Other 'Rules of Purity' in Chinese Buddhism," in Steven Heine and Dale S. Wright, eds., *The Zen Canon* (New York: Oxford University Press, 2004), 275–312. For a critical edition of the Chinese text and an annotated Japanese translation, see Kagamishima Genryū, Satō Tetsugen, and Kosaka Kiyū, eds. and trans., *Yakuchū Zennen shingi* (Tokyo: Sōtōshū Shūmuchō, 1972). For an English translation, see Yifa, *The Origins of Buddhist Monastic Codes in China: An Annotated Translation and Study of the Chanyuan Qinggui*, Kuroda Institute, *Classics in East Asian Buddhism* (Honolulu: University of Hawai'i Press, 2002).

4. See Kagamishima Genryū, *Dōgen Zenji to sono monryū* (Tokyo: Seishin Shobō, 1961), pp. 8–56; and Takeuchi Dōyū, "Shoki sōdan no tenkai: kyōdan," in Kagamishima Genryū and Tamaki Kōshirō, eds., *Dōgen zen no rekishi, Kōza Dōgen* 2 (Tokyo: Shunjūsha, 1980), pp. 2–5.

5. The rarity and high cost of higher grades of incense also resulted in it being used as gifts between monks on formal occasions. In Sōtō Zen today, envelopes containing gifts of cash are euphemistically labeled as "incense."

6. T 82.263a5; 263a21; 263b21–22; 264b8.

7. T 82.262b26–27.

8. The Sacred Monk is the bodhissattva Manjusri (*Monju bosatsu*), who was enshrined in the sangha hall (*sōdō*).

9. Andō Fumihide, *Eihei daishingi tsūkai* (Tokyo: Kōmeisha, 1969), p. 340.

10. Ibid.

11. T 82.264c19–265a4.

12. T 82.307a26–b4.

13. T 82.70b22–23.

14. T 82.70c9–10.

15. Andō Fumihide, *Eihei daishingi tsūkai*, p. 182.

16. T 82.263b3–12.

17. T 82.263b13–14.

18. T 82.263b14–15.

19. Andō, *Eihei daishingi tsūkai*, p. 296.

20. Kagamishima, *Yakuchū Zennen shingi*, p. 308.

21. Ibid.

22. Ibid. The repentance formula I cite above is found in a later section of the *Rules of Purity for Chan Monasteries*, entitled "Text for Receiving Novice Precepts" (*Shami jukai bon*).

23. T 82.276c17–20.

24. T 82.50a1–7.

25. T 82.27c18–19.

26. T 82.58b27–c1.

27. T 82.41c6–11.

28. T 82.41c29–42a2.

29. "Cloud hall" (*undō*) is another name for the sangha hall (*sōdō*).

30. T 80.90a13–91b22.

31. Dōgen was in China from 1223 until 1227.

32. Literally, "[I, Dōgen] made a prostration (*hai*) and asked (*mon*)."

33. "Teachings" (*kyō*) here refers in general to the "houses" (*ke*) or styles of Buddhism that emphasize scriptural exegesis, and to the Tiantai school in particular, which competed with the Chan school for abbacies in Song China.

34. "Descendants of the ancestral teachers" (*soshi no jison*) is another name for dharma heirs in the Zen lineage.

35. My translation is based on the edition of the text found in Takashi James Kodera, *Dōgen's Formative Years in China: An Historical Study and Annotated Translation of the "Hōkyō-ki"* (Boulder: Prajna Press, 1980), pp. 236–237.

36. This is a work completed in 1107 by Juefan Huihong, alias Shimen (1071–1128), a monk who belonged to the Huanglong branch of the Linji lineage.

37. T 82.182c12–28.

38. T 82.15c28–16a1.

39. It is also possible that Dōgen used the "question-and-answer" (*mondō*) format to pose questions to himself, in recognition or anticipation of the sorts of objections his teachings had met or were likely to meet. That was a standard format used by other Zen masters in his day.

40. T 82.16c22–23.

41. T 82.16c25–27.

42. T 82.17a14–b3.

43. T 82.18b22–23.

44. T 82.18b27–18c3.

45. T 82.18a8–27.

46. T 82.18ax15.

47. T 82.143b4–5. Original in classical Chinese.

48. T 82.139a8–14.

49. Dōgen mentions Mazu (Baso), Baizhang (Hyakujō), Huangbo (Ōbaku), and Linji (Rinzai) in this connection.

50. Dōgen mentions Nanyue (Nangaku), Zhaozhou (*Jōshū*), Guishan (Isan), Yangqi (Yōgi), and Daokai (Dōkai) in this connection.

51. Dōgen mentions Mazu (Jp. Baso), Shitou (Jp. Sekitō), Fachang (Jp. Hōjō), Xuefeng (J. Seppō), and Xuansha (Jp. Gensha) in this connection.

52. T 82.142c4–6.

53. T 82.143c10–144a6.

54. T 82.143c10–143a15–16.

55. Zhuoan Deguang, also known as Chan Master Fozhao, was a dharma heir of Dahui Zonggao.

56. T 82.143a19–27.

57. T 82.136a2–9.

58. This is the kōan in its entirety, as cited by Dōgen in "Kankin" (T 82.88b27–88c3). In "Bukkyō," he only cites Prajnatara's answer to the king's question, which begins, "When this humble monk breathes out . . ." (T 82.195a22–24).

59. That is, by seizing on the literal meaning of "sutra reading," one commits an error of interpretation, but it is also a mistake to ignore the literal meaning.

60. This quotation comes from case 43 of the *Gateless Barrier* (Ch. *Wumenguan*, Jp. *Mumonkan*), T 48.298b19. The first sentence also appears in the *Discourse Record of Chan Master Rujing of Jingde Monastery on Mount Tiantong* (*Tendōzan keitokuji nyojō zenji goroku*), T 48:129a17.

61. This quotation comes from the *Extensive Record of Yunmen* (Ch. *Yunmen guanglu*, Jp. *Unmon kōroku*), T 47.572c4.

62. T 82.195a27–b11.

63. T 82.243c17–19. Original in classical Chinese.

64. T 82.243c19; translation by Carl Bielefeldt, based on the edition in Kawamura Kōdō, ed., *Dōgen zenji zenshū*, vol. 2, pp. 177–181: http://hcbss.stanford.edu/research/projects/sztp/translations/shobogenzo/translations/zanmai_o_zanmai/translation.html.

65. "At the beginning of summer" (*nyūge*) can also mean "upon entering the monastic retreat." "Lotus" is also a reference to the true buddha-dharma: the "lotus of the wonderful dharma," and "sun" (*nichi*) can also refer to Japan (Nihon). Thus, this enigmatic phrase can be interpreted to mean, "Here in this monastery, I have made true Buddhism available to the people of Japan."

66. This describes the correct posture for zazen.

67. T 48.136c3–9.

68. For a summary of these two formulas as they appear in Buddhaghosa's *Path to Purification* (*Visuddhimagga*), see Stephan V. Beyer, "The Doctrine of Meditation in the Hinayana," in Prebish, *Buddhism: A Modern Perspective* (Pennsylvania State University, 1975), pp. 142–143.

CHAPTER 4

1. *Dōgen zenji zenshū* I, Kawamura Kōdō, ed. (Tokyo: Shunjūsha, 1991), pp. 145–170 (Part I) and 171–202 (Part II).

2. Yasuraoka Kōsaku, trans., *Shōbōgenzō [Gyōji] jō* (Tokyo: Kodansha, 2002) and *Shōbōgenzō [Gyōji] ge* (Tokyo: Kodansha, 2002).

3. Ishii Shūdō, *Shōbōgenzō [Gyōji] ni manabu* (Kyoto: Zen bunka kenkyūsho, 2007). Another interesting recent study is Itō Shūken, "*Shōbōgenzō-kikigaki-shō* goyaku no kokoromi: 'Gyōji, Ichi,'" *Zen kenkyūjō kiyō*, 31 (2003): 53–85.

4. See Yanagida Seizan, *Shoki Zenshūshi no kenkyū* (Kyoto: Hōzōkan, 1967).

5. T.82: 407c–408a; Kazuaki Tanahashi, ed. *Treasury of the True Dharma-Eye* (Boston: Shambhala, 2010), vol. 2, p. 920.

6. Of the three instances, interestingly enough, the Caodong transmission is the one that is suspect since, unlike Myōzen, Dōgen never received the *pratimoksha* (or Hinayana) precepts, which was a requirement of Chan and other Chinese Buddhist schools, which means that his claim that Rujing transmitted 16 precepts as depicted in "Jukai" is dubious.

7. Hongzhi and Dahui had a complex relationship, as depicted in Ishii Shūdō's article in this volume.

8. Yasuraoka, *Shōbōgenzō [Gyōji] ge*, pp. 436–437.

9. Yasuraoka, *Shōbōgenzō [Gyōji] jō*, p. 3.

10. Nishio Minoru, *Dōgen to Zeami* (Tokyo: Iwanami shoten, 1965).

11. Ishii Shūdō, *Chūgoku zenshūshi wa: Mana Shōbōgenzō ni manabu* (Kyoto: Zen bunka kenkyūsho, 1988).

12. Ishii, *Shōbōgenzō [Gyōji] ni manabu* pp. 597–598. This is complicated by the fact that Tang masters, also cited extensively in "Gyōji," are known primarily through Song sources.

13. Ishii, *Shōbōgenzō [Gyōji] ni manabu*, pp. 22–23. See also Ishii Shūdō, *Sōdai zenshūshi no kenkyū* (Tokyo: Daitō shuppansha, 1987) for a study of Song Chan Buddhism.

14. T.48:204c.

15. Ishii's discussion of Linji includes a section titled *Linji hihan* ("critique of Linji" 臨済批判, pp. 252–258) because he relates the passages in "Gyōji" to other Dōgen writings that criticize Linji, as well as additional masters in rival lineages.

16. Kagamishima Genryū, et al., eds., *Dōgen no in'yō goroku no kenkyū* (Tokyo: Sōtōshū shūgaku kenkyūsho, 1995).

17. Even though the metaphysical material is less significant, because it comes primarily at the beginning of the first part, it often gets more attention than it probably deserves for an overall assessment of the fascicle. The first English translation nearly four decades ago consists of just this brief portion, giving readers the misimpression that "Gyōji" was largely a doctrinal rather than hagiographical work; in Wm. Theodore De Bary, et al., eds., *The Buddhist Tradition in India, China, and Japan* (New York: The Modern Library, 1969), pp. 369–371. An early translation titled "Continuous Practice" consisting of part one of the text only (although this is not mentioned by the translator) first appeared in Francis Dojun Cook, *How to Raise an Ox: Zen Practice as Taught in Zen Master Dōgen's Shōbōgenzō* (Los Angeles: Center Publications, 1978), pp. 175–204. Among the complete translations is the following one titled "[Pure] Conduct and Observance [of Precepts]" that includes very helpful annotations, although the overall phrasing is rather awkward: Gudo Nishijima and Chodo Cross, *Master Dogen's Shobogenzo, Book 2* (London: Windbell Publications, 1996), pp. 129–152 (part I) and 153–184 (part two). One way of counting the themes in the 96-fascicle *Shōbōgenzō* is 42 fascicles on philosophy, 22 on practice, 14 on doctrine, ten on rules, four on tradition, and four on ethics; see http://www.numenware.com/index.php?id=523.

18. As was said of the Shakers' millenarian approach to the building of furniture, a chair was made as if the artisan would die tomorrow but the piece would last a thousand years.

19. Mizuno Kōgen, *Shushōgi no Bukkyō* (Tokyo: Shunjūsha, 1968), p. 11.

20. *Dōgen zenji zenshū* I, p. 146.

21. Other anomalous fascicles that stress practice over doctrine include "Shisho," which deals with Dōgen's experiences in viewing transmission certificates during his travels in China, and "Senmen" and "Senjō," which both focus on monks' everyday behavior, such as washing and cleaning, thereby making these texts seem appropriate for inclusion in the *Eihei shingi*.

22. Reginald A. Ray, *Buddhist Saints in India: A Study in Buddhist Values and Orientations* (New York: Oxford University Press, 1994).

CHAPTER 5

1. For Dōgen's seven major disciples, see Taigen Dan Leighton and Shohaku Okumura, trans., *Dōgen's Extensive Record: A Translation of the Eihei Kōroku* (Boston: Wisdom Publications, 2004), pp. 19–25.

2. See Steven Heine, *Dōgen and the Kōan Tradition: A Tale of Two Shōbōgenzō Texts* (Albany: State University of New York Press, 1994).

3. Leighton and Okumura, *Dōgen's Extensive Record*, pp. 238–239; Kosaka Kiyū and Suzuki Kakuzen, eds. *Dōgen zenji zenshū*, vol. 3 (Tokyo: Shunjūsha, 1989), p. 160.

4. Gene Reeves, *The Lotus Sutra* (Boston: Wisdom Publications, 2008), p. 225.

5. Leighton and Okumura, *Dōgen's Extensive Record*, p. 246; Kosaka and Suzuki, eds. *Dōgen zenji zenshū*, vol. 3, pp. 166–169.

6. William Bodiford, *Sōtō Zen in Medieval Japan* (Honolulu: University of Hawai'i Press, 1993), pp. 30–31.

7. Leighton and Okumura, *Dōgen's Extensive Record*, p. 215; Kosaka and Suzuki, eds., *Dōgen zenji zenshū*, vol. 3, pp. 136.

8. Steven Heine, *Shifting Shape, Shaping Text: Philosophy and Folklore in the Fox Kōan* (Honolulu: University of Hawai'i Press, 1999).

9. Bodiford, *Sōtō Zen in Medieval Japan*, pp. 118, 163.

10. Leighton and Okumura, *Dōgen's Extensive Record*, pp. 257–258; Kosaka and Suzuki, eds., *Dōgen zenji zenshū*, vol. 3, pp. 178.

11. Leighton and Okumura, *Dōgen's Extensive Record*, p. 281; Kosaka and Suzuki, eds. *Dōgen zenji zenshū*, vol. 3, pp. 196.

12. Shohaku Okumura, *Realizing Genjōkōan: The Key to Dōgen's Shōbōgenzō* (Boston: Wisdom Publications, 2010), pp. 2, 75–81.

13. See Taigen Dan Leighton and Shohaku Okumura, trans., *Dōgen's Pure Standards for the Zen Community: A Translation of Eihei Shingi* (Albany: State University of New York Press, 1996).

14. Leighton and Okumura, trans., *Dōgen's Pure Standards*, pp. 121–125.

15. Ibid., pp. 127–204.

16. Taigen Dan Leighton with Yi Wu, trans., *Cultivating the Empty Field: The Silent Illumination of Zen Master Hongzhi* (Boston: Tuttle and Co., 2000), pp. 72–73.

17. See Shohaku Okumura and Taigen Daniel Leighton, trans., *The Wholehearted Way: A Translation of Eihei Dōgen's "Bendōwa" with Commentary by Kōsho Uchiyama Roshi* (Boston: Charles Tuttle and Co., 1997).

18. Okumura and Leighton, trans., *The Wholehearted Way*, pp. 19, 63–65.

19. For translations of "Uji," see Kazuaki Tanahashi, ed., *Treasury of the True Dharma Eye: Zen Master Dogen's Shobogenzo* (Boston: Shambhala, 2010), pp. 104–111; Norman Waddell and Masao Abe, trans., *The Heart of Dōgen's Shōbōgenzō* (Albany: State University of New York Press, 2002), pp. 48–58; Thomas Cleary, trans., *Shōbōgenzō: Zen Essays by Dōgen* (Honolulu: University of Hawai'i Press, 1986), pp. 102–110; or, with extensive commentary, Steven Heine, *Existential and Ontological Dimensions of Time in Heidegger and Dōgen* (Albany: State University of New York Press, 1985), pp. 153–162.

20. See Leighton, *Cultivating the Empty Field*, pp. 8–11, 62, 76–77; Alfonso Verdu, *Dialectical Aspects in Buddhist Thought: Studies in Sino-Japanese Mahayana Idealism* (Lawrence: Center for East Asian Studies, University of Kansas, 1974); and William Powell, trans., *The Record of Tung-shan* (Honolulu: University of Hawai'i Press, 1986), pp. 61–65.

21. Leighton and Okumura, *Dōgen's Extensive Record*, p. 390; Kosaka and Suzuki, eds., *Dōgen zenji zenshū*, vol. 4, pp. 24.

22. Leighton and Okumura, Dōgen's Extensive Record, p. 430; Kosaka and Suzuki, eds., *Dōgen zenji zenshū*, vol. 4, pp. 64.

23. The number 165 for *jōdō* from 1250 through 1252 begins with those from Buddha's parinirvana day, the 15th day of the second month of 1250. Six more were undated after Buddha's Enlightenment day in 1249, the eighth day of the 12th month, and some of these were likely in what we now call 1250.

24. Leighton and Okumura, *Dōgen's Extensive Record*, p. 404; Kosaka and Suzuki, eds., *Dōgen Zenji Zenshū*, vol. 4, pp. 38.

25. Tanahashi, *Treasury of the True Dharma Eye*, p. 260.

26. Leighton and Okumura, *Dōgen's Extensive Record*, p. 423; Kosaka and Suzuki, eds., *Dōgen Zenji Zenshū*, vol. 4, pp. 58.

27. Waddell and Abe, *The Heart of Dōgen's Shōbōgenzō*, pp. 59–98.

28. Okumura and Leighton, trans., *The Wholehearted Way*, p. 22.

29. Leighton and Okumura, *Dōgen's Extensive Record*, p. 466; Kosaka and Suzuki, eds., *Dōgen zenji zenshū*, vol. 4, p. 102.

CHAPTER 6

1. Translator's note: The present chapter is a translation adapted from "Sōdai Zenshūshi yori mitaru Dōgen Zen no ichi," a section contained in Ishii Shūdō, *Dōgen Zen no seiritsushiteki kenkyū* (A Historical Study on the Formation of Dōgen Zen) (Tokyo: Daizō shuppansha, 1991), pp. 293–335. It is based on research that originally appeared in *Nanto Bukkyō* 39 (1977). As the research for this work occurred over 30 years ago, there have been a number of advances in Dōgen studies, especially in Japan. Some, but certainly not all, are anticipated by Ishii here, so although the contents of this chapter are still valid, even ground-breaking to English readers to a large extent, there are, nonetheless, perspectives on a number of issues that the author would likely revise if writing today (examples include the reliability of Dōgen's representation of Rujing's teaching, problems associated with Dōgen's *Hōkyōki*, and a host of other textual issues surrounding the *Shōbōgenzō*—on these the reader is invited to consult Steven Heine's recent work, *Did Dōgen Go to China? What He Wrote and When He Wrote It* [New York: Oxford University Press, 2006]). As a result, discerning readers may wish to regard it as a product of its time, superseded in some respects by contemporary scholarship. Still, it serves as a fine example of Japanese scholarship on Dōgen, by one of its leading experts. To produce a more readable English version, I have taken the liberty of summarizing and slightly abbreviating the primary sources cited by Ishii in places, and take sole responsibility for any changes inadvertently introduced in the process. This is especially true of the section on p. 156, "Kōan-Introspection, Silent Illumination Chan, and Dōgen Zen," in which some lengthy passages from the *Eihei kōroku* have been either abbreviated or omitted. Professor Ishii and an associate at Komazawa University went through the translation carefully and made a few well-advised recommendations to improve the translation, which I have done my best to incorporate. I would also like to thank Morten Schlütter for his assistance in the translation of some of the primary source passages, particularly relating to Hongzhi, and his advice on how to deal with others. Given the degree of difficulty of many of the primary source passages cited, the translation of these should be regarded as tentative in places.

2. Tiantong Rujing was a member of the Chinese Caodong (Sōtō) Chan lineage, with succession as follows: Touzi Yiqing (1032–1083), Furong Daokai (1043–1118), Danxia Zichun (1064–1117), Zhenxie Qinglao (1088–1151), Tiantong Zongjue (1091–1162), Xuedou Zhijian (1105–1192), Tiantong Rujing (1164–1227).

3. Translator's note: Hōkyō is the Japanese pronunciation of the Chinese reign title era name Baoqing, during which Dōgen went to China.

4. Translator's note: Following the interpretation of *inga no shoyū* (literally "the principle of cause and effect") by Itō Shūken and Azuma Ryūshin, *Hōkyōki*, in *Genbun taishō gendaigoyaku Dōgen zenji zenshū*, vol. 16 (Tokyo: Shunjūsha, 2003), p. 3 and p.57n.3. Ikeda Rosan, trans., *Hōkyōki* (for bibliographic information, see the following note), p. 2, interprets this as meaning that Dōgen knew the basics of Buddhism.

5. *Dōgen zenji zenshū* (Tokyo: Chikuma shobō, 1970; hereafter abbreviated as DZZ) 2, p. 371. Translator's note: The translation was done in consultation with Ikeda Rosan, *Hōkyōki: Dōgen no nissō gyūhō nōto* (Tokyo: Daizō shuppansha, 1989; rpt. 2004); Takashi James Kodera, *Dogen's Formative Years in China: An Annotated Translation of the Hōkyō-ki* (London and Henley: Routledge & Kegan Paul, 1980); and Itō and Azuma, trans., *Hōkyōki*, p. 3.

6. DZZ 1, p. 729.

7. DZZ 1, p. 446. Translator's note: See also the Japanese translation by Mizuno Yaoko, *Shōbōgenzō* 5, in Kagamishima Genryū, ed., and Mizuno Yaoko, trans., *Genbun taishō gendaigoyaku Dōgen zenji zenshū*, vol. 5 (Tokyo: Shunjūsha, 2009), p. 190.

8. See Sugio Genyū, "Genjijitsu no hakken—Dōgen Zen sankyū josetsu," *Yamaguchi daigaku kyōiku gakubu kenkyū ronsō*, vol. 26/1 (1977).

9. DZZ 2, *Eihei kōroku* 2, p. 31; written in the third year of the Kangen era (1245). Translator's note: According to Professor Ishii, citing Imaeda Aishin, *Dōgen* (NHK Books), Dōgen's use of the appellation *daibutsu* ("Great Buddha") for himself in the *Eihei kōroku* is confined to the period when the temple was known as Daibutsuji (Great Buddha Temple). After the name of the temple was changed to Eiheiji in 1246, Dōgen referred to himself as "the Old Monk of Eihei[ji]" (*Eihei rōso*); see Ishii Shūdō, *Dōgen Zen no seiritsushiteki kenkyū* (Tokyo: Daizō shuppan, 1991), p. 333n.2.

10. DZZ 2, *Eihei kōroku* 2, p. 35; written in the third year of the Kangen era (1245).

11. DZZ 2, *Eihei kōroku* 4, p. 78; written in the first year of the Kenchō era (1249).

12. DZZ 2, *Eihei kōroku* 5, p. 86; written in the first year of the Kenchō era (1249). Translator's note: "Ascending the Hall" lectures refer to lectures or sermons given by abbots in "dharma halls" (or lecture halls) at Chan monasteries. Regarding this practice, readers may wish to consult T. Griffith Foulk, "Myth, Ritual, and Monastic Practice in Sung Ch'an Buddhism," in *Religion and Society in T'ang and Sung China*, eds., Patricia Ebrey and Peter Gregory (Honolulu: University of Hawai'i Press, 1993), pp. 147–208; and Mario Poceski, "Chan Rituals of Abbots' Ascending the Hall to Preach," in Steven Heine and Dale Wright, eds., *Zen Ritual* (New York: Oxford University Press, 2008), pp. 83–111 and pp. 299–304 (notes).

13. DZZ 2, *Eihei kōroku* 5, p. 101; written in the second year of the Kenchō era (1250).

14. Translator's note: The passage verifying this is cited by Ishii, *Dōgen Zen no seiritsushiteki kenkyū*, p. 295.

15. Translator's note: The statement in brackets has been added by the translator as an implicit assumption intended by the author.

16. Translator's note: The reference here is to Takao Giden, *Sōdai Bukkyōshi no kenkyū* (Kyoto: Hyakkaen, 1975).

17. See Ishii Shūdō, "Dai'e goroku no kihonteki kenkyū [jō] [chū] [ge]," *Komazawa daigaku Bukkyōgakubu kenkyū kiyō* 31 (1973), 32 (1974), and 33 (1975).

18. T 47.921c. Translator's note: I have also consulted Araki Kengo, trans., *Dai'e sho* (*Zen no goroku* 17; Tokyo: Chikuma shobō, 1969), p. 52 in my translation.

19. It is noteworthy that Fu Zhirou (a.k.a., Fu Fengmi) attached a preface to the first edition of a work attributed to Dahui's competitor, Hongzhi Zhengjue, the *Recorded Sayings of Hongzhi* (*Hongzhi yulu*), dated the first year of Shaoxing (1131). Translator's note: Ishii, p. 298, mistakenly identifies the first year of Shaoxing as 1130. Fu Zhirou appears in *Songshi* 375. According to Ishii, *Daie fukaku zenji nenpu no kenkyū*, part 3, p. 145, Fu Zhirou is the same as Fu Fengmi. I am grateful to Morten Schlütter for bringing this to my attention.

20. ZZ 2-31-5.481b-c.

21. See Ishii Shūdō, "Dai'e Sōkō to sono deshitachi (go)—jaku'i to bōkai to iu go wo megutte," *Indogaku bukkyōgaku kenkyū*, vol. 22 (1973).

22. ZZ 2-31-5.481b-c.

23. See Kamata Shigeo, *Zengen shosenshū tojo* (Tokyo: Chikuma shobō, 1971), and *Shūmitsu kyōgaku no shisōshiteki kenkyū* (Tokyo: Tokyo Daigaku shuppankai, 1975).

24. Translator's note: The passage, cited in Ishii's original text, pp. 299–300, has been omitted here. Some liberty has been taken in the translation to fill in background details as a result.

25. Translator's note: On the meaning of the phrase *sheng yuanjia* (Jp. *shō/sei onke*), see Komazawa Daigaku, ed., *Zengaku daijiten* (Tokyo: Daishūkan, 1978), p. 641c; and Iriya Yoshitaka and Koga Hidehiko, *Zengo jiten* (Kyoto: Shibunkaku, 1991), pp. 211b–212a.

26. ZZ 2-31-5.443b-c.

27. Translator's note: See Ishii, p. 301; T 47.837a.

28. Translator's note: See Ishii, pp. 301–302; and *Daie fukaku zenji nenpu no kenkyū*, part 3, p. 143a.

29. Translator's note: The view that Dahui's Kōan-Introspection teaching was formulated in response simply to the rise in influence of the Caodong faction has

been challenged by Hirota Sōgen, "Dai'e Sōkō no *Ben jyashō setsu* ni tsuite," *Zengaku kenkyū*, vol. 78 (2000), pp. 196–229. I am grateful to Professor Ishii for making me aware of this.

30. ZZ 118.74d-75a. Translator's note: What follows is a paraphrase of the passage, recorded in Ishii, pp. 302–303.

31. Translator's note: This is a reference to a passage in the *Lotus Sutra* (see T 9.184c), to the state of the world prior to the appearance of the very first Buddha, Bhishmagarjitasvara, when the world was free of distinctions and oppositions and existed in its true (i.e., formless) form. In Chan lore, it is frequently recast as the "original face, before you mother and father were born."

32. ZZ 2-31-5.429d.

33. T 47.935a-b. Translator's note: Translation follows Araki, trans., *Daie sho*, p. 171. I have omitted an additional citation from Dahui's *Pushuo*, provided by Ishii, p. 305.

34. T 47.498a.

35. ZZ 2-31-5.449d-450b. Translator's note: I have presented a slightly abbreviated version of the passage here.

36. In the three-fascicle *Zheng fayan zang*, Dahui collected the dialogues of truly awakened masters as valued by Dahui.

37. Yanagida Seizan, "Kanna zen ni okeru shin to gi no mondai," *Nihon bukkyō gakkai nenpō*, vol. 28 (1963).

38. Kagamishima Genryū, *Dōgen Zenji to in'yō kyōten goroku no kenkyū* (A Study of Zen Master Dōgen and the Scriptures and Dialogue Records he Cited) (Tokyo: Mokujisha, 1965).

39. See Araki Kengo, *Daie sho*, "kaidai."

40. *Pushuo* 2; ZZ 2-31-5.422d.

41. The *Hongzhi lu* is contained in the library of Senpukuji. The contents of the edition issued in the fifth year of Baoyong, the Zokuzōkyō edition, and the Taishō edition, are the same, but have been reedited into nine fascicles. See Ishii Shūdō, "*Wanshi roku jō*," in *Zenseki zenbon kochū chūshū* (Tokyo: Meicho fukyū, 1984).

42. The poem, cited by Ishii, is found in T 48.100a-b; *Senpukuji* edition, p. 77. Translator's note: A portion of the poem is translated by Morten Schlütter, *How Zen Became Zen: The Dispute Over Enlightenment and the Formation of Chan Buddhism in Song-Dynasty China* (Honolulu: University of Hawai'i Press, 2008), pp. 145–146; and by Taigen Dan Leighton, *Cultivating the Empty Field* (San Francisco: North Point Press, 1991), pp. 52–54. Also, Ishii, *Sōdai zenshū shi no kenkyū: Chūgoku Sōtōshū to Dōgen Zen* (Tokyo: Daizō shuppansha, 1987), pp. 333–336, provides an interpretive translation into modern

Japanese, with commentary. I am grateful to Morten Schlütter for pointing out these references.

43. T 48.98a-b; *Senpukuji* edition, p. 465.

44. T 48.57b; *Senpukuji* edition, p. 237. Translator's note: Following Schlütter, *How Zen Became Zen*, p. 151.

45. T 48.100c; *Senpukuji* edition, p. 80. Translator's note: For an alternate rendering, see Schlütter, *How Zen Became Zen*, p. 150.

46. See also the *Xingyeji*, compiled by Wang Boxiang, T 48.120b; *Senpukuji* edition, p. 319.

47. Fascicle 3 of the *Hongzhi lu*; T 48.36c; *Senpukuji* edition, p. 158. Cited by Ishii, pp. 310–311.

48. ZZ 2-15-31.317c; *Senpukuji* edition, p. 509. Cited by Ishii, p. 311.

49. Translator's note: I read "land in the jar" (*huzhong tiandi* 壺中田地; literally, "fields and earth in a jar") as a variant, or perhaps a copyists error for "realm in a jar" (*huzhong tiandi* 壺中天地; literally "heaven and earth in a jar"), a Chinese idiom derived from a story of the Yuntai Daoist Temple caretaker Zhang Shen from the Latter Han Dynasty (25–220), who always carried a liquor vessel and called the realm inside the jar, "Jar Heaven." Generally speaking, a "realm in a jar" refers to a heaven or idealized realm beyond the dusty and illusory everyday world.

50. T 48.37a; *Senpukuji* edition, p. 159. Translator's note: The translation of the passage is abbreviated here.

51. "*Wanshi kōroku kō*," *Komazawa Daigaku Bukkyō gakubu kenkyū kiyō*, vol. 30 (1972).

52. T 47.925a. Translator's note: Also consulting Araki, trans., *Dai'e sho*, pp. 83–84.

53. T 48.39a; *Senpukuji* edition, p. 167; cited in Ishii, p. 313.

54. For example, this view is seen in Menzan Zuihō's (1683–1769) *Kenkō fusetsu* (*Zoku Sōtōshū zensho, goroku* 2.505a) [cited by Ishii, p. 313]. According to Okada Gihō, in an explanation included in *Zen no hongi*, the *Inscription on Silent Illumination* was compiled in either the 25th or 26th year of the Shaoxing era. The provenance of this view is unclear.

55. ZZ 124.256b-c.

56. Translator's note: The sentence in brackets is the translator's insertion, as implied by the argument.

57. *Sōtōshū zensho* "chūkai" 4.572a.

58. T 45.156a.

59. Hirai Shun'ei, *Chūgoku hannya shisōshi kenkyū* (Tokyo: Shunjūsha, 1976), p. 320, indicates that the most concrete expression for understanding Buddha-wisdom in the Sanlun lineage is Xinghuang Falang's "Buddha-wisdom is Silent Illumination."

60. T 51.457b.

61. This is surely the reason Wang Boxiang compared Hongzhi favorably with the third patriarch when he wrote about Hongzhi's *Inscription at Dayong Hermitage* (*Dayong an ming*) in the *Xingyeji*. T 48.121a; *Senpukuji* edition, p. 322; cited in Ishii, pp. 314–315.

62. ZZ 124.328a. Translator's note: The translation follows Schlütter, *How Zen Became Zen*, p. 128, with minor variation. Regarding Yiyuan, see Schlütter, p. 128, as well.

63. T 48.66c-67a; *Senpukuji* edition, p. 272. Translator's note: The translation follows Schlütter, *How Zen Became Zen*, p. 149.

64. T 48.78a; *Senpukuji* edition, p. 314.

65. T 48.74c; *Senpukuji* edition, p. 301.

66. T 48.74c; *Senpukuji* edition, p. 301.

67. T 48.74a; *Senpukuji* edition, p. 298.

68. T 48.78a; *Senpukuji* edition, pp. 313–314. Translator's note: Hongzhi's use of the phrase *ke zhou ji jian* ("cutting a notch to remember the sword") is a reference to a story in Lü Buwei, *Lushi chunqiu* (*Mister Lu's Spring and Autumn Annals*), indicating the futility of making a mark on a moving boat in order to retrieve a sword that had fallen overboard. The story is as follows:

    There was a man from the state of Chu who was crossing a river. His sword fell from the boat into the river. He quickly made a notch on the boat saying, "This is the place where my sword fell in. When the boat stops, I will go into the water and search for my sword from the spot where I made the notch." The boat was already moving, but the sword had not moved. Is it not suspect to search for the sword in this manner?

    As a result, the saying *ke zhou qiu jian* ("making a notch on the boat to retrieve the sword"), alluded to by Hongzhi here, came to stand for stubborn clinging to something whose time has passed.

69. T 48.98c; *Senpukuji* edition, pp. 466–467.

70. T 48.76a; *Senpukuji* edition, p. 305.

71. T 48.47a; *Senpukuji* edition, p. 197. Translator's note: This is a paraphrase of the lecture cited by Ishii.

72. Translator's note: On the insertion in brackets regarding Zhang Shangying, see Schlütter, *How Zen Became Zen*, p. 119.

73. Translator's note: The reference here is to Bhishmagarjitasvara Buddha, regarding which, see n. 31.

74. See ZZ 2-31-5.466b; T 47.888a. Translator's note: The translation adheres closely to Schlütter, *How Zen Became Zen*, p. 119.

75. "Nyojō to Dōgen," in *Dōgen Zen no shisōteki kenkyū* (Tokyo: Shunjūsha, 1991).

76. This perspective is represented well in Guifeng Zongmi's view of cultivating enlightenment in terms of the actualization of enlightenment in fascicle 13 of the *Jingde chuandeng lu*, T 51.308a.

77. See Kamata Shigeo, *Zengen shosenshu tojo*; and *Shūmitsu kyōgaku no shisōshi teki kenkyū*.

78. *Shōbōgenzō zenshū jō* (hereafter abbreviated as *Zenshū*), vol. 1, p. 595. Translator's note: I consulted Rev. Hubert Norman, O.B.C., trans., *Shōbōgenzō: The Treasure House of the Eye of the True Teaching* (Mount Shasta, CA: Shasta Abbey Press, 2007), p. 891–on line edition, July 23, 2010; and Gudo Wafu Nishijima and Chodo Cross, *Shōbōgenzō: The True Dharma-Eye Treasury*, vol. 4 (Berkeley, CA: Bukkyō Dendō Kyōkai and Numata Center for Buddhist Translation and Research, 2008; originally published, 1994–1999), pp. 132–133.

79. The sermon is entitled *Lidaizhe dan qiqing pushuo*.

80. See ZZ 2-31-5.396a, 398a, 399c, 405c, 411d, 418d, 426b-c, 430d, 451c, etc.

81. Translator's note: See *Shōbōgenzō zuimonki* 5–16, which describes how, when confronting a life-threatening illness, Dahui resolved to practice sitting meditation even harder than before.

82. DZZ 1, p. 359. Translator's note: Following Carl Bielefeldt, *Treasury of the Eye of the True Dharma*, Book 42, "Teaching of the Mind, Teaching of the Nature," hcbss.stanford.edu/research/projects/sztp/translations/shobogenzo/translations/sesshin_sessho/ (Sotoshu shūmuchō, 2005).

83. "Dōgen no Dai'e hyō," in *Dai'e* (Zen sōsho 4; Tokyo: Kōbundō, 1941).

84. DZZ 2, p. 160. Translator's note: Following Taigen Daniel Leighton and Shohaku Okumura, trans., *Dōgen's Extensive Record: A Translation of the Eihei Kōroku* (Boston: Wisdom Publications, 2004), p. 520.

85. DZZ 2, *Fukanzazengi* p. 3.

86. DZZ 1, p. 737.

87. DZZ 2, *Eihei kōroku* 8, p. 161.

88. *Dahui shu* (*Da Xu Sili*), T 47.924c; Araki, trans., p. 81.

89. *Pushuo* 4, ZZ 2-31-5.480b.

90. See Kagamishima Genryū, *Dōgen Zenji to in'yō kyōten goroku no kenkyū*.

91. Translator's note: What follows is a paraphrase of the passage cited by Ishii.

92. Translator's note: According to Leighton and Okumura, *Dōgen's Extensive Record*, the quote is from fascicle 17 of Nagarjuna's *Dazhidu lun*.

93. Translator's note: *Eihei* is the Japanese pronunciation of the Chinese *yongping*, an era name of the Later Han dynasty (58–76 CE), when Buddhism was believed to have first been transmitted to China, and from which Dōgen took the name of his temple Eiheiji.

94. DZZ 2, pp. 136–137. Translator's note: For a translation of this passage, see Leighton and Okumura, *Dōgen's Extensive Record*, pp. 459–460.

95. DZZ 2, p. 384.

96. See Ishii Shūdō, "*Wanshi roku* no rekishiteki seikaku (chū)—Dōgen oshō *Kōroku* no in'yō wo megutte" (The Historical Character of the *Hongzhi lu* [pt. 2], *Shūgaku kenkyū*, vol. 15 (1973).

97. Translator's note: I have omitted a long passage here cited from fascicle 6 of the *Eihei kōroku* (DZZ 2, pp. 109–111; Leighton and Okumura, *Dōgen's Extensive Record*, pp. 386–389), which essentially confirms Dōgen's adherence to the sitting in meditation practice of the Buddhas and bodhisattvas.

98. Translator's note: According to Leighton and Okumura, *Dōgen's Extensive Record*, p. 162 n. 38, the green dragon was the name of a horse in a poem by Tang poet Dufu. The meaning is otherwise unclear, except to highlight the nature of transformation.

99. Translator's note: An apparent reference to the phrase "sun-faced Buddha, moon-faced Buddha," uttered by Mazu Daoyi.

100. DZZ 2, pp. 33–34. Translator's note: Following closely Leighton and Okumura, trans., *Dōgen's Extensive Record*, pp. 162–163.

101. DZZ 2, p. 73.

102. Translator's note: following Carl Bielefeldt, trans., "Lancet of Zazen," *Treasury of the Eye of the True Dharma*, hcbss.stanford.edu/research/projects/sztp/translations/shobogenzo/translations/sesshin_sessho/ (Sotoshu shūmuchō, 2004).

103. T 48.63a; *Senpukuji* edition, p. 257. Translator's note: A second example from Hongzhi's informal lecture, cited by Ishii (pp. 327–328), is omitted here.

104. T 51.460c. Translator's note: The phraseology is exactly the same, save for one character.

105. Takasaki Jikidō, *Kobutsu no manebi: "Dōgen"* (Tokyo: Kadokawa shoten, 1969), argues that Dōgen misunderstood Rujing's phrase "mind and dust are cast off" (modern Japanese pronunciation, *shinjin datsuraku* 心塵脱落) as "body and mind are cast off" (modern Japanese pronunciation, *shinjin datsuraku* 身心脱落), and that Rujing never taught "body and mind are cast off."

106. T 48.40c; *Senpukuji* edition, pp. 172–173. Translator's note: The full passage is cited in Ishii, p. 328.

107. The fact that Dōgen was enthralled with Hongzhi's notion of "completely casting off body and mind" is evident in a sermon by Dōgen, recorded in fascicle 2 of the *Eihei kōroku* (DZZ 2, p. 48), which is based on Hongzhi's sermon.

108. *Eihei kōroku* 3; DZZ 2, p. 65. Translator's note: See also Leighton and Okumura, trans., *Dōgen's Extensive Record*, p. 251.

109. See the *Shōbōgenzō* "Shunjū" fascicle.

110. Translator's note: I have omitted Ishii's citation from a Dharma hall discourse in fascicle 7 of the *Eihei kōroku* (DZZ 2, p. 123; Following Leighton and Okumura, trans., *Dōgen's Extensive Record*, p. 422).

111. Translator's note: "Irrational dialogue" Zen (*muri ewa zen*) refers to the non-sensical utterances found in the in the dialogue records (*yulu*) of many Chan masters, featured prominently in kōan collections; see "Sansuikyō," Mizuno Yaoko, *Shōbōgenzō* 3 (Tokyo: Shunjūsha, 2006), p. 233; and Carl Bielefeldt, trans., "Mountains and Waters Sutra," *Treasury of the Eye of the True Dharma*, Book 29, where the phrase *muri ewa* is translated as "incomprehensible talk."

112. *Eihei kōroku*, fascicle 7 (DZZ 2, p. 74).

113. See Ishii Shūdō, "Busshō Tokkō to Nihon Daruma shū—Kanazawa bunko hōkan *Jōtō shōkakuron* wo tegakari to shite" (*jō*) and (*ge*), *Kanazawa bunko kenkyū*, vols. 222, 223 (1970).

114. DZZ 2, p. 255.

115. DZZ 1, p. 650.

116. DZZ 2, p. 97. Translator's note: see Leighton and Okumura, *Dōgen's Extensive Record*, p. 350.

117. DZZ 2, p. 129. Translator's note: Following Leighton and Okumura, *Dōgen's Extensive Record*, pp. 438–439.

118. See *Bendōwa*.

119. I plan, in future, to write an article that clearly acknowledges the extent to which a disparity exists between the image of Rujing in the *Hōkyōki* and later sources.

CHAPTER 7

1. A characterization put forth by Yanagida Seizan, "Shinzoku toshi no keifu," *Zengaku kenkyū*, vol. 59 (1978), p. 5. For a characterization of this process in terms of the classic Chan work, the *Linji lu* (Jp. *Rinzai roku*), see Albert Welter, *The Linji lu and the Creation of Chan Orthodoxy* (New York: Oxford University Press, 2008).

2. Albert Welter, "Zen Buddhism as the Ideology of the Japanese State: Eisai and the *Kōzen gokokuron*," Steven Heine and Dale S. Wright, eds., *Zen Classics: Formative Texts in the History of Zen Buddhism* (New York: Oxford University Press, 2006), pp. 65–112; see especially, "Eisai's Zen Reform Program: Conventional Buddhism on the Sung-Kamakura Continuum," pp. 97–99.

3. Griffith Foulk, "Ritual in Japanese Zen Buddhism," in Steven Heine and Dale S. Wright, *Zen Ritual: Studies of Zen Buddhist Theory in Practice* (New York: Oxford University Press, 2008), pp. 21–82 and 293–299 (notes).

4. Foulk, "Ritual in Japanese Buddhism," p. 31.

5. Plutarch, "Fraternal Love" in *Moralia* (2.490b).

6. Luther H. Martin, "Of Religious Syncretism, Comparative Religion and Spiritual Quest," in *Perspectives on Method and Theory in the Study of Religion: Adjunct Proceedings of the XVIIth Congress of the International Association for the History of Religions Mexico City, 1995*, Armin W. Geertz and Russell T. McCutcheon, eds. (Leiden: Brill, 2000), pp. 277–286.

7. Judith A. Berling, *The Syncretic Religion of Lin Chao-en* (New York: Columbia University Press, 1980).

8. My views here are the product of a seminar I held in the winter of 2009 at the University of Winnipeg entitled "Syncretism in Chinese Thought." I am indebted to the participants, especially Dragan Majhen, whose M.A. thesis, "Adaptive Pursuit of Harmony in Times of Crisis: Wang Yangming's (1472–1529) Contribution to the Syncretization of Chinese Thought in the Ming Dynasty (1368–1644)," makes a compelling case for understanding syncretism (or syncretization) as a progression of syncretic tendencies.

9. Robert Baird, "Syncretism," in Chapter 5: "Some Inadequate Categories," in *Category Formation and the History of Religions* (The Hague & Paris: Mouton, 1971), pp. 142–154.

10. Martin, "Of Religious Syncretism, Comparative Religion and Spiritual Quest," p. 277.

11. See, for example, Michael Pye, "Syncretism versus Synthesis," in *Method & Theory in the Study of Religion* 6/3 (Berlin: Walter de Gruyter, 1994), pp. 217–229; and Harry Thomsen, "Non-Buddhist Buddhism and Non-Christian Christianity in Japan," in Sven S. Hartman, *Syncretism* (Stockholm: Almqvist & Wiksell, 1969), pp. 128–136.

12. Helmer Ringgren, "The Problems of Syncretism," in Sven S. Hartman, *Syncretism*, pp. 7–14.

13. The *Hōkyōki* is divided variously: Takashi James Kodera, *Dogen's Formative Years in China: an Annotated Translation of the Hōkyō-ki* (London and Henley: Routledge & Kegan Paul, 1980), for example, divides it into 50 sections; Ikeda Rosan, *Hōkyōki: Dōgen no nyūsō kyūhō nōto* (Tokyo: Daitō shuppansha, 1989; reprint edition, 2004), divides it into 42 sections; and Itō Shūken and Azuma Ryūshin, *Hōkyōki*, in *Genbun taishō gendaigoyaku Dōgen Zenji zenshū*, vol. 16 (Tokyo: Shunjūsha, 2003), divides it into 44 sections. Each of these versions treats the section in question as section 2.

14. For an alternate translation, see Kodera, *Dogen's Formative Years in China*, p. 118. I have also consulted the Japanese translations of Ikeda Rosan, *Hōkyōki*, pp. 8–9; and Itō Shūken and Azuma Ryūshin, *Hōkyōki*, pp. 5–6. The original text

of the *Hōkyōki*, written in classical Chinese, is provided in Ikeda, pp. 147–181; and Itō and Azuma, pp. 87–101.

15. On the problems associated with dating the *Hōkyōki* and different theories regarding its dating, see Steven Heine, *Did Dōgen Go to China? What He Wrote and When He Wrote It* (New York: Oxford University press, 2006), pp. 36–38.

16. As Nakaseko Shōdō has indicated in *Dōgen Zenji den kenkyū-sei* (Tokyo: Kokusho kankōkai, 1997), there are some major discrepancies between the way Rujing is represented by Dōgen and Rujing's own writings. For a summary, see Heine, *Did Dōgen Go to China?*, pp. 204–206. As a result, the representation of Rujing's views by Dōgen should be read primarily as Dōgen's own.

17. See Kamata Shigeo, *Zengen shosenshu tojo* (Tokyo: Chikuma shobo, 1971), p. 44.

18. Tamamuro Taijō, *Dōgen* (Tokyo: Shin Jinbutsu Ōraisha, 1971), pp. 210–211.

19. *Dogen's Formative Years in China*, p. 172 n.11.

20. Ikeda Rosan, *Hōkyōki*, p. 52; Itō Shūken and Azuma Ryūshin, *Hōkyōki*, pp. 20–21; and Kodera, *Dogen's Formative Years in China*, pp. 124–125.

21. Mizuno Yaoko, *Shōbōgenzō* 4, in Kagamishima Genryū, ed., and Mizuno Yaoko, trans., *Genbun taishō gendaigoyaku Dōgen zenji zenshū* vol. 4 (Tokyo: Shunjūsha, 2009), pp. 80–81. I have also consulted the translations by Gudo Wafu Nishijima and Chodo Cross, *Shōbōgenzō: The True Dharma-Eye Treasury*, vol. 2 (Berkeley, California: Bukkyō Dendō Kyōkai and Numata Center for Buddhist Translation and Research, 2008; originally published, 1994–1999), p. 70; and Rev. Hubert Norman, O.B.C., *Shōbōgenzō: The Treasure House of the Eye of the True Teaching* (Mount Shasta, California: Shasta Abbey Press, 2007), pp. 301–302.

22. The "actual performance" of the Buddha Dharma here is a translation of *kagō* (literally, "house activities"), referring to the practices one undertakes as a member of a Buddhist monastic congregation.

23. Literally, they do not know what is "internal" (*nai*) and do not know what is "external" (*ge*).

24. Mizuno Yaoko, trans., *Genbun taishō gendaigoyaku Dōgen zenji zenshū*, vol. 5, pp. 81–82. Nishijima and Cross, trans., *Shōbōgenzō*, vol. 2, pp. 70–71; Norman, trans., *Shōbōgenzō*, p. 302.

25. I have written elsewhere on this development; see Albert Welter, *The Linji lu and the Creation of Chan Orthodoxy* (New York: Oxford University Press, 2008), especially pp. 38–42; and *Monks, Rulers, and Literati: The Political Ascendancy of Chan Buddhism* (New York: Oxford University Press, 2006), especially pp. 172–207.

26. See Griffith Foulk, "Sung Controversies Concerning the 'Separate Transmission' of Ch'an," in Peter Gregory and Daniel Getz, eds., *Buddhism in the Sung* (Honolulu: University of Hawai'i Press, 1999), pp. 220–294.

27. On this, see the article by Ishii Shūdō in the present volume.

28. On the influence of the *Zongjing lu* over the teachings of Dainichi Nōnin, see Ishii Shūdō, "Dōgen no Nihon Daruma shū hihan," in *Dōgen Zen seiritsu shiteki kenkyū* (Tokyo: Daizō shuppan, 1991), pp. 626–714, especially the subsection "*Sūgyō roku* to Nihon Daruma shū," pp. 689–693. On the influence of the *Zongjing lu* in Eisai's *Kōzen gokoku ron*, see Albert Welter, "Zen as the Ideology of the Japanese State."

29. Itō Shūken and Azuma Ryūshin, *Shōbōgenzō Zuimonki*, in *Genbun taishō gendaigoyaku Dōgen Zenji zenshū*, vol. 16 (Tokyo: Shunjūsha, 2003), pp. 143–145. I have also consulted the translation by Reihō Masunaga, *A Primer of Sōtō Zen: A translation of Dōgen's* Shōbōgenzō Zuimonki (Honolulu: East-West Center Press, 1971), pp. 13–14. I have discussed the development of this episode in the context of Yanshou's life and biographical image elsewhere, in Albert Welter, "The Contextual Study of Chinese Buddhist Biographies: The Example of Yung-ming Yen-shou (904–975)," Phyllis Granoff and Koichi Shinohara, eds., in *Monks and Magicians: Religious Biographies in Asia* (Oakville, Ontario: Mosaic Press, 1988), pp. 247–268; *The Meaning of Myriad Good Deeds: A Study of Yung-ming Yen-shou and the Wan-shan t'ung-kuei chi* (New York, Bonn: Peter Lang Publishing Inc., 1993) pp. 53–99; and most recently, "Yongming Yanshou: Scholastic as Chan Master," in Steven Heine and Dale Wright, eds., *Zen Masters* (New York: Oxford University Press, 2010), pp. 59–89.

30. Kagamishima Genryū, *Eihei kōroku* vol. 3, in *Genbun taishō gendaigoyaku Dōgen zenji zenshū* vol. 12 (Tokyo: Shunjū sha, 2000), pp. 24–26. Taigen Daniel Leighton and Shohaku Okumura, trans., *Dōgen's Extensive Record: A Translation of the Eihei Kōroku* (Boston: Wisdom Publications, 2004), pp. 438–439. For my translation of this passage, see the article by Ishii Shūdō in the present volume.

31. See Mizuno Yaoko, trans., *Genbun taishō gendaigoyaku Dōgen Zenji zenshū*, vol. 5, pp. 32–65; Norman, trans., *Shōbōgenzō*, pp. 622–640; Nishijima and Cross, trans., *Shōbōgenzō* vol. 3, pp. 87–108.

32. The following characterization of Yanshou's teaching in the *Zongjing lu* follows the more extensive treatment provided in my book, *Yongming Yanshou's Conception of Chan in the Zongjing Lu: A Special Transmission within the Scriptures* (New York: Oxford University Press, 2011).

33. From fascicle 2 of the ZJL (T 48.427b29–c12).

34. The back-to-back reference to Jiangxi and Mazu is odd, given that these are usually understood as appellations for the same person. I know of no other attribution for these terms than to Mazu Daoyi, although the dual reference here is strange. Could it be that Yanshou is adapting materials from different sources, using different, common appellations for the same person?

35. As an example of Yanshou's incorporation of Confucianism and Daoism, see fascicle 3 of the *Wanshan tonggui ji* (T 48.988a3–b9), and my discussion of it in *The Meaning of Myriad Good Deeds*, pp. 229–232.

36. T 48.416b10–11.

37. See, for example, Dōgen's comments in the *Shizen biku* fascicle of the *Shōbōgenzō*. Norman, trans., *Shōbōgenzō*, pp. 1050–1071; Nishijima and Cross, trans., *Shōbōgenzō* vol. 4, pp. 263–287.

38. T 48.416b13–20.

39. One may note in this context the influence of *weishi* (consciousness-only) thought on Yanshou, which posits that all existence is but a manifestation of mind. On the role of *weishi* in Yanshou's thought, see Ran Yunhua (Jan Yun-hua), *Yongming Yanshou* (Taipei: Tung-ta t'u-shu-kuan kung-ssu, 1999), pp. 69–145.

40. Mizuno Yaoko, *Shōbōgenzō* 1, in Kagamishima Genryū, ed., and Mizuno Yaoko, trans., *Genbun taishō gendaigoyaku Dōgen Zenji zenshū* vol. 1 (Tokyo: Shunjū sha, 2002), p. 9.

41. Mizuno Yaoko, *Shōbōgenzō* 1, p. 10.

42. Mizuno Yaoko, *Shōbōgenzō* 1, p. 11.

43. Mizuno Yaoko, *Shōbōgenzō* 3, in Kagamishima Genryū, ed., and Mizuno Yaoko, trans., *Genbun taishō gendaigoyaku Dōgen zenji zenshū* vol. 3 (Tokyo: Shunjūsha, 2006), p. 227. According to Carl Bielefeldt, Mountain and Waters Sutra, "Introduction," the term "expression" *(dō genjō)* should probably be taken in two senses: the words of the Buddha and his practice; hcbss.stanford.edu/research/projects/sztp/translations/shobogenzo/translations/sesshin_sessho/ (Sotoshu Shumucho, 2001). The full translation of the opening paragraph, translated by Bielefeldt, reads:

> These mountains and waters of the present are the expression of the old buddhas. Each, abiding in its own dharma state, fulfills exhaustive virtues. Because they are the circumstances "prior to the kalpa of emptiness," they are this life of the present; because they are the self "before the germination of any subtle sign," they are liberated in their actual occurrence. Since the virtues of the mountain are high and broad, the spiritual power to ride the clouds is always mastered from the mountains, and the marvelous ability to follow the wind is inevitably liberated from the mountains.

44. Mizuno Yaoko, *Shōbōgenzō* 3, p. 130.

45. T 48.418a-b.

46. Mizuno Yaoko, *Shōbōgenzō* 5, pp. 107–108.

47. For references, see Mizuno Yaoko, *Shōbōgenzō* 5, p. 251a-b (p. 107 n.2).

48. Yanagida Seizan, "Dōgen to Chūgoku Bukkyō," *Zen bunka kenkyū kiyō* 13 (1984), pp. 7–29.

49. Kagamishima Genryū, *Dōgen Zenji to inyō kyōten-goroku no kenkyū* (Tokyo: Mokujisha, 1974; originally published 1965).

50. "Dōgen to Chūgoku Bukkyō," pp. 9–10.

51. Abe Chōichi, *Chūgoku Zenshūshi no kenkyū: seiji shakai shiteki kōsatsu* (Tokyo: Kenbu shuppan, 1987, revised edition), pp. 186–210.

52. Ikeda Rosan, "Chōsō Tendaigaku no haikei—Enju kyōgaku no saihyōka," *Komazawa daigaku Bukkyōgakubu ronshū* 14 (1983), pp. 62–81. Yanshou's Tiantai thought is also discussed in Yi-hsun Huang, *Integrating Chinese Buddhism: A Study of Yongming Yanshou's Guanxin Xuanshu* (Taipei: Dharma Drum Publishing, 2005), pp. 96–105.

53. On the sources cited in the *Wanshan tonggui ji*, see Albert Welter, *The Meaning of Myriad Good Deeds*, pp. 121–127; on the sources cited in the *Zongjing lu*, see Albert Welter, *Yongming Yanshou's Conception of Chan in the Zongjing lu: A Special Transmission within the Scriptures* (New York: Oxford University Press, 2011).

54. Welter, *The Meaning of Myriad Good Deeds*, pp. 131–142.

55. Mizuno Yaoko, *Shōbōgenzō* 1, p. 4. Yanagida Seizan, "Dōgen to Chūgoku Bukkyō," p. 12, argues that the influence of the Rinzai monastery, Kennin-ji, founded by Eisai, on Dōgen's training was significant. Dōgen trained there for approximately eight years (according to Yanagida; Dōgen, in the passage year, makes it nine years) before departing for China, and for roughly another three years after his return, so that over ten years of his Buddhist training was carried out at Kennin-ji.

56. See, for example, the references to Linji in the discourses, Dharma talks, etc., recorded in the *Eihei kōroku*, as indexed by Leighton and Okumura, *Dōgen's Extensive Record*, p. 668.

57. Mizuno Yaoko, *Shōbōgenzō* 5, pp. 114–116; Nishijima and Cross, trans., *Shōbōgenzō* vol. 3, pp. 143–145.

58. For a complete list of fascicles containing Dōgen's critiques of the Linji school, see Steven Heine, *Did Dōgen Go to China?*, p. 178, Table 30.

59. Mizuno Yaoko, *Shōbōgenzō* 5, pp. 117–119. Nishijima and Cross, trans., *Shōbōgenzō* vol. 3, pp. 145–146.

60. Mizuno Yaoko, *Shōbōgenzō* 5, p. 119; Nishijima and Cross, trans., *Shōbōgenzō* vol. 3, p. 146.

61. Elsewhere, Dōgen seems to acknowledge Dahui's awakening as legitimate; see the chapter by Ishii Shūdo in this volume.

62. Mizuno Yaoko, *Shōbōgenzō* 7, in Kagamishima Genryū, ed., and Mizuno Yaoko, trans., *Genbun taishō gendaigoyaku Dōgen zenji zenshū* vol. 7 (Tokyo: Shunjūsha, 2009), pp. 20–26.

63. Mizuno Yaoko, *Shōbōgenzō* 7, pp. 124–125; following Nishijima and Cross, trans., *Shōbōgenzō: The True Dharma-Eye Treasury*, vol. 4, pp. 132–133.

64. On this, see Welter, *Monks, Rulers, and Literati*.

65. A reference to "availing oneself of the eyes of a snake" is found in fascicle 7 of a version of the *Shoulengyan jing*, or Surangama Sutra (T 19–945.138c28), but there appears to be no connection to the passage cited here.

66. T 48.418a13–16.

67. T 48.418a16–18.

68. T 48.420a3–8.

69. T 48.420a8–10.

70. T 48.417c20–21.

71. The identification of the Linji faction and "a separate transmission outside the teachings" is discussed in Welter, *Monks, Rulers, and Literati*. Similar concerns are addressed by Yanshou in the *Wanshan tonggui ji*; see Welter, *The Meaning of Myriad Good Deeds*, pp. 208–216 (translations of passages found at T 48.958c-959a, 960b-c, and 961a-b).

72. An early example of this is the *Sijia yulu* (Dialogue Records of Four Clans/ Houses), which places the records of Mazu, Baizhang, Huangbo, and Linji together in a single compilation. The earliest known arrangement of the dialogue records of these four masters is the *Tiansheng Guangdeng lu*, compiled by Li Zunxu in 1029 and issued in 1036. Dōgen follows this tradition, acknowledging that Linji's followers are heirs in Mazu's stream (see the *Gyōji* fascicle, Part 1; Mizuno Yaoko, *Shōbōgenzō* 2, esp. pp. 149–152).

73. Mizuno Yaoko, *Shōbōgenzō* 3, p. 173; Nishijima and Cross, trans., *Shōbōgenzō* vol. II, pp. 142–143.

74. Although the Chan school reached consensus that Huizhong was Huineng's heir, early sources contest this view. The Dunhuang manuscript *Quanzhou Qianfo xinshu zhu zushi song* considers Huizhong the disciple of Qingyuan Xingsi. The *Song Gaoseng zhuan* regards him as a disciple of Hongren. The *Zutang ji* and *Jingde Chuandeng lu* classify him as Huineng's disciple (Albert Welter, *Monks, Rulers, and Literati*, pp. 77–78).

75. Dōgen also held Baizhang (Hakujō) in high regard, as in the "Gyōji" fascicle, where he attributes the success of the Linji faction in Song China in large part to the influence of Baizhang's "profound customs," and the conduct and observances he instituted as practices (Mizuno Yaoko, *Shōbōgenzō* 2, p. 123; Nishijima and Cross, trans., *Shōbōgenzō* vol. II, p. 169), as well as Linji faction masters like Zhaozhou (Jōshū).

76. Mizuno Yaoko, *Shōbōgenzō* 1, pp. 161–172; Nishijima and Cross, trans., *Shōbōgenzō* vol. I, pp. 65–70. This discussion is also noted, in passing, in the *Bendōwa*.

77. Mizuno Yaoko, *Shōbōgenzō* 1, pp. 170–171.

78. Mizuno Yaoko, *Shōbōgenzō* 5, pp. 81–104, esp. pp. 85–91.

79. T 48.418c17–419a2.

80. Other Chan masters honored in fascicle 1 are Mazu Daoyi, Ehu Dayi, and Sikong Benjing.

81. T 48.418c10–17.

82. Steven Heine, *Did Dōgen Go to China?*, p. 58, suggests that the 12-fascicle text of the *Shōbōgenzō*, consisting of revisions of existing fascicles undertaken by Dōgen toward the end of his life, were revised, in part, to emphasize consistency with Sakyamuni's original message.

83. Foulk, "'Rules of Purity' in Japanese Zen," in Heine and Wright, *Zen Classics*, p. 141.

84. Foulk, "Rules of Purity," pp. 143–143; the quotation is taken from p. 143.

85. With regard to Yanshou's perspective on Chan lineage and his failure to assert a lineal identity, see my forthcoming book, *Yongming Yanshou's Notion of Chan in the* Zongjing lu*: A Special Transmission Within the Scriptures* (New York: Oxford University Press, 2011). On Fayan Wenyi's critique of Chan factionalism, see section 2 of the *Zongmen shigui lun* (X 63–1226.37a19–b8); for a translation see Thomas Cleary, *The Five Houses of Zen* (Boston: Shambhala, 1997), pp. 133–134.

CHAPTER 8

1. Originally appeared in *Dōgen zenji kenkyū ronshū*, Daihonzan Eiheiji Daionki Kyoku, ed. (Fukui-ken: Eiheiji, 2002), pp. 1018–1046.

2. An early version of this chapter was first presented at Yale University for the conference, "From Precept to Practice: New Perspectives on Japanese Buddhist Culture," 1998. The encounter between Zhiyi and Bodhidharma occurs in Tōkai's discussion of the Zen school, in *Tōkai kudenshō, Tendaishū zensho*, vol. 9:567–570.

3. Bernard Faure, *The Rhetoric of Immediacy: A Cultural Critique of Chan/Zen Buddhism* (Princeton: Princeton University Press, 1991), pp. 96–131.

4. *Zenmon hōgo shū*, 2 (Tokyo: Kōyūkan, 1921), p. 416. For my translation of this text, see "A Discussion of Seated Zen," in Donald Lopez, ed., *Buddhism in Practice* (Princeton: Princeton University Press, 1995), pp. 197–206; this passage occurs at p. 202.

5. *Zenmon hōgo shū* 2, p. 416.

6. T 48:494a16–17.

7. Ibid., 494b19–27.

8. Ibid., 497a1–9.

9. Ibid., 497b24–26.

10. See, e.g., *Jingde chuandeng lu*, T 51:227b6ff.

11. T 48:497a16–29. Although I attribute this last bit to Yanshou, since the story is not recorded elsewhere, it is not certain just where Farong's answer breaks off and the author's comment begins here. Peng Cheng Wang is not known from other sources.

12. *Putidamo nanzang ding shifei lun*, in Hu Shi, *Shenhui heshang yiji*, rev. ed. (Taipei: Hu shi jinianguan, 1970), p. 275–276. Shenhui's quotation differs slightly from the sutra version quoted here (from T 12:372b26). Since the Dunhuang manuscript is damaged at this point, it is not clear exactly how Shenhui argues from the quotation.

13. *Linji lu*, T 47:499c23–500a12. Linji's quotation is from the Dunhuang commentary to the *Diamond* attributed to Fu Dashi. The "grounded" (or "earth walker") here is likely a play on a term for the flightless sage.

14. *Guzunsu yulu*, ZZ 118:89d2–6.

15. *Jingde chuandeug lu*, T 51:263b12.

16. *Dongshan lu*, T 47.508b2–4; *Liandeng huiyao*, ZZ 136:272b13–c1.

17. *Kōzengokokuron*, in Ichikawa Hakugen and Yanagida Seizan, ed., *Chūsei zenke no shisō, Nihon shisō taikei* 16 (Tokyo: Iwanami shoten, 1976), p. 105b.

18. Ibid., 105b–106a. Maudgalyayana's story appears in the *Dharmaguptaka-vinaya*: *Shibun ritsu*, T 22:568c–569a; there are various versions of *Jingde chuandeng lu*'s story; see, e.g., *Shibun ritsu*, T 22:646b-c.

19. *Kōzengokokuron*, p. 106a.

20. Ibid., p. 105b.

21. Ibid., p. 105a-b. Eisai is here paraphrasing the story appearing in the *Dazhidulun*, T 25:129b29–c18.

22. Eisai's only nod toward the Chan literature here is his passing reference (at 106a) to Yanshou's story of Farong and Peng Cheng—a passage he does not quote but seems to invoke only to point out that the founder of Japanese Tendai, Saichō, was a descendant of the Chan master Farong.

23. "Tenpuku bon," in Suzuki Kakuzen et al., ed., *Dōgen zenji zenshū*, vol. 5 (Tokyo: Shunjūsha, 1989), pp. 11–12.

24. Kawamura Kōdō, ed., *Dōgen zenji zenshū*, vol. 2 (Tokyo: Shunjūsha, 1993), pp. 241–242. The story appears in the *Jingde chuandeng lu*, T 51:244a7–21.

25. I have elsewhere translated the entire fascicle as "Reading Others' Minds," in Donald Lopez, ed., *Buddhism in Practice* (Princeton: Princeton University Press, 1995), pp. 69–79. An earlier version appeared in *The Ten Directions* 13/1 (1992), pp. 26–34.

26. Kawamura Kōdō, ed., *Dōgen zenji zenshū*, vol. 2, pp. 245–246.

27. Ibid., p. 245.

28. Ibid., p. 251.

29. Kawamura Kōdō, ed., *Dōgen zenji zenshū*, vol. 1, p. 392.

30. Ibid., p. 394.

31. Ibid., p. 393.

32. Ibid., pp. 395–396.

33. Ibid., pp. 394–395.

34. Ibid., pp. 396–397.

CHAPTER 9

1. *Shūkyō nenkan* (Tokyo: Bunkachō, 1997), pp. 64–77.

2. Eiheiji is located in Fukui Prefecture (premodern Echizen Province), whereas Sōjiji is now located in Yokohama (near Tokyo). The original Sōjiji is located on the Noto Peninsula in Ishikawa Prefecture.

3. Kagamishima Sōjun, "Kaisetsu," in *Enkyōdo Sōtōshū jiin honmatsuchō* (typeset version of 1747 and 1827 texts; 1944; reprinted and expanded edition, Tokyo: Meicho fukyūkai, 1980). Giin (a.k.a., Kangan or Hōō; 1217–1300) and Meihō Sotetsu (1277–1350) were two prominent leaders within early Sōtō history in Japan.

4. Sakurai Shūyū, ed., *Eiheijishi* (Fukui: Dai honzan eiheiji), vol. 2, pp. 1516–1525.

5. Reliable data on temple relationships prior to the start of Tokugawa-period regulation of religious institutions are unavailable. For an overview, see William M. Bodiford, *Sōtō Zen in Medieval Japan* (Honolulu: University of Hawai'i Press, 1993), pp. 122–139.

6. For example, Takahashi Zenryū, "Honmatsu seiritsu to Tokugawa bakufu no shūkyō seisaku ni tsuite," in the 1980 reprint of Kagamishima Sōjun, ed., *Enkyōdo Sōtōshū jiin honmatsuchō*, p. 5.

7. As John Whitney Hall explained in the pages of this journal (see "Terms and Concepts in Japanese Medieval History: An Inquiry into the Problems of Translation." *JJS* 9, 1983, p. 10), "It is unfortunate that modern times *tennō* (or *tenshi*) has so unquestionably been rendered "emperor." . . . The translation "emperor," whether drawing upon European or Chinese usage, carrie[s] overtones of grandeur and autocratic personal power that the Japanese *tennō* did not possess . . ." Indeed, not only has Japan never possessed a ruler commanding supreme authority (the usual meaning of "emperor") but, except for a brief moment in the 20th century, the Japanese never extended rule over a vast territory approximating an empire. Moreover, in premodern Japanese Buddhist

literature, especially Sōtō documents, the ruler most frequently is designated simply as *ō* ("king"). For these reasons, in this chapter, I refer to the ruler's court and its titles with the adjective "royal" instead of "imperial."

8. *Nobutane kyōki* (diary of Nakamikado Nobutane, 1442–1525), entries for 11.23 & 12.16, in Zōho Shiryō Taisei Kankōkai, ed., *Zōho Shiryō taisei* (Kyoto: Rinsen shoten, 1965), vol. 45, pp. 218b, 221b. Today, on Eiheiji's main gate (*sanmon*), there is a wooden plaque which is said to represent calligraphy by Goen'yū *tennō* (1358–1393), awarded by him to Eiheiji in 1372. It reads: *Nihon Sōtō daiichi dōjō* (literally: "the number one training center of Japan's Sōtō lineage")—not *honchō Sōtō daiichi dōjō*. It is extremely doubtful, however, if Eiheiji actually received calligraphy from Goen'yū or any other royal honors as early as the 14th century. No direct or indirect documentary evidence either among Sōtō or non-Sōtō sources attests to this earlier award. Moreover, if earlier royal calligraphy had established a precedent for use of the word *Nihon*, it is highly unlikely that a subsequent award would have changed it to *honchō*. Other inconsistencies also exist. Nakamikado Nobutane reports that Eiheiji originally had requested a different word order (*honchō daiichi Sōtō dōjō*), which had been rejected, and that the calligraphy was written by the nobleman Sesonji Yukisue (1476–1532), not by a royal sovereign. It is hard to imagine that, in 1507, Eiheiji would have requested an unacceptable word order or would have received calligraphy written by a mere nobleman if the temple already possessed a wooden plaque representing calligraphy awarded by Goen'yū more than 130 years earlier. See Imaeda Aishin, *Chūsei Zenshūshi no kenkyū* (1970; 2nd edition, Tokyo: Tōkyō Daigaku shuppankai, 1982), pp. 395–396, 397 n. 10.

9. The designation "five mountains" refers not to a particular number of places but is the name of a broad category of Buddhist monasteries and temples divided into three levels of status: *gozan* (as many as 11 centers), *jissatsu* (as many as 32), and *shozan* (as many as 186). Except for one or two possible exceptions, Sōtō institutions were not affiliated to the Five Mountains. Regarding *bakufu* fees for appointments to abbotships, see Martin Collcutt, *Five Mountains: The Rinzai Monastic Institution in Medieval Japan* (Cambridge, MA: Harvard University Press, 1981), pp. 228–236. Regarding Eiheiji's case, see Imaeda, *Chūsei Zenshūshi*, pp. 394–397.

10. Bodiford, *Sōtō Zen in Medieval Japan*, pp. 135–136.

11. For these titles, see *Shoshū Chokugōki* (ca. 1311–1660), in Hanawa Hokiichi and Hanawa Tadatomi, eds., *Zoku gunsho ruijū* (1822; reprinted Tokyo: Keizai zasshisha, 1902), vol. 28B.

12. Hirose Ryōkō, "Eiheiji no suiun to fukkō undō," in Sakurai, ed., *Eiheijishi*, vol. 1, pp. 384–386.

13. Bodiford, *Sōtō Zen in Medieval Japan*, pp. 135–138. Ryōan Emyō (1337–1411) was a prominent leader in medieval Sōtō. His name is used to identify one of the smaller networks of Sōtō temples affiliated to Sōjiji.

14. *Eihei Dōgen oshō kōroku* (1598 copy by Monkaku), reprinted in Ōkubo Dōshū, ed., *Dōgen zenji zenshū* (Tokyo: Chikuma shobō, 1970), vol. 2, *jōdō* nos. 184, 249, 274, 276, 342, 384, 515. Regarding the dates of these lectures, see Itō Shūken, "'Eihei kōroku' setsuji nendai kō," *Komazawa daigaku bukkyō gakubu ronshū*, no. 11 (1980), pp. 185–188.

15. See *Giun oshō goroku*, reprinted in *Sōtōshū zensho* (revised and enlarged edition; Tokyo: Sōtōshū Shūmuchō, 1970–1973), vol. 5, "Goroku," no. 1, p. 9a.

16. The observance in Japan of the Chinese sequence of memorial services is discussed by Tamamuro Taijō, *Sōshiki bukkyō* (Tokyo: Daihōrinkaku, 1963), p. 171.

17. *Zuichō hon Kenzeiki* (1552 version of Kenzei's chronicle, recopied by Zuichō in 1589), reprinted in Kawamura Kōdō, ed., *Shohon taikō Eihei kaisan Dōgen zenji gyōjō Kenzeiki* (Tokyo: Taishūkan shoten, 1975), p. 85.

18. There exists a manual for Dōgen memorial services titled *Eiheiji kaisan kigyō hokke kōshiki* that was published in the early 1900s at Eiheiji. According to its postscript, this text was revised by Menzan Zuihō in 1747, based on an original by Giun that had been stored at Hōkyōji. The genealogy of this text, however, remains unknown. In Menzan's otherwise well-documented life, there is no evidence that he ever saw this text. He did not mention it in the manual for Dōgen memorial services (*Jōyō daishi hōon kōshiki*) that he compiled for Dōgen's 500-year memorial in 1752. Moreover, we know that a manual for *hokke kōshiki* (*Lotus Sutra* ceremony) as donated to Eiheiji in 1759 by the abbot of Keiyōji (in Edo) for the express purpose of being used for Dōgen memorial services. That Keiyōji text is the most likely origin of the *Eiheiji kaisan kigyō hokke kōshiki*. See Kumagai Chūkō and Yoshida Dōkō, "Shūtō fukko undō to Eiheiji," in Sakurai, ed., *Eiheijishi*, vol. 2, p. 985.

19. Bodiford, *Sōtō Zen in Medieval Japan*, pp. 70–80.

20. Hirose, "Eiheiji no suiun to fukkō undō," pp. 477–481.

21. The following four documents help reveal Keizan's ambitions for Yōkōji: (1) *Tōkoku dentōin gorō gosoku narabi ni gyōgō ryakki* (originally dated 1323.9.13, but included in a 1718 version of *Tōkokuki*; reprinted in Kohō Chisan, ed., *Jōsai daishi zenshū*, 1937; reprinted and enlarged, Yokohama: Dai honzan sōjiji, 1976), pp. 411–416; (2) *Tōkoku jinmirai honji to nasubeki no okibumi* (originally dated 1318.12.23, but included in the 1515 copy of *Shōbōgenzō zatsubun*; reprinted in Matsuda Fumio, "Keizan Zenji no jinmiraisai okibumi ni tsuite: Yōkōji kaibyaku no haikei," no. 12, 1970), pp. 133–134; (3) *Tōkoku jinmiraisai*

okibumi (originally dated 1319.12.8; reprinted in Ōkubo Dōshū, ed., *Sōtōshū komonjo*, Tokyo: Chikuma Shobō, 1972), no. 163, vol. 2, pp. 120–121; and (4) *Tōkokuki* (copy dated 1432 at Daijōji, reprinted in Ōtani Teppu, ed., "Daijōji hihon 'Tōkokuki,'" *Shūgaku kenkyū*, no. 16 (1974), pp. 231–248. Regarding these documents, see the above cited article by Matsuda Fumio, but note that, at the time of Matsuda's analysis, the 1432 Daijōji copy of *Tōkokuki* had not yet been published and the correct year of Keizan's birth was not yet known. For a comprehensive study of Keizan and his religious world, see Bernard Faure, *Visions of Power: Imagining Medieval Japanese Buddhism* (Princeton: Princeton University Press, 1996).

22. James C. Dobbins, "Envisioning Kamakura Buddhism," in Richard K. Payne, ed., *Re-Visioning "Kamakura" Buddhism*, (Honolulu: University of Hawai'i Press), pp. 32–33.

23. Bodiford, *Sōtō Zen in Medieval Japan*, pp. 95–97.

24. The original text of the *Tōkoku gyōji jijo* probably was compiled by Keizan's disciples at Yōkōji after his death. The earliest surviving copy was completed in two fascicles by Fusai Zenkyū in 1376 and is owned by Zenrinji temple (Fukui Pref.). The standard edition of *Keizan oshō shingi*, which was published in 1680 by Manzan Dōhaku, was edited and enlarged based on texts and practices that were not yet in existence during Keizan's lifetime. It is crucial, therefore, when using the *Keizan shingi* as a source for Keizan's monastic practices to verify each passage by comparison to earlier manuscripts. In the case of Dōgen memorial services, the instructions found in the 1680 published text (fasc. 2, p. 353) can also be found in the earliest extant manuscript copy, *Gyōji jijo* (1376, leaves 31–32). The exact same instructions also are found in versions of this liturgical calendar that were adapted for use at other temples, such as *Shōbō shingi* (1509; reprinted in Sōtōshū Zensho Kankōkai, ed., *Zoku Sōtōshū zensho*, Tokyo: Sōtōshū Shūmuchō, vol. 2, 1974–1977, "Shingi—kōshiki," fasc. 1, pp. 67–68) and *Ryūtaiji gyōji jijo* (1559; reprinted in *Zoku Sōtōshū zensho*, vol. 2, pp. 110–111). The *Kōtakuzan Fusaiji nichiyō shingi* (1527; reprinted in *Sōtōshū zensho*, vol. 4, "Shingi," p. 653a), a completely unrelated liturgical text, likewise gives elaborate instructions for the observance of Dōgen's memorial. Other medieval liturgical manuals, such as the *Seigenzan Yōtakuji gyōji no shidai* (ca. 1582; reprinted in *Sōtōshū zensho*, vol. 4), however, do not include memorial services for Dōgen. Moreover, analysis of monastic events mentioned in medieval-period transcripts of lectures also omit Dōgen's memorial (see Bodiford, *Sōtō Zen in Medieval Japan*, p. 160). Of the four texts mentioned above, two of them were used at temples (Ryūtaiji and Yōtakuji) affiliated with Sōjiji, and two were used a temples (Shōbōji and Fusaiji) that functioned as independent

heads of their own factions. In this regard, it is significant to note that Fusaiji's instructions command the participation of representatives from affiliated branch temples.

25. Hirose, "Eiheiji no suiun to fukkō undō," pp. 472–477.

26. Ibid., p. 527.

27. Ibid., pp. 525–530; and Hirose Ryōkō, "Bakufu no tōsei to Eiheiji," in Sakurai, ed., *Eiheijishi,* vol. 1, pp. 664–665.

28. I was prompted to explore this topic when I read Sakurai's history of Eiheiji (*Eiheijishi,* 2 vols., 1982) and noticed how much of that text is devoted to records of Dōgen memorial services.

29. Hirose Ryōkō, "Bakufu no tōsei to Eiheiji," in Sakurai, ed., *Eiheijishi,* pp. 666–667. The sangha hall (*sōdō*), along with the buddha hall (*butsuden*) and dharma hall (*hattō*), represents the presence of the three jewels (*sanbō*) within the monastery. As such, the translation of *sōdō* as "monks hall" is incorrect. I thank T. Griffith Foulk and Yifa for drawing my attention to this point.

30. For the 1702 and 1752 services, see Kumagai and Yoshida, "Shūtō fukko undō to Eiheiji," in Sakurai, ed., *Eiheijishi,* pp. 836–837, 976–978.

31. Kumagai Chūkō, "Bakumatsuki no Eiheiji," in Sakurai, ed., *Eiheijishi,* vol. 2, p. 1293.

32. Yoshioka Hakudō, "Meiji ki no Eiheiji," in Sakurai, ed., *Eiheijishi,* vol. 2, pp. 1380–1389.

33. Kumagai, "Bakumatsuki no Eiheiji," in Sakurai, ed., *Eiheijishi,* p. 1266.

34. Yoshioka Hakudō, "Taishō-Shōwa ki no Eiheiji," in Sakurai, ed., *Eiheijishi,* vol. 2, p. 1455.

35. Kumagai and Yoshida, "Shūtō fukko undō to Eiheiji," in Sakurai, ed., *Eiheijishi,* pp. 991–992.

36. Kumagai Chūkō, "Koki fukko to Gentō Sokuchū zenji," in Sakurai, ed., *Eiheijishi,* vol. 2, pp. 1017–1022.

37. The designation "Tōshō shinkun" is the exact wording used by Gentō Sokuchū in this document. Although Ieyasu's official posthumous title was that of a local buddha or bodhisattva (*daigongen*), he was just as commonly referred to as the divine ruler. For the regulations in question, see: *Eiheiji sho hatto* (1615), in Ōkubo, ed., *Sōtōshū komonjo,* no. 28, vol. 1, pp. 20–21. Regarding the interpretation of *kakun,* see William M. Bodiford, "Dharma Transmission in Sōtō Zen: Manzan Dōhaku's Reform Movement," *Monumenta Nipponica,* vol. 46, no. 4 (1991), p. 450.

38. For the original documents summarized above, see Kumagai, "Koki fukko to Gentō Sokuchū zenji," in Sakurai, ed., *Eiheijishi,* pp. 1125–1190.

39. Because the preface to this work is dated 1794, that same year usually is erroneously listed as its date of publication. See Kumagai, "Koki fukko to Gentō

Sokuchū zenji," in Sakurai, ed., *Eiheijishi*, pp. 1057–1058. Although the *Eihei shingi* first appeared in print in 1667, Gentō Sokuchū's revised 1799 version became the standard (*rufu*) edition. The history of this text prior to 1667 is not known.

40. Kumagai, "Bakumatsuki no Eiheiji," in Sakurai, ed., *Eiheijishi*, pp. 1291–1311. Reference works disagree as to the exact dates of Gaun Dōryū's life. Here, I provide those given in *Eiheijishi*.

41. Yoshioka, "Meiji ki no Eiheiji," in Sakurai, ed., *Eiheijishi*, p. 1390.

42. Sakurai, ed., *Eiheijishi*, p. 1555.

43. See *Teiho Kenzeiki* (reprinted in reprinted in *Sōtōshū zensho*, vol. 17, "Shiden," no. 2), p. 15. Cf. Kawamura, ed., *Shohon taikō Eihei kaisan Dōgen zenji gyōjō Kenzeiki*, p. 2.

44. Kawamura Kōdō, "Eihei kaisan Dōgen zenji gyōjō Kenzei ki kaidai," in Kawamura, ed., *Shohon taikō Eihei kaisan Dōgen zenji gyōjō Kenzeiki*, p. 201a.

45. Kawamura, ed., *Shohon taikō Eihei kaisan Dōgen zenji gyōjō Kenzeiki*, p. 126.

46. Ibid., p. 136.

47. Kumagai, "Koki fukko to Gentō Sokuchū zenji," in Sakurai, ed., *Eiheijishi*, p. 1223.

48. Ibid., pp. 1222–1223. The *Teiho Kenzeiki zue* (illustrated by Zuikō Chingyū and Daiken Hōju) is reprinted in *Sōtōshū zensho*, vol. 17, "Shiden," no. 2. New editions of this text, some will full-color illustrations were issued recently in time for Dōgen's 750th memorial.

49. Kumagai, "Bakumatsuki no Eiheiji," in Sakurai, ed., *Eiheijishi*, p. 1272.

50. Ibid., pp. 1266, 1271.

51. Ibid., pp. 1276–1281.

52. Kawamura, "Eihei kaisan Dōgen zenji gyōjō Kenzeiki kaidai," pp. 202–204.

53. Bodiford, *Sōtō Zen in Medieval Japan*, pp. 134–135.

54. Yokozeki Ryōin, *Edo jidai Tōmon seiyō* (Tokyo: Bukkyōsha, 1938), p. 825.

55. Ryōin, *Edo jidai Tōmon seiyō*, pp. 909–912.

56. Kumagai, "Koki fukko to Gentō Sokuchū zenji," in Sakurai, ed., *Eiheijishi*, p. 1035.

57. Today, the *Honzan* edition of the *Shōbōgenzō* consists of 95 chapters. Five of those chapters, however, were not added until 1906. In 1796, when publication of the *Shōbōgenzō* as a whole was permitted, publication of five chapters ("Den'e," "Busso," "Shisho," "Jishō zanmai," and "Jukai") remained prohibited because they concerned religious secrets (such as dharma transmission ceremonies). See Kumagai, "Koki fukko to Gentō Sokuchū zenji," in Sakurai, ed., *Eiheijishi*, p. 1035.

58. For most scholarly purposes, the best small edition of Dōgen's writings is Ōkubo, ed., *Dōgen zenji zenshū*, 2 vols. plus a supplement. For detailed textual

investigation of the various premodern versions of Dōgen's *Shōbōgenzō*, though, one must turn to the *Eihei shōbōgenzō shūsho taisei*, 25 volumes plus a supplement (Tokyo: Taishūkan shoten, 1974–1982).

59. Yoshioka, "Meiji ki no Eiheiji," in Sakurai, ed., *Eiheijishi*, pp. 1393–1395.

CHAPTER 10

1. Kagamishima Genryū estimated Tenkei's works appropriately and restored his proper position in the assessment of his work in *Dōgen zenji to sono monryū* (Tokyo: Seishin shobō, 1961). Also, Shibe Ken'ichi published over 30 essays that refer to Tenkei's thought from 1984 to 1999.

2. See, for example, Harada Kōdō, "Kōan kenkyū: Genjōkōan and kosoku-kōan," *Indogaku Bukkyōgaku kenkyū*, vol. 30–32 (1982).

3. Ishii Shūdō, *Sōdai Zenshūshi no kenkyū* (Tokyo: Daitō shuppansha, 1987), pp. 367–369.

4. The outset of analyzing Sōtō studies is the work of Yamanouchi Shun'yū, who published *Sōtōshu ni okeru zaike shūgaku no teishō* in 1990 and since then has been considering continually the contemporary approaches of Dōgen and Sōtō studies.

5. Matsumoto Shirō, "Dentō Shūgaku kara Hihan Shūgaku e," *Shūgaku kenkyū*, vol. 40 (1998), p. 18.

Glossary of Sino–Japanese Terms

General List of Terms Used by Multiple Authors

Baso/Mazu 馬祖

Bendōwa 辨道話

Ben-Gen-Butsu 辨現佛

Bukkyō (Buddhist Teachings) 佛教

Bukkyō (Buddhist Sutras) 佛經

Butsudō 仏道

Daibutsuji 大仏寺

Daigo 大悟

Dainichi Nōnin 大日能忍

Daruma 達磨

Den'e 傳衣

Dōgen 道元

Dōgen zenji zenshū 道元禅師全集

Echizen 越前

Eihei kōroku 永平広録

Eihei shingi 永平清規

Eiheiji 永平寺

Eisai 栄西

Ejō 懷弉

Fukanzazengi 不観坐禅儀

Fushukuhanpō 赴粥飯法

gedō 外道

Genjōkōan 現成公案

Goroku/yulu 語録

Goshō 御抄

Hiei 比叡

Hōkyōki 宝慶記

hongaku 本覺

Hongzhi 宏智

Huineng 慧能

Ishii Seijun 石井清純

Ishii Shūdō 石井修道

jinzū 神通

Kagamishima Genryū 鏡島元隆

Kawamura Kōdō 河村孝道

Keizan 螢山

kōan/gong'an 公案

Kōzengokokuron 興禪護國論

li/ri 理

Linji Yixuan 臨濟義玄

Mana Shōbōgenzō 漢字正法眼蔵

Matsumoto Shirō 松本史郎

Myōzen 明全

Rinzai/Linji 臨済

Rujing 如淨
Senne 詮慧
shikan taza 只管打座
shinjin datsuraku 身心脱落
shōbō 正法
Shōbōgenzō 正法眼藏
Shōbōgenzō kikigakishō
　　正法眼藏聞書抄
Shushōgi 修証義
Sōtō/Caodong 曹洞
Tendai 天台
Yanagida Seizan 柳田聖山
Yongming Yanshou 永明延壽
Yoshizu Yoshihide 吉津宜英
zazen 坐禅
Zazenshin 座禅儀
zenji 禪師
Zhaozhou 趙州

Chapter 1. Bodiford, "Textual Genealo-
　　gies of Dōgen"

Baika shisho 梅花嗣書
Benchū 辨註
Bendōwa monge 辨道話聞解
Beppon 別本
besshū 別輯
Bonsei 梵清
Chinzo 陛座
Chōenji 長圓寺
Daichi 大智
Donki 曇希
Eihei gen zenji goroku
　　永平元禪師語録
Eishōji 永昌寺
Fusan Gentotsu 斧山玄現
Gasan 峨山
Gentō Sokuchū 玄透即中
Gesshū Sōko 月舟宗胡

Giin 義尹
Hōkyōji 寶慶寺
Jakuen 寂圓
Jōkōji 成高寺
Jōrokuji 丈六寺
kan 卷
kana 假字
keji 假字
Kenzei 建撕
Kenzeiki 建撕記
Kōroku 廣録
Kōshō Chidō 光紹智堂
Kōshū 晃周
Kōzen 晃全
kunten 訓點
Kyōgō 經豪
kyūsō 舊草
maki 卷
mana 眞字
Manzan Dōhaku 卍山道白
Meihō 明峰
Monkaku 門鶴
Nenpyō sanbyakusoku funōgo
　　拈評三百則不能語
nissō denbō shamon Dōgen
　　入宋傳法沙門道元
rufu 流布
ryakuroku 略録
Ryūsui Nyotoku 龍水如得
sasshi 冊子
Shigetsu Ein 指月慧印
Shinbōji 眞法寺
shinji 眞字
shinjin datsuraku 心塵脱略 (dropping
　　mind and dust)
shinsō 新草
Shōbōgenzō byakujaketsu
　　正法眼藏闢邪決
Shōbōgenzō monge 正法眼藏聞解

shūi 拾遺

sōan hon 草案本

Sōgo 宋吾

Sotō (or Bankō) Dōki 祖刀 (or 萬光) 道輝

Tenkei Denson 天桂傳尊

Tsūgen Jakurei 通幻寂靈

Tuigeng Dening 退耕德寧

Wuwai Yiyuan 無外義遠

Xutang Zhiyu 虛堂智愚

Yōkōan 永興庵 (a.k.a., Yōkōji 永興寺)

Yōkōji 永光寺

Zenkō 善晧

Zongmen tongyao 宗門統要

zuimon kiroku 隨聞記錄

Chapter 2. Heine, "What Is on the Other Side? Delusion and Reality in Dōgen's 'Genjōkōan'"

ai 愛

aijaku 愛惜

an 案

Bashō 芭蕉

Biyanlu 碧巖録

Busshō 仏性

busshō kenzai ron 仏性顕在論

busshō naizai ron 仏性内在論

busshō shūken ron 仏性修顕論

Changzong 常聰

chōshu 聽取

Dahui 大恵

Denkōroku 伝光録

eto 會取

Fayan Qingliang 法眼清涼

Fujiwara Teika 藤原定価

gaikyo 外境

genjō 現成

genjō shite iru kōan 現成している公案

Hachidainingaku 八大人覚

Hakamaya Noriaki 袴谷 憲昭

hakanashi はかなし

Hihan Bukkyō 批判仏教

hitotsu no koto 一つの事

honshō-myōshū 本証妙修

hō [dharma] 法

hō [side] 方

hongaku shisō 本覚思想

Huanglong 龍

Huineng 惠能

ippō-gūjin 一法究盡

iro 色

Ishii Seijun 石井清純

jiko 自己

Jingde chuandeng lu 景德傳燈

Jingqing 鏡清

jisetsu 時節

jū-hōi 住法位

kanbun 漢文

kanshi 漢詩

Keisei sanshoku 谿聲山色

Kegon Chan 華厳禅

Kentōkagodō 見逃課悟道

kikigaki 聞書

kō 公

koe 声

Komazawa University Daigaku Bukkyōgakubu 駒澤大学佛教学部

Kōshōji 興聖寺

kurashi くらし

Kurebayashi Kōdō 榑林皓堂

Kyōgō 経豪

Lingyun 靈雲

Lu 廬

mayoi (madoi, mei) 迷い

medekeri 愛でけり

mito 見取

mizu no oto 水の音

mujō-kan 無常感 (emotional pain of impermanence)

mujō-kan 無常観 (contemplative observation of impermanence)

Nishiari Bokusan 西有穆山

nokori no kaitoku santoku のこりの 海徳山徳

ōzora 大空

Qingyuan 青原

sangai-yuishin 三界唯心

satori 悟

shinjingakudō 身心学道

shinjin wo kosu 心身を挙す

shō 證

Shōbōgenzō keiteki 正法眼蔵啓迪

shōsuru 證する

shu (to) 取

shūgyō 修行

Shukke 出家

sokushin-zebutsu 即心是物

Su Shi 蘇軾

Tiantong 天童

Tomiyama Sōei 富山祖英

Udonge 優曇華

waka 和歌

ware ni arazaru われにあらざる

Wumenguan 無紋間

Xiangyan 香嚴

xuan (gen) 玄

Yakō 野光

yamanaki kaichū 山なき海中

Yōkōshū 楊光秀

zengo saidan 前後際斷

Zongmen liandeng huiyao 宗門聯燈會要

Chapter 3. Foulk, "'Just Sitting'? Dōgen's Take on Zazen, Sutra Reading, and Other Conventional Buddhist Practices"

ai raihai あい禮拜

akudō 惡道

anraku no hōmon 安樂の法門

Baizhang 百丈

bendō 辨道

bendō kufū 辨道功夫

Bonmōkyō 梵網經

bosatsu kai 菩薩戒

Bukkyōgo daijiten 佛教語大辞典

buppō 佛法

busshin 佛心

Busshō zenji 佛照禪師

busso 佛祖

busso daidō 佛祖大道

busso no e 佛祖の會

butsubutsu soso 佛佛祖祖

butsuden 佛殿

chan 禪

Chanyuan qinggui 禪苑清規

chiji 知事

chishiki 知識

Dahui Zonggao 大慧宗杲

daidai 大大

daiji yori naru gyōji 大慈よりなる行持

daishō ryōjō 大小兩乘

daishu 大衆

daiten sanpai 大展三拜

Daoxuan 道宣

datsuraku no kankin 脱落の看經

dōchō oshō 堂頭和尚

doji 土地

dojijin 土地神

doji ryūjin 土地竜神

Dōkai 道楷

dokkyō 讀經

dokuju 讀誦

dōkyū 道舊

dōshin 道心

Ekō 回向

enju 園頭

enjudō 延壽堂

enza 宴坐

Fozhao 佛照

fusatsu 布薩

fushin samu 普請作務

fuyō 不用

fuyō no kankin 不用の看經

gakori 我箇裏

ganzei 眼睛

ganzeiri 眼睛裏

ge 悔

ge ango 夏安居

gedō no ken 外道の見

Gensha 玄沙

gisoku 儀則

gō 業

gogai 五蓋

goji shōbō 護持正法

goyoku 五欲

Guang Fozhao 光佛照

gudōshin 求道心

gyō 行

gyōji 行持

Gyōji 行持

hai 拜

haimon 拜問

hajime yori はじめより

hakken 法眷

Hannyatara sonja 般若多羅尊者

hatsurō 發露

hishin 非心

hishiryō 非思量

hitasura ni ひたすらに

hō 法

Hōjō 法常

hōki 法器

hōkyaku 抛却

Hōkyō 寶慶

Hōnen 法然

honshō 本證

ichi daiji 一大事

ino 維那

innen 因緣

ittō 一等

ji 持

Jingshan 徑山

jijuyū zanmai 自受用三昧

jinkō 沈香

jō 定

Jōdo 淨土

Jōdo shin 淨土淨眞

jōdō 上堂

jōbutsu sakuso 成佛作祖

jōji 淨治

jōjū 常住

jōshin 淨信

jōten 常轉

Jūundō shiki 重雲堂式

Jūbutsumyō 十佛名

Juefan Huihong 覺範慧洪

jukai 受戒

juko 頌古

jundō 巡堂

jūni hai 十二拜

junsui zen 純粹禪

kafuza 跏趺坐

kaigo 開悟

kaihon 戒本

kaikyō 戒經

kamawazu ni かまわずに

kan 看

Kankin 看經

kankindō 看經堂

kankingen 看經眼

kankin no za 看經の座

kankin sen 看經錢

ke 家

Keisei sanshiki 谿聲山色

ken shukushin dōjō no hai
　　建祝聖道場の牌

kesa 袈裟

Kesa kudoku 袈裟功徳

kesshutsu 抉出

ketsuge 結夏

kin 經

ko 乎

kō ni kunjiru 香に薫じる

kobutsu hō 古佛法

kokoro no taza 心の打坐

kosoku 古則

kosoku kōan 古則公案

kū 空

kudoku 功徳

kuyō 供養

kyo 舉

kyō 經

kyō 教

kyōdō 經堂

kyōke 教家

kyōzō 經藏

kyūhai 九拜

kyūri 究理

kyūri zakan 但究理坐看

Lizong 理宗

meishinteki 迷信的

menpeki 面壁

metsuzai 滅罪

mi no taza 身の打坐

mochiizu もちいず

mon 問

Monju bosatsu 文殊菩薩

mu dōshin 無道心

mujō no daihō 無上の大法

mondō 問答

Mumonkan 無門關

Musai oshō 無際和尚

Mushogo 無所悟

mushotoku 無所得

myōjutsu 妙術

myōri 名利

namu Amidabu 南無阿彌陀佛

nehan myōshin 涅槃妙心

nehandō 涅槃堂

nenbutsu 念佛

nendo 念度

nenju 念誦

nichi 日

Nihon 日本

ninji 人事

Ninnō kyō 仁王經

nisshitsu 入室

nyorai no shōgyō 如來之聖教

nyoze kyō 如是經

nyūge 入夏

rai 禮

raihai 禮拜

Raihai tokuzui 禮拜得髓

rikutsuppoi 理屈っぽい

rinken 隣肩

rintan 隣單

rinzō 輪藏

rōka 廊下

rokudo 六度

rōrō 老老

ryōten sanpai 兩展三拜

ryūten 龍天

sai 齋

Saishō ō kyō 最勝王經

san 懺

sanbō 三寶

sandoku 三毒

sangaku 三學

sange 懺悔

sange no tame 懺悔のため

Sangemon 懺悔文

sangeshiki 懺悔式

Sanji gō 三時業

sanken 參見

sanmapattei 三摩鉢底

sanpachi nenju 三八念誦

sanpai 三拜

sanzen 參禪

sanzen gakudō 參禪學道

sarani さらに

satori さとり

seijō 清淨

sekenteki 世間的

Sekimon rinkanroku 石門林間録

Sekitō 石頭

senbō 懺法

senshi kobutsu 先師古佛

senshi Tendō oshō 先師天童和尚

seppō 説法

Seppō 雪峯

seshu 施主

seshu ekō 施主回向

sha 者

shakku ruitoku 積功累徳

shami 沙彌

Shami jukai bon 沙彌受戒本

shi 之

Shibun ritsu 四分律

shichi butsu 七佛

shie shigō 紫衣師號

shihaku 師伯

shikan 祇管

shikan tasui 只管打睡

Shimen 石門

Shimen linjian lu 石門林間録

shimushiki 四無色

shimushikijō 四無色定

shin 身

shin 心

shingi 身儀 (deported body)

shingi 清規 (monastic rules)

shinjin datsuraku no taza
　　　身心脱落の打坐

shinjin datsuraku suru koto wo eyo 身
　　　心脱落することをえよ

shinnen 心念

Shinran 親鸞

shiryō 思量

shisho 嗣書

Shisho 嗣書

shishuku 師叔

shitoku 始得

shizen 四禪

shō 證

shōe 證會

shōdō 照堂

shōjin 精進

shōjō 小乘

shōken 相見

shoki 書記

shōkō 燒香

shōkō gyōji 燒香行事

shōkō raihai 燒香禮拜

shōkō jisha 燒香侍者

shoku su 觸す

shōnin 聖人

shōsetsu 聖節

shōsō 聖僧

shu 修

shuryō 衆寮

shusan 修懺

shushō 修證

shuso 首座

shūzen 習禪

sodō 祖道

sōdō 僧堂

sokurei sanpai 觸禮三拜

somuku 背く

sonshuku 尊宿

soshi 祖師

soshi no jiso 祖師兒孫

sōshiki 相識

tadashi ただし

tanryō 單寮

tanza 端坐

taza 打坐

tekiteki menju 嫡嫡面授

ten 轉

tendoku 轉讀

Tendōzan keitokuji nyojō zenji goroku 天童山景德寺如淨禪師續語録

tenkin 轉經

tenshin 點心

Tiantai 天臺

tōhai 答拜

tōryō haiga 到寮拜賀

tsūkansu 都監寺

undō 雲堂

Unmon kōroku 雲門廣録

Wuji 無際

Xu gaoseng zhuan 續高僧傳

ya 也

Yōgi 楊岐

yokusu 浴主

za 坐

zagu 坐具

zaikon 罪根

zangi 慚愧

Zanmai ō zanmai 三昧王三昧

zasui 坐睡

zazen bendō 坐禪辨道

zen 禪

zendo 禪度

zendō 禪堂

zenji 禪師

zenke ryū 禪家流

zenna 禪那

zennasu 禪和子

Zennen shingi 禪苑清規

zenshū 禪宗

zenso 禪祖

zensu 禪子

Zhuoan Deguang 拙菴德光

zōsu 藏主

Zuimonki 隨聞記

zunnan 童行

Chapter 4. Heine, "A Day in the Life: Dōgen's View of Chan/Zen Lineage in *Shōbōgenzō* 'Gyōji'"

Chōmei 長明

chuandeng lu 伝灯録

Congrong lu 従容録

Dahui 大慧

Daruma-shū 達磨宗

Deguang 德光

Denkōroku 伝光録

Deshan 德山

Donghan 洞山

en-mitsu-zen-kai 圓密禪戒

Enni 圓爾

Furong Daokai 芙蓉道楷

Gakudōyōjinshū 学道用心集

Ganzei 眼睛

Gyōji 行持

gyōji dōkan 道環

Heike monogatari 平家物語

Hōjōki 方丈記

hongaku shisō 本覚思想

Hongzhi 宏智
Hongzhou 洪州
Hōsshō 法性
Huanglong 黄竜
Ishii Shūdō 石井修道
Jingde chuandeng lu 景徳伝灯録
Kajō 家常
Kenninji 建仁寺
kōso 高祖
Menju 面授
Myōzen 明全
Nishio Minoru 西尾実
Rujing yulu 如浄語録
Sansuikyō 山水経
Senmen 洗面
Senjō 洗浄
Shisho 嗣書
Shitou 石頭
shū 宗
shushō ittō 修証一等
Shushōgi 修証記
taiso 太祖
Tōfukuji 東福寺
Uji 有時
Yasuraoko Kōsaku 安良岡康作
Wuzu Fayan 五祖法演
yūgen 幽玄
zuda 頭陀
zudagyō 頭陀行
zushi 祖師

Chapter 5. Leighton, "Dōgen's
    Approach to Traning in
    Eihei kōroku"

Hatano Yoshishige 波多野義重
hōgo 法語
jijūyū zanmai 自受用三昧
jōdō 上堂

Jōdō Shinshū 浄土真宗
Kanzeon 観世音
ri 理
shōsan 小參
shushō no itto 修証の一等
uji 有時

Chapter 6. Ishii Shūdō, "Dōgen Zen
    and Song Dynasty China"

Anchan 安禪
Ayuwang, Mount 阿育王山
Baoqing 寶慶
Baozang lun 寶藏論
bendō 弁道
benjue 本覺
biguan 壁觀
bu zeng wu 不曾悟
busshō e 仏生会
butsu jōdō e 仏成道会
butsu nehan e 仏涅槃会
Butuoluo, Mount 補陀洛山
Caodong 曹洞
chanbing 禪病
Chanti Weizhao 闡提惟照
Chanyuan zhuquanji duxu
    禪源諸詮集都序
cheng kejiu 成窠臼
Da Fu Fengmi 答富楓密
Da Li Langzhong 答李郎中
Da xu sili 答許司理
Dabei zhanglao 大悲長老
Dahong, Mount 大洪山
Dahui Jue chanshi yulu
    大慧覺禪師語録
Dahui nianpu 大慧年譜
Dahui pujue chanshi taming 大慧普
    覺禪師塔銘
Dahui shu 大慧書

Dahui Zonggao 大慧宗杲

Dahui Zongmen wuku
　大慧宗門武庫

Daibutsu 大仏

Dainichi Nōnin 大日能忍

daiwu chan 待悟禅

daiwu wei ze 待悟為則

Danxia, Mount 丹霞山

Danxia Zichun 丹霞子淳

Danxia Zichun songgu 丹霞子淳頌古

Daohuan 道環

daoli 道理

Dayang Jingxuan 大陽警玄

Dayong an ming 大用庵銘

Dazhidu lun 大智度論

Dōgen no Dai'e hyō
　道元の大慧評

Dōgen zenji zenshū 道元禅師全集

Fang Shuwen qing pushuo
　方數文請普説

fangbian 方便

Fangwai daoyou qing pushuo
　方外道友請普説

fawang 法王

Feng Wenshu 馮温舒

fofo yaoji, zuzu jiyao 佛佛要機,
　祖祖機要

Fozhao Deguang 佛照德光

Fu Zhirou 富直柔

Furong Daokai 芙蓉道楷

Fuzan Gentotsu 斧山玄鈯突

Gakudōyōjinshū 学道用心集

gen 現

guandai 管帶

Guanyin 觀音

Guifeng Zongmi 圭峰宗密

gushi 顧視

Guyun Daoquan 孤雲道權

Heze Shenhui 荷澤神會

Hotsu bodaishin 発菩提心

hua 話

huan 環

huzhong tiandi 壺中田地

hongaku mon 本覚門

Hongzhi guanglu 宏智廣録

Hongzhi yulu 宏智語録

Hongzhi Zhengjue 宏智正覺

Hongzhou Chan 洪州禪

honshō 本証

huatou 話頭

inga no shoyū 因果の所由

jian 鑑

jiangxin dengwu 將心等悟

jiaochan yizhi 教禪一致

jiewai 劫外

jimo 默

Jing, Mount 徑山

Jingde chuandeng lu 景德傳燈録

Jinshin inga 深信因果

Jishō zammai 自証三味

jō 成

jōdō 上堂

kanhua 看話

ke zhou ji jian 刻舟記劍

ke zhou qiu jian 刻舟求劍

kenkō fusetsu 建康普説

Kippō Vihara 吉峰精舎

Kobusshin 古仏心

Kumu Facheng 枯木法成

kyōge betsuden 教外別伝

kyōzen icchi 教禅一致

Letan Wenzhun 泐潭文準

li 李 (square)

Lidaizhe dan qiqing pushuo
　礼待者断七請普説

Lingyin Monastery 靈隱寺

Linji 臨濟

Linji lu 臨濟録

Linji zhengzong ji 臨濟正宗記

Lu, Mount 廬山

Lushi chunqiu 呂氏春秋

Menju 面授

Miaogao tai 妙高台

Mikkyō 密教

Mingyue tang 明月堂

mo er chang zhao 默而常照

momo er zizhao 默默而自照

mozhao 默照

Mozhao ming 默照銘

Mujū Ichien 無住一円

muri ewa zen 無理会話禅

Myōzen 明全

Nengren Chan Monastery 能仁禪寺

Ōsaku sendaba 王索仙陀婆

Panro wuzhi lun 般若無知論

pingshi chan 平實禪

Pudeng lu 普燈録

Pushuo 普説

Puzhao Monastery 普照寺

qidian badao 七顛八倒

qingzuo 靜坐

quan shi jue 全是覺

Renchū 練中

sanjie weixin 三界唯心

sankyō icchi shisō 三教一致思想

Sanlun 三論

Sansuikyō 山水經

Senpukuji 泉福寺

Sengcan 僧璨

sengtang 僧堂

Sengtang ji 僧堂記

Sengzhao 僧肇

Senkō 千光

Sesshin sesshō 説心説性

shangtang 上堂

shen 神

sheng yuanjia 生冤家

shi 事

Shi Wang Tongban daren 示王通判大任

shigaku mon 始覚門

shijue 始覺

Shōben 勝弁

shoshin 初心

shouzuo 首座

Shunjū 春秋

shushō funi 修証不二

sōdō 僧堂

Songshi 宋史

Sōtōshū zensho 曹洞宗全書

Taiping Xingguo Cloister 太平興國院

taming 塔銘

Tendō shōkaku oshō geju shinmeiki monge 天童正覚和尚偈頌箴銘記聞解

Tianning Monastery 天寧寺

Tiantong, Mount 天童山

Tiantong Zongjue 天童宗珏

tenzo 典座

Tenzokyōkun 典座教訓

Touzi Yiqing 投子義青

tuoluo 脱落

Uji Kannondōri-in sōdō kanjin sho 宇治観音導利院僧堂勧進疏

wanfa weishi 萬法惟識

Wang Boxiang 王伯庠

wanghuai 忘懷

watō 話頭

wei momo er zizhao 唯默默而自照

wenzi 文字

wu 悟

Wuji Liaopai 無際了派

wumen 悟門

wushi 無事

wushi chan 無事禪
wushi hui 無事會
wuxingduan 無形段
Xi 奚
Xi 隰縣 (district)
xiaocan 小參
xin 心
xindi famen 心地法門
xing 性
Xinghuang Falang 興皇法朗
Xingye ji 行業記
xinxin ruyi 心心如一
Xinxin ming 信心銘
Xinxin ming niangu 信心銘拈古
Xu'an Huaibi 虛庵懷敝
Xuancheng 宣城
Xuedou Zhijian 雪竇智鑑
Xuefeng, Mount 雪峰山
Xuming 虛明
yan 言
yang 陽
Yangyu Hermitage 洋嶼庵
Yantou 嚴頭
yanyu 言語
yi wu wei ze 以悟為則
yiduan 疑団
yin 隱
Yiyuan 義遠
youhu sanmei 游戲三昧
youjian 游踐
youwu 有無
Yuantong Chongsheng 圓通崇勝禪院
Yuantong Monastery 圓通寺
Yuanwu Keqin 圓悟克勤
yulu 語路
Yunju, Mount 雲居山
Yunju Zhenru Chan Cloister 雲居真如禪院

Yuntai Daoist Temple 雲台道觀
Zhang Jun 張浚
Zhanglu 長蘆
Zhanglu Chongfu Chan Cloister 長蘆崇福禪院
Zhang Shen 張申
Zhao Chao erdashi qing pushuo 照超二大師請普説
Zhao Lingjin 趙令衿
Zhaolun 肇論
Zheng fayan zang 正法眼藏
zhengming 證明
Zhengdao ge 証道歌
zhenshi wuchu 真實悟處
Zhenxie Qinglao 真歇清了
zhiguan 只管
zhiyin 知音
zhiyou 至游
Zhiyou an ming 至游庵銘
zhiyou chan 至游禪
Zhuangzi 莊子
zhuoyi 著意
Zichun 子淳
zizhao 自照
Zōdan shū 雑談集
Zoku Sōtōshū zensho 續曹洞宗全書
zongcheng 宗乘
Zongjing lu 宗鏡録
Zongmen wuku 宗門武庫
zongshi 宗師
zuochan 坐禅
Zuochan zhen 坐禪箴

Chapter 7. Welter, "Zen Syncretism: An Exmination of Dōgen Zen Thought in Light of Yongming Yanshou's Chan Teaching in the *Zongjing Lu*"

Abe Chōichi 阿部肇一

Baizhang Huaihai 百丈懷海

Bankei 盤珪

benyuan xindi 本原心地

Biyan lu 碧巖

Butsukōjōji 佛向上事

Caodong 曹洞

Caoqi 曹溪

Chan 禅

Chanzong 禅宗

chanzong fa 禪宗法

Da zhidu lun 大智度論

Dahui Zonggao 大慧宗杲

Daimitsu 台密

Daizong 代宗

dao 道

Deshan 德山

dō genjō 道現成

Eichō 栄朝

Ehu Dayi 鵝湖大義

Enni Ben'en 圓爾辨圓

Fahua jing 法華經

Fayan Wenyi 法眼文益

fodao 佛道

fofa 佛法

foyi 佛意

foyu 佛語

ge 外

Genbun taishō gendaigoyaku
原文対照現代語訳

Guifeng Zongmi 圭峰宗密

guoshi 國師

Gyōyū 行勇

Hakuin 白隠

Heze 荷澤

Heze Shenhui 荷澤神會

hon menmoku 本面目

hon shugyō 本修行

Hongren 弘忍

Hongzhi 宏智

Huangbo Xiyun 黄檗希運

Huayan jing 華嚴經

Huineng 慧能

Hyakujō 百丈

Ikeda Rosan 池田魯参

Ishii Shūdō 石井修道

Kōzengokokuron 興禅護国論

jia 假

Jiangxi 江西

jiao 教

jiaochan yichi 教禪一致

jiaowai biechuan 教外別傳

jing 經

Jing, Mount 徑山

Jingde chuandeng lu
景德傳燈録

Jingming jing 淨名經

Jishō zanmai 自証三昧

junsui zen 純粋禅

kagō 家業

Kamakura 鎌倉

Kamata Shigeo 鎌田茂雄

Keisei sanshiki 渓声山色

Kenninji 建仁寺

kong 空

Kongōzammai-in 金剛三昧院

kyō bosatsu bō 教菩薩法

kyōge betsuden 教外別伝

liaoyi 了義

Linji Chan 臨濟禪

Jiashe Mateng 迦葉摩騰

Mateng 摩騰

Mazu Daoyi 馬祖道一

miao falianhua 妙法蓮華

Miyan 密言

Mizuno Yaoko 水野弥穂子

Mujō seppō 無情説法

Myōzen 明全

nai 內
Nanyang Huizhong 南陽慧忠
Nanyue 南嶽
Niepan jing 涅槃經
Ōsaku sendaba 王索仙陀婆
Ōbaku 黃檗
Panruo jing 般若經
Qingyuan Xingsi 青原行思
Quanzhou Qianfo xinshu zhu
    zushi song
    泉州千佛新著諸祖頌
Ran Yunhua (Jan Yun-hua) 冉雲華
sanguan 三觀
sanjiao yizhi 三教一致
Sansuikyō 山水経
Shengyan 聖言
shi 事
shikan zazen 祇管座禅
Shingon 真言
Shizen biku 四禅比丘
Shoulengyan jing 首楞嚴經
Sijia yulu 四家語錄
Sikong Benjing 思空本淨
Sishierzhang jing 四十二章經
Sokushin zebutsu 即心是佛
Song 宋
Song gaoseng zhuan 宋高僧傳
Su Dongbo 蘇東坡
Su Shi 蘇軾
Suzong 肅宗
Tamamuro Taijō 圭室諦成
Tan jing 壇經
Tang 唐
ti 體
Tiansheng Guangdeng lu 天聖廣燈錄
Tiantai 天台
Tiantai, Mount 天台山
Tiantai Deshao 天台德韶
wangqing 忘情

wangyou 妄有
wanshan 萬善
Wanshan tonggui ji
    萬善同歸集
weishi 唯識
wenzi 文字
wuliang yi 無量義
Wume guan 無門關
Wuyan 無言
Wuyue 吳越
Xuefeng Yicun 雪峰義存
Yangqi 楊岐
yanjiao 言教
yijiao 義教
yixin 一心
yizong 義宗
yong 用
Yongping 永平
Yunmen 雲門
Zengen shosenshu tojo
    禪源諸詮集都序
Zhanran 湛然
Zhejiang 浙江
Zhiguan fuxing chuan guangjue
    止觀輔行傳廣決
Zhong 中
Zhongyi 忠懿
Zhu Falan 竺法蘭
zong 宗
Zongjing lu 宗鏡錄
zongmen 宗門
Zongmen shigui lun
    宗門十規論
zongzhi 宗師
Zutang ji 祖堂集

Chapter 8. Bielefeldt, "Disarming the
    Superpowers: The *Abhijna* in Eisai
    and Dōgen"

ajari 阿闍梨

baotong 報通

Baizhang Huaihai 百丈懷海

bodai 菩提

bukke no sahan 佛家の茶飯

buppō 佛法

butsu kōjō 佛向上

chaku chaku sōden seru jinzū chie 嫡
　　嫡相傳せる神通智慧

Chūsei zenke no shisō
　　中世禅家の思想

Da'er sanzang 大耳三藏

daigon satta 大權薩埵

dai jinzū 大神通

Dazhidulun 大智度論

Deshan 德山

dixing shentong 地行神通

do 度

Dōgen zenji zenshū 道元禅師全集

Dōgen zenji kenkyū ronshū
　　道元禅師研究論集

Dongshan lu 洞山録

dunwu 頓悟

Enni 圓爾

fanfu 凡夫

fo xiangshang ren 佛向上人

fo liutong 佛六通

Fu Dashi 傅大師

gogen 五眼

Guzunsu yulu 古尊宿語録

hentsū 變通

hokkai kai 法界海

hokkuru shū 北倶盧州

hōni 法爾

hosshin 發心

xin 心

Hu Shi 胡適

huanshi 幻師

Huineng 慧能

Ichikawa Hakugen 市川白弦

itoku 異徳

jian xing cheng fo 見性成佛

jueti 覺體

jin jippō kai 盡十方界

Jingde chuandeng lu 景徳傳燈録

jinsoku 神足

jūriki 十力

junzen 純禅

kenshū 兼修

King Peng Cheng 彭城王

kōmyō 光明

Kōzengokokuron 興禪護國論

kyōge betsuden 教外別傳

kyōshi 經師

Kudenshō 口傳抄

kongsheng 空聲

kongxiang 空相

kyūsan hakkai 九山八海

Liandeng huiyao 聯燈會要

liuru wuji 六入無迹

Linji lu 臨濟録

myōyū 妙用

mokuren 目連

matsudai 末代

matsudai buppō 末代佛法

mitsuyaku 密益

mujin hokkai kai 無盡法界海

muryō asōgi kō 無量阿僧祇劫

Nanyang Huizhong 南陽惠忠

nehan 涅槃

Nihon shisō taikei 日本思想大系

Niutou Farong 牛頭法融

Putidamo nanzang ding shifei lun 菩
　　提達摩南宗定是非論

roku jinzū arakan 六神通阿羅漢

rokugun biku 六群比丘

ronshi 論師

reiken 靈驗

sabanya kai 薩婆若海

saitenjiku koku no dozoku
    西天竺國の土俗

san jidō 三示導

san jigen 三示現

sanmyō 三明

sejin ketsugi 世人決疑

shamon isshaku no shinjitsu tai 沙門
    一隻の眞實體

shen 神

sheng 聖

Shenhui 神會

Shenhui heshang yiji 神會和尚遺集

shentong 神通

shentong zuoyong 神通作用

Shibun ritsu 四分律

shintan koku yori higashi
    震旦國より東

shō jinzū 小神通

shōkai 性海

shu 守

shugyō 修行

sō 相

sokushin jōbutsu 即身成佛

Suzuki Kakuzen 鈴木格禅

Tajinzū 他心通

Tendaishū zensho 天台宗全集

tenma gedō 天魔外道

Tenpuku bon 天福本

Tōkai 等海

Tōkai kudenshō 等海口傳抄

tong 通

uhatsurashiki 優鉢羅色

wu shentong pusa 無神通菩薩

wuyun louzhi 五蘊漏質

wuzhong tong 五種通

wuxiang 無相

wuxin 無心

wuzheng 無生

wuzhu 無主

xiangyi 相異

xin 信

xingqian 形遷

yaotong 妖通

yehu jing 野狐精

yisheng 一乘

yitong 依通

Yuan 緣

Zazen ron 坐禪論

Zenmon hōgo shū 禪門法語集

zheng 證

zheng ke 證果

zhenshi shenbian 眞實神變

zhibian 智變

zhiti 智體

zongji 蹤跡

zui bukesiyi ren 最不可思議人

Chapter 9. Bodiford, "Remembering
    Dōgen: Eiheiji and Dōgen Hagiog-
    raphy"

ango 安居

Busso 佛祖

Chion'in 知恩院

Chōjuin 長壽院

daibonshō 大梵鐘

Daijiji 大持寺

Daijōji 大乘寺

Daiken Hōju 大賢鳳樹

daikō shōden zenji 大功正傳禪師

Dentōin 傳燈院

Dōgen no tekison 道元の的孫

Eihei Dōgen oshō kōroku
    永平道元和尚廣録

Eihei kaisan gogyōjō
    永平開山御行状

Eihei senjū 永平先住

Eihei shō shingi 永平小清規

Eiheiji kaisan kigyō hokke kōshiki 永
    平開山忌行法華講式
Eiheiji sho hatto 永平寺諸法度
fūro 風呂
furōkaku 不老閣
Fusai Zenkyū 普濟善救
Fusaiji 普濟寺
Gasan 峨山
Gaun Dōryū 臥雲童龍
Gentō Sokuchū 玄透即中
Genzō e 眼藏會
Gikai 義介
Giun oshō goroku 義雲和尚語録
Goen'yū tennō 後圓融天皇
gozan 五山
Gyōji jijo 行事次序
hinkan 賓館
Hirose Ryōkō 広瀬良弘
hokke kōshiki 法華講式
Hōkyōji 寶慶寺
honchō Sōtō daiichi dōjō
    本朝曹洞第一道場
Hōnen 法然
Honganji 本願寺
honji 本寺
honzan 本山
hōon jukai e 報恩授戒會
hōtō no honzan 法統の本山
Imaeda Aishin 今枝愛真
Itō Shūken 伊藤秀憲
Jakuen 寂圓
Jishō zanmai 自證三昧
jitō no honzan 寺統の本山
Jōdo Shinshū 浄土眞宗
jōdō 上堂
Jōdoshū 浄土宗
Jōyō daishi hōon kōshiki
    承陽大師報恩講式
Jōyōan 承陽庵

Jōyōden 承陽殿
jūgonen sensō 十五年戰爭
Jukai 受戒
Kagamishima Sōjun 鏡島宗純
Kaisetsu 解説
kakun 家訓
Kan sansetsu 關三刹
Keiyōji 慶養寺
Keizan Jōkin 瑩山紹瑾
Keizan shingi 瑩山清規
Kichijō kō 吉祥講
kinen hai 記念碑
Kohō Chisan 孤峰智璨
koki 古規
Kōtakuzan Fusaiji nichiyō shingi
    廣澤山普濟寺日用清規
kuin 庫院
Kumagai Chūkō 熊谷忠興
kyōzō 經藏
Matsuda Fumio 松田文雄
matsuji 末寺
Meihō Sotetsu 明峰素哲
Minchō karei no shinki
    明朝花麗の新規
Monkaku 門鶴
Myōzen 妙全
Nakamikado Nobutane 中御門宣胤
Nihon Sōtō daiichi dōjō
    日本曹洞第一道場
Nishiari Bokusan 西有穆山
Nobutane kyōki 宣胤卿記
nyo hō e 如法衣
Oka Sōtan 丘宗潭
Ōkubo Dōshū 大久保道舟
Ōtani Teppu 大谷哲夫
rakan 羅漢
Reibaiin 靈梅院
ryō daihonzan 兩大本山
Ryōan 了庵

ryōrō 兩廊

Ryūtaiji gyōji jijo 龍泰寺行事次序

Saian Urin 載庵禹隣

Sakurai Shūyū 桜井秀雄

sanmon 山門

Seigenzan Yōtakuji gyōji no shidai
　　青原山永澤寺行事之次第

Sesonji Yukisue 世尊寺行季

Shingi 清規

Shinran 親鸞

Shisho 嗣書

Shōbō shingi 正法清規

Shōbōgenzō zatsubun 正法眼藏雜文

Shoshū chokugōki 諸宗勅號記

sō honzan 総本山

sōdō 僧堂

Sōjiji 総持寺

sōryō 僧寮

Takahashi Zenryū 高橋全隆

Tamamuro Taijō 圭室諦成

Teiho Kenzeiki 訂補建撕記

Teiho Kenzeiki zue 訂補建撕記圖會

teishō 提唱

Tenkai 天海

Tenshin 天眞

Tō Eizan 東叡山

tōin 塔院

Tōkoku dentōin gorō gosoku narabi ni
　　gyōgō ryakki洞谷傳燈院五老
　　悟則並行業略記

Tōkoku gyōji jijo 洞谷行事次序

Tōkoku jinmirai honji to nasubeki no
　　okibumi
　　洞谷盡未來可成本寺之置文

Tōkoku jinmiraisai okibumi
　　洞谷盡未來際置文

Tōkokuki 洞谷記

Tokugawa Ieyasu 徳川家康

Tōshō shinkun 東照神君

Yōkōji 永光寺

Yokozeki Ryōin 横関了胤

Yoshida Dōkō 吉田道興

zenji 禪師

Zenrinji 禪林寺

Zuichō 瑞長

Zuichō hon Kenzeiki 瑞長本建撕記

Zuikō Chingyū 瑞岡珍牛

Chapter 10. Ishii Seijun, "New Trends
　　in Dōgen Studies in Japan"

Bendōhō 弁道法

Bukkyō no shinzui wo ha-aku seru
　　Dōgen zenji no kyōgi仏教
　　の真髄を把握せる道元禅
　　師の教義

Chiji shingi 知事清規

Daidō Chōan 大道長安

Dentō Shūgaku 伝統宗学

Dōgen no jissen tetsugaku kōzō
　　道元の実践哲学構造

Dōgen no shisō 道元の思想

Dōgen Zenji to sono monryū
　　道元禅師とその門流

Dōgen Zen no honryū 道元禅の本流

Fuyō Rōran 父幼老卵

Fuzan Gentotsu 斧山玄訥

Gendai Shūgaku 現代宗学

Hihan Shūgaku 批判宗学

Hongzhi Zhengjue 宏智正覚

Ida Shoten 井田書店

Iriya Yoshitaka 入矢義高

Kegon 華厳

Kobutsu no Manabi: Dōgen 古仏の
　　まねび道元

Kohō Chisan 孤峰智璨

Koki-fukko 古規復古

Kindai Shūgaku 近代宗学

Kyōgō 経豪

kyōten 経典

Nihon zenseki shiron 日本禅籍史論

Nukariya Kaiten 忽滑谷快天

Ōbaku 黄檗

Okada Gihō 岡田宜法

Ōuchi Seiran 大内青巒

Rinzai-shū 臨済宗

Shibe Ken'ichi 志部憲一

Shōbōgenzō benchū 正法眼蔵弁註

Shōbōgenzō monge 正法眼蔵聞解

Shōbōgenzō na ippō
　　正法眼蔵那一宝

Shūjō 宗乗

Shushōgi 修証義

Shūtō-fukko 宗統復古

Sōtō fushūkai 曹洞扶宗会

Sōtō Shūgaku 曹洞宗学

Taidaikogogejarihō
　　対大己五夏闍梨法

Takahashi Masanobu
　　高橋賢陳

Takasaki Jikidō 高崎直道

Tenkei Denson 天桂伝尊

Tenzokyōkun 典座教訓

Tsunoda Tairyū 角田康隆

Ui Hakuju 宇井伯壽

Zengaku shisōshi 禅学思想史

Zenshūshi 禅宗史

Zongmen tongyao ji
　　宗門統要集

Zutang ji 祖堂集

Index